gave much so that I could be free for my studies. That was certainly the case for my grandparents, Horace Thomas Johnson and Beverly Jean Dozier Johnson, both of whom passed away while I was working on this project. From the day of my birth to the day of their deaths, they were my greatest champions. They often said that their dream for their grandchildren was that they would receive the education that they themselves never had the opportunity to pursue. The existence of this book bears witness to the sacrifices they made to make sure that their dream came true. For this reason, and for countless others, I dedicate it to them.

CU01507348

T&T Clark Studies in Systematic Theology

Edited by

John Webster, King's College,
University of Aberdeen, UK

Ian A. McFarland, Candler School of Theology,
Emory University, USA

Ivor Davidson, University of Otago,
New Zealand

Volume 6

t & t clark

KARL BARTH AND
THE *ANALOGIA ENTIS*

Keith L. Johnson

t & t clark

Published by T&T Clark

The Tower Building   80 Maiden Lane
11 York Road   Suite 704, New York
London SE1 7NX   NY 10038

www.continuumbooks.com

First published 2010
Paperback edition first published 2011

Keith L. Johnson has asserted his right under the Copyright, Designs and Patents Act, 1988, to be identified as the Author of this work.

British Library Cataloguing-in-Publication Data
A catalogue record for this book is available from the British Library

ISBN: 978-0-567-44134-8 (hardback)
ISBN: 978-0–567–34463–2 (paperback)

Typeset by Newgen Imaging Systems Pvt Ltd, Chennai, India
Printed and bound in Great Britain

CONTENTS

CONTENTS

CONTENTS

ACKNOWLEDGMENTS

This book would not have been possible apart from the assistance of many and the sacrifice of a few. This project started out as a dissertation supervised by George Hunsinger, Bruce McCormack, and John Bowlin at Princeton Theological Seminary. Each of them contributed in some way to my work, and while the responsibility for the final product is mine alone, this book would not have been what it is without them. Special recognition is due to Professors Hunsinger and McCormack for the years they invested in my doctoral training. They supported me in countless ways, large and small, and I could not have asked for better teachers. Clifford Anderson, curator of Special Collections at Princeton Theological Seminary, regularly helped me obtain many rare manuscripts through the Karl Barth Centre. I am grateful to Hans-Anton Drewes, director of the Karl Barth-*Archiv* in Basel, Switzerland, for making several unpublished resources available to me and for permission to cite them in this work. A special word of appreciation also goes out to Thomas Kraft at T&T Clark/Continuum, as well as to the editors of the 'Studies in Systematic Theology' series: John Webster, Ian A. McFarland, and Ivor J. Davidson.

My friends and colleagues provided strong support to me while I was working on this project. Space permits me to note only a few names. Kevin Hector is a constant conversation partner and a good friend, and he read through the manuscript and provided invaluable feedback. John Flett and John Drury also provided helpful responses to my work. My teaching assistant, Rachel Neftzer, spent many hours cataloguing and sorting manuscripts on my behalf. The graduate students in my 'Nature and Grace' seminar at Wheaton College worked through the questions involved in this book with me on a weekly basis, and they prompted me to think more deeply about the issues at stake. My colleagues at Wheaton, especially Jeff Greenman and Ann Gerber, also were a constant source of encouragement to me during long days of writing.

The completion of this book stands as a testament to the love and support of my wife, Julie. She has made countless sacrifices on my behalf and put her own dreams aside more than once to further mine. I am who I am today because of her. The same can be said of the rest of my family, many of whom

1

INTRODUCTION

For in Him we live and move and have our being.

– Acts 17.28

Since we have gifts that differ according to the grace given to us, each of us is to exercise them accordingly . . . according to the proportion of his faith.

– Rom. 12.6

The Question at Princeton

While on a tour of the United States in May 1962, Karl Barth delivered the Warfield Lectures at Princeton Theological Seminary.[1] He was warmly received during his visit, and he drew large crowds both for his lecture and for two open forums during which he answered questions from the audience. Early during the first forum, the following question was addressed to Barth:

> Dr. Barth, in your volume in the *Dogmatics* on the Doctrine of God, in your denial of natural theology, you can with honesty deny any *analogia entis*. But later on in the volume you introduced the idea of the *analogia entis* when you discussed the speech of God and the human speech about God. So I must admit that my question is: Will you explain fully to us the modified use of *analogia entis* in the context of grace which you use later on?[2]

---

[1] These lectures were incorporated into *Evangelical Theology: An Introduction*, trans. Grover Foley (London: Fontana Library, 1965). For the details of Barth's visit to America, see Eberhard Busch, *Karl Barth: His Life from Letters and Autobiographical Texts* (Grand Rapids, MI: Eerdmans, 1994), pp. 457–60.

[2] Karl Barth, *Gespräche: 1959–1962*, Gesamtausgabe (Zurich: Theologischer Verlag Zürich, 1995), p. 499. The identity of the questioner is not known.

This question is instructive, because it reflects a shift that occurred in the perception of Barth's interpretation of the *analogia entis* between the early and later parts of his career. The *analogia entis* is a Roman Catholic doctrine that has its roots in the thought of Augustine of Hippo and Thomas Aquinas. It entered into the forefront of modern theology only in the 1920s, however, through the work of the Jesuit theologian Erich Przywara. Through a series of lectures, essays, and books, Przywara used the *analogia entis* as the basis for a 'creaturely metaphysics' that he believed represented the 'fundamental thought form' of all Roman Catholic theology.[3] Przywara's work attracted the attention of both Catholic and Protestant scholars, including Barth. His response to Przywara's theology was definitive: the *analogia entis* was 'the invention of the anti-Christ' and the primary reason why he could never become a Roman Catholic.[4] Barth paid much attention to the *analogia entis* in the early volumes of his *Church Dogmatics* (*CD*), both in the form of criticism and the development of a constructive alternative to it, the *analogia fidei*. Throughout this early period in his career, then, there simply was no doubt about Barth's view of the *analogia entis*: it is a form of natural theology that is to be rejected absolutely and unequivocally.

This clarity left the scene, however, with the volume referenced by the questioner in Princeton: *CD* II/1. There we find Barth just as critical of natural theology, especially in its Roman Catholic formulations, as he had been previously. He also, as the questioner notes, remains critical of the *analogia entis*. At certain points in the volume, however, Barth appears to open the door to the possibility that he could change his mind about the doctrine. One passage in particular stands out in this regard. In the midst of a discussion of a pair of essays by the Catholic theologian Gottlieb Söhngen, Barth indicates that he could be convinced to retract his earlier condemnation of the *analogia entis*.[5] Söhngen had argued that the formulation '*analogia entis* within an *analogia fidei*' represents the true Roman Catholic view, and he insisted that such a view not only stands outside the scope of Barth's

---

[3] See Erich Przywara, *Analogia Entis*, in *Schriften*, vol. 3 (Einsiedeln: Johannes-Verlag, 1962), pp. 23–8.

[4] Karl Barth, *Church Dogmatics* I/1, revised edn (Edinburgh: T&T Clark, 1975), p. xiii; *Die Kirchliche Dogmatik* I/1 (Zürich: Evangelischer Verlag, 1932), pp. viii–ix.

[5] See Gottlieb Söhngen, 'Analogia Fidei: Gottähnlichkeit allein aus Glauben?', *Catholica* 3:3 (1934), pp. 113–36 and 'Analogia Fidei: Die Einheit in der Glaubenswissenschft'. *Catholica* 3:4 (1934), pp. 176–208. He advances similar arguments later in 'Analogia entis oder analogia fidei?' in *Wissenschaft und Weisheit: Zeitschrift für augustinisch-franziskanische Theologie und Philosophie in der Gegenwart* 9 (1942), pp. 91–100; and 'Analogia Entis in Analogia Fidei', in *Antwort: Karl Barth zum Seibzeigsten Geburtstag* (Zurich: Evangelischer Verlag AG, 1956), pp. 266–71.

criticism of Przywara, but that Barth himself actually assumed such a view whether he realized it or not.[6] Barth was impressed enough with the argument to say that if Söhngen's interpretation of the *analogia entis* really represents the Roman Catholic position, 'then naturally I must withdraw my earlier statement that I regard the *analogia entis* as "the invention of the anti-Christ"'.[7] He concludes that he is not ready to take such action yet, however, because he does not believe that Söhngen's position truly represents the Catholic point of view.[8] Regardless of this caveat, a shift had occurred: the door had been opened to the possibility that Barth could change his mind about the *analogia entis*. In the years ahead, many interpreters of his theology began to claim one of two positions: either that Barth *should* retract his earlier position in precisely the way that he suggested or that he already *had* retracted it in private without doing so publicly.

Von Balthasar and Beyond

The figure most responsible for fostering these views is Hans Urs von Balthasar. In his influential book on Barth's theology, von Balthasar builds upon the work of Przywara and Söhngen to make a two-fold case: that Barth's criticism of the *analogia entis* was based upon a misunderstanding of Przywara's theology, and that Barth's account of the *analogia fidei* and *analogia relationis* actually assumes the prior existence of an *analogia entis*. The key to these claims is von Balthasar's argument that Barth's theology operates under the same assumption that underlies the *analogia entis*: that God's act in creation is the presupposition of God's act of reconciliation in Jesus Christ. This shared assumption means that, even though Barth believes that his *analogia fidei* and *analogia relationis* stand in contrast to the *analogia entis*, they actually fall squarely within 'the classical terms of the analogy of being'.[9] Barth's own use of analogy, therefore, demonstrates that he has 'no difficulty' accepting the *analogia entis* when it is conceived

---

[6] See Söhngen, 'Analogia Fidei: Die Einheit', p. 191: 'Do we not meet here in the *analogia fidei* an *analogia entis*, one that admittedly, remains entirely within the *analogia fidei*, [and is] something other than a metaphysical *analogia entis*?'

[7] Karl Barth, *Church Dogmatics* II/1 (Edinburgh: T&T Clark, 1957), p. 82; *Die Kirchliche Dogmatik* II/1 (Zürich: Evangelischer Verlag, 1940), p. 90. Hereafter these volumes will be cited as *CD* II/1 and *KD* II/1 respectively.

[8] Barth says: 'But I am not aware that this particular doctrine of the *analogia entis* is to be found anywhere else in the Roman Catholic Church or that it has ever been adopted in this sense. Indeed, we may well ask: can this conception possibly be approved by wider circles in Roman Catholic theology, let alone by the teaching office of the Church?' See *CD* II/1, pp. 82–3; *KD* II/1, pp. 90–1.

[9] Hans Urs von Balthasar, *The Theology of Karl Barth: Exposition and Interpretation*, trans. S. J. Edward T. Oakes (San Francisco: Ignatius Press, 1992), p. 164.

'within the context of an overarching analogy of faith' – even if Barth himself fails to realize that this is the case.[10]

The merits of von Balthasar's interpretation of Barth will be discussed in due course. His relevance at this point lies in the fact that, after the publication of his book about Barth, von Balthasar's claims about Barth's relationship to the *analogia entis* quickly gained currency. This interpretation of Barth was attractive for at least three reasons. First, von Balthasar's view represented a mediating position between the extremes of Przywara's *analogia entis* and Barth's *analogia fidei*. This position was appealing both to Roman Catholic theologians, who were looking for new avenues for dialogue with Protestants in the years leading up to Vatican II, and to Protestant theologians, who were seeking ways to overcome their disagreements with Catholicism and the division that had opened between Barth and Emil Brunner over the issue of natural theology.[11] Second, Barth himself praised von Balthasar's book as a helpful and incisive analysis.[12] His praise gave Barth's fellow Protestants the reason and motivation to accept von Balthasar's mediating position as an alternative to Barth's early, more polarizing, position. The third and perhaps most important reason for the shift in opinion, however, is the fact that after von Balthasar's book, Barth simply stopped discussing the *analogia entis* in print. His silence led many to believe that von Balthasar's arguments had been convincing to Barth himself.[13] At the same time, Barth's development of the *analogia relationis* in *CD* III/1–2 indicated that analogy was playing a larger part in his theology than ever before. When all of these factors were considered in the light of Barth's apparent openness to the possibility of changing his mind, it became clear to many if not most interpreters that Barth's position on the *analogia entis* had shifted, and that it had done so because he realized that his early condemnation of it was based upon a mistaken interpretation. This new reading of Barth's interpretation of the *analogia entis* was easy to adopt, because it

---

[10] *Ibid.*, pp. 163–4.

[11] After reading Barth's account of the *analogia relationis*, Brunner concludes that Barth's thought on the *analogia entis* 'has changed'. He notes that this shift means that their former disagreements can be resolved: 'This is exactly what I said in my pamphlet *Natur und Gnade*, some time ago. I am happy to know that this controversy, which caused so much discussion, may now be regarded as settled'. See Emil Brunner, *The Christian Doctrine of Creation and Redemption: Dogmatics Volume II* (Philadelphia: Westminster Press, 1952), pp. 42–5.

[12] See Barth's remarks from 1958 in the preface to his book, *Anselm: Fides Quaerens Intellectum: Anselm's Proof of the Existence of God in the Context of His Theological Scheme*, trans. Ian W. Robertson (Richmond, VA: John Knox Press, 1960), pp. 11–12.

[13] Jung Young Lee, for example, argues that Barth's silence about the *analogia entis* stems, in part, from his recognition of 'the validity of von Balthasar's criticism'. See Lee, 'Karl Barth's Use of Analogy in his *Church Dogmatics*', *Scottish Journal of Theology* 22 (1969), p. 150.

was ecumenically minded and seemed to stand in line with Barth's most recent comments and concerns.

This is not to say that von Balthasar's interpretation of Barth went unchallenged. G. C. Berkouwer, for example, argued that von Balthasar fails to recognize that the 'fundamental intentions of Barth's opposition to the *analogia entis*' are rooted in basic Reformed commitments, and this blind spot prevents him from recognizing that Barth never deviates from his 'original intention', even in the later volumes of the *CD*.[14] Eberhard Jüngel took the same position from a different angle by arguing that von Balthasar's argument is based upon a category mistake. The mistake is the incorrect assumption that 'being' and 'faith' are 'different species within a common proximate genus', when in reality, 'the opposition of the *analogia entis* and the *analogia fidei* has to do with as unrelenting a contradiction as the opposition of δικαιοσύνη ἐχ νόμου [righteousness from the law] and δικαιοσύνη ἐχ πίστευς [righteousness from faith]'.[15] Any formula that attempts to bring them together, therefore, does so only by denying this difference. Eberhard Mechels also argued that the two concepts are contradictory, at least when understood on Barth and Przywara's terms. He argued that the '*analogia fidei* in Barth contains no *analogia entis*. The thesis "*analogia entis* within an *analogia fidei*" . . . has no basis in either the interpretation of the *analogia entis* of Przywara or the interpretation of the *analogia fidei* of Barth'.[16] In other words, von Balthasar's mediating position is an impossibility.

These arguments, however, did little to slow the questions about the accuracy of Barth's interpretation of Przywara or about a shift in his position on the matter over time. Ironically, after von Balthasar, it was Jüngel who did the most to foster the impression both that Barth made a mistake and that he changed his mind. In his influential book *God as the Mystery of the World* – written 15 years after the remarks cited above – Jüngel laments the fact that many Protestant theologians criticize the *analogia entis* 'with an astonishing lack of understanding and horrifying carelessness'.[17] The problem, he says, is that these scholars believe that, in the *analogia entis*,

---

[14] G. C. Berkouwer, *The Triumph of Grace in the Theology of Karl Barth* (Grand Rapids, MI: William B. Eerdmans Publishing Co., 1956), p. 193.

[15] Eberhard Jüngel, 'Die Möglichkeit theologischer Anthropologie auf dem Grunde der Analogie', in *Barth-Studien* (Gütersloh: Benzinger Verlag, 1982), p. 211.

[16] Eberhard Mechels, *Analogie bei Erich Przywara und Karl Barth: Das Verhältnis von Offenbarungstheologie und Metaphysic* (Neukirchen-Vluyn: Neukirchener Verlag, 1974), p. 266. Jüngel notes that this book stands as the exception among Protestant literature because it provides a careful and sympathetic examination of Przywara's theology. He rightly notes, however, that it is 'too schematic' in its approach to the two figures. See Jüngel, *God as the Mystery of the World: On the Foundation of the Theology of the Crucified One in the Dispute between Theism and Atheism* trans. Darrell L. Guder (New York: T&T Clark, 1983), p. 282, fn. 1.

[17] Jüngel, *God as the Mystery of the World*, p. 281.

'God, world, and man, or creator, creation and creature, are drawn together into a structure of being which then makes it possible to understand God on the basis of the ordering of the created world under him'.[18] But this interpretation is incorrect. In fact, as Jüngel notes, this criticism is 'directed against the very thing against which [the *analogia entis*] *itself* is directed'.[19] He notes that these interpreters are 'strengthened in their imperturbability by Karl Barth's blunt statement' labelling the *analogia entis* 'the invention of the anti-Christ' – a remark, he insists, that has 'often been cited but little understood'.[20] While he places part of the blame for this misunderstanding on Barth himself, he places the majority of it upon the 'Barthian school' that has failed to note the 'change [in Barth's view] which was caused precisely by his discovery of the analogy of faith as the precondition for the possibility of proper talk about God'.[21] In other words, the Barthians not only have failed to understand the *analogia entis*, they have failed even to understand Barth.

This analysis, offered by one of Barth's most prominent interpreters, has been influential for scholars on both sides of the debate. It is important to note, however, that Jüngel aims his criticism in this passage at Barth's *interpreters* – not at Karl Barth himself. Indeed, note what Jüngel does *not* say in this passage: he does not say that *Barth* misunderstood the *analogia entis*. In fact, his claim that the Barthians have 'little understood' the meaning of Barth's statement in *CD* I/1 suggests that their misinterpretation of the *analogia entis* does not, in fact, correspond to Barth's original statement. Jüngel also does not say that Barth's 'change' late in his career marks a retraction of his prior rejection of the *analogia entis*; indeed, he explicitly notes that Barth 'still adhered to his rejection' of the *analogia entis* even *after* this change.[22] This 'change', therefore, refers to something *other* than a retreat from Barth's previous position. Such nuance, however, was lost on most readers of Jüngel's book. The important point was that one of Barth's most prominent interpreters had admitted that Barth's statement in *CD* I/1 was problematic and that his views on the *analogia entis* had changed. That he had done so in a book in which Przywara is treated positively and which shares the title of a lecture in which Przywara prominently defends the *analogia entis* only strengthened the impression of a Barthian retraction.[23] When read in the light cast by von Balthasar's interpretation,

---

[18] *Ibid.*, p. 282.

[19] *Ibid.*, pp. 281–2, emphasis added.

[20] *Ibid.*, p. 282.

[21] *Ibid.*

[22] *Ibid.*

[23] See Erich Przywara, 'Gottgeheimnis Der Welt: Drei Vorträge über die Geistige Krisis der Gegenwart', in *Schriften*, vol. 2 (Eisiedeln: Johannes-Verlag, 1962), pp. 121–242. Jüngel's positive opinion of Przywara is clear throughout the book, such as when he

Jüngel's statements provided an opening for Barth's critics to strengthen their condemnation of his views, and it also gave Barth's more sympathetic interpreters even more of a reason to embrace von Balthasar's thesis.

We see evidence of both lines of thought among contemporary interpretations of Barth. Remarks from two contemporary interpreters of Przywara's theology, David Bentley Hart and John Betz, stand as a case in point. Hart views Barth's rejection of the *analogia entis* as a 'barbarous' act that is 'nothing but an example of inane (and cruel) invective' and 'speaks only of Barth's failure to understand Przywara'.[24] Barth's 'misunderstanding of the term and of Przywara's project', Hart says, led him to oppose Przywara with a 'vehemence bordering on the demented', but this mistaken reading and Barth's own 'disastrous' alternative 'render his complaints vacuous'.[25] For his part, Betz argues that Barth's remarks about the *analogia entis* show that he had a 'scant understanding of Przywara's doctrine' and 'never grasped what a first reading of the relevant texts should have revealed'.[26] He concludes that 'the solecisms in [Barth's] critique are so numerous (and have been repeated so often) that an entire book would be required to sort them out'.[27] Among Barth's more sympathetic interpreters, the trend is to follow von Balthasar's lead and argue that developments in Barth's later theology reveal that the distinction between his doctrine of analogy and the Roman Catholic doctrine are exaggerated. Stanley Hauerwas, for example, argues that 'the decisive issue for Barth was what he took to be the presumption of the *analogia entis* that we shared a common "being" with God', but recent developments in Catholic theology have undermined this critique and made 'many of the past formulas and stereotypes comparing "Catholic" and

---

says that Przywara's *Analogia Entis* is 'a work which cannot be admired enough'. See Jüngel, *God as the Mystery of the World*, p. 262, fn. 1.

[24] David Bentley Hart, *The Beauty of the Infinite: The Aesthetics of Christian Truth* (Grand Rapids: William B. Eerdmands Publishing Co., 2003), p. 241.

[25] David Bentley Hart, 'The Offering of Names: Metaphysics, Nihilism, and Analogy', in *Reason and the Reasons of Faith*, ed. Paul J. Griffiths and Reinhard Hütter (New York: T&T Clark, 2005), p. 285, fn. 14. Why is Barth's alternative 'disastrous'? Hart explains: 'Rejection of the analogy of being, properly understood, is a denial that creation is an act of grace that really expresses God's love, rather than a moment of alienation or dialectical negation; it is a rejection, that is, of Acts 17.28, and ultimately, of Gen. 1.1 (and everything that follows from it). If the rejection of the *analogia entis* were in some sense the very core of Protestant theology, as Barth believed, one would still be obliged to observe that it is also the invention of antichrist, and so would have to be accounted the most compelling reason for not becoming a Protestant'. See Hart, *The Beauty of the Infinite: The Aesthetics of Christian Truth*, p. 242.

[26] John R. Betz, 'Beyond the Sublime: The Aesthetics of the Analogy of Being (Part Two)', *Modern Theology* 22, no. 1 (2006), pp. 3, 11.

[27] *Ibid.*, 5.

"Protestant" views on analogy not only wrong but irrelevant'.[28] In line with these new interpretations, Hauerwas concludes that Barth's 'similarities with Catholicism make it all the more difficult to distinguish Barth's account of the *analogia fidei* from [the] *analogia entis*'.[29] Peter Oh draws a similar conclusion in a recent monograph on Barth's use of analogy. Late in his career, Oh argues, Barth 'finally admits the shortcoming of the *analogia fidei* and the one-sidedness of his interpretation of the *analogia entis* after being convinced by Hans Urs von Balthasar'.[30] This leads Oh to conclude that '[i]t is certain that Balthasar's affirmation of the complementary concept of analogy, "*analogia entis* within *analogia fidei*", has sufficiently convinced Karl Barth himself'.[31] These remarks from scholars both critical and sympathetic to Barth demonstrate the broader trend with respect to Barth's interpretation of the *analogia entis*. This trend has at least one important consequence: if accepted as an accurate portrayal of Barth's views, it frees theologians to talk about the *analogia entis* without engaging Barth's arguments against it or his alternative to it. After all, if Barth's rejection of the *analogia entis* was a 'demented' and 'barbarous' act, if his interpretation was 'mistaken' and 'one-sided', and if his alternative to it is a 'disastrous' and 'vacuous' solecism that secretly presupposes the *analogia entis* anyway, then why should anyone listen to what Barth has to say about the *analogia entis*?

Answering Two Questions

It is into this context that this study enters. There are many ways in which one could discuss the *analogia entis* in the theology of Karl Barth. One could examine the topic of analogy in general, and its use in the work of Barth in particular, to determine how Barth's use of analogy is related to its use by others, including Roman Catholic theologians like Przywara.[32] Alternatively, one could summarize the use of analogy in thinkers like Przywara, Barth, Söhngen, von Balthasar, and Jüngel and then bring them into conversation with one another to make an argument about how analogy is used in each thinker, which use is the most adequate, and how this study might apply to

---

[28] Stanley Hauerwas, *With the Grain of the Universe: The Church's Witness and Natural Theology* (Grand Rapids: Brazos Press, 2001), p. 185, fn. 24. This account of the motivation for Barth's critique corresponds to Jüngel's description of the view of Barth's interpreters, but not his account of Barth's own reasons for rejecting the *analogia entis*. As we will see, Barth's rejection of the *analogia entis* was not motivated by this concern.

[29] *Ibid.*, p. 158, n. 37.

[30] Peter Oh, *Karl Barth's Trinitarian Theology: A Study in Karl Barth's Analogical Use of the Trinitarian Relation* (London: T&T Clark, 2006), p. 15.

[31] *Ibid.*, p. 16.

[32] For a study of this sort, see Battista Mondin, *The Principle of Analogy in Protestant and Catholic Theology*, 2nd edn (The Hague: Martinus Nijhoff, 1968).

our constructive work in the future.[33] Or again, one could look at Barth's use of analogy throughout his career, from the use of analogy in his discussion of the cross in the second edition of his commentary on Romans to his use of it in the later volumes of the *CD*.[34] All of these projects would shed light in some way or another on Barth's interpretation of the *analogia entis* and the alternative he offers to it. They would not, however, address the two questions that are driving most contemporary interpretations of Barth's relationship to the *analogia entis*: (1) Did Barth's rejection of the *analogia entis* result from a mistaken understanding of it? and (2) Did Barth, either in response to the realization that he had made a mistake or due to changes in his theology, withdraw his critique of the *analogia entis* and accept some form of it into his own theology? These are the two questions that this book intends to answer, and it will do so by means of a two-part argument. The first part will address the question of whether or not Barth's rejection of the *analogia entis* was predicated upon a mistaken interpretation of it, while the second part will address the question of whether or not Barth changed his mind about the *analogia entis* from the early to the late part of his career.

Two claims will be defended. First, I will argue that Barth's rejection of Przywara's *analogia entis* is not the result of a mistaken interpretation. That is to say, Barth understood the *analogia entis* accurately and he rejected it on grounds that are theologically coherent and justified. His rejection was neither 'demented' nor based on a 'scant understanding' of the principle, but rather, it was a well-reasoned and consistent rejection stemming from valid theological concerns that make sense within the context of Barth's own theological development and his Protestant commitments. This first claim will be defended by way of a four-chapter narrative that leads us to Barth's condemnation of the *analogia entis* as 'the invention of the anti-Christ' in the preface to *CD* I/1. In Chapter 2, I will argue that the disagreements that culminated with the publication of Przywara's *Analogia Entis* and Barth's *CD* I/1 in 1932 have their basis in the divergent responses that Barth and Przywara had to the tragedy of World War I. I will explain this claim by examining the development of Barth's theology through the second edition of Barth's commentary on Romans in 1921 and the development of Przywara's theology through the essay 'God in us or above us?' in 1923. In Chapter 3, I argue that the key elements of the debate that culminated

---

[33] See Joseph Palakeel, *The Use of Analogy in Theological Discourse: An Investigation in Ecumenical Perspective* (Rome: Pontificia Università Gregoriana, 1995) and Philip A. Rolnick, *Analogical Possibilities: How Words Refer to God* (Atlanta, GA: Scholars Press, 1993).

[34] Bruce McCormack has provided much material for this topic, although there is much left to pursue. See McCormack, *Karl Barth's Critically Realistic Dialectical Theology: Its Genesis and Development, 1909–1936* (Oxford: Oxford University Press, 1995).

in 1932 were in place by 1926. Specifically, Barth's engagements with the Reformed tradition, as well as his desire to respond to Przywara's criticism of his Romans commentary, lead him into a new understanding of the relationship between God and humanity that is revealed for the first time in his dogmatic lectures at Göttingen; at the same, Przywara's desire to avoid the mistakes of Protestant theology and meet the challenges of the contemporary culture lead him to a particular account of the *analogia entis* in his book *Religionphilosophie katholischer Theologie*. This account transitions into the argument of Chapter 4. There I examine the circumstances of Przywara's visit to Barth's seminar on Thomas Aquinas in Münster in February 1929. I argue that this visit helps us see that Barth had more than just a 'scant' understanding of Przywara's *analogia entis*; rather, he had an in-depth knowledge of it delivered to him by Przywara himself. I also examine Barth's first critical response to Przywara's *analogia entis* by means of a close reading of his lectures 'Fate and Idea in Theology' and 'The Holy Spirit and the Christian Life'. These two lectures not only show us the background of Barth's later and more prominent criticism of the *analogia entis*, but they also show us that his criticism is based upon concrete and justified theological distinctions and concerns. These criticisms lead him into the definitive rejection of the *analogia entis* found in the preface to *CD* I/1. The first part concludes with Chapter 5, where the claim will be that Przywara's account of the *analogia entis* in *Analogia Entis* does not mark a break with his prior formulations of it.[35] Barth's prior reasons for criticizing the principle, therefore, remain justified.

The second claim of the book will build upon the insights gained in the first part. The central argument will be that, while Barth never changed his mind about his rejection of Przywara's *analogia entis*, he did change his response to the *analogia entis* in three ways. First, he drops his polemic against the *analogia entis* because he becomes convinced that the Roman Catholic description of it has changed. Specifically, Söhngen and von Balthasar convince Barth that Przywara's interpretation of the *analogia entis* is not *the* Roman Catholic interpretation, and Barth came to believe that their accounts of the *analogia entis* were built, in part, upon insights that *he* had given them. Second, Barth acknowledges that his *analogia fidei* necessarily implies a participation in 'being', and that he must account for a 'participation in being' in his theology. However, because his account of this 'participation in being' stands in line with the same distinctions that he used to justify his initial rejection of the *analogia entis*, it does not mark a change of mind about that rejection. Third, Barth's view develops because, in his mature theology, he finally accepts that there is a relationship of ongoing continuity

---

[35] Throughout this book, the title of Przywara's volume, *Analogia Entis*, will be capitalized, while the doctrine *analogia entis* will be in lowercase.

between God and humanity. His account of this divine–human continuity does not correspond to Roman Catholic accounts, however, because while Catholic accounts are based upon the notion that God's act of reconciliation in Jesus Christ presupposes God's prior act in creation, Barth's account works in reverse: for him, the human as created stands in continuity with the human in grace precisely because Jesus Christ's justification of sinners is the condition of the possibility of creation. This means that what humans know of God and themselves through reflection upon their created nature is not the precondition for the fulfilled and perfected knowledge that they have by means of God's revelation in Christ; rather, because what humans are *internally* is, at every moment in time, a function of the *external*, justifying relation of God to them in Jesus Christ, this relation is something that can be known through the revelation of Christ alone. Barth's mature account of divine–human continuity, therefore, does not mean that he has adopted a version of the analogy he initially rejected, but rather, it stands as the strongest possible rejection of such an analogy, because nothing at all like that analogy is conceivable on Barth's terms. In short, Barth's mature theology *fulfils* his early rejection of Przywara's *analogia entis* rather than retreats from it. These arguments are defended by way of a two-chapter examination of Barth's mature theology in conversation with Roman Catholic critiques of it. In Chapter 6, I examine the first two changes in Barth's response to the *analogia entis* by means of an account of Barth's account of the *analogia fidei* in *CD* I/1, Gottlieb Söhngen's critique of it, and Barth's response to Söhngen. In Chapter 7, I explain the third shift in Barth's response by interacting with von Balthasar's interpretation of Barth and by analysing how Barth's doctrine of analogy functions within the doctrine of reconciliation in *CD* IV/1–3. The conclusions of these chapters leads to Chapter 8, where I make the case that these conclusions provide a new starting point for the debates about Barth's interpretation of the *analogia entis*.

A New Starting Point

This potential for a new starting point brings us back to the question posed to Barth at the forum at Princeton in 1962, and to his answer:

> Yes. Exactly speaking it is true that in the first volume of *Church Dogmatics* I said something very nasty about the *analogia entis*. I said it was the invention of the anti-Christ. Later on I began to see that the notion of analogy cannot totally be suppressed in theology. I didn't at first speak of an *analogia entis*. I spoke of *analogia relationis* and then in a more biblical way of the analogy of faith. And then some of my critics said: 'Well, after all, an *analogia relationis* is also some kind of *analogia entis*'. And I couldn't deny it completely. I said: 'Well, after

all, if *analogia entis* is interpreted as *analogia relationis* or analogy of faith, well, then I will no longer say nasty things about the *analogia entis*. But I understand it in *this* way'. So I have not changed my mind.[36]

This book will prove that Barth's interpretation of his own development with respect to the *analogia entis* is accurate. It also will show that the debate about Barth's interpretation of the *analogia entis* should begin from the basis that Barth's criticism of the *analogia entis* was not based on a mistake, and that he did not change his mind about his rejection of it over the course of his career. This new starting point changes the terms of the discussion in positive ways, and it opens up new possibilities for a true dialogue between Protestants and Roman Catholics because it clears the ground from many of the misconceptions that have shaped this debate for decades.

---

[36] Barth, *Gespräche: 1959–1962*, p. 499.

2

THE BACKGROUND
TO THE DEBATE

'God is in heaven and thou are on earth'. The relation between such a God and such a man, and the relation between such a man and such a God, is for me the theme of the Bible and the essence of philosophy.
– Karl Barth[1]

God nearer to me than all the world. God nearer to me than I am to myself; God more real than all the world, God more real than myself: God all in all, Deus meus et omnia!
– Erich Przywara, S. J.[2]

Introduction

The debate about the *analogia entis* reached its zenith in the summer of 1932 with the publication of Karl Barth's *Church Dogmatics* I/1 (*CD* I/1) and Erich Przywara's *Analogia Entis*. The debate of that summer can be understood rightly, however, only when it is viewed in the context of the previous two decades. This chapter stands as the first of a four-chapter narrative that examines the events of those two decades in order to explain why Barth and Przywara arrived at the point they did in 1932. This narrative will show that Barth and Przywara's divergent trajectories were set in place early in their careers and that neither thinker would have written what he did in 1932 apart from his engagement with the other. It also will put us in a position to address one of the two major questions driving

---

[1] Karl Barth, *The Epistle to the Romans*, 6th edn, trans. E. C. Hoskyns (London: Oxford University Press, 1933), p. 10.
[2] Erich Przywara, 'Gottgeheimnis Der Welt: Drei Vorträge über die Geistige Krisis der Gegenwart', in *Schriften*, vol. 2 (Eisiedeln: Johannes-Verlag, 1962), p. 230.

this study: Was Barth's condemnation of the *analogia entis* as 'the invention of the anti-Christ' simply the result of a misunderstanding?

This chapter begins this narrative by looking at the events that shaped Barth and Przywara's early theology. The central claim of this chapter is that the disagreement of 1932 had its roots in Barth's and Przywara's divergent responses to the church's role in the tragedy surrounding World War I. Specifically, while Przywara believed that the church had done too *little* in the face of this tragedy, Barth believed that it had done too *much*. In response, Przywara sought a theology that would help the church engage the modern world instead of retreat from it; Barth, in contrast, sought a view of God that would prevent the church and its theologians from enlisting God on their side as they engaged in social and political endeavours. These divergent responses shaped the way each thinker understood the nature of the theological task, and it meant that while they shared much in common in their understanding of the church's failures in the modern world, they differed fundamentally in their formulation of a theological solution to correct these failures. Their divergence, as we will see, took place along the same fault lines that had divided Protestants from Roman Catholics four centuries earlier, and it set the stage for the key theological distinctions that would separate Barth's Protestantism from Przywara's Catholicism in the decades that followed.

This claim will be made concrete as the argument progresses. It will proceed in two sections. First, I will provide an account of how Barth's response to the errors of his liberal Protestant teachers drove him to develop a theology that emphasizes God's distinction from the world. I will argue that this response led Barth to emphasize God's transcendence at the expense of his immanence – an error brought to Barth's attention, among other things, by Przywara's critique of Barth's early theology. Second, I will show that, prompted by his belief that the Catholic Church was failing to engage modern culture, Przywara sought a unifying theological principle that would lead the Church to precisely this kind of engagement. Przywara's chief inspiration in this matter was Cardinal John Henry Newman, but Newman was simply a vehicle for the insights of the two pillars of the Catholic tradition – Augustine of Hippo and Thomas Aquinas – both of whom led Przywara to the *analogia entis*. I will argue, however, that Przywara formulated the *analogia entis* in the way that he did in part because he was responding to the dangers he saw in the resurgent Protestantism represented by Barth.

These two sections will set the stage for the arguments in the following chapters. In Chapter 3, I argue that Barth and Przywara's theologies were intertwined with one another inasmuch as each was responding to a theological challenge posed by the other. Specifically, I show that Barth turned to a more robust understanding of the doctrines of revelation and the incarnation in part to respond to questions raised by Przywara; at the same time, Przywara worked to develop a theology of the human consciousness centred upon the *analogia entis* in part to overcome the deficiencies he saw in Barth's commentary on Romans. This argument continues in Chapter 4, where I argue that Barth's initial critique of Przywara's *analogia entis* reveals that he did not misunderstand Przywara's principle, and I also show that this critique propelled Barth into the arguments of *CD* I/1. In Chapter 5, I demonstrate that Przywara's *Analogia Entis* does not invalidate Barth's prior criticism and that the condemnation found in the preface of *CD* I/1 is the culmination of this previous criticism. This argument will put us in the position to address the question about whether or not Barth's criticism was based on a misunderstanding.

Barth's Break with Liberalism

To say that Barth thought that the church had done too *much* in the face of the tragedy of the war is to express his deep disappointment that his former professors not only failed to oppose the political forces that led to the war but actually *endorsed* them on the basis of their theological convictions.[3] Indeed, Barth noted later that his teachers' support for the war was the key motivation for his break with the liberal theology they espoused.[4] In this critical moment, he thought, his teachers' theology had finally 'unmasked itself' for what it truly was, and Barth's rejection of it was decisive.[5] 'I could

---

[3] This account of Barth's break from the liberal theology of his teachers is limited in scope, because it focuses primarily upon specific insights of Barth during this period that were central both to his subsequent criticism of the *analogia entis* and to his constructive response to it. For a comprehensive account of Barth's break with liberalism, see Bruce L. McCormack, *Karl Barth's Critically Realistic Dialectical Theology: Its Genesis and Development, 1909–1936* (Oxford: Oxford University Press, 1995), pp. 31–203. Like many Barth scholars, I am deeply indebted to McCormack's account of Barth's theological development, and its influence on my account of Barth's development in this and the following chapter is substantial.

[4] While this event was the catalyst that pushed Barth away from his teachers, Barth's break with their theology actually began years before as he struggled with sermon preparation. Barth says as much in the preface to the second edition to *Romans*: 'I myself know what it means year in year out to mount the steps of the pulpit, conscious of the responsibility to understand and interpret, and longing to fulfil it; and yet, utterly incapable, because at the University I had never been brought beyond that well-known "Awe in the presence of History" . . . It was this miserable situation that compelled me as a pastor to undertake a more precise understanding and interpretation of the Bible'. See Karl Barth, *The Epistle to the Romans*, p. 9.

[5] Karl Barth, 'Concluding Unscientific Postscript on Schleiermacher', in *The Theology of Schleiermacher: Lectures at Göttingen, Winter Semester of 1923/24*, ed. Dietrich Ritschl (Grand Rapids, MI: William B. Eerdmans Publishing Co., 1968), p. 264. Barth's break was not decisive in the sense that he immediately turned to a new insight that corrected his teacher's failures. Rather, as Eberhard Busch notes, his break was decisive in that it

15

not any longer follow either their ethics and dogmatics or their understanding of the Bible and of history'.[6] What had been 'unmasked' was his teachers' critical error: the placement of religious experience at the centre of theological reflection. The centrality of experience had enabled supporters of the war to appeal to their own 'religious war "experience"' to validate their cause, and for Barth, the fact that this cause so clearly stood in opposition to the character of God meant that this kind of theology could only be false at its core.[7] In fact, Barth makes this point explicitly in a sermon delivered only a month after the beginning of the war. He tells his congregation that any religion that uses its experience of God to justify its own side in a war is engaging in an act 'completely alien to the innermost being of God'.[8] That such a misinterpretation can take place, he says, also demonstrates that 'the innermost being of God is also completely alien to humankind'.[9] God's will, in other words, cannot be known by way of theological reflection that is grounded upon human experience, because by nature it stands utterly apart from all human understanding.

This insight marks an important development in Barth's thinking, and the fact that Barth points to the distinction between God and humanity in his initial response to his teachers' error shows that the theological trajectory he would travel over the next few years was determined very soon after his break with liberalism – even if it took Barth himself a few years to discern the full implications of it. Indeed, Barth spends the months and years of the war pondering the ramifications of his basic insight more seriously. As he sees it, his initial task is to figure out how a God so utterly 'other' than the human can be known by the human at all. In other words, if God is not

---

caused him to begin 'a long and exciting *search*'. This search, as we will see throughout the course of this book, took him in the directions that he never expected to go. See Eberhard Busch, *The Great Passion: An Introduction to Karl Barth's Theology*, trans. Geoffrey W. Bromiley (Grand Rapids, MI: William B. Eerdmans Publishing Co., 2004), p. 19.

[6] Karl Barth, 'Evangelical Theology in the 19th Century', in *The Humanity of God* (Louisville: Westminster John Knox 1960), p. 14.

[7] On this point, see Barth's letter to his teacher Wilhelm Hermann on 4 November 1914: 'Especially with you, Herr Professor (and through you with the great masters – Luther, Kant, and Schleiermacher), we learned to acknowledge "experience" as the constitutive principle of knowing and doing in the domain of religion. In your school it became clear to us what it means to "experience" God in Jesus. Now however, in answer to our doubts, an "experience" which is completely new to us is held out to us by German Christians, an allegedly religious war "experience"; i.e. the fact that German Christians "experience" their war as a holy war is supposed to bring us to silence, if not demand reverence from us'. See Karl Barth, *Karl Barth-Martin Rade: Ein Briefwechsel*, ed. Christoph Schwöbel (Gütersloh: Gütersloher Verlagshaus Gerd Mohn, 1981), p. 115.

[8] See Barth's sermon from 6 September 1914, in Karl Barth, *Predigten 1914*, Gesamtausgabe (Zürich: Theologischer Verlag Zürich, 1974), p. 465.

[9] *Ibid.*

known in the way that his teachers claim, then how is God known? He also believes that his answer to this question must have a practical shape, because both the immediate political realities and his responsibilities to his congregation demanded that he spell out what true knowledge of God looks in practical terms.

'The Righteousness of God'

Barth's process of discernment took place in the following months in conversation with his friend Eduard Thurneysen.[10] Two contributions by Thurneysen stand out during this period. First, Thurneysen introduced Barth to the eschatological theology of Christoph Blumhardt, who rejected religion, defined in ritualistic and institutional terms, in favour of a clearer recognition of the revolution brought about by the Kingdom of God.[11] When he read Blumhardt, Barth believed that he finally had found a thinker who 'starts out from God' rather than 'climbing upwards to Him by means of contemplation and deliberation'.[12] This 'above to below' movement was new to Barth, and it stimulated his own constructive thinking as he was pondering an alternative to the theology of his teachers. Second, Barth found in Thurneysen a dialogue partner who would keep him motivated and focused as they turned again to the primary sources, both theological and biblical.[13] Together they read the 'old orthodoxy' of Luther and the

---

[10] Thurneysen's influence both on Barth's rejection of liberalism and his formulation of a constructive alternative to it can hardly be overstated. Barth recalled that it was Thurneysen who 'once whispered the key phrase to me, half aloud, when we were alone together: what we needed for preaching, instruction, and pastoral care was a "wholly other" theological foundation'. The next morning, Barth says, 'I sat down under an apple tree and began, with all the tools at my disposal, to apply myself to the *Epistle to the Romans*'. See Barth, 'Concluding Unscientific Postscript', p. 264.

[11] For an account of Barth's meeting with the Blumhardt brothers, see Eberhard Busch, *Karl Barth: His Life from Letters and Autobiographical Texts* (Grand Rapids, MI: William B. Eerdmans Publishing Co., 1994), pp. 84–5. See also the autobiographical sketch Barth composed in 1927 for the Münster Faculty Album, reprinted in Karl Barth and Rudolf Bultmann, *Karl Barth-Rudolf Bultmann Letters 1922–1966*, ed. Bernd Jaspert, trans. Geoffrey W. Bromiley (Grand Rapids: William B. Eerdmans Publishing Co., 1981), pp. 151–7. For a more in-depth analysis of the Blunhardts' influence on Barth's development, see Christian T. Collins Winn, '"Jesus is Victor!": The Significance of the Blumhardts for the Theology of Karl Barth' (Unpublished Doctoral Dissertation, Drew University, 2006).

[12] Karl Barth, *Action in Waiting* (Rifton, NY: Plough Publishing House, 1969), pp. 23–4.

[13] This turn back to the sources was driven by the problems that Barth had writing his sermons after turning way from his previously held theology. See his remarks in the Münster Faculty Album: 'But beyond the problems of theological liberalism and religious socialism, the concept of the kingdom of God in the real, transcendent sense of the Bible became increasingly more insistent, and the textual basis of my sermons,

Reformed tradition, and Barth noted that whereas it has previously been 'present to us only in the caricatures in which it had been taught to us at the university', a fresh reading led to new and provocative insights.[14] With Thurneysen encouraging him along the way, Barth also dove deeply into the Bible, and he soon found himself 'surrounded by a stack of commentaries' while reading Paul's letter to the Romans.[15] This study, of course, would result in the publication of his commentary on Paul's letter a few years later. In the meantime, however, his reading, conversations with Thurneysen, and preaching led to new insights that were beginning to shape the way he thought about God's relationship with human beings.

One lecture in particular – 'The Righteousness of God', delivered at Thurneysen's church in Aarau on 16 January 1916 – stands out as marker of the way Barth's thought was developing.[16] The subject matter of the lecture is the human's relationship to God, and the question animating the lecture is a practical version of the main question he had been pondering since he broke away from his teachers: How is God known, and what does true knowledge of God look like in practical terms? Barth's answer is to turn to the human conscience, which is, he says, the 'only place between heaven and earth in which God's righteousness is manifest'.[17] One of the reasons this is the case, he explains, is that humans have a deep longing for God that pushes them to reach for an 'existence higher than joy and deeper than pain'.[18] Ideally, this longing would be fulfilled by God's righteousness, but this way 'has long since been obstructed'.[19] The problem stems from the fact that every person, in some form or another, resents the notion that the righteousness that fulfils human life must be found in *God* rather than in his or her own life.[20] Barth explains that, as the one who is 'wholly other', God comes to us as something 'different and new', and he 'seeks entrance into our life and our world'.[21] We resent this intrusion in our lives and reject it, and we respond by creating alternative paths to righteousness such as systems of morality, the creation of the state and its laws, and the practice of religion. Each one of these attempts fails on its own merits, however,

---

the Bible, which hitherto I had taken for granted, became more and more of a problem'. See Barth and Bultmann, *Karl Barth-Rudolf Bultmann Letters 1922–1966*, p. 154. See also Busch, *Karl Barth*, pp. 89–91.

[14] Barth, 'Concluding Unscientific Postscript', p. 264.

[15] Barth and Bultmann, *Karl Barth-Rudolf Bultmann Letters 1922–1966*, p. 155.

[16] Karl Barth, 'The Righteousness of God', in *The Word of God and the Word of Man*, ed. Douglas Horton (Gloucester, MA: Peter Smith Publishing, 1978), pp. 9–27.

[17] *Ibid.*, p. 10.

[18] *Ibid.*, p. 11.

[19] *Ibid.*, p. 15.

[20] Barth explains that, as humans, we simply 'do not dream of appealing beyond ourselves for help in our need and anxiety'. See *Ibid.*, p. 14.

[21] See *Ibid.*, pp. 13, 16–17.

and the result is that despite all our efforts, we have 'gone no further than to play sleepily with shadow pictures of the divine righteousness'.[22] We have, Barth argues, created nothing more than a false god and a 'tower of Babel' by which we can delude themselves that we do not 'have to deal with reality' – the reality that God alone is the source of the righteousness that fulfils the deepest human longing.[23] 'This', Barth says, 'is our despair'.[24]

What should we do in response to this situation? Barth argues that we cannot overcome this despair by *doing* anything at all, since humanity has done little more than make 'a veritable uproar with our morality and culture and religion'.[25] Rather, the only way forward is simply to stand in *silence* before God. By 'letting God speak within', Barth argues, we learn to recognize that God's will is not a 'continuation of our own' human will; it exists, rather, as a 'wholly other' will that prompts a 're-creation and re-growth' of our human will into something it could not have become on its own.[26] This new will, Barth says, takes the form of faith.

> Then begins in us, as from a seed, but an unfailing seed, the new basic something which overcomes unrighteousness. Where faith is, in the midst of the old world of war and money and death, there is born a new spirit out of which grows a new world, the world of the righteousness of God . . . For now something real has happened – the only real thing that can happen: God has now taken his own work in hand.[27]

This work of God, Barth says, is something that 'breaks forth' and 'prevails' upon the earth from heaven – from above to below – but, even so, it manifests itself primarily within and through the human will. In this sense, Barth believes that the righteousness of God becomes concrete for the human in a way that the various other human efforts to obtain righteousness could not.[28] Barth concludes by instructing his listeners that the war should be seen as a shaking of the tower of Babel that had been built in Europe over the course of the previous decades, and this shaking should awaken the people of Germany to move beyond to the fallacy of their efforts to achieve righteousness under their own power. He cautions, however, that it remains to be seen whether true faith will result from the present trials.

---

[22] *Ibid.*, p. 21.
[23] *Ibid.*, pp. 21–2. Barth puts it thus: 'it becomes evident that we are looking for a righteousness without God, that we are looking, in truth, for a god without God and against God . . . It is clear that such a god is not God . . . He is an idol. He is dead'.
[24] *Ibid.*, p. 17.
[25] *Ibid.*, p. 24.
[26] *Ibid.*, pp. 24–5.
[27] *Ibid.*, p. 26.
[28] *Ibid.*

Four aspects of this lecture stand out for our purposes. First, it is interesting to note that Barth's appeal to the human conscience as the starting point and centre of God's work in history parallels the move that Erich Przywara will make in his own theology just a few years later. In other words, in their initial responses to the theological crisis at hand, Barth and Przywara start in the same place. The story of why Barth abandons this trajectory in the years that follow – and why Przywara believes that one must stay on this trajectory – provides the foundation for a clear understanding of the motivations behind Barth's rejection of Przywara's *analogia entis* and the theological distinctions that separate them. Second, this lecture shows how difficult it was for Barth to shed liberal patterns of thought early on after his break with Protestant Liberalism. Even with his insistence that God's will cannot be a continuation of the human will, Barth still adopts the basic patterns of his teachers by looking to the human conscience as the locus of divine activity. As Barth will soon realize, this starting point leaves him planted on the same theological terrain that he had just rejected, as any talk of looking 'within' inevitably causes him to think about God's relationship with humanity from 'below to above', from the human to God. In the years ahead, Barth will work hard to shut the door to this kind of thinking, and this shift, as we will see, shapes both Przywara's formulation of the *analogia entis* as well as Barth's response to it. It is important to note, however, that even though he had not yet completely shed his former way of thinking, Barth had broken away from the theology of his teachers in significant ways. This is the third important aspect: this lecture shows traces of key distinctions and categories that would become permanent features of Barth's mature theology. The insights that God is 'wholly other', that God breaks into human life from above, and that human faith results from an act of God rather than the human each remain with Barth in the years that follow, even though each of these ideas will develop and change over time, especially following Barth's encounter with Przywara.[29] Thus, while Barth had not completely shed the patterns of thought he had inherited from his teachers, he was moving in significant ways towards doing so. The fourth important aspect of this lecture builds upon this point: this lecture shows that, unlike his former teachers, Barth's interpretation of the status of human history and culture is fundamentally negative. The state and its law, religion, and even the church are not seen as manifestations of God's activity in the world; they are seen, rather, as being in some sense *antithetical* to God. This perspective will develop later on into one of the most prominent points of disagreement between Barth and Przywara, especially since Przywara

---

[29] McCormack makes a similar point: 'Barth's theological development from this point on represented a more-or-less continuous unfolding of a single theme: God is God'. See McCormack, *Karl Barth's Critically Realistic Dialectical Theology*, p. 134.

increasingly interpreted the events of history and culture as a manifestation of God's self-revelation to the world. As we will see in later chapters, Barth's view of history and culture grows more positive as his theology matures, but it will do so only near the end of Barth's career and only after he has proceeded through the fires of his own critique of this position. For now, the experience of the war strongly motivates Barth to avoid any direct correlation between God's activity and the activities of human culture. Indeed, while Barth's worry about their connection plays only a subtle part in this lecture, it becomes central to his theology as he works through his commentary on Paul's Epistle to the Romans.

Romans I

Barth began concentrated study on Paul's Epistle to the Romans a few months after delivering 'The Righteousness of God'. The experience was slow-going, at least by the standards of his later output.[30] The extra time spent on the manuscript, however, meant that Barth's understanding of the distinctions and categories that had been working subtly throughout 'The Righteousness of God' had time to develop and mature to the point where they could become more prominent and central to his theology. We see the fruit of this development in the final manuscript of the first edition of Barth's commentary on Romans.[31] One of Barth's concerns as he works through Paul's text is to explain how the relationship between God and humanity can be a relationship-in-distinction.[32] His goal, as becomes clear

---

[30] He began his work in June 1916 and finished the final manuscript a little over two years later. The longer time frame was partly due to the interruptions of his pastoral duties. See Busch, *Karl Barth*, pp. 101–6.

[31] I will refer to the first edition as *Romans* I and the second edition as *Romans* II. A full account of the theology of Barth's *Romans* is not necessary here. My goal, instead, is simply to bring to the fore the distinctions and themes that will play a central role in Barth's debate with Erich Przywara in the years ahead. These themes also are important because they provide the lens through which Przywara read and interpreted Barth. It is not far off the mark to say that, for Przywara and many other Catholics of the period and the decades that followed, 'Barth's theology' was one and the same as the theology of *Romans* II. This eventually becomes problematic because, while Barth's theology changed and developed over time, many of his critics still viewed him through the lens of his earlier positions.

[32] Or, as Barth puts it, his goal is to explain the logic of the claim: 'World remains world. But God is God'. For Barth – in contrast to thinkers like Thomas Aquinas or Przywara – the tautology 'God is God' indicates something about God's *essence* rather than his existence, as it signifies the absolute distinction of God's essence from everything that other than God. The phrase above is used by Barth in the lecture, 'Kriegszeit und Gottesreich' delivered on 15 November 1915, cited in Herbert Anzinger, *Glaube und kommunikative Praxis: eine Studie zur vordialektischen Theologie Karl Barths* (München: Chr. Kaiser Verlag, 1991), pp. 120–2. For more on Barth's use of the phrase

21

in the text, is to find a way to remove the human consciousness from the centre of our understanding of the creator–creature relationship while also upholding some way of talking about true human knowledge of God. Barth is convinced that human knowledge of God cannot be conceived as something constant or always available – since this leaves it under human control – but rather, it must be understood as something that comes afresh and anew in each moment. But what does this kind of knowledge look like in practical terms? In other words, how can one see God as, on the one hand, existing prior to and apart from all human knowledge of him, and, on the other, as one who really is known by the human?

In *Romans* I, Barth's answer to this question takes the form of two sets of distinctions: first, the distinction between 'so-called' history and 'real' history; and second, the distinction between a relationship of 'immediacy' to God, which occurred before the Fall, and the post-Fall relationship which takes the form of 'organic growth' as the human returns to the original relationship.[33] These distinctions were intended to work in concert to show how the human can know God even though God remains 'wholly other' and distinct from the knower at every moment. In the first distinction, Barth understands 'so-called' history as the history of the world as it can be known through academic disciplines such as science, history, and psychology.[34] Barth explains that this history arose only after the Fall, and as such, it has always been marked by alienation from God and its true end. This history, he says, is an 'objectless' history.[35] Its highpoint thus comes with the arrival of the Law, because the Law shows a way towards something better.[36] Inasmuch as this way has not been followed, however, the Law remains unfulfilled, and 'so-called' history reveals itself as nothing more than a sign of the world's judgement: '[t]he culture', Barth says, 'devours us'.[37] In contrast, 'real' history is *God's* history. Human life in 'real' history is not marked by death but by 'immediacy' to God – and thus by true life. 'Real' history intersects with 'so-called' history only at the cross of Jesus Christ, where a turn takes place from one history to the other. From this moment on, whenever human beings say 'Yes' to the word spoken to them

---

'God is God', see Eberhard Busch, 'God is God: The Meaning of a Controversial Formula and the Fundamental Problem of Speaking about God', *Princeton Seminary Bulletin*, no. 7 (1986), pp. 101–13.

[33] For a more thorough summary of these distinctions, see McCormack, *Karl Barth's Critically Realistic Dialectical Theology*, pp. 135–83, especially pp. 141–55.

[34] See Karl Barth, *Römerbrief. Erste Fassung, 1919*, ed. Hinrich Stoevesandt, Gesamtausgabe (Zurich: Theologischer Verlag, 1985), p. 64.

[35] *Ibid.*

[36] *Ibid.*, 83.

[37] *Ibid.*, 34.

in Christ, the world stands not in 'so-called' history but in 'real' history.[38] This means, Barth argues, that 'real' history is present in the midst of 'so-called' history as its true meaning and significance. 'The divine history of the world', he says 'is now growing *within* the human history of the world'.[39] This means that 'real' history acts, at every moment, to push 'so-called' history forward towards its true end in God. The relationship between the two histories, however, is strictly eschatological in nature: God's presence in 'so-called' history occurs from above as he irrupts into the world, meaning that while God acts *in* the world, he is not *of* the world. This action takes place in the life of every individual as she is confronted by the decision about which history she will live in. 'Real' history, therefore, cannot be understood as being of the same type as 'so-called' history, and the events of this history cannot be the subject of historical investigation like the events of 'so-called' history. This means that 'real' history is fundamentally distinct from 'so-called' history, and it stands as a 'hidden history' that determines the shape and meaning of human life without being subject to human control or evaluation.[40] Hence, while Barth sees a relation between 'real' history and 'so-called' history, this relation does not alleviate the stark difference between them.

The second distinction – the one between the nature of the pre-Fall and post-Fall relationship between God and humanity – follows a similar pattern. Humans originally had a relationship of 'immediacy' with God, meaning that a real relation of 'intimate and life-giving fellowship' existed between them.[41] This relationship was broken by the Fall, which, Barth says, resulted in an 'ungodliness which completely pervaded the substance of our life and culture'.[42] The Fall thus led to death, which, because it was not only physical but spiritual, entailed the surrender of the immediacy between humans and God.[43] The Fall and the loss of immediacy defines human life in the present, but this loss was reversed at the cross of Jesus Christ. The cross reverses the Fall by setting in motion the reconciliation of the world – manifested as the Kingdom of God – in which death and sin

---

[38] *Ibid.*, 64: 'Then the new people of God belong . . . in [the history] in which the criterion of God is executed'.

[39] *Ibid.*, 24, emphasis mine.

[40] See Barth, *Römerbrief. Erste Fassung, 1919*, p. 88: 'The meaning of history was always available, but it was covered up by the absurdity of "history".'

[41] McCormack, *Karl Barth's Critically Realistic Dialectical Theology*, p. 149. As a real relation, Barth believes this notion precludes any idea that the creature is an emanation of God. As we will see, however, one of Przywara's lines of criticism against Barth is that his view of the relationship between creature and creature inevitably falls into precisely this error.

[42] Barth, *Römerbrief. Erste Fassung, 1919*, p. 258.

[43] *Ibid.*

are overcome and immediacy with God is restored. Barth sees the Kingdom ushered in by Christ as a kind of 'seed' that will continue to grow until it reaches maturity at the end of time.[44] This is what he means by his use of the phrase 'organic growth': the Kingdom of God develops and matures through time until it is fulfilled at the *eschaton*. As such, the Kingdom is *in* this world but not *of* it; it truly exists only eschatologically. It thus cannot be linked to any human enterprise, such as a church, state, or even religion: 'Our theme, which you have known and understood and which we now have called back into memory is no *religion* but the Kingdom of God.'[45] This Kingdom thus must be seen strictly as a 'divine possibility' that exists as God acts to redeem the world in Christ. Like the presence of 'real' history in the midst of 'so-called' history, therefore, the Kingdom of God constitutes a 'hidden history' in the world: it breaks into the world and changes it, but at no moment does it become part *of* it.

While more can be said to flesh out these two distinctions, we already are in a position to see how Barth's theology has developed in the years since he delivered 'The Righteousness of God'. Barth maintains many of the key theological distinctions he used previously, but he uses them in a more advanced and consistent manner – even if, at the time, he presses the limits of language and logic to do so. In *Romans* I, Barth is trying to address the question of how one can see God as a reality who exists prior to and apart from human knowledge of him while also seeing him as One who can truly be known. He recognizes that the answer to this question lies in the notion of God as *self*-revealing, because if God maintains control of divine revelation at every moment while still actually revealing himself to the human knower, then one can hold that God remains independent from the knower without abandoning the notion that God can be known at all. The distinction between 'real' history and 'so-called' history moves in the direction of showing how this self-revelation is possible, because while the human becomes a participant in 'real' history, she is never able to control or master this history. It always remains a 'hidden' part of human existence because it breaks into that existence moment-by-moment without becoming a permanent feature of it. 'Real' history, therefore, remains at all times something that occurs by God's action and decision alone. Likewise, by drawing a distinction between the pre-Fall and post-Fall relationship with God, Barth is able to describe this relationship in terms of the 'organic' growth of the Kingdom of God in history. The relationship thus can be seen as something that occurs *in* history, but because it at all times comes from above as that which *will be* consummated, it can never be directly identified with anything

---

[44] Jesus Christ, he says, 'is the seed of the new world'. See *Ibid.*, p. 91.
[45] Barth, *Römerbrief. Erste Fassung, 1919*, p. 576. He warns: 'Watch out for the demons of religion! They could come back!'

human or creaturely. This means that the possibility of the knowledge of God can never be grounded in the believer's consciousness or in anything else immediately available to the knower, but only in God's free act.

These distinctions help us see how the patterns governing Barth's thought about the creator–creature relationship are functioning at this point. Barth is firmly committed to a vision of a 'wholly other' God who becomes part of history without becoming *of* it, and he also wants to maintain that the human knower has real knowledge of God, although he makes this knowledge a constant *need* rather than something the human can ever have or hold as a possession. One worry with his construal, however, is that while Barth affirms the possibility of human knowledge of God, he does not explain in detail *how* it occurs. Barth recognized this problem as the reviews of the book came in and he realized that some of the distinctions he had used, especially the notions of 'immediacy' and 'growth', had caused more confusion than clarity. These notions, of course, stand in line with Barth's arguments in the 'The Righteousness of God' about humanity's 'deep longing' for God and the 'seed' of righteousness that develops over time. By using them, Barth had intended to create space in history for God's activity in the world, and he had hoped that he could do so in such a way that God could no longer be enlisted for human endeavours. He began to worry, however, that such notions simply did not go far enough in distinguishing God from the world. He realized, in other words, that he had not completely closed the door to the errors that lead to his teachers' failures.[46]

For this reason, when the opportunity to write a second edition of *Romans* arrived, Barth eagerly seized it. He had realized that the theology of *Romans* I needed to be 'completely reformed and consolidated' before he could answer the question of how can God be known to human beings while remaining at all times the agent of that knowledge.[47] This reform was

---

[46] See George Hunsinger's remark that the Barth of *Romans* I 'had seen a kind of dialectical identity between divine and human praxis in the historical emergence of God's kingdom'. The existence of this identity points to the problem Barth found as he read the reviews of the book. He had intended to close the door to precisely these kinds of views, but in actuality, his notions of 'immediacy' and 'organic growth' fostered them. See Hunsinger, 'Toward a Radical Barth', in *Karl Barth and Radical Politics*, ed. George Hunsinger (Philadelphia: The Westminster Press, 1976), p. 211.

[47] See Barth's remarks in the preface to the second edition, found in Barth, *The Epistle to the Romans*, p. 2. McCormack articulates the questions that were driving Barth's revisions: 'If God is to be known by humans, God must somehow make Himself to be "objective" to the human knower; He must place Himself within the range of "objects" which can be intuited by human beings. But how could God become an "object" of human intuition without making Himself subject to the control (the disposition, the management) of the human knowing apparatus? How could God be known by human beings without ceasing to be God, to be the master of the relation between God and humankind? How can "God be God" – not only before revelation, but during

undertaken with a sense of urgency.[48] After years of trying to discern a way forward past the mistakes he saw in his teachers' theology, Barth finally began to see a clear way forward. His goal was to transform what he now realized was the 'nebulous and speculative' argument of *Romans* I into an argument defined by 'sharply contoured antitheses'.[49] This would occur, he believed, only through an audacious reconfiguration of the relationship between God and humanity. He dedicated himself, therefore, to present once again – and in a new way – precisely how it is that God 'cuts sharply through all human sense of possession' and how human knowledge of God remains a divine event at every moment.[50]

Romans II

Barth's reformulated argument in *Romans* II centres upon the notion that the doctrine of justification provides the template for theological epistemology.[51] That is, in order to guard against the idea that the knowledge of God can be obtained, possessed, or controlled like other types of human knowledge, Barth makes it the result of grace alone. The knowledge of God, he says, occurs only as the 'impossible possibility', meaning that it 'exists as the possibility of *God* and as his possibility only'.[52] God's revelation breaks forth into human existence as 'a pure, absolute, vertical miracle' in the form of an 'undimensional line of intersection' between God and the world.[53] Its 'undimensional' nature means that it is an event completely

---

and after it?' These were not different questions than Barth had been attempting to answer in *Romans* I; he was just answering them in a different way. See McCormack, *Karl Barth's Critically Realistic Dialectical Theology*, pp. 207–8.

[48] Busch records that Barth wrote the book in eleven months, 'sending the pages straight off to the publisher as he finished them'. Barth wrote to Thurneysen that he lived that summer 'like a drunken man back and forth between desk, dinner table and bed, travelling every kilometre with my eye already on the next one'. See Karl Barth and Eduard Thurneysen, *Karl Barth – Eduard Thurneysen Briefweshsel: 1921–30*, Gesamtausgabe, vol. V (Zürich: Theologischer Verlag Zürich, 1974), p. 508.

[49] These remarks are taken from a self-portrait written by Barth in 1964, cited in Busch, *Karl Barth*, p. 118.

[50] Barth, *The Epistle to the Romans*, p. 92.

[51] One of the implications of this insight in *Romans* II is that, apart from grace, all human speech about God is revealed to not actually be speech about God at all. Przywara pushed back against this notion because he believed that a properly formulated doctrine of analogy provided a way to avoid the errors Barth was trying to avoid without denying the ability of humans to say something true about God. Barth would move in a similar direction in the *Church Dogmatics*, but he would do so without abandoning the commitment to the *diastasis* between God and humanity that is driving his insights here.

[52] Barth, *The Epistle to the Romans*, p. 62, emphasis added.

[53] Barth, *The Epistle to the Romans*, p. 60.

unique and distinct from all historical events; it is an event, Barth thinks, that *touches* the human world without ever becoming part *of* that world.

This event occurs in and through the person of Jesus Christ, the one who stands at the point where 'the unknown world cuts into the known world'.[54] In Jesus alone, Barth says, God intersects with the world and makes himself an object of human knowledge. This knowledge, however, is unique because human history and God's history 'are separated absolutely' from one other even in Jesus.[55] That is, while God makes himself known in Jesus, he does so only *indirectly*, because the historical man Jesus of Nazareth is not the revelation of God but the *medium* of revelation. 'The revelation which is in Jesus', Barth says, 'because it is the revelation of the righteousness of God, must be the most complete veiling of His incomprehensibility. In Jesus, God becomes veritably a secret: He is made known as the Unknown, speaking in eternal silence.'[56] Note Barth's word choices here: 'veiling', 'incomprehensibility', 'secret', and 'silence'. He is pushing the limits of paradox and dialectic, and he is doing so to make sure his reader gets the point: all human knowledge of God is the result of God's self-revelation rather than any inherent human ability to come to that knowledge. Jesus, as a historical person, marks the place where God intersects the world and reveals himself to it; however, because revelation can only be the event by which 'the *Unknown* God dwelling in light unapproachable' makes himself known, the knowledge of God available in Jesus is not like other human knowledge.[57] At every moment, the knowledge of God remains indirect, veiled, and distinct from every other type of knowledge. Such knowledge has no substance, no before and no after; it is simply *event*.

To make this idea concrete, Barth turns to the resurrection. This is an important move, because it allows Barth to walk the tightrope he wants to walk between God and humanity without falling on either side of the divide. He argues that the resurrection is a 'non-historical event'.[58] That is, he claims it is an event that occurs *in* history without becoming *of* history, because it reveals God without making that revelation a part of the world of human knowledge. Barth asserts this idea near the beginning of *Romans* II:

The Resurrection is the revelation: the disclosing of Jesus as the Christ, the appearing of God, and the apprehending of God in Jesus.

---

[54] *Ibid.*, p. 29.

[55] *Ibid.*, p. 77.

[56] *Ibid.*, p. 98.

[57] *Ibid.*, p. 35. Robert Jenson summarizes the implication of Barth's move here: 'The *Commentary on Romans* represents in theology the end of historical religion'. See *God after God: The God of the Past and the God of the Future, Seen in the Work of Karl Barth* (New York: The Bobbs-Merrill Company, 1969), p. 51.

[58] Barth, *The Epistle to the Romans*, p. 205.

> The Resurrection is the emergence of the necessity of giving glory to God: the reckoning with what is unknown and unobservable in Jesus, the recognition of Him as Paradox, Victor, and Primal History. In the Resurrection the new world of the Holy Spirit touches the old world of the flesh, but touches it as a tangent touches a circle, that is, without touching it. And, precisely because it does not touch it, it touches it as its frontier – as the new world. The Resurrection is therefore an occurrence in history, which took place outside the gates of Jerusalem in the year A.D. 30, inasmuch as it there 'came to pass,' was discovered and recognized. But inasmuch as the occurrence was conditioned by the Resurrection, in so far, that is, as it was not the 'coming to pass,' or the discovery, or the recognition, which conditioned its necessity and appearance and revelation, the Resurrection is not an event in history at all . . . There is here no merging or fusion of God and man, no exaltation of humanity to divinity, no overflowing of God into human nature. What touches us – and yet does not touch us – in Jesus the Christ, is the Kingdom of God who is both Creator and Redeemer.[59]

Barth believes that human beings really are able to 'apprehend' and know God in the resurrection of Jesus, but he insists that they cannot place this knowledge in the same category as the rest of their knowledge. The reason is that the resurrection straddles history: it is the event that at once 'lies on the frontier of that which is not history' as well as 'on the frontier of history'.[60] In one sense, it can be seen as a historical event that *actually* occurred 'outside the gates of Jerusalem in the year A.D. 30'. It thus has to do with the central experiences of human existence – that is, with the experience of life and death – and it can be seen as a bodily and human event. We really can know something in this event. In another sense, however, it is the event in which the 'Kingdom of God has become actual'.[61] The chains of sinful human history are broken here, and the world as humans know it has been opened up to a new history – one above and beyond human life. As such, the resurrection is a *non*-worldly event. It marks the in-breaking of the Kingdom of God that stands on the frontier of this world and looks into another. In the resurrection, the two worlds come together, but there is no 'merging or fusion' between them; they remain in stark opposition to one another at every moment.[62] In the resurrection, then, humans stand 'before an irresistible and all-embracing dissolution of the world of time and

---

[59] *Ibid.*, 30.

[60] *Ibid.*, p. 222.

[61] *Ibid.*, p. 30.

[62] The Kingdom of God cannot be seen, as Barth says, 'merely as improved worldliness'. Rather, it brings the world something absolutely new and other that stands over against all that already is. See *Ibid.*, p. 108.

things and men'; they stand 'before the supremacy of a negation by which all existence is rolled up'.[63] In short, the place where God is revealed to the world is the place where the world in and of itself – that which Barth had previously named 'so-called history' – is negated.

These are the ideas that capture how Barth understands the knowledge of God and the creator–creature relationship in *Romans* II. He is pushing the limits of time and eternity to articulate how God can be known but not possessed by the human who receives God's self-revelation. The result is an understanding of the knowledge of God that finally slams the door on *any* notion that could be used to establish *any* kind of continuity between God and humans. This marks an important shift from Barth's argument in 'The Righteousness of God' and *Romans* I. In 'The Righteousness of God', Barth worked with the idea of God's distinction from the world, but he had not yet figured out how to articulate this distinction in terms other than what he had learnt from his teachers, because notions of 'longing' and 'seeds' occupied centre stage. In *Romans* I, Barth moved further in the direction of the distinction between God and the world while trying to answer the question of real human knowledge of God. He still had not found a way of saying it that closed the door entirely on the merging of God and humanity, however, because 'immediacy' and 'organic growth' left room for just such an interpretation. Now, in *Romans* II, Barth has finally sealed himself off from this way of thinking altogether. He has established that there is *no* connection between God and humanity apart from God's revelation in Jesus Christ, and because this revelation is by 'grace alone' in the same sense that justification is by 'grace alone', this revelation is protected from human control of any kind. To this end, even Jesus himself is seen not in terms of the material and concrete events of his human life but in terms of his resurrection: this event is the one event, eschatological in nature, in which God's revelation truly occurs. It is an event that cannot be captured on the plane of other human events; God's Kingdom comes into contact with the world at this point without merging or blending into the world in any way.[64]

---

[63] *Ibid.*, p. 91. Barth, of course, sees an existence that is 'rolled up' as one that is *reconciled.* Jenson captures this insight: The relationship between God and humanity 'is not the standing relation between two realities, but rather the *critique* of the one by the other, the denial of the one reality by a freedom so completely to be able to affirm by the denial; it is the justification of the ungodly'. The denial of human existence, in other words, is its salvation. See Jenson, *God after God*, p. 27.

[64] The lack of attention to incarnate life of Jesus serves, in part, as the foundation for Jenson's criticism that, because the gospel must have a 'narrative content', *Romans* II stands as an *anti*-gospel book: 'A consistent policy based on the *Commentary on Romans* would be a portentous silence, which might be religiously impressive, but would mark the cessation of the gospel'. Barth himself expressed worries later on about his tendency to move the 'humanity of God . . . from the center to the periphery' in

Hence in *Romans* II, Barth has finally figured out how to eliminate the notion of a connection between God and humanity that takes anything other than the form of a particular and unique movement from God to the human, from the other world to this world, from above to below. There is no 'relative relation between God and man', no possibility for understanding the knowledge of God as something manifested in the human consciousness or possessed by the human in such a way that the human could control it.[65] Those lines of thinking have been banished, and the result is that the creature finally has *no* role to play in the establishment or maintenance of the relationship with God.[66] Even faith itself is negated, as Barth describes it merely as 'a void, an obeisance before that which we can never be, or do, or possess'.[67] The history of the world in Christ, therefore, can no longer be seen as the 'beginning of a new, a second, epoch'; rather, God's history confronts the history of this world and judges it by negating it.[68] God does not develop the potential already present in human life by meeting the human at the point of their deepest longing. Rather, God *annihilates* that life by confronting it with the truth of the resurrection. It is in this judgement and negation of the world – when God truly and finally is recognized as *God* – that faith becomes real and the true relationship between God and humanity occurs. In this sense, the negation of the world by God and God's faithfulness in spite of it is the world's *true*

Romans II. As we will see, however, he will correct this problem in the *Church Dogmatics* not by retracting his arguments from *Romans* II but by making the *same* argument 'even better'. See Jenson, *God after God*, pp. 30–1; and Karl Barth, "The Humanity of God", in *The Humanity of God* (Louisville: John Knox Press, 1960), pp. 38–45.

[65] Barth, *The Epistle to the Romans*, p. 108.

[66] Hence Barth: 'If relationship with God were to produce an enhancement of human being and having and doing in this world, rather than a weakening, or even a deprivation, of these things, God would become visibly and concretely a spiritual or historical element in the midst of other elements, differing only relatively from these other notable spiritual or historical powers with which men have been endowed.' See Barth, *The Epistle to the Romans*, p. 113.

[67] *Ibid.*, p. 88. He continues: 'it is devotion to Him who can never become the world or man, save in the dissolution and redemption and resurrection of everything which we here and now call world and man.'

[68] *Ibid.*, p. 77. Barth is at great pains throughout *Romans* II to close to door to any misinterpretation like the one that plagued the idea of 'growth' in *Romans* I. See, for example, his emphasis that 'the creation is a *new* creation; it is not a mere new eruption, or extension, or unfolding, of that old "creative evolution" of which we form a part, and shall remain a part, till our lives' end'. See Barth, *The Epistle to the Romans*, p. 102.

history: it is the 'crimson thread which runs through the whole course of the world'.[69] Barth's picture of God, then is of the One who is

> the pure and absolute boundary and beginning of all that we are to have and do; God, who is distinguished qualitatively from men and from everything human, and must never be identified with anything which we name, or experience, or conceive, or worship as God . . . the Unknown, who is never a known thing in the midst of other known things; God, the Lord, the Creator, the Redeemer: this is the Living God . . . Above and beyond the apparently infinite series of possibilities and visibilities in this world there breaks forth, like a flash of lightning, impossibility and invisibility.[70]

This God is not one who could ever be enlisted on the side of a human war; he is not one who can be found in the recesses of the human ego or in the concrete visibility of the church; and he cannot be handled or manipulated or made to serve any human cause – even the cause of human salvation. This God is the God who is wholly other than the world, who judges the world, and who stands over the world as the one whose action marks the death of the present world and the resurrection of a new one. Such is the God that Barth turned to after the war – the Unknown God who is seen in the flash but is gone before we can make him our own.

Przywara: Towards a Renewed Roman Catholic Church

At about the same time that Barth was turning away from the theology of his teachers, Erich Przywara was encountering a theological crisis of his own. In contrast to Barth, however, Przywara's crisis was fostered by his

---

[69] Barth, *The Epistle to the Romans*, p. 77. This captures an important insight: while Barth seeks to negate any notion that God can be present in the various forms of human striving in history, this negation has the positive function of pointing to the source and manner of the world's true redemption. In later years, Barth would latch onto the 'crimson thread' more and more and make it the emphasis of his theology. T. F. Torrance captures this when he says that *Romans* II was 'more than a "corrective" . . . it pointed out, if not the actual road ahead, at least the direction in which it lay'. See Torrance, *Karl Barth: An Introduction to His Early Theology 1910–1931* (London: T&T Clark, 2000), p. 54.

[70] Barth, *The Epistle to the Romans*, pp. 330–1. Busch notes that Barth's use of 'invisibility' in *Romans* II is directed against Schleiermacher's 'intuition' (*Anschauung*), which saw God as already posited from the outset in the religious self-consciousness as well as any notion of a subsequent positing of God in the self-consciousness. See Busch, *The Great Passion*, p. 22.

conviction that the church had done too *little* in the face of the tragedy caused by the war. This belief stemmed from his disappointment that, after the advent of the modern world, the Catholic Church had retreated from the culture instead of engaging it with the truth of the gospel. This retreat had left the Church incapable of playing a constructive role within society in the years after the war, and in Przywara's view, the culture suffered as a result. In light of this situation, Przywara believed that the only viable option for Catholic Church was to institute reforms that could put it in position to live up to its responsibility to exist as the body of Christ in the modern world. The key to these reforms would be a renewal of the Church's theology.

That Przywara would have this perspective makes sense when his ideas are seen within the context of his personal and intellectual development. Born in 1889 in Kattowitz, located in what today is Poland, Przywara entered the Society of Jesus as a young man in 1908. Although he lived in Germany at the time, he was educated in Valkenburg, Holland, because the Jesuits were outlawed in Germany during this period.[71] The fact that Przywara chose to join an ostracized group speaks to his personality as an 'outsider' not only with respect to German culture, but also within the Roman Catholic Church itself. Unlike many Catholic theologians of his time, Przywara did not align himself with a distinctive interpretative school, such as those of Augustinian, Thomist, Scotist, or Molinist variety. His interests instead ranged across the entire spectrum of Catholic thought and the Western philosophical tradition. Rather than immersing himself in one interpretative tradition, Przywara consciously tried to pull together different strands of the tradition into something *new* that would stand over and above the individual elements that comprised it. This approach meant that Przywara tended to work outside of the Catholic mainstream, but it also meant that he had a unique perspective that often enabled him to see the failures and promise of Catholic theology in a way that those working within mainstream could not.[72]

This unique perspective was fostered, in part, by the diverse nature of his academic studies. He had a strong interest in philosophy, reading widely

---

[71] This education took place between 1910 and 1921, with a delay during the war. The Jesuits were outlawed in part because they had been accused of being 'un-German'. For more details about his education, see Thomas F. O'Meara, *Erich Przywara, S.J.: His Theology and His World* (Notre Dame: Notre Dame University Press, 2002), pp. 4–5.

[72] On this point, Gertz offers an insight that will become clearer as we trace out Przywara's theology: 'His basic openness to the mystery of the "ever greater God" excludes in advance any limitation to a given school theology. Przywara does not let himself to be classified in a given school; he also does not form "a school" . . . in any *similarities* of particular theologies . . . the greater *dissimilarity* must be recognized theoretically and practically.' See Bernhard Gertz, *Glaubenswelt als Analogie: Die Theologische Analogielehre Erich Przywaras und ihr Ort in der Auseinandersetzung um die Analogie Fidei* (Düsseldorf: Patmos-Verlag, 1969), p. 417, emphasis added.

and deeply among the great thinkers in the Western tradition. He also had a passion for music and poetry.[73] These interests combined to give him a distinct perspective on the Western intellectual tradition and the Catholic Church's role in it, and he was not averse to sharing his perspective on how the two traditions might interact with one another. Indeed, despite his youth, he published several articles and essays during and shortly after the war that not only marked him as a rigorous and interesting thinker, but as someone who was pushing the Catholic Church to view the contemporary cultural crisis as an opportunity rather than a threat.[74] It is perhaps because of these unique views that, despite academic interests and obvious intellectual gifts, no academic post could be found for Przywara after his ordination. The lack of a teaching position left him, as always, an 'outsider' in the Catholic intellectual world. As he waited for an opportunity to arise, Przywara stayed busy by studying Ignatian spirituality as well as by editing a German edition of John Henry Newman's works.[75] Finally, in 1922, he was given the opportunity to serve on the staff of the Jesuit periodical, *Stimmen der Zeit*. It was a perfect match. Przywara embraced his work at the journal, and he would remain in his position until war ended the journal's publication in 1941.

Stimmen der Zeit became Przywara's outlet for dozens of reviews, essays and articles over the next few years. It was not uncommon, in fact, for him to contribute several pieces in a single issue. Many of his contributions are long and perceptive reviews of recently published books brought together under a single theme for examination. These reviews demonstrate Przywara's keen insight, and they also show that he read widely. Indeed, the intellectual freedom that his position at the journal provided him gave him the time

---

[73] In fact, when his studies were interrupted by the war, Przywara made a living by teaching music at the Jesuit preparatory school Stella Matutina in Feldkirch, Austria. He even published a book of hymns during this time. As would be the case with Barth, music was important to all aspects of his life, including his theology. He reflected later, in fact, that '"Music as form" is the real birthplace of what later I took up as "polarity", and then "unity in tension", and finally as "analogy" at the center of my thinking'. In a passage found only in the second edition of *Analogia Entis*, Przywara describes the *analogia entis* as 'the mystery of this musical rhythm – just as the fugues of Bach's "Art of the Fugue" are interwoven toward a great silence.' See Erich Przywara, *Analogia Entis*, in *Schriften*, vol. 3 (Einsiedeln: Johannes-Verlag, 1962), p. 210. See also Bernhard Gertz, 'Erich Przywara (1889–1972)', in *Christliche Philosophie im katholischen Denken des 19. und 20 Jahrhunderts*, vol. 2, ed. Emerich Coretch (Graz: Styria, 1988), p. 572.

[74] The most important of these early writings is *Eucharistie und Arbeit*, published in 1917, which was reprinted as, *Eucharistie und Arbeit*, in *Schriften*, vol. 1 (Eisiedeln: Johannes-Verlag, 1962).

[75] His reading of Newman, as we will see, will be one of the most formative experiences of his life. See Erich Przywara, *A Newman Synthesis* (New York: Longmans, 1931).

and opportunity to become one of the most well-read Catholic thinkers of his time.[76] It also made him an attractive and available guest lecturer, and Przywara made up for not having an academic post by lecturing regularly in universities and institutions across Germany. The combination of his editorial position, his writings and lectures, and the originality of his insight made him 'a leading spokesman for Catholicism during the whole period between the two world wars' – at least among a certain group of Catholics.[77] He was influential among younger thinkers who were 'seeking their futures in a new, culturally open Catholicism', but he was not embraced as openly by those who held a more traditional view of the Catholic Church's role and function.[78] Among these thinkers, Przywara was viewed as someone who spoke less for the Church and its tradition than for himself.[79]

Towards the *analogia entis*

It was during these years that, in response to the challenges of his time, his work at the journal, his perception of the needs of the next generation

---

[76] His tremendous output, both in the journal and in his books, explains some of his influence, especially before the war. Leo Zimny lists over 800 publications in *Erich Przywara: Sein Schriftum, 1912–1962* (Eisiendeln: Johannes-Verlag, 1963). Nielsen notes that during his most active years in Munich, Przywara either lived alone or only with a few members of his order. This isolation, along with the lack of pastoral duties, meant that he had time for intensive study and research. See Niles C. Nielsen, 'The Analogia Entis of Erich Przywara' (Unpublished Doctoral Dissertation, Yale University, 1951), p. 495.

[77] James V. Zeitz, 'Erich Przywara: A Visionary Theologian', *Thought* 58 (1983), p. 147.

[78] O'Meara, *Erich Przywara*, p. 7. For example, Karl Rahner and Hans Urs von Balthasar regularly and publicly noted Przywara's influence on their thought. This influence has been felt in post-Vatican II Catholic theology, but even so, it is important to remember Przywara himself was a Vatican I theologian in every sense, as his theological commitments and the form of his thought took their shape in adherence to this council. It is hard to argue, however, that Przywara had no influence at all on the proceedings at Vatican II, given the scope of his influence in Germany during the years before World War II. Martha Zechmeister puts it well: Przywara is 'someone whose lectures and writings gave decisive impetuses for a Catholic restoration, a precursor of Vatican II'. See Martha Zechmeister, 'Przywara, Erich S. J. (1908)', in *Lexikon für Theologie und Kirche*, vol. 9 (Freiburg: Herder, 1999), p. 688.

[79] The consequences of Przywara's isolation would be felt in the years after World War II when he fell into disfavour with the officers in the Society of Jesus and was denied any position, teaching or otherwise, within the Catholic Church. His superiors pushed him away in part because they believed that his theology – which involved the synthesizing of new ideas from diverse (and often non-Catholic) streams of thought – was exactly what the Church did *not* need at the time. Przywara noted his isolated position in Catholic theology later in his career in 'Die Reichweite der Analogie als katholischer Grundform', in *Schriften*, vol. 3 (Einsiedeln: Johannes-Verlag, 1962), pp. 247–51. Also see Nielsen, 'The Analogia Entis of Erich Przywara', p. 23.

of Catholics – and interestingly, his reading of Karl Barth – Przywara began to turn to the *analogia entis*. Przywara later recalled that his first encounter with the principle occurred in 1912–13 while studying Thomas Aquinas' *Quaestiones disputatae* and *De Ente et Essentia*, and the basic insights he gained from this encounter stayed with him in the years that followed as he began to think about the Catholic Church, its tradition, and its role in the world.[80] His love for the rhythms patterns of music and poetry influenced his thinking during this time, and these influences combined with the analogical insights he learnt from Thomas to shape how he was absorbing the ideas he was encountering in figures like Augustine, pseudo-Dionysus, and the German Mystics.[81] These thinkers provided many of the important distinctions and categories he later would use in his formulation of the *analogia entis*. The event, however, that helped him put the pieces in place so that he could formulate his interpretation of the *analogia entis* was his work on the collected volume of Newman's writings.

Przywara became convinced that Cardinal Newman was one of the few thinkers who recognized what it meant to truly be Catholic in the modern world. He referred to him as an '*Augustinus redivivus* of modern times' – a figure who stood 'amidst the torrent which bears all things to their doom' with a gaze 'calmly fixed upon the God of the end'.[82] Przywara found this image appealing as he considered the 'torrent' that the post-war years had brought to the Catholic Church in Germany. The Church's crisis, Przywara noted later, had its roots in the 'terrible experience of the war years, when this deified world exploded in shreds, humanity – which had constricted and anthropomorphized God – appeared as a carnivorous beast, and creation itself appeared as a volcano'.[83] In response to the philosophical and

---

[80] See Przywara, *Analogia Entis*, p. 7.

[81] See James Collins, 'Przywara's "*Analogia Entis*"', *Thought*, no. 65 (1990), p. 267. Przywara's love for poetry is well known. During these early years, he published two collections: *Unsere Kirche* in 1915 and *The Divine Majesty* in 1925.

[82] Erich Przywara, 'St. Augustine and the Modern World', in *A Monument to Saint Augustine* (London: Sheed & Ward, 1930), p. 286. Przywara develops these themes in a series of major essays on Newman, many of which are collected in *Ringen der Gegenwart: Gesammelte Aufsätze 1922–1927*, Band II (Augsburg: Filser, 1929), pp. 802–79. In these essays, Przywara defends Newman against charges that he is guilty of 'modernism' by demonstrating the potential benefits of Newman's living and experiential emphasis on faith. Newman's *An Essay in Aid of a Gramma of Assent* (New York: Longmans, 1947) and *An Essay on the Development of Christian Doctrine* 6th edn (Notre Dame: University of Notre Dame Press, 1989) were particularly important for Przywara.

[83] Erich Przywara, 'Die religiöse Krisis in der Gegenwart und der Katholizismus', in *Katholische Krise: In Zusammenarbeit with dem Verfasser herausgegeben und mit einem Nachwort versehen*, ed. Bernhard Gertz (Düsseldorf: Patmos-Verlag, 1967), p. 47.

theological questions this situation raised, the German Catholic Church split into two groups, with conservative factions arguing that the Church should posture itself *against* the culture and progressives seeking to reform the Church so that it might reach out *to* the culture more effectively. Przywara – who described the difference between the groups as the distinction between the 'narrow rules and narrow ideas' of a 'ghetto' Catholicism and the 'the creative freedom' of the 'Catholicism of the future' – identified with the progressive side, and he regularly argued that Catholics should seek to redeem the culture rather than take a protective or reactionary stance over against it.[84] The Catholic Church would relate rightly to the world, he believed, only when Catholics were able to recognize the hand of God at work *in* the world, especially in their own lives. For this reason, they not only must be able to recognize the 'towering distinctiveness of God', but they also should recognize 'the self-communication of God reaching from creation to the human person'.[85] In other words, while Catholics should retain a firm commitment to the notion that God is utterly distinct from them, they also should keep their eyes open for the ways that God is working in and through their lives and, by extension, through the culture as a whole. For Przywara, then, the unsettling events that were shaking the foundations of the culture in general and the Church in particular were more an opportunity to be seized than a trial to be suffered. Catholics would respond appropriately to these events when they learnt to 'stand in the middle of the storm of the times' – that is, when they recognized that these events were the direct result of the activity of God and joined with this activity by participating in it.[86]

How could the Catholic Church arrive at such a perspective? Przywara thought that the answer was to develop a comprehensive philosophical-theological system that combined the metaphysical foundation of the Scholastics with the scientific and psychological elements of modern thought. Such a system, he believed, would provide Catholics the theological foundation they needed to prompt them to meet the intellectual and cultural challenges they were facing with confidence instead of fear. More specifically, Przywara was convinced that the resources of the Catholic tradition had much to offer the larger world of philosophy, especially as it considered the problem of God. This problem, in his view, was the foundation of the other problems, political and cultural, that Europe faced at the time, and Przywara believed that this problem could be addressed if a robust Catholic theology could be translated into modern idiom and brought to bear upon it. If a theology

---

[84] Erich Przywara 'Katholizität', in *Katholische Krise: In Zusammenarbeit with dem Verfasser herausgegeben und mit einem Nachwort versehen*, ed. Bernhard Gertz (Düsseldorf: Patmos-Verlag, 1967), pp. 20–1.

[85] Przywara, 'Die religiöse Krisis in der Gegenwart und der Katholizismus', p. 47.

[86] Przywara 'Katholizität', p. 38.

of this sort, built upon the best insights of the Catholic tradition, could be formulated in the midst of such an unsettling period in history, then the Church would be freed to reach out to the world with the resources of its tradition and show the world that, in fact, God remained an active force in it and was working even now to redeem it.

Przywara was convinced that Cardinal Newman pointed Catholics towards just such a system. In the face of a modern world torn between the 'comprehended Hegelian God, Who is therefore not God' and 'the unattainable God of Kierkegaard, of Whom therefore man must despair', Newman pointed to a 'God Who is at once without and within'.[87] Przywara saw Newman's idea as a modern reformulation of Augustine's 'one God exterior and interior' – a notion he believed was central not only to the spiritual life of Catholics, but to the entire history of philosophy.[88] Newman, Przywara argues, follows in the footsteps of Augustine in his turn to the concepts of the conscience, to implicit reasoning, and in his defence of 'the validity of the ordinary man's unreflective response to the moral and physical universe'.[89] Przywara sees these 'modern' psychological reflections on the human self as wholly consistent with traditional Catholic thought because, he argues, they function simply as a subjective, concrete, and personal expression of traditional Catholic theological principles.[90] Newman, in other words, has taken the best of the Catholic tradition and made it relevant by translating it into a conceptual framework familiar to the modern world. Indeed, Przywara believes that Newman's more subjective approach – when combined with the rationality of Catholic thought in the tradition of Thomas Aquinas – points to a way forward for modern Catholics because it shows them how Catholic thought can contribute to and ultimately resolve the problems which have shaped not only the history of philosophy, but the contemporary world as well. Newman thus provides an example that could lead the Catholic Church to address the cultural and philosophical problems that led to modern tragedies such as the War.

In short, for Przywara, Newman's synthesis points Catholics towards a vision for a Church that embraces rather than simply stands over against the modern world. This vision was compelling for him because it demonstrates

---

[87] Przywara, 'St. Augustine and the Modern World', p. 279. This dichotomy between two sides with a mediating Catholic position in the middle was a pattern that would be repeated in Przywara's thought throughout his career.

[88] *Ibid.* 'It should be obvious', Przywara says, 'where alone in this modern age [Augustine's] spirit finds its perfect reincarnation.' This helps explain why Przywara chose to translate Newman's works into German; he was, in effect, providing German Catholics a role model of how to live as a Catholic in the modern world.

[89] Collins, 'Przywara's "Analogia Entis"', p. 268.

[90] See Erich Przywara, 'J. H. Newmans Problemstellung', in *Ringen der Gegenwart*, pp. 826–34.

that reflection upon the subjective and individual elements of the Christian life can be used to combine contemporary insights – especially those related to human subjectivity and experience – with the basic commitments of the Catholic tradition. This is why Przywara saw Newman as the new Augustine: just as Augustine developed his 'most sublime vision' in 'the presence of the fall of the old world', Newman was able to see 'man, the world, and history from the already almost prophetic perspective revealed to him by that final struggle between Christ and Antichrist legible on the countenance of the modern world'.[91] Newman himself summarized his approach in a phrase often quoted by Przywara: 'My unchangeableness here below is perseverance in changing'.[92] Przywara interpreted this phrase as representing a vertical, God-centred approach that concurrently embraces the realities of a horizontal world, and this vertical–horizontal pattern became a model for him as he began to develop his own version of the same insight, the *analogia entis*.

'God as the Mystery of the World'

Newman's influence upon Przywara can be seen in an important series of lectures he delivered in August 1923 at Ulm entitled 'God as the Mystery of the World'.[93] The subject matter of these lectures was nothing new for him. In fact, by this point, Przywara had been writing about the same themes and topics for over a year. For example, in 'The Experience of God and the Demonstration of God' – an essay written nearly a year before he delivered 'God as the Mystery of the World' – Przywara offers his earliest account of the relationship between the history of Western philosophical thought, Roman Catholic theology, the idea that God is both 'above' and 'in' creation, and the *analogia entis*. He argues that an analysis of the contrasts found in the history of philosophical thought shows that, in the end, the finite world must be seen as wholly dependent upon 'something immutable and infinite, which is essentially distinct from them'.[94] This relationship should be interpreted within the context of creation's ongoing relationship with the immutable God who is both 'in' and 'above' it. While God is 'in all things', Przywara says, he also is 'beyond all things, a God who is comprehensible in creatures, who are in the divine image, and yet incomprehensive

[91] Przywara, 'St. Augustine and the Modern World', p. 286.

[92] See John Henry Newman, *Meditations and Devotions of the Late Cardinal Newman* (London; New York: Longmans, Green,, 1893), pp. 508–9. See also Erich Przywara, 'Gottgeheimnis Der Welt', p. 241.

[93] For a description of the circumstances of these lectures, see O'Meara, *Erich Przywara*, pp. 41–5.

[94] Erich Przywara, 'Gotteserfahrung und Gottesbeweis', in *Schriften*, vol. 2 (Eisiedeln: Johannes-Verlag, 1962), p. 7.

in his innermost being'.[95] He argues that the *analogia entis* is the concept that best captures the nature of this relationship because it represents the 'origin, the ground of truth, [and] the content and extent of our natural knowledge of God', but he is not clear on exactly what the concept entails.[96] He picks up this argument again in a series of lectures delivered at the University of Leipzig in February 1922, and he takes it further by drawing out its implications for the life and work of the Catholic Church more specifically.[97] The lectures that comprise 'God as the Mystery of the World' are simply a further refinement of these same ideas. They stand, therefore, as a marker along the way of Przywara's ongoing attempt to refine and clarify his one basic argument about the history of philosophy, the Catholic Church, and their relationship with one another. These lectures are distinct, however, because of their high level of clarity and comprehensiveness, and for this reason, they are representative of Przywara's best insights during this period.

Przywara delivered these lectures to the Catholic Student's Union, and he was in his element, because Catholic youth often were sympathetic to his perspective about the need for reform in the Church. His overall goal in these lectures is to provide the theological and philosophical foundation that would be necessary to begin to institute the kind of reforms these students were seeking. Specifically, Przywara wants them to see the movement of God in their own lives as well as in the wider patterns of history – especially philosophical history – more clearly. He tells the students that the most constructive vision for the future is for Catholics not to simply be a *part* of the German culture, but to *embrace* it as the context of the movement of God in history. In fact, he argues, the philosophical movement shaping post-war German culture 'seeks us' and, 'whether we ourselves know it or not, we are, in our own internal Catholic problems, already a part of this movement'.[98] In other words, as Przywara sees it, the German culture – characterized most directly by the questions and problems posed by its philosophers – is, at the prompting of God, seeking the truth about God. The Catholic Church, which exists in tune with that same God, participates in this same divine movement, and as such, it is both equipped and called by God to give the world the answers it needs. For this reason, Przywara argues, the Church commits a disservice both to God and the world when it chooses to be content with either an 'undignified running in the background' or a 'purely negative protest' – activities which Przywara

---

[95] *Ibid.*

[96] *Ibid.*, p. 10.

[97] Przywara's 1922 lectures were published later on as *Gott: Fünf Vorträge über das religionsphilosophische Problem* (Köln: Oratoriums-Verlag, 1926), and they were reprinted as *Gott*, in *Schriften*, vol. 2 (Eisiedeln: Johannes-Verlag, 1962), pp. 243–372.

[98] Przywara, 'Gottgeheimnis Der Welt', p. 124.

calls the twin 'illnesses' of the Church.[99] Instead, the task and mission of the Church is to engage the world positively – on the world's own terms – with the truth of the Catholic faith, and it is to do so under the presupposition that the culture itself is the primary context of God's redemptive work in history.

How can the Catholic Church change its perspective and reach out to the world in this way? Przywara lifts up Thomas Aquinas as an example, because in his view, Aquinas consistently demonstrates the kind of 'inner rhythm' and 'Catholic balance' that is required if one is to engage the culture.[100] In the modern Catholic Church, he says, this rhythm and balance already manifests itself in the Catholic liturgy as it 'bears, in its unexplored depths, those contrasting tensions' that pervade both the Church's inner life and the culture as a whole.[101] It also finds expression, he tells his young audience, in the German Catholic youth movement, especially since this movement has reawakened ideas about the value of the individual and his role in society.[102] The influence of Newman's turn to the human consciousness and experience can be seen in Przywara's argument at this point. Przywara insists that each individual realizes his own inner nature as he moves towards God, but this realization does not mean – as he believes Martin Luther's theology implies – that Christ is now 'locked into the interior world' of the individual.[103] The movement of the world towards God, he says later in the lecture, cannot be 'a program of one individual or of a limited community. It is the philosophy of humanity, one for all the various kinds of human beings; all peoples will have their own contributions to bring forward as gift'.[104] Przywara's vision for the Church, therefore, is not focused on the Church alone but on the world as the context for the Church's work. The Catholic Church, prompted by God's commission, is enlisted to go out into a world in which God already is moving, and, through the rhythm of its own inner life, it is to prompt and direct the world to discover its *own* true life of rhythm and movement with God. Przywara, therefore, is not merely offering a vision of how *Catholics* are to live in the world; he is putting forth a Catholic vision for *the world* to become its true self as a result of the insights that the Catholic tradition offers to it. This means that the life, work, and teaching of the Catholic Church, which exist as the focal point of the Catholic life, stand at the centre of this redemptive vision as the instrument by which God culminates his work in human history.

---

[99] *Ibid.*, p. 137.

[100] *Ibid.*, p. 156.

[101] *Ibid.*, p. 144.

[102] *Ibid.*, pp. 145–56.

[103] *Ibid.*, p. 147.

[104] *Ibid.*, p. 238.

Przywara argues that the best way to interpret this vision is in terms of the 'miracle of the "*analogia entis*", the polarity of similarity and dissimilarity between God, who according to the Apostle "is all in all" and "works all in all" . . . and the creature in its own being and working'.[105] Przywara explains this idea by way of a lengthy examination of the philosophical tradition from the ancient Greeks to the Scholastics and beyond. He argues that the primary story to be told about the history of philosophy involves the failure of the great philosophers to resolve the problem of the relationship between the immanence and transcendence of God.[106] From Plato and Aristotle to Descartes, Kant, and Hegel, every major philosopher has emphasized either divine immanence or transcendence at the expense of the other, and in every case, the result has been the collapsing of the being of God into the being of the world. However, Przywara insists, by recognizing these back-and-forth movements within philosophical history, the modern Catholic thinker stands in a position to 'come ever closer to that ideal philosophy that is able to view both the image of God and the world, so to speak, from the point of view of all the individual types'.[107] In other words, he believes that by seeing the errors of both extremes throughout history, a Catholic thinker can discern that the right way forward involves finding the proper balance between the two emphases. The result of discovering this balance is a 'program on whose realization the one *philosophia perennis* has labored up until today'.[108] This 'program' presents the true alternative to the false 'either-or' offered by the philosophers: a view of God that maintains God's distinction from the world while also situating the human as one whose very being is at every moment oriented towards God as her final end.

Such a view of God, Przywara argues, is maintained throughout the history of the Catholic tradition when seen as an organic whole. That is, when the teachings of figures like the Church Fathers, Augustine, Aquinas, Scotus, and Newman are read in light of one another, it becomes clear the Catholic tradition's concept of God maintains precisely the type of balance that the philosophers had not been able to discern, because it holds together both the distinction and the unity – the transcendence and the immanence – that marks the human relationship with God. The Catholic view, he says,

> forms, beneath the illuminating sun of the revelation of the creation of the world 'out of nothing' and 'in the beginning' – as well as the revela-tion of the providence of God – that wonderful patristic concept of

---

[105] Przywara, 'Gottgeheimnis Der Welt', pp. 213–14. Przywara here draws a connection between the *analogia entis* and the work of Augustine, Thomas Aquinas, and Duns Scotus.

[106] See Przywara, 'Gottgeheimnis Der Welt', pp. 157–212.

[107] *Ibid.*, p. 161.

[108] *Ibid.*, p. 238.

God as the 'God exterior and interior', the towering God of both incomprehensibility and the unutterable indwelling within all creation: God in us and above us. Transcendence and immanence no longer dissolve into one another, but they are bound to one another as two poles in living unity in tension.[109]

This 'tension' manifests itself in the unresolved contrast between God's distinction *from* human beings with his intimate and constant relationship *to* them. The ground of such tension, as Przywara develops in detail near the end of the lecture, is the incarnation. Jesus Christ, fully divine and fully human, demonstrates in his person the polarity which defines human life in general, and the Catholic Church – as the body of Christ in the world – continues to exist in this polarity in and through its sacramental life.[110]

Przywara explains how this polarity manifests itself in the lives of individual Catholics by pointing his students to a theme that Newman adopted from Augustine: the notion that 'fear and love must go together'.[111] Fear corresponds to the exteriority of God while love corresponds to the believer's internal experience of God, and both are necessary components of the Christian life because each one tempers the extremes of the other, and a denial of either pole would mean the removal of the distinction between God and creature. If fear and love are kept together in the proper tension within Christian life, Przywara says, the result is that the 'wonderful reflection of loving nearness and reverential distance, of fearing love and loving fear, as Augustine formulates it in a genial antithesis, this deepest ethos of Christianity, is now anchored in a decisive source – in God himself'.[112] This 'unity-in-tension' constitutes Przywara's comprehensive vision for Catholic life, and it stands as the unique Catholic contribution to the history of philosophy. This kind of life, he believes, builds upon the foundation the basic Catholic insights of Aquinas and Newman, both of whom stood on the shoulders of Augustine.[113] Indeed, in a remark that foreshadows emphases he would develop more thoroughly in his later writings, Przywara

---

[109] *Ibid.*, p. 193.

[110] See *Ibid.*, pp. 229–38. Przywara here returns to an idea he had developed more thoroughly in a 1922 lecture, 'Gott der Idee und der Geschichte'. See Przywara, *Gott*, in *Schriften*, vol. 2, pp. 282–97.

[111] Augustine, *The Confessions*, trans. O. S. B. Maria Boulding, Vintage Spiritual Classics (New York: Vintage Books, 1997), pp. 201–16 (Book 10.6–19).

[112] Przywara, 'Gottgeheimnis Der Welt', p. 193.

[113] Note the final paragraph of Przywara's lecture: 'Must we choose Thomas *or* Newman in this unhealthy epoch, struggling as it is between integralism and modernism . . . No, the choice of this hour as we stand at the central point of the spiritual crisis of our time is not Thomas or Newman, but, true to the spirit of Catholic polarity, Thomas *and* Newman.' See *Ibid.*, p. 242.

explicitly echoes Augustine in his description of what the believer's disposition before God should look like:

> To be sure, such is the fundamental disposition of human knowledge of God: God nearer to me than all the world, God nearer to me than I am to myself; God more real to me than all the world, God more real than I am to myself: God all in all, *Deus meus et omnia*! But precisely out of the implicitness of this knowledge of God, out of this – shall we say, psychological immediacy to God – grows that disposition of awe-struck longing, that inextinguishable *Inquietum*, that never satisfied but always blessed infinite restlessness toward God, which is: *quaeritur inveniendus et invenitur quarendus*, I seek in order to find, and I find in order to seek.[114]

The vision Przywara is casting for his student audience is clear: they should live as awe-struck believers who not only find their *telos* in God, but exist even now in a restless movement *towards* God in concert with God's work in history. This vision, when applied to the Catholic Church as a whole, provides a picture of a Church that does not retreat from the world but *embraces* it as the locus of God's redemptive activity. It also provides a compelling vision for the Church to demonstrate to the world the shape of the world's own life and existence before God by means of the Church's tradition, liturgy, and spiritual life. With this basic theological foundation in hand, Przywara hopes, the Catholic Church can be motivated to reach out to the world with the truth of the gospel. If it does, then perhaps the horrors of the past can be averted in the future, because the despair that drove events like the war can be dissipated. This result can occur, however, only if the Catholic Church meets the challenges that face it with confidence instead of fear and love for the world in which God is at work.

'God in Us or Above Us?'

At the same time Przywara was delivering his 'God as the Mystery of the World' lectures, another lecture entitled 'God in Us or Above Us?' was being published in *Stimmen der Zeit*.[115] There are two important differences in Przywara's argument in this lecture as compared to the much longer 'God

---

[114] *Ibid.*, p. 230. See Saint Augustine of Hippo, *The Trinity*, trans. Edmund Hill (Brooklyn, NY: New City Press, 1991), pp. 395–6 (*De Trinitate* 15.2).

[115] Erich Przywara, 'Gott in uns oder über uns? (Immanenz und Transzendenz in heutigen Geistesleben)', in *Stimmen der Zeit*, 105 (1923), pp. 343–62. A revised version of this essay was reprinted under the title, 'Gott in uns und Gott über uns', in *Ringen der Gegenwart*, Band II, pp. 543–78. All citations will be from the original *Stimmen der Zeit* version.

as the Mystery of the World'. First, while the challenge posed by Protestant theology is mentioned briefly in 'God as the Mystery of the World', it occupies the central place in this lecture. Przywara's primary goal still is to offer a vision that enriches Catholic life and practice, but in this lecture, he also wants to show that Catholic theology provides a better way to meet the challenges of the modern world than Protestant theology. Specifically, Przywara worries that Protestant theology in the tradition of Martin Luther inevitably leads the church to 'shrink back' from the culture rather than engage it, and he is convinced that this is precisely what the church should *not* be doing during this critical period in history.[116] The theologian Przywara worries about the most in this regard is Karl Barth. He notes, in fact, that Barth and other 'dialectical' theologians are ushering in a 'genuine rebirth of Protestantism', saying that '[o]f any group in present-day Protestantism, Luther belongs to them and is their father'.[117] In other words, Przywara believes that Barth and his colleagues have recaptured the basic theological principles and insights that prompted the Reformation, most notably the 'wholly other' God of Luther.[118] As a result, they pose a stark alternative to Przywara's own uniquely Catholic vision of God and God's relationship to the world.

This insight points to the second important difference between these two lectures: Przywara's decision to frame his account of human life more explicitly in relation to his doctrine of God. He is convinced that the divisions between Protestants and Roman Catholics are less the result of ecclesiological differences than they are of fundamentally different understandings of the nature of God.[119] As he interprets it, Luther and the other Reformers were seeking a transcendent God to correct the errors they saw in the Catholic Church, while the Catholic Church – especially after the recovery of the tradition at the Council of Trent – sought God in terms of the balance between divine transcendence and immanence. The latter approach is the correct one, Przywara believes, and this means that the key

---

[116] Przywara, 'Gott in uns oder über uns?', p. 350. Przywara had offered a similar critique of Luther and his heirs, including Barth, in his lectures at the University of Leitzpig in 1922. See Przywara, *Gott*, in *Schriften*, vol. 2, pp. 285–308.

[117] *Ibid.* This 'rebirth' was a positive development, in Przywara's view, because it finally allowed him to pinpoint the 'root' of the differences between Protestants and Catholics. In Barth, Przywara sees a theologian who understands that both these differences and the answer to the crisis facing the modern church have their root in a proper understanding of God relationship to his human creatures. Barth thus provided sparring partner, of sorts, with whom Przywara could engage and against whom he can draw clear distinctions.

[118] *Ibid.*

[119] *Ibid.*, pp. 343–4. On the distinction between Protestants and Roman Catholics, Przywara says: 'The final basis lies in the concept of God'.

to both a proper understanding of God's relationship with humanity as well as to a right account of the nature and task of the church in the world is to develop the concept of the 'God of the *analogia entis*, the "God above us and in us"' more fully.[120] It is for this reason, above all others, that Przywara attempts to articulate the meaning and content of the *analogia entis* more fully than he does in 'God as the Mystery of the World'. His goal in doing so is to articulate the key difference between Protestants and Catholics – as well as the true nature of the Catholic alternative – in a clearer and more comprehensive way.

Przywara highlights these distinctions in his lecture by explaining that the phrase 'God in us and God above us' captures the 'Catholic middle' – illustrated best by Augustine – which finds the balance between the extremes of emphasizing either God's transcendence or immanence at the expense of the other.[121] This understanding of God supplies, once again, the theological foundation for Przywara's vision for the role that Catholic Church can and should play in the modern world. Just as the incarnation reveals the central truth and pattern of God's relation to the world, this relationship now takes the shape of the Catholic Church's life as the 'body of Christ' in the world. The Church can fulfil this role, however, only if it conforms its own life and action to the life and action of God who is both 'in' and 'over' creation. In other words, the Church lives in line with its purpose, and with God's overall relationship to creation, when it corresponds to the unity-in-tension of God's immanence and transcendence by being 'in' but not 'of' the world.

Przywara argues that this incarnation-centred vision for the Catholic Church stands in opposition to any vision that would be possible under the theology of those Protestants like Barth who are following the insights of Luther. While he believes that these thinkers correctly understand the 'God above us' part of the equation by holding that God is utterly distinct from humanity, they fail to balance this emphasis with an account of God's involvement in and connection to creation. The result is a theology that posits God as the 'all-determining reality' and 'sole effective' agent in the world.[122] Such a view, Przywara thinks, leads to two errors that, while seeming to be opposite, actually are identical. On the one hand, Przywara believes that a direct line exists between Luther's view of God and those philosophies, such as the ones offered by Spinoza and Hegel, in which everything

---

[120] *Ibid.*, p. 344.

[121] *Ibid.*, p. 345.

[122] *Ibid.*, p. 347. As Przywara notes, his interpretation of Luther is not based upon a direct reading of Luther's works but upon essays by Franz Xavier Kliefl, a Catholic theologian at the University of Wurzburg, and Ernst Troeltsch, a Protestant teaching at Heidelberg, which had appeared simultaneously in October 1917.

that occurs in nature and history is the direct consequence of God's activity.[123] This argument is an early form of the charge of 'theopanism' that Przywara would regularly issue against Barth in the years ahead. That is, if God is seen as the sole effective cause of everything that happens in history, then creation as such ultimately cannot be distinguished from God because it is merely an extension of God's will.[124] On the other hand, in reaction to such a view, Przywara holds that other thinkers – represented by Kant and more starkly by Nietzsche – created philosophies that finally collapsed creaturely activity into divine activity.[125] In either case, the result is the same: God and the world are brought into direct identity with one another. Instead of the 'Catholic balance between transcendence and immanence', Luther and his heirs offer a transcendence which 'capsizes immanence only to again capsize transcendence' – meaning that, in their desire to preserve God's distinction from the world, theologians like Luther and Barth have actually made God and the world one and the same.[126]

Przywara insists that this error is the direct result of Luther's obsession with obtaining an 'absolute assurance of salvation', because to acquire this view, Luther had to downplay human action to such an extent that 'the visible world and visible humanity are visible only as "sin" and "the devil's work"'.[127] In other words, Luther's fear of works-righteousness led him to emphasize God's transcendence *over* creation to such an extent that he completely lost God's immanence *within* creation. Without any notion of immanence to balance transcendence, Luther began to view the world – and the Christian life – solely in terms of divine agency. The result was doubly tragic. In the realm of theology and philosophy, the door was opened to seeing human action as indistinguishable from divine action, and the trajectory thus was set for the eventual blurring of the distinction between God

---

[123] Przywara will later make this criticism more pointed: 'The internal dialectics of Reformation religiosity have been uncloaked as the prime cause of the dialectics of the modern age.' See Przywara, 'Die religiöse Krisis in der Gegenwart und der Katholizismus', p. 51.

[124] Przywara explains: 'Transcendence and immanence are no longer bound together in a "tension of opposites" but have been made identical. In that the hidden, incomprehensible God, the *Deus absconditus* as Luther liked to say, is not merely "all in all" but rather "everything alone". He is the essence of the creature, and all activities of the creature, insofar as they are understood to be "essential", are His work alone.' See Przywara, 'Gott in uns oder über uns?', p. 348.

[125] *Ibid.*, p. 351. Przywara views Nietzsche's 'superman' as the clearest representation of 'man as God'.

[126] *Ibid.*, p. 351.

[127] *Ibid.*, pp. 349–50. Przywara sees a direct line between Luther's theology and that of the 'Barth-Gogarten-Thurneysen' school, whom he says, argues that 'God is yes but the creature is no; God is life but the creature is death; God is holy, but the creature is sin'. See Przywara, *Gott*, in *Schriften*, vol. 2, p. 286.

and the world. More practically, because the being and action of the human – and, by extension, the being and action of the church – were seen as simply 'unconnected' to God in the sense that they were no longer seen as having any real or distinct role in the outworking of God's salvation in the world, they were completely devalued.[128] Przywara sharpens his criticism by drawing a contrast between such a view and the Roman Catholic *analogia entis*:

> It happens also – and here we see the actual contrast to the Catholic concept of God – that in the place of the 'analogy' between God and the creature, there is put pure 'negation'. If the *analogia entis* of the Catholic concept of God means the mysterious tension of a 'similar-dissimilar,' corresponding to the tension of the 'God in us and above us', then in the Protestant concept of God, the 'similarity' has been completely crossed out.[129]

Przywara's meaning is clear. With all notions of similarity 'crossed out', Luther and his heirs have downplayed God's involvement in human life to such an extent that life in the world, including the life of the church itself, simply fails to matter. This kind of theology, he believes, stands in contrast to the basic truth of the incarnation of Jesus Christ, where the visible world of the human was united, in one person, with the invisible world of God.[130] It also leaves no room for a vision of the church as a continuation or manifestation of the incarnation in the modern world. The final consequence – and here we return to the motivations underlying Przywara's argument – is that the church is left without reason to do anything other than retreat from the world, abandoning it to its present state, while looking to the God who stands above in judgement over it. Such a theology is tragic, Przywara believes, because it signifies a surrender of the church's true mission. What the church needs instead is a theology that holds to a proper understanding of God's relation to the world, one in which God's dissimilarity to the world is kept in balance with God's similarity to it. Such tension, Przywara believes, is precisely what the Catholic *analogia entis* maintains. By describing human existence in relation to a God who exists both above us and in us, the *analogia entis* promotes a view of the Catholic Church

---

[128] Przywara, 'Gott in uns oder über uns?', p. 350. Also see Przywara, *Gott*, in *Schriften*, vol. 2, pp. 298–308.

[129] Przywara, 'Gott in uns oder über uns?', p. 350.

[130] Hans Urs von Balthasar echoed this critique in his analysis of the theology of the second edition of Barth's *Epistle to the Romans*: 'the very heart of Christianity, its most crucial doctrine, the Incarnation, becomes impossible . . . there can be no such thing as the *life* of Christ, but only a *death* of Christ'. See Balthasar, *The Theology of Karl Barth: Exposition and Interpretation*, trans. S. J. Edward T. Oakes (San Francisco: Ignatius Press, 1992), p. 72.

whose relation to the world follows precisely the same pattern: it is a Church *above* the world, in the sense that exists in distinction from the world, but it also is a Church *in* the world, in the sense that its inner life is bound together with its outwardly focused mission to reach out to the world with the truth of the gospel.

In the years ahead, Przywara would continue to be driven by this vision for the Catholic Church, and as a result, he would turn his efforts to articulating the *analogia entis* more fully. This doctrine, he believed, was the key both to addressing the philosophical questions hanging over modern European society and to meeting the challenges posed by the resurgent Protestant theology, typified by Karl Barth, that was dominating the theological scene. That Przywara would formulate this principle, in part, to respond to the challenge Barth's theology presented to his own vision for the role of the Catholic Church shows how intertwined the formation and development of his version of the *analogia entis* would be with Barth's theology. As we will see, Barth's own theological development is bound together with Przywara's theology as well.

A Stage Set for the Future

Barth read 'God in us or above us?' shortly after receiving a letter from Thurneysen, who commended it:

> Acquire for yourself a copy of Issue 11 of *Stimmen der Zeit*, August 1923, Herder Freiburg. There is a remarkably discerning and detailed essay about us from the side of the Catholic partner. It is interesting because he makes the Catholic standpoint very clearly visible. There are also essential and detailed remarks on Augustine. It is an expert who speaks there. We come off very well, even though our real concern is not seen.[131]

Thurneysen likely thought that the 'Dialectical Theologians' came off well because they had been identified as the definitive Protestant theologians of their day and as Luther's proper heirs. Barth, however, may not have had such a positive view of how he had been portrayed. As we will see in the next chapter, Barth had spent the years after the publication of *Romans* II teaching theology at Göttingen, where he had been invited to serve as an 'Honorary Professor of Reformed Theology'.[132] We will see that his studies

---

[131] Barth, *Karl Barth – Eduard Thurneysen Briefwechsel: 1921–30*, p. 190.

[132] Barth had been selected for this position because of the contribution of *Romans* I; the second edition would be published only after his arrival. For details of Barth's invitation and his transition to Göttingen, see Busch, *Karl Barth*, pp. 123–38.

of the writings of the Reformed tradition led him to realize that it was possible to articulate a theology that maintained God's distinction from the world while also maintaining a real relationship between God and humanity. These new ways of thinking had prompted Barth to rethink the construal of the relationship he had offered in *Romans* II. When Przywara's critique of his position came across his desk, therefore, it reached Barth at vulnerable point. Was Przywara not correct? Barth indeed *had* 'crossed out' any similarity between God and humanity in *Romans* II, and he had done so for good reasons – at least he thought so at the time. But had he not also avoided talk of the incarnate Jesus' human life in *Romans* II in favour of an emphasis on the resurrection? Had he not, in other words, downplayed the incarnation out of fear that it might open the door to errors he desperately wanted to avoid? Did that move leave him with little room for a real incarnation at all? If so, what does that mean for his understanding of the purpose and role of the church? Had he so downplayed its role that it no longer had any real value at all? Were there other ways to secure the distinction between God and the world without abandoning the possibility of any real relationship between them?

We have reason to think that these kinds of questions became central for Barth because only a few months after he read Przywara's essay, he wrote in the preface of the fourth edition of Romans that it was 'obvious that the book needs to be rewritten'. He mentions that the changes have been prompted, in part, by 'Catholic reviewers' who have 'displayed a genuine understanding of the point at issue'. Among these reviewers, he lists Przywara and Joseph Engert, and he notes that while Przywara reads him as a modern version of the old Reformers, Engert says that the commentary 'does not differ from the teaching of Thomas Aquinas, of the Council of Trent, and of the Roman Catechism'. Obviously, Barth notes, 'the two reviewers are clearly not saying quite the same thing'. Once he can get a clear picture of the true Catholic response, he says, 'we should be bound to answer them'.

> Meanwhile, I cannot help saying that I regard it as a most hopeful sign for both sides that an opportunity should now be provided of entering into genuine theological, as opposed to merely historical, discussion with the theologians of the Old Church. Those, like ourselves, who are moving in the world of the theology of the Reformation, for this very reason, ought not – and indeed do not – cast in the teeth of others that they are moving with conviction in the world of medieval theology.[133]

---

[133] See Barth, *The Epistle to the Romans*, pp. 20–1. Barth's attitude on this dialogue is captured by a quote from his first lecture during his seminar on Zwingli at Göttingen: 'Opponents have sharp eyes, as a rule sharper than partisans and always sharper than the so-called impartial or neutral'. We can discern here that Barth's hope for a

This statement can be read as one that outlines the spirit of the dialogue that would take place between Barth and Przywara over the next decade. It was a dialogue that has its roots in the fact that their divergent responses to the tragedy of World War I led Barth and Przywara in different directions. While Barth rejected Protestant Liberalism's broad starting point in favour of a narrower one, Przywara looked for a way to bring Catholicism out of its narrow confines and put it into conversation with the wider history of philosophical thought about God. Thus, whereas Barth was narrowing the parameters upon which true theology could be performed, Przywara was extending them. Yet their motivations were similar: Przywara thought that Roman Catholicism had answers that the world needed, if only it could meet the world where it was. Barth thought that neither the world nor the church knew what its problems were until they were told about them by God, and he wanted to lead the church to the point where it would finally listen.

Barth may have been convinced that the construal of *Romans* II needed to be changed, but he also was convinced that the alternative Przywara offered in 'God in us or above us?' did not provide an acceptable alternative. He needed to find a new way forward, and he would begin the process at Göttingen. He would do so, however, in a spirit of hope that the dialogue would be beneficial for both sides. He knew that he had much to learn, and he welcomed dialogue with someone, like Przywara, from whom he could learn much. For his part, Przywara had already found his way forward. The errors of *Romans* II, among other things, convinced him more than ever that he had to formulate a uniquely Catholic view of the world for the sake of the world. Barth's eschatological negation of the world, if it took hold, would only lead Christians to hand human history over to those who would destroy it. The world needed another vision: one that taught the world that all human existence stood in connection to the God above. In the years after 'God in us or above us?' Pryzwara began working towards a full articulation of the *analogia entis* as the centre of this vision. This view would culminate in the publication of *Religionphilosophie katholischer Theologie* in 1926. This book would lead him to an engagement with Barth once again, and it would set the stage for the exchange of 1932.

'genuine discussion' with his Catholic interlocutors did not only involve a desire to proclaim his own views, but also a sincere hope that he could learn from his opponents. See Karl Barth, *Die Theologie Zwinglis 1922/1923: Vorlesungen Göttingen Wintersemester 1922/1923*, Gesamtausgabe (Zurich: Theologischer Verlag Zürich, 2004), p. 5.

3

INCARNATION AND ANALOGY

No, when God reveals himself . . . it is an event with which what we do in our own sphere may well be in analogy but cannot be in continuity, as though our thinking and feeling were a kind of outflow or continuation of revelation.

– Karl Barth[1]

Religion is thus fundamentally not so much 'creature-feeling before God' but rather, it is consciousness of 'God in me and I in God' as the fundamental character of the creature.

– Erich Przywara, S. J.[2]

Introduction

The previous chapter discussed how Karl Barth moved from the liberal theology of his teachers to the theology of *Romans* II following his teachers' embrace of the German cause in World War I. It also explained how, in that book, Barth rejected the possibility of an inherent or ongoing connection between God and humanity in favour of a relationship seen purely in terms of negation. This negation leaves Jesus Christ – understood not in terms of his incarnate life as much as his eschatological resurrection – as the sole point of connection between God and creation. The chapter ended with Barth's comment, prompted in part by Erich Przywara's criticism, that this portrayal needed to be 'rewritten'. The chapter also showed that Przywara's

---

[1] Karl Barth, *The Göttingen Dogmatics: Instruction in the Christian Religion*, ed. Hannelotte Reiffen, trans. Geoffrey W. Bromiley, vol. 1 (Grand Rapids, MI: Eerdmans, 1991), p. 94.

[2] Erich Przywara, *Religionsphilosophie katholischer Theologie*, in *Schriften*, vol. 2 (Eisieldeln: Johannes-Verlag, 1962), p. 410.

vision for the Roman Catholic Church after the war was missionary in nature. That is, his goal in these early years was to formulate a theological framework that could help the Catholic Church engage the world instead of retreat from it, because he believed the Church's theological tradition had resources that could address the philosophical problems facing German culture. The chapter noted that Przywara saw Barth's theology as a threat to his vision for the Church, and we examined how he posited the *analogia entis* as an alternative to Barth's construal of the creator–creature relationship.

This chapter will continue the narrative of the previous one in the service of three goals. First, I will make the case that Barth's engagement with the Reformed tradition led him to move beyond the formulations of *Romans* II without fundamentally breaking from them. This move occurs as Barth develops a doctrine of revelation founded upon a more robust understanding of the incarnation, and it takes its final shape as a result of his deep engagement with the Reformed tradition. This development addresses Przywara's criticism of the theology of *Romans* II, sets the stage for their personal encounter in 1929, and provides the foundation for Barth's eventual formulation of the *analogia fidei* in *Church Dogmatics* I/1 (*CD* I/1). Second, I demonstrate that the next step for Przywara as he sought to develop a vision for how the Catholic Church could engage the world was to turn more explicitly to the human consciousness as the foundation for his presentation of the *analogia entis*. This formulation of the *analogia entis*, presented fully in *Religionsphilosophie katholischer Theologie*, enables Przywara to overcome traditional philosophical problems about the question of God and God's relationship with creation in a uniquely Catholic way, and it allows him to coherently describe the creator–creature relationship in terms of similarity within an ever greater dissimilarity. This description, he believes, provides the framework from which the Catholic Church finally can reach out to the world with the answers that the world cannot discover on its own. Third, I argue that, with Barth's developments at Göttingen and the insights of Przywara's *Religionsphilosophie*, all of pieces are in place for the debate that will occur between Barth and Przywara in the years that followed. That is, Barth's criticism of Przywara's *analogia entis*, culminating in his condemnation of it in the preface of *CD* I/1, simply consists of drawing out the insights first articulated at Göttingen; likewise, Przywara's mature presentation in *Analogia Entis* builds upon but does not fundamentally depart from the presentation of the principle in his *Religionsphilosophie*. This argument will culminate in Chapters 4 and 5.

Barth at Göttingen

Although he felt unprepared for the classroom, Barth accepted the position as 'Honorary Professor of Reformed Theology' at Göttingen because he felt that 'my place was among the theological students of Germany'.[3] He found the shift from the pastorate to a teaching position, however, more difficult than he initially had supposed. He noted later that his new position meant that he could no longer engage simply in 'attacking all kinds of errors and abuses', but that he now had 'to say what we really thought'.[4] This challenge was complicated by the fact that Barth simply was not prepared to give academic lectures on the subjects he was assigned. It was to his advantage, however, that his position called for a scholar of Reformed theology, because he soon found himself engaging in a close and careful study of the most important figures and texts in the Reformed tradition. In addition to courses on several books of the Bible, Barth taught seminars on the Heidelberg Catechism, Calvin, Zwingli, the Reformed Confessions, and Schleiermacher during his first two years at Göttingen.[5] His preparation for these lectures was hurried but rich, and the manuscripts reveal a depth to Barth's thinking that had not been present before. They also reveal something Barth himself discovered: that his theology 'was more Reformed and Calvinistic than I realized'.[6]

Two of Barth's seminars – the seminar on Ulrich Zwingli and the seminar on the Reformed Confessions – stand out as particularly instructive for Barth's development with respect to his later debate with Przywara about the *analogia entis*. These seminars help us see that Barth's view of the relationship between God and human creatures shifts without fundamentally changing direction during these early years in Göttingen. That is to say, while Barth did not abandon the *diastasis* of *Romans* II – he never would do that – he did enrich it with a different understanding of God's relationship to humanity. These early seminars show why and how this shift began to occur. They also demonstrate how Barth's studies during this period laid the groundwork for his rethinking of the incarnation and its implications

---

[3] He noted later: 'I did not even possess the Reformed confessional writings, and had certainly never read them'. See the autobiographical sketch in 1927 for the Münster Faculty Album in Karl Barth and Rudolf Bultmann, *Karl Barth-Rudolf Bultmann Letters 1922–1966*, ed. Bernd Jaspert, trans. Geoffrey W. Bromiley (Grand Rapids: William B. Eerdmans Publishing Co., 1981), p. 156.

[4] Cited in Eberhard Busch, *Karl Barth: His Life from Letters and Autobiographical Texts* (Grand Rapids, MI: Eerdmans, 1994), p. 126.

[5] A list of Barth's courses from his time at Göttingen can be found in Bruce L. McCormack, *Karl Barth's Critically Realistic Dialectical Theology: Its Genesis and Development, 1909–1936* (Oxford: Oxford University Press, 1995), pp. 293–4. The most important work on Barth's time in Göttingen is by Matthias Freudenberg, who offers an analysis of Barth's engagement with the Reformed tradition in these seminars. See Matthias Freudenberg, *Karl Barth und die reformierte Theologie: Die Auseinandersetzung mit Calvin, Zwingli und den reformierten Bekenntnisschriften während seiner Göttinger Lehrtätigkeit* (Neukirchen-Vluyn: Neukirchener Verlag, 1997).

[6] Barth and Bultmann, *Karl Barth-Rudolf Bultmann Letters 1922–1966*, p. 156.

for the creator–creature relationship after Przywara's arguments against the theology of *Romans* II. We will look briefly at each of these seminars and then turn to Barth's arguments from 'Instruction in the Christian Religion', his first attempt to lecture on dogmatics.

The Theology of Zwingli

Barth's seminar on Ulrich Zwingli took place early in his time at Göttingen, during the winter semester of 1922–23. That he was just beginning his teaching duties may explain the fact that, as John Webster notes, the quality of his lectures are disappointing: 'Barth does not have a firm hold on the structure of his exposition, broaching issues which will be treated at length later and then passing on from them in a rather unsatisfactory way, covering the same ground two or three times in some instances'.[7] A particular theme in these lectures, however, helps us see how Zwingli's theology was pushing Barth to consider the relationship between God and humanity differently than he had before. As the semester progresses, we see Barth growing more and more intrigued by Zwingli's construal of the relationship between God and the creature on ethical rather than ontological grounds. For Zwingli, Barth notes, human action stands at the centre of the Christian life, but it does so only because this action is demanded by God as a consequence of God's justifying act. Human action plays a part in the relationship between God and the creature, in other words, but it does so only as a function of God's prior act rather than any inherent characteristic of the human being.[8] Barth recognized that this move enabled Zwingli to posit a 'real relation' between God and the creature without violating the integrity of either party. This relation meant that the 'majesty and transcendence of God allowed, [and] even required, humankind to live on the earth in an *earthly* way'.[9]

This move was intriguing to Barth because he recognized that it made human action a constitutive element of the relationship between God and the human while also maintaining the proper distinction between God and the creature: the human being has a role to play in the relationship, but this role does not impinge on God's distinction from the world in any way. Like Barth in *Romans* II, therefore, Zwingli upholds God as God and the world as the world. The errors that Barth had tried to avoid while writing *Romans* II were not present in Zwingli: God and the creature did not enter into a mystical communion with one another, nor is there some kind of mediation of God's being to the creature or a 'third thing' between them in which both

---

[7] John Webster, *Barth's Earlier Theology* (New York: T&T Clark International, 2005), p. 26. My description of the lectures is indebted to Webster's account.

[8] See Karl Barth, *Die Theologie Zwinglis 1922/1923: Vorlesungen Göttingen Wintersemester 1922/1923*, Gesamtausgabe (Zurich: Theologischer Verlag Zürich, 2004), p. 90.

[9] *Ibid.*, p. 91, emphasis mine.

participate.[10] Instead, in Zwingli's construal, the fellowship between God and the creature takes *moral* form as God and the creature engage in corresponding activity while remaining 'fully what they are' at all times.[11] Thus, unlike Barth's account in *Romans* II, human being and action *matters* in the relationship between God and the world because the human has a real part to play in the relationship as her action is called forth by God. In Zwingli, then, Barth discovered a thinker who held on to the importance of human history and life while simultaneously upholding God's transcendence. Such a view was new to Barth, and while he did not immediately embrace Zwingli's theology as his own, the patterns and distinctions that Zwingli gave him would remain with him in the years ahead as he sought a way to address the challenges of the *analogia entis*.[12]

The Theology of the Reformed Confessions

Barth taught the seminar on the Reformed Confessions in the summer following the Zwingli seminar. This class becomes significant for a consideration of his engagement with Przywara and the *analogia entis* because it prompts Barth to explore the Reformers' reasons and justification for their break with the Roman Catholic Church more closely than he had before. This study colours his interpretation of Roman Catholicism for the rest of his career, and it will also provide the framework from which Barth would issue his initial response to the *analogia entis* after he encounters it for the first time in 'God in us or above us?' later in the year.

For the Reformed, Barth argues, the Reformation was 'not the legitimate organic continuation and further development of the medieval world and church but rather virtually a complete *break* with it'.[13] The fault line of this break falls upon the doctrine of God. He explains that the insight 'God is *God*, has burst upon [Reformed theologians] like an armed warrior, as something totally new, alien, and surprising. *This* is what has drawn them

---

[10] Barth, *Die Theologie Zwinglis*, p. 101.

[11] Barth, *Die Theologie Zwinglis*, p. 96. Webster argues that Barth's description of Zwingli stands closely in line with the account that Barth would offer later in the *Church Dogmatics*. See Webster, *Barth's Earlier Theology*, p. 35 as well as Webster's fuller treatment of Barth's mature ethical thought in his *Barth's Ethics of Reconciliation* (Cambridge: Cambridge University Press, 1995).

[12] In this sense, I concur with Webster that, even though Zwingli 'only rarely appears in Barth's writings after 1923, his theology is "latent" in much of what Barth later thought'. Specifically, I believe that the theological patterns that Barth first learnt from Zwingli determined the shape of his account of the 'covenant of grace' from *Church Dogmatics* II/2 onward. See Webster, *Barth's Earlier Theology*, p. 35.

[13] Karl Barth, *The Theology of the Reformed Confessions*, trans. Darrell Guder and Judith Guder, Columbia Series in Reformed Theology (Louisville: Westminster John Knox Press, 2002), p. 10.

into an irreconcilable contradiction to the old church'.[14] While the same emphasis on God can be found in the great theologians of the Catholic past such as Anselm, Peter Lombard, Bonaventure, and Thomas Aquinas, Barth argues that it was 'lacking in relevance' and 'very much in the background' for the Catholic Church in the time of the Reformers.[15] He argues, in fact, that the past formulations had been transformed into something altogether different for the Catholic Church: they now serve as 'the foundation of a great theological-ecclesial system of harmoniously arranged mediation of grace, the peaceful alignment of nature *and* grace, immanence *and* transcendence, human *and* divine freedom'.[16] The result was a theology that distorts the 'two-sidedness of the matter, the dialectic of the connection' between creator and creature because it makes 'sanctification into the outflow of justification and *vice versa*'.[17] Barth notes that the Reformed argue for a connection between creator and creature as well, but their connection is one in which 'there is no cooperation' between God and humanity.[18] Instead, the Reformed see grace and faith – and thus both sides of the relation – in terms of 'God's action upon man'. This point of view, however, supplies them with 'the necessary distance in order *then* to establish that faith is not God's only action upon man. This same God also makes man obedient for his service'.[19] On this basis, Barth concludes that 'the center of Christianity' for the Reformed is 'not only justification, not only faith, but without mixture and yet undivided the doublet: faith *and* obedience'.[20] Reformed theology, in short, leaves room for both God *and* the human. Barth labels this construal 'the positive doctrine of Reformed Christianity'.[21]

---

[14] *Ibid.*, p. 79. Since the principle 'God is God' had been driving Barth's own view since his break with the theology of his teachers, Barth clearly sees his own work as a modern instantiation of this same view.

[15] *Ibid.*, p. 80.

[16] *Ibid.* The language parallels descriptions Barth will later give of Przywara's theology.

[17] *Ibid.*, p. 148. As we will see, Barth will issue this same critique against Augustine and Przywara in his lecture, 'The Holy Spirit and the Christian Life'.

[18] *Ibid.*

[19] *Ibid.* Webster notes: 'The key word here [for Barth] is connection (*Zusammenhang*), which not only sums up what Barth sees as the particular genius of Reformed Christianity, but also provides a first draft of what will later present itself with such dogmatic grandeur in his theological dramatics of the covenant.' As was the case with his lectures on Zwingli, then, Barth's study of the Reformed Confessions supplied him with the insights, distinction and categories that would later be used as the building blocks for his 'covenant of grace'. All he needed was a framework that could help him put all of these various pieces together. He would find just such a framework in Pierre Maury's lection on predestination in 1936. See Webster, *Barth's Earlier Theology*, p. 53 and Pierre Maury, *Predestination*, trans. Edwin Hudson (Richmond: John Knox Press, 1960).

[20] Barth, *The Theology of the Reformed Confessions*, p. 149.

[21] *Ibid.*, p. 148.

Note that Barth has discovered in the Reformed Confessions something very similar to what he found in Zwingli: a theology that establishes a connection between God and the creature. This connection, however, differs from the one found in Roman Catholicism – or, for that matter, Protestant Liberalism – because it takes *moral* form as God's grace demands a corresponding act of obedience from the human recipient of it. As we will see, Barth quickly recognizes that this view opens the door to a theology that makes divine revelation the starting point for understanding the connection between God and humanity, and he also realizes that this starting point means that a whole host of problems that have worried him about such a connection can be avoided. He notes, for example, that the Reformation 'begins with revelation, with the Word, and with faith', focusing on 'God's interest in the human person' rather than the human's interest in God. As such, he says, it 'proclaims the human is *not* the measure of all things, least of all Christianity, and positions him before the reality *of God*'.[22] Such a view stands in line with the view that Barth himself wants to uphold, and the fact that it does so while also positing a more robust relationship between God and the creature than Barth maintained in *Romans* II undoubtedly stimulated Barth's thinking, because he saw that it was possible to have a theology that was fully God-centred that also makes human being and action important.

> All of Reformed Christianity is to be understood as the attempt to understand the human person, who through the Reformation was again placed before the immediate reality of God, as *human*, in the *world*, in *history*, but not at peace with so much as at *war* with the world, and yet in *relationship* to it . . . it is looking at *modern* man, at the *modern* world.[23]

Here we see that, by way of his study of the Reformation, Barth has moved beyond his initial theological response to the tragedy of the war and his teachers' theological failures. God does not just stand in a relationship of otherness and negation to the creature; rather, God compels the human to engage in real, obedient, and meaningful action *in* the world in response to the divine act of grace. By extension, the Christian not only is commissioned to stand in *contradiction* to the world because of her status in Christ, but she also is enlisted to be in *relationship* with the world and participate in its history precisely because of her status in Christ. This theological perspective – which was only beginning to be developed at this point – put Barth in a position to recognize the truth of Przywara's criticism that Barth had

---

[22] *Ibid.*, p. 208.
[23] *Ibid.*, p. 209.

'crossed out' the relationship between God and humanity when that criticism arrived at the end of the summer.[24] Given what he was learning from his lectures in Reformed theology, it is not surprising that Barth took Przywara's criticism seriously. The seriousness of the critique was compounded by the fact that Barth had realized from his studies that it was possible to conceive of the relationship between God and humanity without surrendering the basic commitment – namely the *diastasis* between God and creature – that had driven the argument of *Romans* II. The question was how to formulate such a theology for his own time on his own terms.[25]

The Göttingen Dogmatics

Barth sought to answer this question as he prepared for his first series of lectures on dogmatics in the spring of 1924. The work was difficult, and he soon found himself frustrated while reading hundreds of pages from a diverse list of thinkers that included Aquinas, Strauss, Schweizer, and Hermann.[26] Help would come, however, in the form of Heinrich Heppe's *Reformed Dogmatics* – a collection of excerpts from post-Reformation theologians covering the major areas of doctrine. In this 'out of date, dusty, [and] unattractive' book Barth found 'an atmosphere in which the way through the Reformers to Holy Scripture was more meaningful and natural than in the atmosphere of the theological literature which had been stamped by Schleiermacher and Ritschl'.[27] The phrase 'through the Reformers to Holy Scripture' points us to what Barth discovered in these thinkers: the path to a *doctrine of revelation*. It was in this doctrine, Barth realized,

---

[24] Erich Przywara, 'Gott in uns oder über uns? (Immanenz und Transzendenz in heutigen Geistesleben)', in *Stimmen der Zeit* 105 (1923), p. 350.

[25] For Barth, simply repeating the answers of the Reformers was never an option. As he argues in his opening lecture on dogmatics, the key question is 'What are *you* going to say? Not as one who knows the Bible or Thomas or the Reformers or the older Blumhardt, but responsibly and serious as one who stands by the words that are said: you? And *what* are you going to say? Not how impressively or how clearly or how well adapted to your hearers or to the present age – these are all secondary concerns – but *what*? You? What? These are the questions of dogmatics.' See Karl Barth, *The Göttingen Dogmatics*, p. 6.

[26] Barth said later: 'I shall never forget the spring vacation of 1924. I sat in my study at Göttingen, faced with the task of giving lectures on dogmatics for the first time. No one can ever have been more plagued than I then was with the problem, could I do it? and how?' See 'Foreword', in Heinrich Heppe, *Reformed Dogmatics* (Grand Rapids: Eerdmans, 1978), p. v. Also see Barth's letters from this period in Karl Barth and Eduard Thurneysen, *Karl Barth – Eduard Thurneysen Briefweshsel: 1921–30*, Gesamtausgabe (Zürich: Theologischer Verlag Zürich, 1974), p. 243.

[27] Barth, 'Foreword', p. iii.

that the answer to Przywara's criticism and the way forward for his own theology would come.

As he developed this doctrine through the course of his lectures, Barth's goal was similar to the one that had driven his work in *Romans* I and *Romans* II: he wanted to speak of God as one who can truly be known by human beings, but to do so in such a way that God would remain the subject of this revelation at every moment. To this end, he was prompted by his reading of the post-Reformation sources to employ the notion of *Deus dixit* – 'God speaks' – as the governing concept of his theology. He argued that it was impossible to speak about God 'in the sense of metaphysical or philosophical thinking'; instead, 'speaking about God can refer only to an original speaking *by* God'.[28] Theology, in other words, must be able to talk about God without first resorting to metaphysics. But how is such talk possible? Barth sought to address this question by advancing a new emphasis on God's speech described in terms of the three-fold Word of God: 'revelation, scripture, and preaching – the Word of God as revelation, the Word of God as scripture, and the Word of God as preaching, neither to be confused or separated'.[29] Both the verbal character of revelation and the trinitarian pattern of his thinking here is clear, and each aspect works to govern his construal of the relation between the three forms. Just as the Son and Holy Spirit proceed from the Father, scripture and preaching proceed from revelation; likewise, just as the Son and the Holy Spirit are as fully God as the Father, so scripture and preaching are as fully the Word as revelation. Scripture and revelation stand as God's speech, therefore, in precisely the same sense as the Logos does, although they are secondary and derivative in relation to it.[30]

The important aspect of the pattern for our purposes is the inclusion of preaching. 'The preaching of God's Word *is* God's Word' – such a claim stands in line, Barth thinks, with the basic commitments of the entire Reformed tradition.[31] *God's* Word is proclaimed in the human word inasmuch as this human word proceeds from scripture and revelation. But

---

[28] Barth, *Göttingen Dogmatics*, p. 12, emphasis mine.

[29] *Ibid.*, p. 14.

[30] There are, of course, important qualifications to be made to this formula, and Barth will develop and modify this pattern in *Church Dogmatics* I/1. He would not fundamentally depart from this basic insight, however, and this pattern governed his understanding of revelation from this point forward. For a discussion of this pattern as it relates to the Word of God as Scripture, see Bruce L. McCormack, 'The Being of Holy Scripture is in Becoming: Karl Barth in Conversation with American Evangelical Criticism', in *Evangelicals and Scripture: Tradition, Authority and Hermeneutics*, ed. Vincent E. Bacote, Laura C. Miguélez, and Dennis L. Okholm (Downers Grove, IL: InterVarsity Press, 2004), pp. 55–75.

[31] Barth, *Göttingen Dogmatics*, p. 32. He points specifically to the Second Helvetic Confession as an example.

how can a *human* word be *God's* word? Barth's discussion of the question is instructive:

> Should one not at least gather from this confident assertion the question whether there might not be words which – although they are human words, mere words like any others – are also *more* than that on account of the knowledge or recognition to which they lead, [and] on account of their impartation of truth from one person to another? The fact that they are human [words] does not entail a humanizing of the divine. From the very first, Protestantism meant: to believe in the becoming-human of the Logos precisely in spoken human *words*.[32]

Note that the human words are not in and of themselves God's Word; they have no special attribute or characteristic that makes them God Word. Rather, they are God's Word only in a qualified sense: 'on account of the knowledge' to which they lead and 'on account of their impartation of truth'. That is to say, they are God's Word only when *they reveal God*, and this revelation occurs only by a specific *act* of God upon the recipient.[33] Barth thus believes that God can and does take up creaturely realities, including human language, to reveal himself, but he qualifies this claim by the fact that this 'taking up' occurs only when God does so as an act of *self-revelation*. In this way, he thinks, God remains God at every moment in his act of revelation through creaturely realities, and there is no room for the possibility of the deification of the creature. That is, the creaturely reality – whether it be scripture or the preacher – remains merely creaturely even as it becomes God's Word in its correspondence to God's self-revealing act. These creaturely realities reveal God, therefore, only by participation as God takes them up in his self-revealing act and the creaturely reality corresponds to this act.[34]

---

[32] *Ibid.*, pp. 32–3, translation modified. See Karl Barth, *Unterricht in der christlichen Religion: Erster Band: Prolegomena, 1924*, in Gesamtausgabe (Zurich: Theologischer Verlag, 1985), p. 40.

[33] The focus on the present tense nature of the event would be something would change in Barth's theology as it matured. He moved away from the 'here and now' and more towards the 'there and then'. For this reason, McCormack argues that 'though the ground of his later theology was clearly Christological, his theology was largely pneumatocentric'. It would only be after Barth's development of his doctrine of election in 1936 that his theology would be a 'Christologically grounded, christocentric theology'. See McCormack, *Karl Barth's Critically Realistic Dialectical Theology*, p. 328.

[34] Barth's argument here follows the contours of John Calvin's description of the sacraments, because Barth has many of the same motivations as Calvin does in his account. See John Calvin, *Institutes of the Christian Religion*, ed. John T. McNeil (Philadelphia: The Westminster Press, 1960), pp. 1276–303 (Book IV.14).

Barth grounds this idea on the 'becoming-human' of the Logos, meaning that the doctrine of the incarnation is determining his notion of how creaturely realities function the way that they do in the act of revelation. Barth's account of the implications of the incarnation is made clear in subsequent lectures. As was the case in *Romans* I and *Romans* II, he is committed to the notion that divine revelation can never be something controlled or possessed by human beings. At no point can there be a 'humanizing of the divine', he believes, because the content of the revelation must be God himself. In other words, by avoiding this error, Barth maintains that the notion that the revelation of God truly is the revelation of *God* can be secured, because it means that revelation can be 'identical in subject and object'.[35] He explains:

> Either God speaks, or he does not. But he does not speak more or less, or partially, or in pieces, here a bit and there a bit . . . If God *speaks*, then *God* speaks, and we have to do with the one Logos that the prophets and apostles received, the one revelation in the incarnation which the people of the Bible know and attest as either promised or manifested.[36]

The reference to the 'one Logos' is instructive, because it directs us to the doctrine that is governing Barth's thoughts about revelation at this point: the *anhypostatic/enhypostatic* Christological doctrine. This idea, which Barth derived through his study of Heppe's book, construes the incarnation in terms of the Logos, the second Person of the Trinity, who took upon himself human nature in its entirety and lived a human life in and through it.[37] Barth interpreted this formula to mean that the humanity of Jesus had no reality independent of God the Son, and thus, as a result, Jesus Christ's human personality can be understood only in the light of the personality of the Logos. The result of this construal, Barth thinks, is that the revelation occurring in the historical person Jesus of Nazareth can be revelation only in a qualified sense. '[T]he *Deus dixit*', he explains, 'is the meaning and content of the incarnation'.[38] The human Jesus reveals God only when God,

---

[35] Barth, *Göttingen Dogmatics*, p. 95.

[36] *Ibid.*, p. 92. He repeats this again more sharply: 'Revelation is either the whole revelation of God or it is not revelation' (p. 93).

[37] See McCormack, *Karl Barth's Critically Realistic Dialectical Theology*, pp. 327–8. I am indebted to his account for the arguments here. For a more thorough account of the *anhypostatic/enhypostatic* doctrine, Barth's innovative reading of it, and its influence upon Barth's mature Christology, see Paul Dafydd Jones, *The Humanity of Christ: Christology in Barth's Church Dogmatics* (London: T&T Clark, 2008), pp. 19–26.

[38] Barth, *Göttingen Dogmatics*, pp. 90–1. This is the reason that Barth can argue that we 'must dare to be less christocentric and therefore to be more objective and valiant by

as the Logos, unveils himself by speaking his Word to the human knower through the veil of human flesh. The humanity of Jesus thus does not in and of itself reveal God; only the Logos as he speaks in and through the human Jesus reveals God. Or, as Barth puts it: 'even in the humanity of Christ the content of revelation as well as the subject is God alone'.[39] For this reason, Barth argues that the revelation of God in Jesus Christ should be seen in terms of a dialectic of God's veiling and unveiling: God remains hidden and incomprehensible in revelation because he remains the subject of that revelation at all times, but he is the subject, Barth says, 'not alongside or behind revelation but *in* it'.[40]

Barth would wrestle with the implications of this claim for the rest of his career. For our purposes, the important development lies in the fact that Barth believes that this formula allows him to preserve an absolute distinction between God and humanity without completely separating God from humanity at the same time. That is to say, because the incarnate Jesus Christ stands as the revelation of the hidden God, Barth can now speak of God as revealed in the human person Jesus in such a way that God still remains the subject of that revelation at every moment. This insight supplies him the room he needs to formulate a robust doctrine of the incarnation, because the same God who is the transcendent Lord *over* human existence is the one who is *in* human existence in Jesus Christ. Then, with this doctrine of the incarnation in hand, Barth is in a position to talk about the creator–creature relationship in ways that maintain his prior emphasis on the 'wholly other' God without completely negating any real or ongoing connection between God and humanity.

Barth moves in this direction later in his lectures as he returns to the question of how creaturely realities can remain creaturely even as they become God's Word in God's Self-revealing act. In the same way that God can take up the humanity of Jesus as God's Word, Barth believes that God can take up human words in the act of preaching so that these human words *are* God's Word. As in the incarnation, these human words are the Word in the qualified sense that they are God's Word only inasmuch as God bears witness to himself in and through them in the event of his self-revelation. Yet, because these words correspond to God's Word in this event, there is a real relation between God's Word and the human words. This relation takes the form of analogy.

---

again giving God the significance that is his due precisely according to his revelation through the historical fact of Jesus of Nazareth, namely, that he *alone* is the content of revelation'.

[39] *Ibid.*, p. 90. Hence, Barth says, 'the historical phenomenon of Jesus as such is a creature of the triune God'.

[40] *Ibid.*, p. 93.

No, when God reveals himself, this means that God himself, known and making known, speaking and hearing, is present on the stage, and no matter whether we call this revelation or faith, it is an event with which what we do in our own sphere may well be in analogy but cannot be in continuity, as though our thinking and feeling were a kind of outflow or continuation of revelation . . .".[41]

Here we see analogy entering into Barth's theology in a way that will become prominent later on. Indeed, McCormack concludes that '[w]hat we see emerging here is the first tentative articulation of the *analogia fidei* in the strict sense in which Barth would later employ the term'.[42] Barth's new understanding of the incarnation – as well as the corresponding notions of God's relationship to the creaturely world – has opened up a new way of thinking for him. No longer does God's transcendence mean that any relationship between God and the creature is 'crossed out', as Przywara had charged. Now, as a function of his fresh articulation of the doctrine of revelation, Barth views God's transcendence *over* human existence hand-in-hand with God's revelation *in* human existence. By the end of his Göttingen lectures, Barth was only a short distance away from describing the relationship between God and humanity in terms of the *analogia fidei*, and this account that would set the stage for a radical enrichment of his understanding of that relationship. Before Barth could come to that point, however, his thinking on the subject would need to be sharpened. This would occur by way of a personal encounter with Erich Przywara.

Przywara's Religionsphilosophie katholischer Theologie

In the months following the publication of 'God in us or above us?' Przywara continued to develop the themes he had been working on for years. In his essays and lectures from this period, we find him expanding and refining his arguments about the failures of Western philosophy, the challenge posed by Protestant theologians like Barth, the proper role of the Catholic Church in the modern world, and the *analogia entis*. The highpoints of his thoughts during these months are the lectures 'Catholicity' and 'The Contemporary Religious Crisis and Catholicism', because in them, Przywara spells out the motivation behind his programme more clearly than ever before.[43] He remains focused on the goal of prompting reform within the Roman Catholic Church so that it can meet the challenge posed

---

[41] Barth, *Göttingen Dogmatics*, p. 94.
[42] McCormack, *Karl Barth's Critically Realistic Dialectical Theology*, p. 341.
[43] See Erich Przywara, 'Katholizität' and 'Die Religiöse Krisis in der Gegenwart und der Katholizismus' in *Katholische Krise: In Zusammenarbeit with dem Verfasser*

by a culture that had lost its way to God. To serve this end, he poses a sharp question to his fellow Catholics: 'What does Catholicism have to say?'[44] If the Catholic Church has a clear vision of the God that the culture so desperately seeks – and Przywara believes that it does – then is the Church capable of communicating this truth to the culture in such a way that it will listen to it? This is the key question facing the Roman Catholic Church, in Przywara's view, and he continues to look for a way to provide Catholics the theological framework from which to begin to address it.

Przywara's thoughts along these lines culminate with the publication of the volume *Religionsphilosophie katholischer Theologie* in 1926.[45] This book is one of Przywara's greatest works, and it represents his most comprehensive attempt thus far both to describe the meaning and purpose of the *analogia entis* and to position it as Catholicism's key contribution to the questions hanging over modern philosophy. This book also is important, as we will see, because it provides a clear picture of the way in which Przywara was talking about the *analogia entis* in the months and years leading up to his visit to a seminar that Barth was teaching in Münster in February 1929. In fact, this book – along with Przywara's description and defence of its arguments in conversation with Barth and his students – becomes the primary source from which Barth's understanding of Przywara's *analogia entis* is derived, and Barth's criticism of the *analogia entis* in the years leading up to the publication of *CD* I/1 is based upon the arguments found here.

Przywara's Methodology

Przywara's *Religionsphilosophie* stands out among his works because it offers the most incisive engagement with the philosophical tradition that he had produced up until that point. His approach to this tradition in this book can be understood more clearly if it is seen in the light of remarks that he offered about his methodology later in his career. In his book *In und Gegen*, Przywara describes his method in terms of the dynamic of 'in' and 'against'.[46]

---

herausgegeben und mit einem Nachwort versehen, ed. Bernhard Gertz (Düsseldorf: Patmos-Verlag, 1967), pp. 20–53.

[44] Erich Przywara 'Katholizität', p. 21.

[45] See Erich Przywara, *Religionsphilosophie katholischer Theologie* (Münich: Oldenbourg, 1926). This volume was reprinted in the 1962 edition of Przywara's collected works. See Przywara, *Religionsphilosophie katholischer Theologie*, in *Schriften*, vol. 2 (Eisieldeln: Johannes-Verlag, 1962). The original volume was translated into English as *Polarity: A German Catholic's Interpretation of Religion*, trans. A. C. Bouquet (London: Oxford University Press, 1935). These works will hereafter be cited as *Religionsphilosophie* and *Polarity*, and the translation will correspond to the text in *Polarity* unless otherwise noted.

[46] See Erich Przywara, *In und Gegen* (Nürenberg: Glock und Lutz, 1955), pp. 8–9. Also see James V. Zeitz, 'Erich Przywara on Ultimate Reality and Meaning: "Deus Semper

His goal when he encounters a text or movement is to venture *into* it by means of a close and careful study and then to stand *against* it by critically evaluating it in light of its historical context. If he overemphasizes either the 'in' or the 'against' as he investigates his subject, then his study of it becomes too one-sided; when these two elements are kept in tension, however, he is able to discern his subject's 'immanent synthesis'. This synthesis provides him a picture of the centre or 'rhythm' of his subject, and this picture allows him to see both his subject and everything in relation to it from a new and 'grounded' perspective.[47]

This idea of obtaining a 'grounded' perspective provides insight into an important aspect of Przywara's approach to the *analogia entis* in *Religionsphilosophie* and later in *Analogia Entis*. Despite the often-abstract nature of his thought, Przywara believes that his formulations are the direct result of a careful interpretation of the contours of philosophical and theological thought throughout history, especially within the Catholic tradition. On this point, Przywara is clearly influenced by John Henry Newman's book *An Essay on the Development of Christian Doctrine*.[48] There Newman argues that the full meaning of Christian doctrine can be established only when it is understood within its historical context. That is, while the church is other than the world, it also exists *in* the world, and therefore, Church doctrine can be understood rightly only when it is seen in the light of the particular historical context in which it was developed. In other words, for Newman, the context within which a doctrine was formed is an elemental part of that doctrine's meaning. Przywara adopts a similar view: history *matters* for theology. The history of past ages, however, is not the only history that matters. Christians are making history in the *present*, and the context in which they work matters for the formulation and interpretation of their doctrines as well. A proper theological approach, therefore, is one that takes the best insights of the past and brings them together in a synthesis that addresses the historical context of the present. In *Analogia Entis*, Przywara describes this as the 'method of critical reflection':

> There remains only one thing: to live now and today within the stream, within the life of the sources. That might be designated as the method

---

Major"', *Ultimate Reality and Meaning* 12 (1989), pp. 193–4 and Zeitz, *Spirituality and the Analogia Entis According to Erich Przywara, S.J.* (Washington, DC: University Press of America, 1982), pp. 118–20.

[47] See Przywara, *In und Gegen*, pp. 129–30.

[48] John Henry Newman, *An Essay on the Development of Christian Doctrine*, 6th edn (Notre Dame: University of Notre Dame Press, 1989). Niles C. Nielsen calls this book 'a prerequisite to an understanding of Przywara's position'. See Nielsen, 'The Analogia Entis of Erich Przywara' (Unpublished Doctoral Dissertation, Yale University, 1951), pp. 388–91.

of critical reflection. The method is 'critical' in so far as one remains conscious of the distinction between the contemporary formulation of questions and the formulation made by the founders of the tradition. 'Reflection' occurs when such an incisive critique still contains the positive meaning that makes the pulsating stream of the tradition perceptible for contemporary life. This produces a third [thing]: the maximum possible unity [of meaning] from all the stages of time working itself out through this one stream. This will happen in the ideal case, when the relevant metaphysics becomes, so to speak, a metaphysics of this one stream – that is, a metaphysics of the most basic law in which the stream of tradition, from past to present to future, exists as one stream in all its differentiation.[49]

This vision for how the thinking of the past can be linked together with the best insights of the present to address contemporary problems explains why Przywara believes that he can offer something completely unique – namely, his innovative interpretation of the *analogia entis* – and still claim that it is the 'fundamental thought form' of Roman Catholic theology past and present. It also explains why Przywara believes that the Catholic Church's theological tradition cannot be the only resource for the formulation of Catholic theology in the present. Following Newman, he believes that the development of Catholic tradition must be interpreted in the light of the context of the history of *all* human thought about God. If the basic form of this tradition can be described in terms of the *analogia entis* – as Przywara believes that it can be – then any account of it must be the final product of an 'in' and 'against' study of with the entire spectrum of thought about God throughout history.[50] That it does so from the perspective of the Catholic tradition indicates simply that this tradition is the one tradition that has the resources by which the 'one stream' that makes up the history of thought about God can be interpreted.

This account of Przywara's method helps explain both the goals and the structure of his *Religionsphilosophie*. In the preface to the book, Przywara outlines the two main tasks he hopes to accomplish through his study. He will begin, first, by setting forth 'the metaphysical foundations for belief in God' by way of an 'exposition of a general synthetic philosophy', and then, second, he will engage in some 'real theology' in order to provide an account of the 'final structure' of the 'Catholic system of culture, morals,

---

[49] Erich Przywara, *Analogia Entis*, in *Schriften*, vol. 3 (Einsiedeln: Johannes-Verlag, 1962), p. 56.

[50] Edward Oakes thus is correct when he says that Przywara believed that 'at the heart of all religious thought . . . one could detect an implicit metaphysics of the God-world relation'. See Edward T. Oakes, *Pattern of Redemption: The Theology of Hans Urs von Balthasar*, 2nd edn (New York: Continuum, 1997), p. 3.

and dogma'.[51] There is 'common ground' for both tasks, he says, because philosophy and theology are united by their shared focus upon the question of the relationship between God and humanity. This unity between the two disciplines explains the structure of the book. In the first part, Przywara provides a typological survey of philosophical thought about God through-out history (the 'in'), and in the second part (the 'against'), he indicates that the solution to the problems in the philosophical accounts is 'found in the fundamental thesis upon which the Catholic religion is based', the *analogia entis*. These two parts lead into a concluding section that provides a 'survey of the historical implications of this thesis'.[52] This section marks Przywara's attempt to unite philosophical and Catholic thought about God together into 'one stream'.[53] In the end, Przywara thinks that this account demonstrates that the unresolved tensions in philosophical thought about God can be solved by the truth of the Catholic tradition and, at the same time, it should motivate Catholics to reach out to the culture with the truth of the *analogia entis*.

The Problem of God in History

Przywara begins the first part by noting that human attempts to obtain knowledge of the nature of the relationship between God and creation centre upon the problem of essence (*Soseinsproblem*) and the problem of existence (*Daseinsproblem*).[54] While this distinction eventually will serve as the axis around which Przywara's *analogia entis* turns, in this section, Przywara uses it simply as a framework by which to examine the history of philosophical thought about God. He describes the *Soseinsproblem* as horizontal in nature, because it involves 'the configuration of the relation-ship of men to God', while the *Daseinsproblem* is vertical because it denotes 'the accomplishment of the relationship of men to God' which occurs from either 'above to below' or 'below to above'.[55] Since both of these problems involve the human relationship to God, he says, each one must be addressed by means of 'a consideration of consciousness as its point of departure', and this means that the examination must unfold 'within the bounds of the unceasing tension of consciousness between its self-containedness (Immanence) and its essential orientation upon a being independent of its

---

[51] Przywara, *Religionsphilosophie*, p. 375; *Polarity*, p. 1, translation mine. He notes that these two tasks serve to answer the same question: 'What is the fundamental meta-physical presupposition regarding subject and object, and their correlation, which brings together philosophy and theology in the eyes of the Catholic, and unites them as organically one?'

[52] *Ibid.*

[53] See the passage from Przywara, *Analogia Entis*, p. 56, cited above.

[54] Przywara, *Religionsphilosophie*, p. 376; *Polarity*, p. 2.

[55] *Ibid.*, translation mine.

consciousness (Transcendence)'.[56] What Przywara means is that the problems of essence and existence are, in fact, different forms of same problem: the nature of God's relationship to humanity. This problem has been governed by the tension of those who seek God *within* creation and those who seek God *beyond* it, and a survey of the history of philosophical thought about God shows that thinkers have swung from one extreme to the other. Przywara's goal is to start with the competing tensions that have led to this duality and then overcome them by locating them within a larger, unified framework. He uses the human consciousness as his starting point both because it is the place where the immanence and transcendence of God is realized within human life and because it has been the traditional focus of philosophical reflection. As such, the consciousness provides a point of contact between philosophy and theology.[57]

With this framework in mind, Przywara argues that the problem of essence has been approached in one of three ways, with each way representing a type of religious philosophy.[58] All three types fail to reach an adequate notion of God's relation to humanity, he says, but they fail for different reasons. The *immanence type* is characterized by passivity towards God: the human seeks God by turning inward, and she 'finds Him in that mysterious depth of the seas of consciousness'.[59] The *transcendence type* moves in the opposite direction as the human looks outside her own being in her quest for God. This occurs by way of what Przywara describes as 'essentially objective apprehension and reflection', which is characterized by the 'state of being open to receive impressions leading to the experience of this content [God] in sensation and perception'.[60] The third option, the *transcendentalist*

---

[56] *Religionsphilosophie*, p. 376; *Polarity*, p. 2.

[57] Przywara's account of the consciousness is influenced by the work of Edmund Husserl and Max Scheler. Przywara was drawn to their phenomenological approach because, in his view, it prioritized the reality of the world standing *over against* human experience as opposed to the transcendental philosophies that absorbed the world *into* experience. For more on the influence of Husserl and Scheler on Przywara's thought, see Bernhard Gertz, *Glaubenswelt als Analogie* (Düsseldorf: Patmos-Verlag, 1969), pp. 152–8; and Thomas F. O'Meara, *Erich Przywara, S.J.: His Theology and His World* (Notre Dame: University of Notre Dame Press, 2002), pp. 90–8.

[58] *Religionsphilosophie*, p. 377; *Polarity*, p. 4.

[59] *Religionsphilosophie*, p. 380; *Polarity* p. 7. He identifies this view with Schleiermacher and his followers, in whom, he says, 'God makes Himself known in the process whereby the consciousness more fully renders itself explicit. He is the Infinite Content, to which the infinity of consciousness crystallizes'.

[60] *Religionsphilosophie*, pp. 378–9; *Polarity*, p. 5. Przywara points to European deism as the chief representative of this type. God is above the creature, and there is thus no relationship between God and the creature, or any relationship of grace or power. Instead, God is simply a result of 'a purely prosaic scientific process of deduction'. See *Religionsphilosophie*, p. 381; *Polarity*, p. 8.

type, is defined by 'becoming-actualness', which Przywara describes as a 'continuous endeavor and struggle' that 'bears within itself its meaning and its goal'.[61] Like the transcendence type, the transcendentalist type maintains the otherness of God inasmuch as God is understood as something outside the human towards which she strives. However, since the striving itself is the goal of this type, Przywara argues, this view ends up collapsing into a version of the immanence type.[62] This collapse marks the failure of religious philosophy, because while the contrast of the first two types clearly demonstrates the 'necessity of a higher connection between their opposites', the third type fails to provide this connection because it 'infinitely extends the problem'.[63] As a result, when considered from the perspective of the problem of essence, the solution to the problem of God provided by religious philosophy makes a 'life with God appear impossible'.[64]

The problem of existence raises a different question: 'Does religion, as relation between God and humanity, come into being from above downwards, as ultimately an "act of God", or is it formed from below upwards, from man, and therefore ultimately as an "act of man?"'[65] This question has been problematic, Przywara explains, because the tendency has been to choose one answer to the exclusion of the other. Here Przywara follows arguments he had developed in earlier essays and lectures. On the one hand, those who emphasize that the relationship is the result of an 'act of God' rob the world of its own reality by making the human relationship with God – and thus human existence itself – an extension of divine action. The result is that creation becomes nothing more an extension of God's own life. This is the error of 'theopanism', and Przywara associates it with Luther and his modern heirs, including Barth.[66] On the other hand, those who argue that this relationship is the product of an 'act of man' commit a form of pantheism because God merely becomes the 'ultimate basis for all rationality' and the 'ideal meaning of humanity'.[67] In the end, Przywara insists, the two errors merge into one as theopanism 'appears at bottom to be only camouflaged' pantheism.[68] While pantheism is built on the rationalism of the *active* human being, theopanism is the rationalism of the *passive* human

---

[61] *Religionsphilosophie*, p. 379; *Polarity*, p. 5.

[62] *Religionsphilosophie*, pp. 381–2; *Polarity*, pp. 9–10. Przywara argues that this view finds historical expression in some types of Kantianism, as well as in the philosophy of Fichte and Nietzsche.

[63] *Religionsphilosophie*, p. 388; *Polarity*, p. 15.

[64] *Religionsphilosophie*, p. 399; *Polarity*, p. 27.

[65] *Religionsphilosophie*, p. 395; *Polarity*, p. 22.

[66] *Religionsphilosophie*, p. 396; *Polarity*, p. 24.

[67] *Religionsphilosophie*, pp. 396–7; *Polarity*, pp. 23–5. Przywara clearly has Kant in his sights here, as he calls this 'religion within the limits of humanity'.

[68] *Religionsphilosophie*, p. 398; *Polarity*, p. 26.

being; underneath these surface differences, however, they are nothing more than 'two forms of one and the self-same rationalism'.[69] God becomes simply 'the cloak of an inward dialectic', meaning that once again, any notion of true communion with God has proven impossible.[70]

The Analogy of Being as the Solution to the Problem

The failures of the various philosophical accounts of God's relationship with humanity demonstrate that religious philosophy has failed to adequately address the problem of God and that it has no hope to do so. In response, Przywara moves to the second part of his argument by claiming that humanity needs to move 'outside the tangle of problems' and discover a resource that reduces the 'whole tangle to a unity'.[71] Roman Catholic theology, he says, provides just such a resource. He argues that one of its key attributes is the fact that Catholics see the relationship between God and creation as 'open upwards'.[72] That creation is by nature 'open' to God testifies to the fact that it is 'a revelation of God from above to below' and 'the similitude of [God's] being'.[73] Even so, the fact it is open *'upwards'* means that, even in its similarity to God, creation 'testifies from itself to a God who is beyond similitude'.[74] This similarity within an even greater dissimilarity, Przywara argues, is the key insight captured by the Roman Catholic *analogia entis*, which is the underlying principle of the 'open upwards' concept. For this reason, it marks an advance over all other attempts to describe the relationship between God and humanity.

But in what sense does the *analogia entis* strike this balance? How can Przywara claim that creation is a revelation of God while also holding that God is utterly distinct from creation? And why does he believe that this concept solves the problem of God in a way that every other option in the history of philosophy has failed to do? The key to understanding Przywara's argument is to unpack the meaning and content of the *analogia entis* itself, and that requires an examination of the Thomist metaphysics working behind it.

When Thomas Aquinas came onto the scene, the most common way of thinking about being was in terms of gradations of being, such as in Plotinus' view of the One who alone truly 'is' and the various levels of being that

---

[69] *Religionsphilosophie*, p. 399; *Polarity*, p. 27.
[70] *Ibid.*
[71] *Religionsphilosophie*, p. 400; *Polarity*, p. 29.
[72] *Ibid.*
[73] *Religionsphilosophie*, pp. 401–2; *Polarity*, pp. 30–1, translation mine.
[74] *Religionsphilosophie*, p. 401; *Polarity*, p. 30.

creatures have as they emanate from this One.[75] Such views, of course, are problematic for a theologian who wants to maintain the kind of distinction between God and creation that follows from the doctrine of *creatio ex nihilo*. At the same time, creation cannot be seen as completely *unconnected* to God, both because it comes from God and because it has its continuing existence in connection to him. How, then, can creation's distinction from God be maintained alongside its connection to God? Aquinas addressed this problem by arguing that God does not share the same being that creatures have, as if there were three entities – God, the creature, and 'being' – that are interrelated to one another in some way. Instead, God *is* being, and as such, he is wholly distinct from all creatures who nevertheless have *their* being by participation in his being.

Aquinas works out this notion by drawing a distinction between the essence and existence of God and the essence and existence of creatures. The logic of the distinction, as least as Przywara interprets it, works as follows. Each creature that *is*, exists. Each creature that exists has a set of special characteristics that are its own, and this set of characteristics is the creature's *essence* – that in virtue of which the creature is what it is.[76] So, for example, the essence of a horse is that set of characteristics that make it a horse: the horse's 'horseness'. The horse's 'horseness', however, does not cause the horse to exist. That is why a creature is a creature: a creature's *existence* is something altogether different from its *essence*, because its existence is not something it has but something it receives from outside of itself. This means, as Aquinas puts it, that 'all beings apart from God are not their own being, but are beings by participation'.[77] One implication of this idea is that essence and existence are not identical in the creature, because while essence subsists in the creature, existence is something the creature receives. In contrast, God's essence *is* to be, meaning that God's essence and existence are one and the same.[78] Thus, as Aquinas says, 'God alone is being identical with

---

[75] Przywara interprets this tradition as the result of the ancient conflict between the views of Heraclitus, who held that being was in constant flux, and Parmenides, who held that being was unchanging and that the material world, because it changed, was an illusion. Both of these options were held in tension in the various attempts by later thinkers to resolve the differences between them. See Erich Przywara, 'Gottgeheimnis Der Welt: Drei Vorträge über die Geistige Krisis der Gegenwart', in *Schriften*, vol. 2 (Eisiedeln: Johannes-Verlag, 1962), pp. 59–81. For an account of the history of the concept 'being' with Przywara's development in mind, see Edward Oakes, *Pattern of Redemption*, pp. 15–33.

[76] Here I am following Etienne Gilson, *Being and Some Philosophers*, 2nd edn (Toronto: Pontifical Institute of Medieval Studies, 1952), p. 175.

[77] Thomas Aquinas, *Summa Theologicae*, trans. Father of the English Dominican Province (New York: Benziger Brothers, Inc., 1948), I.44.1.

[78] See Aquinas on God's simplicity, *Summa Theologicae* I.3.3–4.

essence, [while] in every creature . . . there must be found its essence or nature on the one hand, and its being on the other, which it acquires from God whose essence is his being'.[79] While creatures have being by 'participation', God is the 'one First Being, Who possesses being most perfectly'.[80] Creatures are composite because they are the combination of their essence and existence; God is simple because his essence and existence are one and the same. Inasmuch as they have essence and existence, creatures are similar to God who also has essence and existence; creatures are distinct from God, however, not only because they have a different essence than God, but also because creaturely existence is derived while God's existence is not.

This framework is working in the background of Przywara claims about the 'open upwards' nature of the creature's relationship to God and the meaning and content of the *analogia entis*. His argument is that, like God, the creature has a unity of essence and existence, but unlike God, the creature's unity is one of 'tension' rather than identity.[81] This tension stems from the fact that the creature's essence is an 'inward process essentially within existence'.[82] That is to say, the creature's essence appears within the context of existence only as becomingness, because its essence is realized only 'over or above existence' – meaning that it cannot be considered apart from its relationship with God, in whom the creature has its being.[83]

This idea is the key to understanding why Przywara believes that the *analogia entis* solves the problem of God that religious philosophy had failed to answer. In reality, he explains, the human is

> similar to God through the possession of a unity of essence and existence, but even in this similarity it is essentially dissimilar to God

---

[79] Thomas Aquinas, *Scriptum super libros Sententiarum* 1.8.5.1. See Gregory P. Rocca, *Speaking the Incomprehensible God: Thomas Aquinas on the Interplay of Positive and Negative Theology* (Washington, DC: Catholic University of America Press, 2004), p. 250.

[80] Thomas Aquinas, *Summa Theologicae* I.44.1.

[81] *Religionsphilosophie*, p. 403; *Polarity*, p. 32. Przywara argues that this rules out two common misconstruals of the likeness between creator and creature. First, creation does not have an 'eternal essence to which God in the act of creation has lent a developing existence'. This would leave creation 'in a sort of coeternal relationship with God'. Second, this likeness is not one in which creation 'flows forth immediately from the depths of the divine *actus*' in some sort of emanation from God.

[82] *Ibid*. Betz summarizes Przywara's point here: 'God is who he is, whereas creatures are forever becoming who they are'. See John R. Betz, 'Beyond the Sublime: The Aesthetics of the Analogy of Being (Part Two)', *Modern Theology* 22, no. 1 (2006), p. 29.

[83] Betz argues that while Przywara is consistent with Aquinas here, he also 'takes his thought further to the degree that the real distinction is stated in expressly dynamic terms'. The reason is that the creaturely being is 'never identical to its essence – i.e., never in complete possession of itself, but fundamentally ecstatic'. See Betz, 'Beyond the Sublime (Part Two)', pp. 21–2.

because, in God, the unity of essence and existence is that of identity, whereas in the creature the unity of essence and existence is one of tension. Now since the relation of essence and existence is the essence of 'being,' so God and the creature are in 'being' similar and dissimilar – that is, they are analogous to one another: and this is what we mean by *analogia entis*, analogy of being.[84]

This passage provides one of the clearest accounts of Przywara's understanding of the meaning and content of the *analogia entis*, and he sees two immediate implications of it. The first implication simply fleshes out the logic of his line of thought: because the creature's being cannot be considered apart from its relationship with God, the creature's being as such *reveals* God. This idea again captures the sense of Przywara phrase 'open upwards'. On the one hand, it means the very fact of the creature's existence testifies to God as its source, but, on the other hand, because the creature remains dependent upon God for its existence at every moment, God remains utterly distinct from it. Or, as Przywara puts it: 'God as the pure "Is" is, on the one side, so inward to the creation that the transient "is" of the creation is only *from* him and *in* him – and yet on the other side, differentiated from the creation, above it as the pure "Is", for whom no relationship to anything which is "becoming" is in any way possible'.[85] On this basis, Przywara argues that the creature's being is itself a revelation of both the immanence *and* the transcendence of God. Specifically, he says that the *analogia entis* is simply 'the philosophical expression' of both *creatio ex nihilo* and *creatio continua* that Thomas Aquinas originally had been trying to maintain.[86] The doctrine of *creatio ex nihilo* is maintained by the fact that creation comes from God but in no way has any sort of eternal existence alongside God or emanates from God; rather, it depends at every moment upon God for its continuing existence. The doctrine of *creatio continua* is maintained by the fact that God truly is immanent in creation. Since every human being is dependent on God for her moment-by-moment existence, she exists in relation to the God who, from above to below, freely acts in her at every moment.

The fact that the creature's being reveals both the immanence and transcendence of God points to the second key implication of this analogy for Przywara: the connection that it provides between the project of

---

[84] *Religionsphilosophie*, p. 403; *Polarity*, p. 32, translation mine.

[85] *Religionsphilosophie*, p. 404; *Polarity*, p. 33. Also see Przywara, *Analogia Entis*, pp. 131–2 and pp. 171–3.

[86] *Religionsphilosophie*, p. 403; *Polarity*, p. 32. On this point, Betz concludes: 'what Przywara means by the *analogia entis* is simply an explication of Thomas' own teaching in this regard and in no sense a new-fangled doctrine . . . if one is to condemn Przywara, one must also condemn Aquinas himself'. See Betz, 'Beyond the Sublime (Part One)', p. 41.

philosophical history and the tradition of the Roman Catholic Church. 'God is the Creator of the universal nature and of human nature,' Przywara explains, 'and therefore he is discernable in its entire expanse'.[87] This means that anyone – philosopher or theologian – who reflects upon this creation can discern at least part of the truth about God and God's relationship with it. That is, when 'seen from the standpoint of the Catholic *analogia entis*, the creature in its totality is the window whereby, in an analogy which transcends all analogy, we see into the being of God who is beyond all analogy'.[88] Przywara explains this idea in an important passage:

> For the *analogia entis* does not denote an ascertainable God contained in the limits of the creature, but a reverent looking towards God as to the One to whose self-condescension is already [what marks] this creation as creation, so that the creature, far from signifying an externally imposed limit to this creative power, is nothing more than the preliminary boundary which He Himself has freely set to this His own voluntary self-condescension. On this principle, the Incarnation of God is (and especially so in the midst of a true incarnation-cosmos), on the one hand, neither ascertainable, nor, on the other, contradictory. The Incarnation of God, in the midst of a true incarnation-cosmos, appears much more as the crown of the process of the self-condescension of God.[89]

This paragraph – which caught Barth's attention when he read it – makes the full implications of the *analogia entis* for Przywara's project of reform in the Catholic Church clear.[90] The human being, in her analogous relationship to God's being, does not provide a *direct* revelation of God, as would be the case in either pantheism or theopanism as Przywara understands them. Rather, the human in her 'open upwards' existence before God serves as an *indirect* revelation of God because – since her very existence demonstrates

---

[87] *Religionsphilosophie*, p. 411; *Polarity*, p. 41. This is why, he explains, 'Catholicism finds no contradiction between the supernatural and the Incarnation, on the one hand, and natural forms of divine revelation and impartation on the other' (*Religionsphilosophie*, p. 404; *Polarity*, p. 33). This enables Przywara to say, as he does elsewhere, that '[c]ommon to "metaphysics" and "religion" is the central point of the *analogia entis* and the presupposition of the natural self-revelation of God in his creation, so that on the one hand metaphysics bears within itself an element of religion (the presupposition of the self-revelation of God) as, on the other hand, religion contains an element of metaphysics (the criterion for recognition of the *analogia entis*)'. See Przywara, 'Metaphysik und Religion', in *Schriften*, vol. 2 (Einsiedeln: Johannes-Verlag, 1962), p. 22.

[88] *Religionsphilosophie*, p. 442; *Polarity*, p. 73, translation mine.

[89] *Religionsphilosophie*, p. 442; *Polarity*, pp. 73–4, translation mine.

[90] See Karl Barth, *Church Dogmatics* I/2 (Edinburgh: T&T Clark, 1956), pp. 144–5; *Die Kirchliche Dogmatik* I/2 (Zürich: Evangelischer Verlag, 1938), p. 158.

her relationship with God – she exists as a 'window' through which God's being is revealed. Special revelation is not required to obtain this knowledge of God, in Przywara's view, because one can arrive at this knowledge by reflecting upon the same object as the philosophers did: the human consciousness. 'Religion', he explains, 'when we acquaint ourselves with it by means of the ultimate sense of the *analogia entis*, signifies the active consciousness of the divine origin of the creature, the consciousness that in its ultimate essence it is the self-revelation and self-condescension of God'.[91] The human consciousness thus marks the connecting point between the philosophical attempts to discover the relationship between God and humanity and the answer provided by the Roman Catholic Church.

This connection points to the great advantage, in Przywara's mind, of his vision: the fact that 'the creature is already in this "natural" religion objectively ready for the religion of the actual incarnation'.[92] In other words, Przywara believes that the strength of the *analogia entis* is that, because there is a clear point of connection between the philosophical project of discerning the nature of God's relationship with creation and the Catholic answer to that question, any self-reflective human is prepared to encounter the Christian message that centres upon Jesus Christ. Indeed, because the human as such already exists within the polarity of the immanence and transcendence of God described by the *analogia entis*, she models within her own created being what God 'becomes Himself' in the incarnation.[93] This points to the fact that the whole of creation is an 'incarnation-cosmos' (*Menschwerdungskosmos*) and is just as much a self-revelation of God as the incarnate Jesus Christ was, because the direction of the revelation is the same: 'above to below'.[94] The knowledge of God available through

---

[91] *Religionsphilosophie*, p. 442; *Polarity*, p. 74. Betz summarizes well: 'Przywara's analogy of being, which at face value appears to be purely abstract metaphysical doctrine, is therefore nothing of the kind, but grounded in a concrete phenomenology of finite being and consciousness.' See Betz, 'Beyond the Sublime (Part Two)', p. 25.

[92] *Religionsphilosophie*, p. 442; *Polarity*, p. 74, translation mine.

[93] *Ibid*. Betz explains: 'Przywara sees the order of grace as the fulfilment (through Christ) of what is foreshadowed by the order of nature (in spite of its corruption).' See Betz, 'Beyond the Sublime (Part Two)', p. 9.

[94] Betz interprets Przywara's claims about God's self-revelation here as evidence that 'Barth's criticisms of the *analogia entis* as an attempt conceptually to lay hold of God independently of his self-revelation . . . have no warrant whatsoever'. Of course, the question of whether or not Barth's claims are warranted depends on how one defines 'God's self-revelation'. Przywara here explicitly defines it in terms of the *Menschwerdungskosmos*, a term which extends God's self-revelation to the *whole of the created order*. Barth, as we will see, offers severe criticism to this definition, and this criticism becomes the basis for his rejection of the *analogia entis*. For his part, Betz thinks that Barth's unwillingness to accept Przywara's *Menschwerdungskosmos* is 'a wonder of the first order' and a sign that Barth rejects 'any openness whatsoever of the creature

reflection upon the human consciousness is not the result of a 'below to above' movement which starts from the human and then ascends to God, but rather, God's revelation in the consciousness moves from 'above to below' because it is not the creature as such but the creature in her relationship to God that reveals God.[95]

On this point, Przywara explains that one of the key attributes of the *analogia entis* is that it 'knits all that is creaturely together into a total likeness to God, and yet to such a likeness as in its ultimate essence is in a condition of *potentia oboedientialis* (to use an old theological expression), that is, a condition of the tool in the hand of the artificer'.[96] Przywara's use of the *potentia oboedientialis* recalls Aquinas' employment of that term, which references a creature's passive potency in relation to an extrinsic active agency. A debate exists among Thomists, however, about what 'passive potency' means with respect to the creature's relationship with God, so it is necessary to be clear about which reading Przywara is aligned with.[97] Some Thomists argue that Aquinas uses the term to indicate the creature's susceptibility to a divine miracle, because this view maintains grace as an extrinsic and unmerited event distinguished from a creature's natural capabilities.[98] Others contend that Aquinas uses it to indicate a capacity already intrinsic to the creature before any additional miracle of grace. The creature, for example, is seen as having an obediential potency for the supernatural

---

to God, and thus any natural desire (*desiderium naturale*) for God'. He thus concludes: 'But if *this* is what it meant by the *analogia entis*, then it *is* the faith of the Catholic Church, and so Barth is right to identify Przywara with it; it is also the faith of Scripture (cf. Eccl. 3.11a) and the unanimous faith of the Church fathers. Thus, in rejecting it, *if* indeed it *is* to be rejected, Barth is quite consistent in rejecting the Catholic Church as "heresy".' As we will see, I agree with Betz that Barth is being consistent here. See Betz, 'Beyond the Sublime (Part Two)', pp. 6–7.

[95] Przywara makes this point clear: 'The final secret of the Catholic religion is not to be found in approximation from below to what is above as visible from the side of creation, but solely in reverent regard for the God who is over all created things, and so a process from God hitherwards.'. See *Religionsphilosophie*, p. 442; *Polarity*, p. 74.

[96] *Religionsphilosophie*, p. 404; *Polarity*, p. 33.

[97] This definition is taken from the one provided in Stephen A. Long, 'On the Possibility of a Purely Nature End for Man', *The Thomist* 64, no. 3 (2000), p. 213.

[98] Denis Bradley offers an example of this type of reading when he argues that Aquinas teaches that the human's 'natural desire to see God is *implicitly* contained in the natural desire for the perfect good or happiness that structures the will'. Humans, then, have an implicit natural desire for a supernatural end – meaning that they have a natural desire for that which can be achieved only by divine miracle. This understanding of human nature provides the lens through which he reads obediential potency. See Denis Bradley, *Aquinas on the Twofold Human Good* (Washington, DC: The Catholic University of America, 1997), pp. 445–9.

gift of friendship with God, because it is capable of friendship with God by nature even though that friendship itself is possible only if receives a gift of grace that enables it to reach that end.[99] A creature's 'passive potency', then, would be its capacity to be aided by God.[100]

This second interpretation stands closer to the way Przywara employs the term, and it explains why he thinks the revelation of God in the human consciousness is an 'above to below' event as well as why he believes that the *analogia entis* provides a solution to philosophy's problems. From the perspective of the *analogia entis*, the human's movement towards God is already essentially a movement from God to the creature, because 'the creature unveils itself as arising through and in the mysterious and incomprehensible movement of God Himself, wherein He remains God (the pure "Is") and yet the creature proceeds from Him (as "becoming")'.[101] This ascent to God does not require a second act of grace to be actualized, since the creature's movement towards God occurs simply as a consequence of 'being' at all. 'This natural religious endowment', Przywara explains, 'contains in itself the whole correlation, since even the so-called natural cognition of God presupposes a self-revelation of God (in creation *qua* creation)'.[102] In other words, the fact that creation has 'being' at all marks creation as such as an 'above to below' event, and by extension, it means that the human has an intrinsic capacity for the revelation of God built into his being.

This point also explains why Przywara thinks the *analogia entis* can meet the philosophy of religion on its own ground and offer a solution that is comprehensible to it. It is not offering an insight about human existence that is comprehensible only under the terms of grace, from the gift of special revelation, or in the context of the Catholic Church; it is offering an insight

---

[99] A stone, by contrast, would be incapable of such friendship even with the aid of grace because friendship is beyond its nature. For this example, see Long, 'On the Possibility of a Purely Nature End for Man', p. 214. He offers a more in-depth account in an earlier essay: see Stephen A. Long, 'Obediential Potency, Human Knowledge, and the Natural Desire for God', *International Philosophical Quarterly* 37, no. 1 (1997), pp. 49–51.

[100] Such a view stands in line with statements Aquinas often makes about human nature, such as when he says that the beatific vision and knowledge of God 'are to some extent above the nature of the rational soul, inasmuch as it cannot reach it on its own strength; but in another way it is in accordance with its nature, inasmuch as it is capable of it by nature, having been made in the likeness of God'. See Thomas Aquinas, *Summa Theologicae* III.9.2.ad.3; cited in Long, 'On the Possibility of a Purely Nature End for Man', pp. 215–16, who says that this statement 'conforms perfectly to the doctrine of an obediential potency to grace and glory'.

[101] *Religionsphilosophie*, p. 444; *Polarity*, p. 75.

[102] *Religionsphilosophie*, p. 447; *Polarity*, p. 79.

that is available to anyone who has eyes to see human existence for what it really is.[103] As he explains:

> By virtue of the objective and actual 'God over us and God in us' of the *analogia entis*, *all* aspiration after God, and *all* experience of God which solves its riddles, is the dynamic and contemplative consciousness of a Being described by Paul in the words, 'He created the human race . . . if haply they might feel after God and find him, though He be not far from every one of us; for in Him we live and move and have our being' (Acts 17.26–28). Thus *all* movements towards God, *all* illumination by God of the human experience which seeks to enlighten itself, presupposes a tranquil condition of 'God in me and I in God', because precisely by reason of the nature of the *analogia entis*, the relationship between God and man is not a function of man's activity, but of God's condescension.[104]

Przywara's move is clear: he has adopted the starting point of general religious philosophical reflection – the human consciousness – but unlike the philosophers, he has turned it into the very place where the *transcendence* of God is realized. This makes the *analogia entis* at its core a missionary principle, because it leads the human who recognizes the nature of his true existence to strive towards God who is infinitely beyond him. In some sense, this movement is similar to the one found in Hegel's system, as the human moves towards God in an 'endless striving' and 'unceasing motion-in-becoming' (*Werde-bewegtheit*).[105] The difference, however, is that in the *analogia entis*, this striving presupposes God's prior movement to the creature from above. The striving is thus a *gift* from God that occurs as a consequence of the creature's always 'becoming' in the very act of its existence. Hence, while the creature's striving is a striving *towards* God, it is also a striving *in the presence* of God because the creature is 'endowed with its own separate essence and separate existence' as something other than God.[106] This striving thus takes the reverent form of Augustine's *quaerere inveniendum et invenire quaerendum* (seeking to find, and finding to seek),

---

[103] Przywara's desire to engage the modern world on its own terms come to the fore here. He does not want to retreat inside the walls of the Church and offer a solution that only makes sense to those inside it. Instead, he wants to offer a solution that, while based on the Catholic Church's teaching, speaks about human existence in such a way that anyone who engages in the task of philosophy can understand and benefit from. It is in this sense that the *analogia entis* is a missionary enterprise: it attempts to meet the world on its own ground rather than insist that the world move to its ground.

[104] *Religionsphilosophie*, p. 410; *Polarity*, pp. 39–40, emphasis mine.

[105] *Religionsphilosophie*, p. 422; *Polarity*, p. 52.

[106] *Religionsphilosophie*, pp. 422–3; *Polarity*, pp. 53–4.

which Pzrywara calls the 'expression of the fundamental Catholic position' and 'deep and ultimate meaning of all Catholic ethic and civilization'.[107] Human life, he says, takes the form of 'a never-ending (relatively infinite) unveiling of the absolute infinite God in and above the never-ending (relatively infinite) self-evolution of life in Him'.[108] There is thus a 'twofold unity' between the 'experience of the infinity of God *in* the endless rhythm of life' and the 'adoration of the same infinity *above* the endless rhythm of life'.[109] The human who exists in analogy to God stands before God as one who adores and worships him as the God who is always above and from whom the human has all that she has. This explains why Przywara says that, of the various models of God proposed by religious philosophy, '[t]he God of Catholicism alone is the truly transcendent God'.[110] He alone is a God who can be worshipped.

Przywara believes that this account of the *analogia entis* is consistent with the teachings of the First Vatican Council in that it follows from the basic insight that, while God is separate and distinct from all that is external to him, everything other than him was 'in its entire essence and existence derived from him'.[111] This is why he believes that the *analogia entis*, as the philosophical expression of this basic Catholic insight, provides the definitive 'Catholic solution of the religious problem of the relationship between essence and existence'.[112] It reduces the 'tangle' of religious philosophy into a 'unity' because 'in the self-same act in which man, in the likeness of a creature, becomes "within" God, he also becomes "within" him who, in likeness, is above all comparison'.[113] This unity is not one of identification – as is

---

[107] *Religionsphilosophie*, p. 423; *Polarity*, p. 53.

[108] *Religionsphilosophie*, pp. 430–1; *Polarity*, p. 61. David Bentley Hart summarizes Przywara's point well here: 'In *him* we live and move and have our being. Every creature exists in a state of tension (as Przywara likes to put it) between essence and existence, in a condition of absolute becoming, oscillating between what it is and that it is, striving toward its essence and existence alike, receiving both from the movement of God's grace while possessing nothing in itself, totally and dynamically dependent, sharing in the fullness of being that God enjoys in infinite simplicity, and so infinitely other than the source of being.' See David Bentley Hart, 'The Offering of Names: Metaphysics, Nihilism, and Analogy', in *Reason and the Reasons of Faith*, ed. Paul J. Griffiths and Reinhard Hütter (New York: T&T Clark, 2005), p. 285.

[109] *Religionsphilosophie*, p. 431; *Polarity*, p. 62.

[110] *Religionsphilosophie*, p. 408; *Polarity*, p. 38.

[111] *Religionsphilosophie*, p. 402; *Polarity*, p. 31. Specifically, Przywara has in mind the affirmation from the *Constitutio Dogmatica de Fide Catholica* that God 'must be declared to be, in reality and in essence, distinct from the world' and but that God also created the world 'in order to manifest his perfection by the good things which he bestows on what he creates'.

[112] *Religionsphilosophie*, p. 404; *Polarity*, p. 33.

[113] *Religionsphilosophie*, p. 404; *Polarity*, pp. 33–4.

found in the 'unity' offered by the philosophers – but of the proper tension between immanence and transcendence.

Catholicism and History

This argument leads into the third and final section of the book, where Przywara makes the case that the whole of the Catholic tradition, especially its major figures, manifests both the basic truth of the *analogia entis* and its relevance for the questions of philosophy. Of course, he admits, the *analogia entis* itself was not employed by every Catholic theologian, but even so, the tensions operative within it can be seen in the work of every major thinker, early to late, within the tradition. He explains that the various expressions of the principle in history can finally be reduced to two streams – the Augustinian and the Thomist – with the Augustinian stream emphasizing God's immanence and the Thomist stream emphasizing God's transcendence. These streams represent 'two forms of accentuation' within the Catholic tradition, and when viewed together, they capture the tension of the *analogia entis*.[114] In fact, he insists that the existence of these two streams reveals that, in its historical expression, there is an '"analogy" within the *analogia entis* itself'.[115] That is, within the concrete history of the Catholic Church, the *analogia entis* is manifested as the principle which both 'forms its content' and 'determines its shape' by 'determining the relationship of its various schools of thought to one another'.[116] In other words, for Przywara, the *analogia entis* defines the shape of Catholic history as well as Catholic theology.

With this account of the tradition in hand, Przywara turns to illustrating how Catholicism stands as the fulfilment of the history of religious philosophy. He again works through the various antitheses within the problems of essence and existence outlined in the first part of the book, and he demonstrates how the Catholic faith – and specifically its theology and liturgy – resolves these tensions.[117] The *analogia entis* stands at the centre of this account, and because it is the unifying principle of both philosophy and Catholic theology, it represents 'the unity of *all* wisdom regarding God and creation'.[118] Przywara even makes the case that the philosophies of 'Eastern wisdom' can be brought together with Western thought when they are interpreted in the light of the tension of human likeness and unlikeness to God, so that the 'antithetical fabric of the world-wisdom of the East and

---

[114] *Religionsphilosophie*, p. 482; *Polarity*, p. 117.

[115] *Religionsphilosophie*, p. 484; *Polarity*, p. 119.

[116] *Ibid.*

[117] *Religionsphilosophie*, pp. 484–511; *Polarity*, pp. 119–49.

[118] *Religionsphilosophie*, p. 484; *Polarity*, p. 127, emphasis mine.

West is redeemed and brought to the unity of the *Una Catholica*'.[119] There truly is 'no salvation outside the Church', he concludes, because the central principle of the Catholic Church is, in fact, the governing principle of the whole of creation.[120]

Two Competing yet Related Visions

This point leads us back to the motivation lying behind Przywara's argument. As he sees it, the central problem facing European culture after the war was the inability of modern thinkers to determine the nature of the human relationship with God. Without a clear way forward, modern thinkers finally collapsed God into the creature, which meant that God simply became the expression or projection of humanity's own desires. The destructive consequences of this type of thinking became obvious with the war and the despair of the post-war years. Now, in the face of this challenge, Roman Catholics have to find their voice once again and address the world. The *analogia entis* stands as Przywara's attempt to give Catholics something to say. By interpreting the whole of human existence in the shape of analogy, Przywara thinks that he has found a way to transcend the false alternatives that have plagued human thought about God. In the *analogia entis*, while God truly is other than the creature, he also is in relationship with the creature. Human existence itself, because it occurs within the tension of this relationship, pushes the creature towards God as the One in whom it lives and has its being. Not only has the historical dichotomy been overcome, therefore, but it has been overcome in a uniquely *Catholic* way, because life before God takes the form of the rhythmic liturgy which reflects both the immanence and transcendence of God. For Przywara, this vision addresses a critical need in the world, and it also provides the Catholic Church the motivation it needs to address the world's basic needs with the best insights of the Catholic tradition itself. Przywara, in other words, believes that a clear recognition of the *analogia entis* changes the nature of the relationship of Catholics and the world from one of caution and retreat to one of confidence and mission. In this sense, the *analogia entis* of *Religionsphilosophie* is the fulfilment of Przywara's original vision, inspired by Newman, of a Catholic Church that faces the 'torrent' of modernity with its gaze 'calmly fixed upon the God of the end'.[121] It is a vision, in short, of a Church that meets the challenges of the modern world by showing that it has the answers which that world has failed to find on its own.

---

[119] *Religionsphilosophie*, p. 511; *Polarity*, p. 149.
[120] *Ibid*.
[121] Przywara, 'St. Augustine and the Modern World', in *A Monument to Saint Augustine* (London: Sheed & Ward, 1930), p. 286.

Karl Barth also thought that he had the answers the world was seeking. He, too, held to a God who was utterly distinct from the world; and he, too – in part, as a response to Przywara's criticism – sought to formulate theological expressions that maintained this 'wholly other' God's connection to the world. These commitments, however, led him down a different road than the one Przywara travelled. Whereas Przywara turned to the best insights of the Catholic tradition to help him articulate a way for the Catholic Church to be the kind of church the modern world needed, Barth turned to the insights of the Reformation to help him accomplish the same thing; whereas Przywara's project took him in the direction of human experience, Barth's took him in the direction of a particular view of divine revelation; whereas Przywara turned to the *analogia entis*, Barth turned to the incarnation. These same distinctions would divide them from this day forward. Indeed, by the time Barth finished his lectures at Göttingen and Przywara finished his *Religionsphilosophie*, all of the key ideas and concepts were in place to set the stage for the debate that would culminate in 1932 with Barth's condemnation of the *analogia entis* in the preface of *CD* I/1. The debate would become more complicated in the years ahead – and there still were many turns left in the road – but its course was set in 1924 and 1926.

4

THE NATURE OF BARTH'S
REJECTION OF
THE *ANALOGIA ENTIS*

Common to 'metaphysics' and 'religion' is the central point of the
analogia entis *and the presupposition of the natural self-revelation of*
God in his creation, so that on the one hand metaphysics bears within
itself an element of religion (the presupposition of the self-revelation
of God) and on the other hand, religion contains an element of meta-
physics (the criterion for recognition of the analogia entis*).*

– *Erich Przywara, S. J.*[1]

God has made us. We have scope and stability alongside the reality of
God. But even because this is a fabulous marvel, because we hold our
existence within the sheer blinding light of the existence of the God who
created us out of nothing, we are unable to understand our own exist-
ence, not even in the view of it as 'being made for God', as Augustine
said.

– *Karl Barth*[2]

Introduction

With an account of Barth's lectures at Göttingen and Przywara's *Religions-*
philosophie katholischer Theologie in hand, all of the pieces are in place
for an evaluation of the differences between the two thinkers and an
analysis of the question of whether Barth's rejection of the *analogia entis*
was the result of a mistaken understanding of it. In this chapter, I will

---

[1] Erich Przywara, 'Metaphysik und Religion', in *Schriften*, vol. 2 (Einsiedeln: Johannes-
Verlag, 1962), p. 22.
[2] Karl Barth, *The Holy Spirit and the Christian Life: The Theological Basis of Ethics*,
trans. R. Birch Hoyle (Louisville: Westminster/John Knox Press, 1993), p. 7.

argue that Barth rejected Przywara's *analogia entis* precisely because he understood it, and I will show that this rejection stems from legitimate theological concerns arising directly from his Protestant theological commitments. Specifically, Barth realized that the basic insights of the *analogia entis* are built upon an account of the doctrines of revelation, justification, and sanctification that he could not accept on Protestant theological grounds. He recognized that Przywara's construal posits continuity between God and the human, not between God's being and human being, but between God's justifying act and human moral acts. Barth's rejection thus stands in line with the convictions that had been propelling his thought since his break with the theology of his teachers; it corresponds to his affirmation in Göttingen that creaturely realities can be 'in analogy but cannot be in continuity' with God's revelation;[3] it is consistent with the basic motivations of the Protestant tradition; and it stands in line with the convictions that governed his theology until the end of his life. In short, Barth's rejection of the *analogia entis* was not a mistake that could or would be corrected at a later date; rather, it was the fulfilment of his most basic theological insights.

Barth and Przywara in Münster

In 1925, Barth moved from Göttingen to the University of Münster, and this move was more than just a change in scenery. Whereas Göttingen was a predominantly Lutheran city, Münster was a Catholic one, and this new context gave Barth the opportunity to engage with Roman Catholic theology more deeply than he ever had before. For example, he participated in a lay Catholic reading group, and he also taught seminars about pre-eminent Catholic thinkers like Anselm and Aquinas so that he could learn more about them.[4] It is clear as well that Barth continued to think about Przywara's theology and the *analogia entis*. Evidence for this is found in the unpublished sections of his second cycle of dogmatics which were delivered in 1927

---

[3] Karl Barth, *The Göttingen Dogmatics: Instruction in the Christian Religion*, ed. Hannelotte Reiffen, trans. Geoffrey W. Bromiley, vol. 1 (Grand Rapids, MI: Eerdmans, 1991), p. 94.

[4] See Wilhelm Neuser, *Karl Barth in Münster 1925–1930* (Zürich: Theologischer Verlag Zürich, 1985), pp. 37–8. For a list of the courses Barth taught at Münster, see Bruce L. McCormack, *Karl Barth's Critically Realistic Dialectical Theology: Its Genesis and Development, 1909–1936* (Oxford: Oxford University Press, 1995), p. 378. The fact that the two major Catholic theologians Barth taught seminars on were the ones who had given the most convincing natural proofs for God's existence as not accidental. During his Münster years, Barth took an interest in the possibility of a natural theology, and he explored the best sources he could find on the subject. This fact makes his forceful rejection of all natural theology all the more striking.

and 1928.[5] These lectures reveal an openness to the insights and contributions of Catholic theology that is surprising in light of both Barth's previous thought and his future writings. This newfound openness is perhaps most clear in his surprising decision to utilize the *analogia entis* in his *own* dogmatic theology.

As we saw in his lectures in Göttingen, Barth believes that God can and does take up creaturely realities in his act of self-revelation, and we noted that these realities may 'be in analogy' but not 'in continuity' with this revelation.[6] This notion was left underdeveloped in Göttingen, however, and as Barth worked through these same questions for his lectures on dogmatics in Münster, he again faced the problem of explaining how divine revelation can occur in and through creaturely realities without becoming part of these realities in such a way that it can be subject to human possession or control. Barth continues to hold that one of the distinctions between God and humanity lies in the fact that, while the human participates in creaturely realities simply because the human is a creature, God participates in these same realities through the dialectic of veiling and unveiling as he takes them up in the event of his self-revelation.[7] Working through this question again, however, prompted Barth to seek a way to articulate this distinction more thoroughly and precisely. How can God be in relationship with humanity – including in the incarnation and in the event of divine revelation – without simply becoming an object in the world like any other object? It is in his attempt to address this question that Barth, surprisingly, turns to the *analogia entis*. He argues:

> Creaturely 'being' participates precisely as 'being', but without therefore being divine 'being'; it exists *analogia entis* in the 'being' out of which it exists, that is, in the original, divine 'being' . . . that God is and has so *completely different(ly)* from the creature makes it necessary to speak of incommunicable attributes. That he is and has [his attributes] so completely differently from the creature – for this reason the communicable attributes are set; [they are] perfections in which

---

[5] These lectures are known as Barth's 'second cycle' of dogmatics, the 'Christian Dogmatics', or the 'Münster Dogmatics'. Only the prolegomena, consisting of §§1–26, has been published. See Karl Barth, *Die christliche Dogmatik im Entwurf* (München: Chr. Kaiser Verlag, 1927). The unpublished portions, consisting of §§26–45 and §§46–64 have recently undergone an extensive analysis by Amy E. Marga, and my discussion of the text here relies upon her research. See Amy E. Marga, 'Karl Barth's Second Dogmatic Cycle: Münster 1926–1928: A Progress Report', *Zeitschrift für dialektische Theologie* 21, no. 1 (2005), pp. 126–37, and Marga, 'Partners in the Gospel: Karl Barth and Roman Catholicism, 1922–1932' (Unpublished Doctoral Dissertation, Princeton Theology Seminary, 2006), pp. 124–93.

[6] Barth, *Göttingen Dogmatics*, p. 94.

[7] Marga, 'Partners in the Gospel', pp. 160–1.

God allows the creature to *participate*, and with which they, because every perfection is one in the being of God, then they also participate in the incommunicable attributes *as such*. That there are such communicable attributes of God, that we have life, power, knowledge and will, *analogia entis*, in common with God, makes a community between God and the human possible.[8]

It is clear that Barth's use of the *analogia entis* here is imprecise. He seems to be trying to make the same sort of move Przywara makes when the latter employed Aquinas' distinction between the essence and existence of God and the essence and existence of the creature, but Barth makes this move with much less success than Przywara did. For Barth, God and the creature are utterly distinct from one another, and this distinction is marked by God's 'incommunicable attributes'. No creature can participate directly in these incommunicable attributes, but there are 'communicable attributes' that God allows the creature to participate in. Yet, because God is utterly simple – that is, because 'every perfection is one in the being of God' – the creature can participate in the incommunicable attributes of God by way of his participation in God's communicable attributes. For Barth, this participation is by analogy – the *analogia entis* – and it means that the God and the human can have true community with one another as they both participate in the one creaturely reality.

What is happening here? Dogmatically, Barth has not moved beyond the question that drove his discussion of analogy in the Göttingen lectures: he is simply trying to explain how God can take up creaturely realities in the act of his self-revelation. This explanation has its roots in the question that drove his earliest theology: how can God truly be known by human beings while all the time remaining the subject of that knowledge? In Göttingen, Barth had turned to the incarnation to answer this question, but he had not developed his insights fully there. Now, in his attempt to make his answer more specific, he adds to his previous formulations new insights he had learnt from Catholic theology, including the *analogia entis*. This move, however, reveals confusion. Barth's talk of human participation in the 'being' of God seems to indicate that he thinks that humans can come to knowledge of God simply by reflecting upon their created being alone; at the same time, Barth still wants to maintain the notion of God's veiling and unveiling in the event of his self-revelation so that God remains the subject of divine

---

[8] Karl Barth, 'Münster Dogmatics I' (unpublished manuscript in the Karl Barth Archive, Basel), pp. 128–9; cited in Marga, 'Partners in the Gospel', p. 161. 'Münster Dogmatics I' refers to §§26–45 of Barth's lectures. This citation comes from §30, and the page numbers refer to the typed version of Barth's original handwritten notes available in the Archive. For an explanation of the complex numbering system of the unpublished manuscripts from Münster, see Marga, 'Partners in the Gospel', p. 124, fn. 1.

revelation at every moment. Barth, in short, is trying to have it both ways. This is clearly a mistake, and it is one that Barth himself would recognize quickly. In her analysis of the original handwritten manuscripts of these lectures, Amy Marga notes that 'Barth became more apprehensive about using the term [*analogia entis*], for he added an exclamation point in the margin by every occurrence of the term'.[9] Barth, in other words, seems to be worried that, once again, something is not right in his portrayal, and that he needs to find a new way forward.[10] He appears to think that the *analogia entis* may provide that way forward, but he clearly is worried that he misunderstands it.

Przywara's Visit to Barth's Seminar

These worries help explain why, in February 1929, Barth invited Przywara to visit the seminar he was teaching on the *prima pars* of Thomas Aquinas' *Summa Theologicae*. Perhaps Przywara himself could explain the *analogia entis* to him more clearly and give him the insights he needed to address the question of how God can be both above creation and yet intimately related to it.

We know that Barth took Przywara's visit to his seminar seriously, because in the two weeks leading up to Przywara's arrival, Barth led his students in a close reading of Przywara's *Religionsphilosophie*.[11] A record of their

---

[9] Marga, 'Partners in the Gospel', p. 161, fn. 88.

[10] Barth's comment about the published version of *Die christliche Dogmatik im Entwurf* in the preface to *Church Dogmatics* I/1 is instructive here: 'When the first volume was before me in print, it showed me plainly – whatever may be the experience of others, much more plainly than a manuscript lying in a cupboard could ever have done – how much I myself have still to learn both historically and materially.' He also notes that in the new version, 'I have excluded to the very best of my ability anything that might appear to find for theology a foundation, support, or justification in philosophical existentialism'. That this statement appears in the same paragraph that he issues his condemnation of the *analogia entis* is not a coincidence. See Karl Barth, *Church Dogmatics* I/1, rev. edn, trans. Geoffrey Bromiley (Edinburgh: T&T Clark, 1975), pp. xi, xiii; *Die Kirchliche Dogmatik* I/1 (Zürich: Evanglischer Verlag, 1932), pp. vii–viii.

[11] The students discussed their reading in seminars on 25 January and 1 February, 1929. As we will see below, this strengthens McCormack's claim that Barth's 'Fate and Idea' should be read as a direct response to Przywara, even though McCormack's claim was made with the idea that it was Barth's personal encounter with Przywara, rather than his reading of the book, that prompted the response in 'Fate and Idea', because he locates Barth's reading of Przywara's *Religionsphilosophie* in the period *between* 'Fate and Idea' (February) and 'The Holy Spirit and the Christian Life' (October). With the information provided by the protocols, we can now date Barth's reading of the manuscript earlier than McCormack did, and this enables us to read 'Fate and Idea' as a much more specific response to Przywara than McCormack supposed. See McCormack, *Karl Barth's Critically Realistic Dialectical Theology*, pp. 384–90.

discussions of the book exists in the form of student protocols that docu-
mented the seminar proceedings, and these protocols show that Barth's
class read the first two parts of the book critically and with an attention
to detail. For example, on the second week of their reading, a student presented an account of Przywara's description of the *analogia entis*.[12] In it,
she works carefully through Przywara's distinction between the essence
and existence of God and that of the creature, and she points out that, in
the *analogia entis*, the dissimilarity between God and the human is due to
the difference between the *identity* of God's essence and existence and the
tension of the human's essence and existence. She makes it clear that this
tension is what Przywara means when he talks about human existence as
'open upwards' to God.[13]

It also is clear from the protocols that Barth's students are impressed
with Przywara's argument and with his book as a whole. They have questions, however, about his starting point. They note that Przywara begins by
focusing upon the human consciousness and using it to demonstrate both
the failures of modern religious philosophy and the successes of the *analogia
entis*.[14] The students worry that, by focusing on the human consciousness in
this way, Przywara ends up with an abstract picture of human being instead
of with the concrete reality of the human situation. Human being, they
argue, is determined at every moment by the reality of human sin. Przywara,
however, never talks about sinful human being at all. For him, the pattern of
the relationship between God and humanity – the one defined most clearly
by the *analogia entis* – results from God's act of creation, and this pattern
remains intact despite our sin and apart from a second act of grace. The
class worries that this view is a distortion. They argue that it is impossible
to talk about human being in relation to God without beginning with
God's revelation in his Word, because this Word reveals both the reality of
human sin and the human need for reconciliation and grace. The students
conclude that, because it ignores the reality of sin, Przywara's description
of the human is based upon an *ideal* human rather than the *actual* human.
The result is that, even though Przywara uses human consciousness as a
basis for his discussion of the *analogia entis*, by ignoring the reality of sin,
he never really discusses true human consciousness, or being, at all.[15]

Three aspects of these seminar discussions should be noted. First, it is clear
that both Barth and his students carefully read and considered Przywara's
work in advance of his visit, and it is also apparent that the questions they
raised were not based on a 'scant' understanding of his proposal. Rather,

---

[12] 'Thomas Aquinas Seminar Protocol' (unpublished manuscript in the Karl Barth Archive,
Basel), p. 199. The student is 'Frauline von Aschoff'.

[13] *Ibid.*, pp. 199–200.

[14] 'Thomas Aquinas Seminar Protocol', p. 192.

[15] *Ibid.*, pp. 206–7.

they engaged Przywara's book on its own terms, and they took his argument seriously by listening to it carefully and raising critical questions about it. This leads to the second aspect: the objections raised against Przywara's *analogia entis* by the class were not polemical but theological. The Protestant tradition has always asserted that, when considered in light of the present situation, human being must be seen as fallen, and thus any construal of the human that neglects to address the reality of sin fails to address true human *being* at all. The worries that Barth's students had with Przywara's argument, therefore, make sense within the context of the Protestant tradition in which Barth was teaching. As we will see, Barth will take up his students' arguments as his own in just a few weeks, and he will make them more specific. At this point, however, it is important to note that these criticisms are raised not to attack Przywara but to come to an understanding of the root of the difference between the Przywara's Roman Catholic approach to theology and their own distinctively Protestant approach. The students, in other words, made the distinction in order to learn from Przywara rather than assail him. Third, inasmuch as we can assume that the seminar discussion in some sense reflects the trajectory of Barth's own thought, we can see that his views about the *analogia entis* have become more precise and more critical than was apparent in his use of it in his lectures on dogmatics the year before. Barth has not yet rejected the *analogia entis* in the manner that he will reject it in just a few weeks' time, but he no longer appears to be as open to it as he was just a few months earlier.

Barth and his students had a chance to address their questions to Przywara in person when he visited the seminar the next week for a lecture and seminar discussion.[16] His visit began on the evening of February 5 with a lecture entitled 'The Catholic Church Principle'.[17] In light of the questions raised by Barth's class, one aspect of Przywara's argument in this lecture stands out. Przywara explains to Barth's students that one of the distinctions between Protestant and Roman Catholic theology lies in their understanding of how God relates to human beings.[18] From the Catholic point of view,

---

[16] When Barth invited Przywara for the visit, he suggested that Przywara alone deliver a lecture because that would allow more time for discussion than if they each delivered a lecture. He also noted that the Catholic faculty at Münster were worried that Przywara did not represent the official Catholic view. Przywara responded that he would speak only for himself. See the letter from Barth to Przywara on 6 November 1928 as well as the letter from Przywara to Barth on 18 November 1928 (unpublished manuscripts available in the Karl Barth Archive, Basel).

[17] Barth arranged the publication of this lecture in *Zwischen den Zeiten* shortly after Przywara's visit. See Erich Przywara, 'Das katholische Kirchenprinzip', *Zwischen den Zeiten* 7 (1929), pp. 277–302.

[18] *Ibid.*, pp. 277–8.

he says, God's revelation occurs visibly in the Catholic Church, and it does so precisely because the Church exists as the continuing manifestation of the incarnation in the world. In a very real sense, then, the Catholic Church is the 'creaturely-visible form of God' in history.[19] As such, its existence testifies to the pattern of God's relationship to the world, and every other manifestation of this relationship – including its manifestation in God's relation with human beings in particular – follows the same pattern we see in the Catholic Church.[20] This argument illustrates how Przywara would address the questions from Barth's students about his starting point. He believes that he is justified in beginning his study with a reflection upon the human consciousness because the whole of human existence before God follows the same pattern that is visible in God's relationship to the Catholic Church. This pattern is best described by the *analogia entis*, and with this doctrine in hand, a theologian is justified in starting anywhere in history – including with the human consciousness – because any other manifestation of God's relationship with the world will follow this same pattern. From Przywara's point of view, therefore, his starting point is not abstract; it is based, rather, upon the reality that every form of God's revelation in history corresponds to the revelation of 'God in Christ in the Church'.[21] In his mind, he is simply moving from the visible manifestation of God's revelation within the Catholic Church to its visible manifestation in the human con-sciousness by applying the pattern of God's activity former to the one visible in the latter.

In his discussion with Barth's students the following morning – again, as recorded in the protocols – Przywara defends this idea by appealing to the Catholic principle 'grace does not destroy but supports and perfects nature'.[22] In his view, this principle provides the theological basis for understanding how and why the knowledge of God available in the Catholic Church stands in line with the knowledge of God humans can have through reflection upon their own created existence.[23] The necessity of God's justifying grace, he argues, does not mean that nature is 'abolished or dropped' as if sin negates the reality that creatures have their being by participation in God's being.[24] Instead, Przywara says, grace must be seen 'doubly' – both as created and

---

[19] *Ibid.*, p. 283.

[20] *Ibid.*, p. 289.

[21] *Ibid.*, p. 283.

[22] Later on, Przywara favourably compared this discussion with debates he had with advocates of 'evangelical Catholicity'. The difference was that, while his discussion with Barth allowed him to draw clear distinctions, the other discussions inevitably ended up 'smudging differences'. See Erich Przywara and Hermann Sauer, *Gespräch Zwischen den Kirchen* (Nürnberg: Glock und Lutz Verlag, 1956), p. 7.

[23] See 'Thomas Aquinas Seminar Protocol', p. 213.

[24] *Ibid.*

uncreated – meaning that the grace of creation cannot be contrasted with the grace of reconciliation.[25] For Przywara, the creation of the world is a concrete act of grace in which Gods reveals himself: 'the concrete God', he tells Barth's students, 'reveals himself in *this* concrete way'.[26] For this reason, he says, we are justified in saying that the knowledge of God available through philosophical reflection upon God's revelation in creation – and specifically, by philosophical reflection upon human existence and being – stands in line with, and can be perfected and fulfilled by, the knowledge of God and God's relationship with humanity available through God's revelation in the Church. 'Revelation', he insists, 'does not destroy but supports and perfects reason'.[27] Of course, it is impossible to arrive at a full understanding of God through philosophical reflection upon created human existence alone; but when this act of creation is considered from the standpoint of God's subsequent revelation in Christ and in the Catholic Church, it is clear that, in fact, this philosophical reflection leads directly to the God who is both in and over our existence.

These ideas again explain why Przywara's argument in *Religionsphiloso-phie* takes the form that it does: the imperfect knowledge provided by the philosophical tradition's reflection upon the relation between the human consciousness and God is perfected by the revealed knowledge found in the Roman Catholic Church's tradition – and specifically by its central principle, the *analogia entis*. For Przywara, it is simply wrong to dismiss the possibility of obtaining knowledge of God from reflection upon God's act in creation because of the more perfect revelation found in the Church. Rather, he insists, God's revelation in creation and his revelation in the Catholic Church work hand-in-hand, with the latter revelation perfecting the former. This is precisely why human consciousness can serve as a 'window' through which we see the self-revelation of God in his relationship to creation; we know that it functions in this way because we have eyes to see it once we have the pattern and rhythm of the *analogia entis*.

Barth found both Przywara's lecture and his visit to the seminar stimulating. He had discovered a Roman Catholic interlocutor who would not accept compromises but defended his positions vigorously as the *correct* positions to hold. From such a person there could only be much to learn. Przywara's lecture, Barth wrote to Thurneysen, was 'a masterpiece', and he noted that Przywara 'shone' in the seminar while answering the students'

---

[25] *Ibid.*, p. 222.

[26] 'Thomas Aquinas Seminar Protocol', p. 222, emphasis mine. As Betz notes, the *analogia entis* is a 'principle based in the *revelation of creation*'. See John R. Betz, 'Beyond the Sublime: The Aesthetics of the Analogy of Being (Part Two)', *Modern Theology* 22, no. 1 (2006), p. 15.

[27] 'Thomas Aquinas Seminar Protocol', p. 214; also see p. 221.

questions.[28] He also described Przywara's visits to his home on the evenings of February 5 and 6:

> he 'overwhelmed' me . . . just as, according to his doctrine, the dear God overwhelms people with grace (at least within the Catholic Church) so that the formula 'God in-above the human from God's side' is, at one and the same time, the shorthand of his existence as well as the dissolution of all Protestant and modernist, transcendental and immanent stupidity and tension in the peace of the *analogia entis*.[29]

The language of Barth's recollection is consistent with Przywara's own terminology, and it seems clear both from Barth's descriptions of the event and from the protocols that Przywara had been given ample opportunity to present and discuss his theology at length and in great detail. But did Barth truly understand Przywara's theology in general and the *analogia entis* in particular?

To address this question, it will be helpful to summarize what we know of Barth and Przywara's encounters thus far. We know that Barth had positive feelings for Przywara personally, both from their letters to one another and from Barth's remarks in his letter to Thurneysen. It is clear as well that Barth did not have a negative preconception of the *analogia entis* before he read Przywara's book and met him personally, because he had used the principle in his own dogmatic theology. We know that Barth read at least the first two parts of Przywara's *Religionsphilosophie* carefully and discussed it at length during two seminar sessions; we know that he listened to a lengthy lecture from Przywara about Roman Catholic ecclesiology; we know that he sat with Przywara for a two-hour discussion of Przywara's theology in his seminar; and we know that Barth and Przywara spent two evenings together in Barth's home for one-on-one discussions of theology. If Barth had misconceptions about the *analogia entis*, therefore, Przywara had ample time to disabuse Barth of them. We also know that Barth had long since proven himself to be a perceptive and insightful reader of theological texts. His lectures on Zwingli, Calvin, and Schleiermacher at Göttingen stand as examples of his perceptive insight, and the same can be said for his book on Anselm and the lectures that would become *Protestant Theology in the Nineteenth Century*, which were originally delivered in 1929–30 in Münster and continued in 1932–33 in Bonn. Throughout this period, Barth showed an attention to detail, an ability to recognize the contours of a theologian's argument and the underlying motivation for it, and

---

[28] Karl Barth and Eduard Thurneysen, *Karl Barth – Eduard Thurneysen Briefweshsel: 1921–30*, Gesamtausgabe (Zürich: Theologischer Verlag Zürich, 1974), p. 652.
[29] *Ibid.*

a willingness to let a theologian's work speak for itself.[30] He showed himself, in other words, not to be merely a polemicist who saw in texts what he wanted to see.

On the basis of all of this evidence, therefore, it is clear that Barth was in position to obtain an accurate idea of what Przywara meant by the term *analogia entis*, what the implications of the principle were, and how it fit into Przywara's larger theological project. It is also clear that Barth did not approach Przywara or the *analogia entis* in a polemical, or for that matter, a 'demented' way.[31] He approached Przywara as someone representing another tradition, to be sure, and it is clear that Barth recognized points of disagreement between their views. He did not see Przywara as an enemy, however, but as a kindred spirit, albeit one with whom he could not always agree.

In short, at this point, we have every reason to conclude that Barth's eventual rejection of the *analogia entis* was based not upon a lack of understanding or upon an unfair approach to Przywara's theology or to *analogia entis* itself. Of course, the evidence derived from Barth's own written response to the *analogia entis* will have to bear this preliminary conclusion out. We must turn to that response, therefore, before we can draw a definitive conclusion to the question.

Barth's Initial Response: 'Fate and Idea in Theology'

At the end of February, just a couple of weeks after Przywara's visit, Barth delivered a four-part lecture series at the Hochschulinstitut in Dortmund entitled 'Fate and Idea in Theology'. Although he is never mentioned by name in these lectures, Przywara clearly serves as Barth's interlocutor at every turn.[32] These lectures, therefore, deserve extended treatment both

---

[30] See, for example, John Webster's remark that in *Protestant Theology in the Nineteenth Century*, Barth engages in 'respectful, courteous listening, intense questioning and counter-questioning, and more than anything, a submission of both past and present to judgment by the object of theology which is the unifying factor in its history'. See Webster, *Barth's Earlier Theology* (New York: T&T Clark, 2005), p. 101.

[31] See David Bentley Hart, 'The Offering of Names: Metaphysics, Nihilism, and Analogy', in *Reason and the Reasons of Faith*, ed. Paul J. Griffiths and Reinhard Hütter (New York: T&T Clark, 2005), p. 285, fn. 14.

[32] Bruce McCormack has the same view: '[W]hen the essay is read in the light of the situation-in-life in which it was written, it is hard to avoid the impression that Erich Przywara is the silent conversation partner throughout'. He also notes that this essay marks the first time that Barth criticized the *analogia entis* in print, and 'the understanding of it which unfolds here would remain characteristic of Barthian polemics in the future'. See McCormack, *Karl Barth's Critically Realistic Dialectical Theology*, p. 385.

because they provide a glimpse of Barth's initial response to Przywara's *analogia entis* after Przywara's visit to his seminar and because, in this lecture, seeds are planted that will later blossom into Barth's definitive rejection of the *analogia entis*. These lectures, in other words, reveal that Barth's statement in the preface of *Church Dogmatics* I/1 (*CD* I/1) did not occur in a vacuum but was predicated on real concerns raised for the first time in print here. They also point us to the central doctrine – justification by grace alone through faith alone – that propels and shapes Barth's criticism of the *analogia entis* through the end of his career.

Theology and Philosophy

That Przywara was on Barth's mind is apparent in the first lecture as Barth explains the title and his objective for the talk. The title, Barth explained, refers to the 'two boundaries of human thought', realism and idealism, which form the 'basic problem of all philosophy'.[33] Barth's goal is to use these 'boundaries' as the framework from which to ask questions about the proper relationship between philosophy and theology. To flesh out his reason for taking up this task, he draws an analogy between the relationship between theology and philosophy and that of the church and the state. Just as 'the church finds itself in the framework of the state but does not exist in competition with it . . . so theology understands itself as (the) fundamental reflection about human existence as discussed within the framework of philosophy'.[34] Theology is a human enterprise, and as such, it uses the same tools of language, concepts, and categories that philosophers use in their own attempts to describe the human situation. This correspondence leads to a temptation, Barth says, because while the theologian can speak about the human situation only in the 'crabbed, constricted and paradoxical way' forced upon it by its adherence to divine revelation, the philosopher 'is in a position to say it all so much better, more freely, more universally'.[35] This situation places the theologian 'under the insufferable pressure of a situation where [he] can speak only humanly and where this occurs so much better in philosophy'.[36] Hence, just as the church must deal with the temptation of trying either to become the state or be absorbed into it, theology

---

[33] Karl Barth, 'Fate and Idea in Theology', in *The Way of Theology in Karl Barth: Essays and Comments*, ed. H. Martin Rumscheidt (Allison Park, PA: Pickwick Publications, 1986), p. 25.

[34] *Ibid.*, p. 27.

[35] *Ibid.*, p. 30. He explains: 'Indeed philosophy manages to speak profoundly in human language without hearing the Word, without the troublesome connection to Bible and church, and without the recurrent counter-question that constantly casts doubt upon the idea of a divine miracle confirming a human word.'

[36] *Ibid.*

must deal with the temptation of trying either to become philosophy or be absorbed into it. The fact that the shift from theology to philosophy occurs by only a 'few small shifts in accent' or a 'few minor adjustments' makes it all the more dangerous.[37] Theology can avoid these dangers, Barth says, only if it realizes its true task: adhering to God's Word. He will develop what this means in more specificity as the lecture progresses, but at this point, he simply means that theology proper is that which 'thinks and speaks not about those boundaries of human thought, but with all possible objectivity about God'.[38]

The fact that Przywara's project centres upon the relationship between philosophy and theology – and their point of connection in the *analogia entis* – is working in the background of Barth's thoughts here, and the way that he frames this relationship points to a key difference he recognizes between Przywara's project and his own. As we have seen, Przywara's account of the *analogia entis* is built upon the notion that philosophical thought about God failed to recognize the proper relationship between the boundaries of divine immanence and transcendence and thus failed to arrive at any true knowledge of God. The *analogia entis* is then posited as the alternative that resolves the false dichotomy left by philosophy, since it maintains the proper 'tension' between immanence and transcendence. This argument stands directly in line with the Catholic dictum that Przywara cited in Barth's seminar: 'revelation does not destroy but supports and perfects reason'. That is, Przywara describes the problem of philosophy, which works from reason, and then proffers the *analogia entis*, which was derived from divine revelation in Jesus Christ and the Catholic Church, as the solution to that problem. Revelation, in short, works in concert with reason because the two are engaged in the same basic task, and revelation 'fulfils and perfects' reason because the Catholic *analogia entis* accomplishes, on the philosophers' own terms, what the philosophers themselves could not.

Barth seems to have this argument in mind when he says that, if a theologian were able to establish true point of connection between philosophy and theology, then it would be an admirable accomplishment.

> Good for him if in the framework of philosophy he is nothing but a human thinker, a *philosophus* among others, reflecting fundamentally on the conception of human existence, and yet is still a witness to thinking based on divine revelation. Good for him if in the shroud of the completely similar, which he too can think and say by himself,

---

[37] *Ibid.*, p. 31.
[38] *Ibid.*, p. 32.

he speaks of the completely dissimilar; if in the shroud of what is merely relatively extraordinary, in which he has a right to speak, that absolutely extraordinary reality becomes manifest which only God can speak; if while speaking in the world yet not of this world, he nonetheless even in the full humanity of his words really speaks of God.[39]

Even if such a system occurred, however, Barth insists that it is the result of a 'miracle of God . . . not the nature or art of the theologian'.[40] That is, theological formulations correspond to the truth of God only as a result of God's grace rather than the theologian's precision or skill. Here the concerns that have been driving Barth since *Romans* II again become apparent. In Barth's view, the problem that goes along with creating a theological system that centres upon an examination of human existence lies precisely here: there is a tendency for the theologian to forget that this system is not *his* achievement, so that '[h]e might dare to say it not on the basis of the fact that it is said to him [by God], but in the confidence that he is basically in a position to say it of his own accord'.[41] That is to say, Barth worries that a theologian who is able to draw a direct line between insights developed through philosophy, which does not require divine revelation, and theology – which, by definition, must correspond to divine revelation – may begin to think he is able to offer theological insights without turning to divine revelation to do so. Danger lies on the philosopher's side as well, as there is little to prevent the philosopher who encounters this kind of theology from taking it simply as 'a welcome and deep enrichment of what he knows already about human reality' rather than as a Word from God.[42] For Barth, only a short distance lies between such thinking and an account of God and God's relationship with the world that is crafted in the theologian's own image. After all, he had already encountered this kind of thinking in the theology of his former teachers.

Barth's central worry, then, lies in the possibility that God's self-revelation would be seen as an inherent human capability rather than as a miracle of grace. On the one hand, he cannot help but sympathize with the attempt to connect philosophy and theology, because even though theology is a discipline focused on God, it also is a *human* discipline that 'involves a fundamental reflection upon reality by means of that very same thought

---

[39] *Ibid.*, p. 28. Note here the use of the words 'existence', 'similar', and 'dissimilar' here: the language echoes Przywara's own.
[40] *Ibid.*, p. 29.
[41] *Ibid.*
[42] *Ibid.*

which is also the tool of the philosophers'.[43] On the other hand, however, he worries that this kind of system will inevitably fail to stay focused on its true object.

> At this point the critical question is decided as to whether we are doing theology or only philosophy. Here is where the temptation or danger is or is not resisted. Here we do or do not get stuck on that two-fold aspect of reality which shows up in thinking not governed by the Word of God. To put it concretely: here is where we face the temptation of seeking and finding God in fate or God in idea. On the strength of the fact that our thinking is governed by God's Word, we are tempted to surpass the relativity of this two-fold aspect – not through a conceptual synthesis of our own, but by attributing this aspect to God himself as the Lord of all reality.[44]

Here one part of Barth's initial response to Przywara's *analogia entis* – as well as to his own earlier formulations of the *analogia entis* in his Münster dogmatics – can be seen. Like Przywara, Barth wants to surpass the boundaries that have plagued human thought about God, but unlike Przywara, he wants to do so not by a 'conceptual synthesis' but by looking strictly to God's special revelation. Barth is not dismissing the validity of Przywara's project altogether, at least at this point. Rather, he is rejecting the specific approach and method Przywara uses, and he reasserts the correctness of the method he has been working with since his dogmatics in Göttingen.

Barth believes that despite Przywara's claims to the contrary, Przywara is working from 'below to above' by beginning with the human and then working up to God; Barth, in contrast, seeks to work solely from above to below. Przywara, of course, would disagree with that assessment, and the dividing line between them is their divergent interpretations of the nature of God's revelation to humanity. Przywara, because he locates revelation in the doctrine of creation, sees the *analogia entis* as an 'above to below' enterprise, while Barth, because he locates revelation strictly in Christology on the basis of his understanding of human sin and the doctrine of justification, sees the *analogia entis* as moving in the opposite direction, from 'below to above'. In the end, Barth believes that systems like Przywara's which attempt to surpass the limits of human knowledge about God inevitably fall short – collapsing into a view of God as either fate or idea – while his own view, based upon the miracle of God's Word, succeeds in overcoming these limits.

---

[43] *Ibid.*, p. 32.
[44] *Ibid.*

Barth against Realism

As Barth turns to 'fate', or realism, in the second lecture, Przywara's *analogia entis* again takes centre stage. At its heart, Barth thinks that the *analogia entis* is a realist enterprise, and he points to the Thomist distinction between essence and existence that funded Przywara's project as the reason why this is the case. Theologians, he argues, inevitably run up against the tendencies of realism in the fact that they obviously are advancing towards something objective, real, and actual – namely God, who exists prior to and apart from human knowing of him. This objective enterprise, Barth says, leads to a certain line of deductive thinking about God, God's existence, and how creatures relate to him:

> 'God is' – what does that mean if not that God takes part in being? Then of course the next proposition leads to the idea that God is himself being, the origin and perfection of everything that is. In their classical form, as set forth by Thomas Aquinas, these propositions combine with a third which can logically be regarded as the consequence, namely, everything that is as such participates in God. Everything that is exists as mere creature in greatest dissimilarity to the Creator, yet by having being it exists in greatest similarity to the Creator. That is what is meant by *analogia entis*.[45]

It is important to spend time examining this passage, because it provides critical insight into the question of whether Barth accurately interprets Przywara's *analogia entis*. Note what Barth does *not* say here: he does not say that God and humans participate in some larger 'structure of being' and that an analogy can be drawn between God and humans on the basis of this shared participation.[46] Barth recognizes that such an account misrepresents both Aquinas and Przywara's view, and he did not describe the *analogia entis* in this way even in his otherwise confused use of it in his dogmatics at Münster. Instead, Barth works through Aquinas' logic in *precisely* the same way that Przywara does in the *Religionsphilosophie*: God *is* being, and everything other than God exists only by participation in God's being. Because creatures exist by participation, they are distinct from God; but because their being is derived from God, they also exist in similarity to him. In other words, Barth's summary description of 'what is meant' by *analogia entis* corresponds directly to Przywara's description of it.

---

[45] Barth, 'Fate and Idea in Theology', p. 33.

[46] Recall Eberhard Jüngel's accusation that many Barthians – but notably, not Barth himself – offer just such an interpretation of the *analogia entis*. See Jüngel, *God as the Mystery of the World*, trans., Darrell L. Guder (New York: T&T Clark, 1983), p. 282.

With this definition in hand, Barth then argues that this view means that God can be 'inferred from the given' – namely human existence – which means that 'we stand in relation to God by virtue of the fact that we *are*'.[47] Once again, this description stands in line with Przywara's account of the *analogia entis*. As we saw above in the summary of the argument of Przywara's *Religionsphilosophie*, the *analogia entis* is built upon the notion that, because they participate in God's being, humans stand in an intrinsic relationship to God and can thus come to some knowledge of God simply by reflecting upon the 'given' of their own existence. The consequence of this view, as Barth sees it, is that 'the experience of God becomes an inherent human possibility and necessity'.[48] Again, this follows Przywara's own account, although Przywara, of course, would want to add more nuance to it. For example, he would want to supplement Barth's description so that the creature's dissimilarity to God is emphasized even more, since he would say that the similarity itself points to the fact that God is wholly other than creation and beyond similitude. He would thus want to expand and develop Barth's account further; he would *not*, however, need to correct it as a mistaken portrayal of his own view. Barth portrays the central insight of Przywara's principle accurately here, and his description of the consequences of the tensions of the human's 'essence in-over existence' for her knowledge of God stands in line with how Przywara described them both in his book and in Barth's seminar. Przywara does, in fact, believe that the experience of God is an inherent human capability on the basis of God's act of creation, that a human can come to real knowledge of God through reflection upon the 'given' of her own existence, and that the human can arrive at this knowledge by reflecting upon the analogy between the unity of her essence and existence (one of tension) and the unity of God's essence and existence (one of identity). In short, Barth's description of Przywara's *analogia entis* fits the account that Przywara elaborated in his book and in Barth's seminar. Barth does *not* misrepresent Przywara's view. He simply believes, contrary to what Przywara himself would believe, that the *analogia entis* carries all the marks of realism because it is built upon the 'confidence that via certain precise formulations God can be found in a subjective-objective givenness' of creation.[49]

---

[47] Barth, 'Fate and Idea in Theology', p. 33.

[48] *Ibid.*, 39. This account stands in line with the way that Barth's students interpreted Przywara's book.

[49] *Ibid.*, p. 38. McCormack notes that 'Barth could not have been unaware of the fact that Przywara's doctrine of analogy was developed in the closest possible connection to the formula of the Fourth Lateran Council and that his patron saint was Augustine' – whom, as we will see, Barth thinks is the chief representative of an idealist theologian. Przywara, in other words, would have seen himself as leaning more towards the idealist side than the realist side, although he would have believed that the rhythm of

Barth's worry with Przywara's argument is the assumption necessary to get it off the ground. That is, one has to assume that the human, by virtue of his or her createdness, is in a position to make a principle like the *analogia entis* the basic orientation for theology. Here Barth is expressing the same concerns raised by his students in his seminar. Przywara's version of the *analogia entis* is true, Barth believes, only if one holds that God's revelation in Jesus Christ confirms and reinforces a 'presupposed human capacity and necessity apparently somehow given with our existence as such'.[50] In other words, one has to assume that what we know about God by reflecting upon our created existence corresponds to, and is fulfilled by, what we know of God in Jesus Christ in the church.

To illustrate why this view is problematic, Barth turns to the very same principle that Przywara himself used to defend his project: 'grace does not destroy but supports and perfects nature'. For Barth, this principle stands on the mistaken presupposition that the human experience of God is included in and with human nature as such, even if it needs to be perfected by grace. This type of realism is wrong, Barth argues, for two reasons. First, it misunderstands the nature of God's revelation. When theologians talk about God, he argues, they do not mean 'God as such' but 'the God of the Christian church, the God revealed in his Word'.[51] To talk about God at all, therefore, is to talk about the God who 'entered into our own particular mode of being'.[52] This means, Barth says, that 'Jesus Christ as the Word of God to us and therefore himself as God is the content of revelation. And also the Holy Spirit, who illumines the Word for us and us for the Word, is himself God, is the content of revelation.'[53] In other words, Barth believes that Przywara's understanding of divine revelation, which encompasses and connects God's acts in creation *and* reconciliation, is too broad. For Barth, revelation cannot be seen as something that confirms, reinforces, or

---

his analogy maintained both tendencies in their proper tension. McCormack suggests that by 'correlating the *analogia entis* more closely with the *similitudo Dei* of the realists than with the *major dissimilitudo* of the idealists', Barth was 'indicating that the phrase *analogia entis* carries more freight than Przywara personally would allow' – that is, that he is closer to Aquinas than Augustine. This is certainly true, although Barth thinks that the *analogia entis* not only carries more 'freight' than Przywara realizes, but that this freight – and more importantly, the *way* it is carried (i.e., the fact that Przywara's project is centred on human experience as its point of departure) – precluded him from offering a true account of the *major dissimilitudo* at all. The question, then, is less about Przywara's intentions and more about the way his method prevents him, in Barth's estimation, from carrying those intentions out. See McCormack, *Karl Barth's Critically Realistic Dialectical Theology*, pp. 388–9.

[50] Barth, 'Fate and Idea in Theology', p. 38.
[51] *Ibid.*, p. 35.
[52] *Ibid.*
[53] *Ibid.*

completes knowledge that is already available to humans by virtue of their creation. Instead, he says,

> God's Word announces something new to them. It comes to them as light into the darkness. It always comes to them as sinners, as forgiving and thus as judging grace. In relation to it human beings are never once those who are already pardoned, and thus those to whom God's Word no longer or only partially proclaims something new. If they hear something that they basically already know, then they certainly hear something other than God's Word.[54]

The revelation of God, in other words, is God's reconciling grace in Jesus Christ. As such, it is not something that has always been available to us as a result of our existence; nor is it the 'crown of the process' that has been ongoing since creation.[55] There is no 'inherent grace or capacity for grace' but only the particular 'grace which encounters sinners' in a specific event of the person of Christ.[56] Barth argues accordingly that God's self-revelation cannot be understood or made accessible by 'precise conceptual formulations' like the one available in Przywara's *analogia entis*. Revelation is not, he argues, something 'given to us in the givenness of history nor in . . . [the givenness of] our own consciousness'.[57] If this were the case, he says, 'God could not be distinguished from a hidden feature of reality as such', and there would be no need for God to speak to humans at all.[58]

This points to the second reason Barth believes that the realism he finds in Przywara's version of the *analogia entis* is wrong. True theological realism, Barth believes, posits God's givenness or objectivity not as a natural state of being but as *self*-givenness.[59] That is, it makes the possibility and necessity of an experience of God a function of God's free will and act instead of human capacity. Human experience must be 'taken up, negated and transformed' by God so that the experience of God 'is a revealing and not a state of being revealed'.[60] The 'negated' aspect of the equation is the important part, because it signifies that the human is fundamentally incapable of

---

[54] *Ibid.*, p. 39.

[55] See Erich Przywara, *Religionsphilosophie katholischer Theologie*, in *Schriften*, vol. 2 (Eisieldeln: Johannes-Verlag, 1962), p. 442; *Polarity: A German Catholic's Interpretation of Religion*, trans. A. C. Bouquet (London: Oxford University Press, 1935), p. 74.

[56] Barth, 'Fate and Idea in Theology', pp. 39–40.

[57] *Ibid.*, p. 40.

[58] *Ibid.*

[59] Barth's ideas on this point foreshadow insights he will develop more fully in §§25–8 *Church Dogmatics* II/1. The fact that these insights were developed in conversation with Przywara's *analogia entis* reveals how important Przywara was to Barth's own development.

[60] Barth, 'Fate and Idea in Theology', p. 40.

knowing God: the human *in actu* is a sinner. Barth here is affirming his students' objection as his own. The 'negated' aspect is also important because it shows that knowledge of God is not derived from reflection upon human existence but from God's direct act in human existence. This experience of God occurs by the power of the Holy Spirit who works on the human heart, and it corresponds to the act of Jesus Christ, the one who entered into human existence. In contrast to *this* type of true theological realism, Barth believes, the realism of Przywara's *analogia entis* proceeds from the foundation of an abstract view of God's grace. It is built upon the notion of a static God who is 'there' rather than the concrete and specific God who 'comes'. It claims to be able to ascertain, on the basis of its analysis of human existence, what is or is not revelation and how Jesus Christ fits into that already-determined category.[61] It posits a generic God more identifiable with fate – something that stands over human beings as the 'hidden feature of reality' or the ultimate destiny from which they cannot escape – rather than the God who comes to the sinner.[62]

This is even true, Barth thinks, of its construal of Jesus Christ himself. If Przywara's description of the incarnation as 'the crown of the process' of divine revelation is kept in mind, Barth's question is striking: 'Doesn't realism come dangerously near to conceiving of God as given by fate at the very point where God has nothing in common with fate, namely, at the point of his coming?'[63] In other words, because Jesus Christ is seen as standing in continuity with the 'given' that can be read of the face of creation, does he not simply become another part of that 'given'? In Barth's view, the fact that such questions can be raised of the *analogia entis* shows the peril of the type of realism it represents, and he concludes that when a theologian makes revelation a function of human experience, he fails to consider God at all. 'Wouldn't it perhaps be better', Barth asks, 'for this God to be called simply nature? And might it not be better for the theology of this particular God to be called demonology rather than theology?'[64] Here we see an early precursor to Barth's condemnation of the *analogia entis* as the 'invention of the anti-Christ'. For now, his criticism takes interrogative form. Barth would become more sure of this critique in the years that followed, and this section helps us see that Barth's famous condemnation in the preface to *CD* I/1 is no mere rhetorical device or polemic; it stands, rather, a serious charge rooted in substantive theological concerns – one first expressed by his students who were working out of basic Reformed theological principles.

---

[61] Barth notes that this view does this 'as though they had at their disposal a criterion by which they might recognize and acknowledge Christ'. See *Ibid.*, p. 42.

[62] *Ibid.*, p. 35.

[63] *Ibid.*, p. 42.

[64] *Ibid.*

Barth and Idealism

Whereas Barth's discussion of 'fate' consisted largely of a criticism of the *analogia entis* as a realist enterprise, his turn to the topic of 'idea' takes a more positive form. This section of Barth's lecture complements the first two sections in that Barth builds upon the prior criticism to issue constructive suggestions about how a theologian can approach the knowledge of God without falling into the perils he finds in the realism represented by the *analogia entis*. To put it another way: Barth finally is ready to offer his own alternative to the theological programme he believes is represented by Przywara's *analogia entis*. That he does so in conversation with idealism does not mean, as we will see, that he identifies with idealism more than with realism. He does not. Barth believes that *both* tendencies have to be in conversation with one another in a theology if it is to do justice to its object, the God who is both hidden *and* revealed. This section, therefore, not only solidifies Barth's criticism of the *analogia entis* by filling in the theological framework that motivates it, it also corrects the wrong turn Barth had taken in his Münster dogmatics and moves Barth in a direction that he will develop more fully in the *Church Dogmatics*. This direction, as we will see, stands as the fulfilment of the basic insights discovered at Göttingen.

Idealism, Barth says, is 'thinking that has been chastened and strengthened by critical reflection'.[65] It is predicated on the worry that the realists have naïve confidence about the relation between subject and object, and it asks questions not about the given but about that which is *non*-given – which is, in other words, the essential content of the given. This worry, Barth argues, puts idealism and theology in relation to one another. He explains that philosophical idealism took the shape it did only because the concept of God provided the 'impetus for carrying through the project', and likewise, because *God* is its object, and because it can only use human words to describe God, 'no theology has ever avoided the general problem of idealism'.[66] The chief consequence of idealist tendencies for theology has been the notion that God must be recognized as wholly distinct from creatures. This is true, he says, even for a realist enterprise like the *analogia entis*, which holds that, because God cannot be placed in a genus, 'God's givenness must not only be distinguished, but fundamentally distinguished, from all other being'.[67] Barth thinks, in short, that idealism is an inescapable part of every theological enterprise.

---

[65] *Ibid.*

[66] *Ibid.*, p. 43. Not only has theology been unable to avoid the problem, Barth believes, it should not avoid it, because Kant's notion about how human knowledge interacts with empirical reality was correct.

[67] *Ibid.*, p. 44.

There are both positive and negative aspects to this relationship. On the negative side, idealism can run rampant in theology and lead to what Barth calls 'ideology', where God becomes identified with the timeless truths of reason.[68] On the positive side, however, idealism assists theology in that it facilitates the development of the idea of revelation: because idealism helps theologians recognize that God is not a given like other givens in the world, they hold that God must be revealed if we are to have any knowledge of him at all. Barth describes this effect in terms of a hyperbola: idealist thought leads the knower away from the real (the given) into the 'realm of truth', but truth leads the knower back to the real as the context in which truth is found. Hence, 'in its own way genuine idealism does not exclude but includes the given' in theology, because it leads the knower to a 'critical understanding of revelation's givenness'.[69] It leads the knower, in other words, to recognize that the knowledge of God is not something always available but rather is something that can be received only in a unique and particular event of revelation. Barth says, therefore, that idealism leads to the 'chastening [of] the knowledge of the given for the sake of its strengthening', meaning that because the knower realizes that all knowledge of God is revealed instead of 'inferred from the given', the true basis of the knowledge of God – that is, its status as *grace* – is restored.[70]

It is for this reason, Barth argues, that '[i]dealism is the antidote to all demonology passing itself off as theology'.[71] Given that the previous references to 'demonology' were in reference to the *analogia entis*, Barth seems to be saying that the negative tendencies of the realism of the *analogia entis* can and should be corrected by a healthy dose of theological idealism. What does this 'antidote' look like? Barth puts forth three characteristics. First, a proper theological idealism will be grounded in a right understanding of revelation. While the philosophical idealist posits that the truth is 'open and accessible at all times to everyone', the theological idealist knows that 'accessibility' here 'can only mean the possibility of God's access to us, not of our access to God'.[72] This access occurs, Barth thinks, in the particular event of the Word of God in Jesus Christ as attested in the scripture and the church's witness to him. Nothing else, be it human reason, consciousness,

---

[68] Hegel seems to be on Barth's mind here. McCormack summarizes: 'Where idealism fails to perform its critical function, where it all too positively treats its access to the world of ideas as if it were access to God Himself, there God has become indistinguishable from the Idea: *Deus sive ratio*'. See McCormack, *Karl Barth's Critically Realistic Dialectical Theology*, p. 388.

[69] Barth, 'Fate and Idea in Theology', p. 46.

[70] *Ibid.*

[71] *Ibid.*, p. 47.

[72] *Ibid.*

nature, or history, can serve as a source of revelation; the apex of the hyperbola, where reality and truth meet, is Jesus Christ himself.

Second, the idealist theologian must maintain 'respect for the boundaries of human existence'.[73] Theology's object, Barth says, 'is the Word dwelling in inapproachable light. Theology neither reproduces nor articulates it. It bears witness to it'.[74] The notion of witness is important, because it moves the theologian away from a focus on her own task or system and directs her instead to focus solely on her object. The theologian is thus not creative but simply faithful. The idealist theologian's faithfulness to her object, Barth insists, is precisely the opposite of what occurs in a theology that claims 'its dialectic as the meaning towards which it aims'.[75] Przywara's *analogia entis*, which directs focus to the rhythm of human existence that in turn reveals God, is clearly in Barth's sights here. The question he seems to be asking is this: does a system like the *analogia entis* actually direct us to God, as is claimed, or does it inevitably point towards itself?

Third, the idealist theologian will realize that truth is determined by God's action alone. 'When it comes to the knowledge of God', Barth asks, 'is he willing to abandon the notion of "tension" between divine *and* human action?'[76] He argues that the fact that revelation and truth are determined solely by the act of God does not mean that faith is 'strictly a passive matter', a comment that calls to mind Przywara's critique of the Reformers' 'theo-panism'. In fact, Barth insists that faith 'cannot be reduced to a trance-like condition', because the existence of such a condition works only if one assumes that divine and human action exist on the same plane and thus stand in reciprocity with or antithesis to one another.[77] This is not the case, however. Rather, the relationship between the human and God is one of command and 'spontaneity' as the human exists in obedience to God.[78] Barth, in other words, refuses to waver from the position that all action is performed by God alone, but he does not accept the charge that this means that the human becomes simply an instrument or extension of God's

---

[73] *Ibid.*, p. 49.

[74] *Ibid.*

[75] *Ibid.*

[76] Barth, 'Fate and Idea in Theology', p. 49, emphasis mine. The use of 'tension', of course, seems to be an intentional mirror of Przywara's language, and it points to the type of continuity that Barth is challenging when he opposes the *analogia entis*. He rejects any continuity in which God's saving actions are placed on the same plane as human actions.

[77] *Ibid.*, p. 50.

[78] *Ibid.* Barth hints here at an insight that he will develop more fully in the *Church Dogmatics*: that divine and human action do not stand in competition with one another but instead occur in completely different planes or spheres. While Barth had not worked out the details of this proposal yet, his instincts are leading him in the direction he will pursue later.

will in the process. He instead moves back towards the line of thought he had learnt first from Zwingli and then from the Reformed Confessions: a relationship of divine act and human correspondence to it where God and the human remain distinct from one another, and where God's action is not in any sense in competition with human action.

Who is the best example of an idealist theologian who fulfils all three characteristics, in Barth's view? Ironically, he points to a figure central to Przywara's project: Augustine, whom he calls the 'great idealist among the theologians'.[79] Barth appeals to Augustine to correct the realist tendencies of the *analogia entis* because he reads Augustine as standing in line with John Calvin – both of whom, he says, 'placed themselves under rather than over the Word'.[80] This insight is key for Barth: the distinction between the realism of the *analogia entis* and the idealism of Augustine is found in their conception of divine revelation. The problem with the *analogia entis* is that, despite Przywara's motivations or intentions, it functions more from the basis of Aquinas' realism, whose notion of revelation was centred around the doctrine of creation, than it does from Augustine's idealism, whose notion of revelation, Barth believes, is centred upon Jesus Christ. Of course, the question of which of these understandings is correct falls along the fault line of the central doctrine of the Reformation: justification by faith alone. This doctrine is Barth's central concern in the fourth and final part of his lecture.

Returning to Protestant Soil

Having delineated both realism and idealism and the way they shape the theological task, Barth turns in this final section to the question of how one can strike a proper balance between the two tendencies. Selecting one over the other is not an option for a theologian, because each tendency in theology needs to be tempered by the other, since 'demonology' results from a theology too close to realism and 'ideology' results from one too close to idealism. The central question, then, is not whether one tendency must be balanced by the other but rather *how* that balance is to be achieved. In philosophy, Barth observes, striking the right balance 'always means pro-posing and promoting, or at least attempting, a synthesis – that is, some third postulate superior to the two opposites'.[81] That Barth is making a reference to Przywara's own synthesis becomes clear as he proceeds. He argues that the task for theology takes a different form, as it 'must refrain from all reaching – however ingeniously, piously or covertly – for a grand

---

[79] *Ibid.*, p. 45. As we will see, Barth's opinion of Augustine will change very quickly.
[80] *Ibid.*, p. 48.
[81] *Ibid.*, p. 52.

synthesis of opposites'.[82] The reason lies in the fact that theology simply cannot be anthropology. It cannot, in other words, fall into the trap of creating a synthesis that overcomes the limits of *human* knowledge; rather, it must be focused on the conditions set for it by God's revelation in his Word. Theology thus 'can proceed only in the form of a thinking *from* rather than a thinking *toward*'.[83] In other words, theology must begin with divine revelation and think about human experience in light of what has been revealed instead of beginning with human experience and then turning, through reflection upon that experience, to God.[84] Theologians are living in an 'illusion', Barth argues, if 'they think they can really discover God in action through human self-reflection'.[85] But this is precisely what Przywara's *analogia entis*, in Barth's view, attempts to do. By looking at the rhythm of human existence, the *analogia entis* posits that the human points to the God who is 'wholly other' because the human's similarity to God is bound up with an ever greater dissimilarity. The problem is that

> [t]his particular 'wholly other' – the one that is only our mirror image, the keystone in the arches of our culture and for that reason no 'wholly other' at all, but simply the last in a long line of human works – this 'wholly other' can be nothing for us but judgment without grace. For precisely when we want to find God in it, believing we have spoken our ultimate word, we remain alone with ourselves, shut up in our prison of distance, alienation and hostility toward God . . . To want to speak a human word at the very point where everything depends on letting God's Word be spoken is fatal 'self-assertion' *(seipsum interponere)*. Theology must therefore resist the impulse to devise a grand synthesis of opposites.[86]

For Barth, therefore, the primary error to which the *analogia entis* and any other theology that takes the human consciousness as its starting point commits is that it begins with a human word instead of God's Word in Jesus Christ. This is true, he thinks, even if this one believes that this Word is found in God's act of creation.

---

[82] *Ibid.*, p. 54.

[83] *Ibid.*, emphasis added.

[84] This move of course centres on Jesus Christ: 'Begin, in other words, where God's Word has and does concretely come to us: In truth, because it is God's Word. In reality, because it was made flesh.' It is in Jesus Christ, then, that we find the basis from which to properly balance theological realism and idealism, the forces of fate and idea. See *Ibid.*, p. 60.

[85] *Ibid.*, p. 54.

[86] *Ibid.*, p. 56.

This point leads to the insight that the language of alienation and grace above hinted at: the doctrine most central to the knowledge of God is not creation but *justification*. The theologian properly engages in her task when she realizes that her reflection upon God is 'justified only by obedience' – that is, when she conforms her reflection upon God to the Word of God revealed in Jesus Christ, the one who came to save sinners.[87] Any reflection upon God not built upon the foundation of this revelation is 'shut up' in the prison of 'distance, alienation and hostility' because it is constrained by the fallenness and essential inwardness of human nature. 'A theology', Barth says, 'ignorant that even its best concept of God, informed by the pinnacle of human thought, is in itself no witness to God can only be, strictly speaking, a witness to the devil'.[88] This is true, Barth believes, even for a theology built upon the foundation of God's revelation in creation – that is, from the foundation that human beings have an intrinsic relation to the God from whom they have their being – because, quite simply, it neglects to account for the destructive effects of humanity's fall into sin and its need for the grace of Jesus Christ. This is why Barth concludes 'for theology there is no other justification than justification by faith'.[89] By necessity, a theology that truly corresponds to its object will begin not with creation, therefore, but with Christology.

Here we see in full measure Barth's response to Przywara in 'Fate and Idea' – and it is a version of the same response that his seminar gave when they read Przywara's book. All knowledge of God, he believes, stems from the miracle of God's revelation, and this revelation is a unique event that cannot be understood as if it were like other human events. Barth thus stands in contradiction to the principle Przywara evoked in Barth's seminar: revelation does not destroy but supports and perfects reason. For Barth, rather, when we talk about human reason we are talking about *fallen* human reason, and there is no bridge between this reason and the knowledge of God other than the miracle of God's Word in Jesus Christ. This Word is a reconciling Word: it comes to sinners and judges them, negating them in their sin, and restoring them to new life. This is the miraculous way to knowledge of God, and it is a very particular way. When we talk of God, therefore, we talk of the God who came in Jesus Christ to justify sinners; and when we talk of humans who stand before God, we speak of sinners who have been redeemed by Jesus Christ. In short, when we talk about human existence and human consciousness, we talk about it first by

---

[87] *Ibid.*, p. 60.

[88] *Ibid.*, p. 59. Again, we see the roots of Barth's charge that the *analogia entis* is the 'invention of the anti-Christ'. His critique is a theological one: such a theology is a 'witness to the devil' because it shuts the human up in her own alienation from God.

[89] *Ibid.*, p. 60.

talking about Jesus Christ. Any other talk of human existence is talk about a chimera.

This rejection of the *analogia entis* does not take the form of a polemic. It is also not based on a simple mistaken interpretation, as if Barth would change his mind if only someone could explain the *analogia entis* to him more clearly. No – Barth's portrayal of Przywara's view is accurate even to the point that he evokes the same Catholic principles Przywara had used to defend his view in Barth's seminar just three weeks earlier. Barth is *not* making a mistake here. Rather, he is rejecting Przywara's position solely on the basis of his own Protestant theological commitments. This rejection is a substantive and coherent, theologically based rejection that occurs along the fault line of an old divide: on one side is the view that grace perfects our imperfect nature, and on the other is the view that grace judges, negates, and then redeems our fallen nature.

Barth's Second Response: 'The Holy Spirit and the Christian Life'

'Fate and Idea', delivered only three weeks after Przywara's visit with Barth in Münster, gives us an important glimpse into Barth's early understanding of and reaction to the *analogia entis*. In the months that followed, Barth continued to think seriously about Przywara's principle, and his engagement with the topic influenced the direction of his constructive work. He had originally planned to spend the summer months of a sabbatical preparing volumes II and III of *Die christliche Dogmatik in Entwurf*. Now he knew, however, that he would have to completely revise what he had said there. Instead of working on those volumes, therefore, Barth spent the summer reading. He focused especially on the works of Augustine and Luther, and this choice points to their respective importance for how Barth was approaching the *analogia entis* during this time.[90] Now that he was convinced that Przywara's principle was wrong, Barth wanted a better understanding of *why* it was wrong and specifically where Przywara's Catholic theology had gone off track. As we will see, his study of Augustine gave Barth the answers he was looking for, and his reading convinced him that the lines of critique against the *analogia entis* that he had only touched upon in 'Fate and Idea' were well-founded. By turning to Luther, Barth was able to arrive at a clearer understanding of how to think about God's righteousness and grace as it meets the human sinner. Luther pushed Barth in a

---

[90] See McCormack, *Karl Barth's Critically Realistic Dialectical Theology*, pp. 389–90. Also see Barth and Thurneysen, *Karl Barth – Eduard Thurneysen Briefweshsel: 1921–30*, pp. 559–60.

new and more purely theological direction that would enable him to respond more effectively than he had been able to in 'Fate and Idea'.

As the summer wound down, Barth had the opportunity to demonstrate what he had learnt. He was invited to lecture on 'The Holy Spirit and the Christian Life' at Elberfeld, Germany on 9 October 1929 as part of a 'theological week' – a continuing education course, of sorts, for pastors and students who had previously been trained in theology.[91] The event was a family affair for Barth, as his brother Heinrich had lectured the previous day on 'The Concept of "Spirit" in German Idealism'. Barth's lecture was expected to supply the theological counterpart to his brother's philosophical study, and while he lived up to that billing, he did not give his audience exactly what it expected. It was not German idealism but Roman Catholicism that was on Barth's mind during the lectures. Indeed, in a letter written to Paul Althaus while he was composing the lecture, Barth said that the lecture 'is implicitly and explicitly the most anti-Catholic piece I have ever written'. The reason, he explains, was his increasingly negative view of Augustine: 'I believe that as long as we do not root Augustinianism completely out of the doctrine of grace, we will never have a Protestant theology'.[92] This is a dramatic statement, of course, but it is no mere polemic: it is a statement that stands in the tradition of Luther, and it represents an attempt to get at the heart of the theological issues at stake when one talks about God's grace.

Barth's negative perspective on Augustine is apparent throughout the lecture, and because he sees Przywara as one of Augustine's 'followers in modern times', Przywara also functions as one of Barth's explicit interlocutors in every section.[93] Barth begins by challenging their shared understanding of the theological implications of the doctrine of creation. His choice to focus upon this doctrine demonstrates – as was the case in 'Fate and Idea' – that Barth believes the mistaken direction of Augustine's and Przywara's theological programmes stems from their misunderstanding of what creation entails for the relationship between creator and creature.

---

[91] For an account of the circumstances of the lectures, see Robin W. Lovin, 'Foreword', in *The Holy Spirit and the Christian Life* (Louisville, KY: Westminster/John Knox Press, 1993), pp. ix–xx.

[92] See the letter from Karl Barth to Paul Althaus, 14 September, 1929 (unpublished manuscript in the Karl Barth Archive, Basel); cited in McCormack, *Karl Barth's Critically Realistic Dialectical Theology*, p. 390.

[93] Barth, *The Holy Spirit and the Christian Life*, p. 24. Barth's worry with Augustine centres upon Augustine's remarks in 'The Spirit and the Letter' that, despite the 'wound' of sin, the Holy Spirit enables humans to 'do works of righteousness' that contribute in some way to their justification. See 'The Spirit and the Letter', in *The Works of Saint Augustine*, vol. 23, ed. John E. Rotelle, trans. Roland J. Teske (Hyde Park, NY: New City Press), pp. 175–84.

Specifically, Barth thinks that Augustine's doctrine of creation betrays an inconsistent understanding of the distinction between God and humanity, and that this mistaken view leads to a problematic portrayal of justification and sanctification. Here Barth's reading of Luther pays dividends. He frames Augustine's inconsistency in terms of how he understands the Holy Spirit. On the one hand, he notes, Augustine repeatedly states that he believes that the Holy Spirit is not identical with the human spirit – and here, of course, Barth thinks that Augustine stands on solid theological ground. On the other hand, however, Barth shows that Augustine regularly places the Holy Spirit 'in continuity with man's created spirit' by looking to the moral standing of his soul as the locus of God's saving work in his life.[94] He points to the fact that while Augustine teaches justification by faith, he also insists that a believer's justification must be actualized through good works that are manifest in his life as he progresses in the faith, because these works stand as visible signs of the inflow of divine grace and forgiveness. This means, Barth says – echoing the Reformers' critique of Roman Catholicism – that Augustine has 'made justification pass into sanctification'.[95] That is, Augustine understands Christian existence as a constant struggle between the forces of grace and the power of sin in the human soul that takes place over the course of the believer's life. The believer is saved only gradually as she is slowly transformed from a sinner into a non-sinner by the work of the Holy Spirit who imparts 'a divine quality' into her soul.[96]

Luther, of course, rejected this kind of view because he thought it meant that a believer's righteousness before God depended upon her own moral action. Barth shares this critique, and in line with it, he points to three negative consequences that follow from this kind of theology. The first consequence is that the Christian life is construed in terms of an 'ascent' in which the believer slowly rises up to God as she becomes more and more righteous in her moral life. While the Holy Spirit functions as the fuel for this ascent, the Spirit also works *with* the human being who manifests the effects of divine grace through her good works.[97] The result, Barth says, is a type of synergism which 'places man's own work . . . under the prefix

---

[94] *Ibid.*, pp. 3–4.

[95] *Ibid.*, p. 21.

[96] *Ibid.*, p. 23. Barth is referring to the Council of Trent's phrase, picked up from Augustine, of God's 'grace inhering in man'. See Session Six, Canon 11 in *Canons and Decrees of the Council of Trent*, ed. H. J. Schroeder (Rockford, IL: Tan Books and Publishers, 2009), p. 43.

[97] Barth, on this point, has in mind Augustine's statement that reconciliation depends 'both on human will and God's mercy'. See Augustine, *The Augustine Catechism: Enchiridion of Faith, Hope and Love*, The Augustine Series, vol. 1, ed. John E. Rotelle (Hyde Park, NY: New City Press, 1999) p. 64.

of predestination and of grace and of the loftiest humility'.[98] Second, sin is seen more as a disease to be cured rather than as a sign of spiritual death. Barth points to the fact that Augustine portrays sin primarily in terms of 'pride' or 'living for the creaturely good', as well as to the fact that Augustine thinks sin can be overcome by an increase in 'good intentions' manifested in practical activity in the believer's life.[99] This represents a fundamental misunderstanding of sin and its effects, in Barth's view, and it is the same mistake Przywara made by ignoring the effect of sin in his account of the human consciousness in his *Religionsphilosophie*. For them, sin is 'only a wound' or a 'derangement within the undisturbed continuity of man with God'; it is thus more of an imperfection to be corrected than something that fundamentally separates the human from God.[100] This directs us to the third negative consequence: for Augustine, because justification has become sanctification – and because sanctification requires a constant inflow of divine grace into a believer's life – the believer exists at every moment in a state of continuity with God. That is, if an inflow of grace is constantly needed for the Christian to *be* Christian and to move towards God, then the relationship between God and the Christian must be a *constantly-available* one characterized by various levels of distance and closeness. Barth, in a phrase that mimics Przywara's language in *Religionsphilosophie*, describes this relationship as a '"tranquil, assured" continuity' between God and the

---

[98] Barth, *The Holy Spirit and the Christian Life*, p. 23. Barth concludes that 'in this manner sin at the same time speaks sanctimoniously, and the sovereignty of grace is made null and void'. It is for this reason that Barth says that Augustine 'did not realize that righteousness by works as such was contained in this idea of God'. He also points out that Augustine's 'idea of grace could not be so plain as to have made the Reformation doctrine unnecessary'. Note that his engagement with Augustine is taking the form of a clarification of his ideas (one via the Reformation) than a rejection of Augustine altogether. In other words, he does not seek to dismiss Augustine as much as reform him. See *Ibid.*, p. 4.

[99] *Ibid.*, pp. 23–4.

[100] *Ibid.*, p. 23. In a footnote on this point, Barth points to a passage in Przywara's *Religionsphilosophie* where Przywara praises Thomas Aquinas' 'tranquil self-possession' in the face of sin. This perspective, Przywara explains, stems from the fact that he sees creation as something opposite to God, or as 'hitherward from the Creator'. He thus knows 'how to endure the sin of the world', because he understands that 'God, in creating that which was "other than" Himself created also, so to speak, "the possibility of sin", and so "permits" actual sin. Hence follows as a consequence . . . a dual kind of rhythmical motion with the one *analogia entis*'. For Barth, this means that sin merely damages human nature, and the continuity between God and humanity that results from creation remains intact. On this view, Barth comments: 'You may cure a wound by such treatment but you cannot restore a dead man to life'. See Przywara, *Religionsphilosophie*, pp. 483–4; *Polarity*, pp. 118–19; also see Barth, *The Holy Spirit and the Christian Life*, pp. 23–4.

human.[101] In short, he thinks that the roots of Przywara's description of the *analogia entis* are found precisely in Augustine's construal of the relationship between grace, sin, and the Christian's moral standing. Luther's sharp thought on these issues has helped Barth get to the root of the problem with Przywara, and it has further convinced him that his rejection of the *analogia entis* in Przywara's form is correct on Protestant theological ground.

To the Doctrine of God

The central problem, in Barth's view, lies in Augustine's and Przywara's account of the doctrine of God. Specifically, he argues that Augustine and Przywara see the Holy Spirit as merely distinct from but not opposed to human being and action, and this allows them to open the door to a synergistic cooperation between the Holy Spirit and the human. That is, while creation marks a distinction between the Holy Spirit and the human spirit, this distinction does not preclude seeing the Spirit's actions and human action as standing on the same plane with one another as the believer gradually becomes more and more righteous through the course of her life. This critique is critical for understanding Barth's relationship to the *analogia entis*, because this continuity between divine and human action is precisely what Barth is rejecting when he rejects Przywara's version of the *analogia entis*.

For Barth, the Holy Spirit does not cooperate with human action but establishes 'a barrier against all that is our own action'.[102] This opposition stems, he says, from the fact that any emphasis on human action in one's relationship with God reveals a form of unbelief, as it manifests a refusal to 'live by God's giving mercy' alone.[103] The human does not exist open and ready before God by virtue of his creation; he exists as one who is dead in his sins, and he must 'be made open, prepared and made fit for God by God'.[104] The believer's reconciliation thus cannot be construed in terms of an upward movement along the continuum of an always-existing relationship. If this were the case, Barth argues, then sin could be seen as Augustine and Przywara see it: as a 'disturbance' that exists at one moment but then 'can be quite as easily taken as removed again' by an infusion of grace and subsequent moral improvement.[105] For Barth, however, 'we can as little

---

[101] Barth, *The Holy Spirit and the Christian Life*, p. 22.

[102] *Ibid.*, p. 20. The roots of Barth's eventual rejection of sacramentalism are already present here, although it will take him nearly three decades to reach that conclusion by working out the implications of these insights.

[103] *Ibid.*, p. 28.

[104] *Ibid.*, p. 20.

[105] *Ibid.*, p. 24.

think of such sins being easily removed as think of curing a corpse'.[106] Sin must not be seen as 'this or that act' but 'resistance to God's law, opposition to his gracious pronouncement of acquittal and guilt'.[107] Under the conditions of sin, human existence as such is defined by this resistance and opposition. Any relationship with God, therefore, does not take place within the contours of our created existence, but rather, it 'cuts *against* the grain of our existence all through'.[108]

Barth, in other words, agrees with his students: Przywara has failed to account for the reality of human sin. That is, Przywara sees the human relationship with God as a constantly available feature of human existence that occurs because humans have their created being by participation in God's being. For him, grace must be seen 'doubly' – that is, it must be seen both in God's act of creation and his act in reconciliation – and that is why he can speak of God's revelation in creation as standing in continuity with the revelation in the Catholic Church that fulfils and perfects it. It is also the reason why he believes that what we can know of God through philosophical reflection upon our own human existence stands in continuity with what we can know of God by his revelation in the Church. For Barth, however, this means that human action stands in continuity with God's saving action, because what the human can know and do naturally is perfected and fulfilled by what God reveals and does in Jesus Christ. For Barth, grace cannot be seen 'doubly'; grace is strictly God's reconciling act in Jesus Christ. God's relationship with humanity, he says, is not a function of 'an original endowment' that the creature has by virtue of her creation; it is a 'second miracle in addition to the miracle of [the creature's] own existence', one that is realized 'moment by moment' in 'a process of revelation' as God freely acts to relate to her in Christ by the power of the Holy Spirit.[109]

Barth explains his view – and its difference from the one offered by Augustine or Przywara – by turning to Luther's doctrine of justification. For him, the radical intersection of human lives by the Holy Spirit occurs when the sinful human becomes fully righteous *in* Christ, and this intersection is an intrusion into human existence rather than a permanent feature of it.

---

[106] *Ibid.* Luther's influence can be felt here.

[107] *Ibid.*, p. 27.

[108] *Ibid.*, p. 32, emphasis in the original. Barth draws the distinction between his view and Augustine's clearly: 'The truth of grace, which falls plumb down from above, is our judgment and our justification. But its reality – the reality of our sanctification – consists in this vertical line falling upon and cutting the horizontal life of our existence. At the point where our horizontal way becomes – nay, *is cut into* by – this vertical line (but this is really a mathematical point), there arises the problem of Christian obedience.' See *Ibid.*, pp. 33–4.

[109] *Ibid.*, pp. 5, 11.

Indeed, the Christian is *simul peccator et iustus*, and the surmounting of this irreconcilable contradiction does not lie in the Christian – not even in the most secret sanctum of his existence, nor does it happen in any of the hours of his life's journey, not even in those hours most moved and profound, of conversion and death – but it is the action of the Word of God, the action of Christ, who is always the One who makes him out to be a sinner, in order to make him, though a sinner, into a righteous man. But the two things, the acknowledgement of this contradiction and the knowledge of its being surmounted, are not our own business but are the Holy Spirit's.[110]

Barth, in short, is asserting the traditional Protestant notion that there is an 'irreconcilable contradiction' between God and the human, and that this contradiction remains even for the Christian who has been justified. This view stands in opposition to what Barth sees as Augustine's and Przywara's presentation of the traditional Catholic view. Augustine and Przywara offer a vision in which God and humans have a relationship of continuity; that is, their vision is one in which God's grace produces real human merit so that the sinful human slowly develops a 'divine quality' in her soul and actually becomes righteous as she grows into her sanctification. Barth, standing in the footsteps of Luther, presents an alternative vision: one in which the relationship between God and the human is an *irreversible* one that moves in one direction alone – from God to the creature, from sin to forgiveness, from death to life. There is no continuity between divine and human action in this view, because the human remains totally sinful, even as, at the same time, she is counted as totally righteous by her participation in the alien righteousness of Jesus Christ. The distinction between Przywara's and Barth's views, therefore, falls along the line of the same distinctions that had been separating Protestants from Roman Catholics for nearly four hundred years.

Barth realizes that root of this disagreement lies in his rejection of Augustine's and Przywara's view that creation stands in distinction from but not in opposition to God, and he recognizes that this view of creation explains why they frame justification and sanctification differently than he does. It is in the doctrine of creation, therefore, that Barth must strike the blow and set a new trajectory, and he does so, interestingly enough, by offering an alternative form of the *analogia entis*. Unlike his attempt in his dogmatics at Münster, however, this version is not confused and cannot be seen as a misstep with regard to the rest of his theology.

---

[110] *Ibid.*, p. 31. The language of 'existence' and 'life's journey' allude to Przywara and Augustine respectively.

If the creature is to be strictly understood as a reality willed and placed by God in distinction from God's own reality, that is to say, as the wonder of a reality which by the power of God's love, has a place and persistence alongside God's own reality, then the continuity between God and it (the true *analogia entis*, by which he, the uncreated Spirit, can be revealed to the created spirit) – this continuity cannot belong to the creature itself but only to the Creator *in his relation* to the creature. It cannot be taken to mean that the creature has an original endowment in his makeup, but only as a second marvel of God's love, as the inconceivable, undeserved, divine *bestowal* on his creature. Man as creature is not in a position from which he can establish and survey (e.g., in a scheme of the unity of like and unlike) his relation to God and thereby interpret himself as 'open upwards', as Erich Przywara says, and consequently describe his own knowledge as if it meant that God's revealedness were within the compass of his own understanding by itself. The sayings 'God has made us for himself' and 'man made in the image of God' are not to be taken as meaning an abiding and sure fact of revelation that we have once and for all made our own, but it is a process of revelation, which, in the strictest sense, is first coming to us and to come, moment by moment, if, as we should, we have taken seriously what it means by the *Deity* of the *Creator* Spirit.[111]

This passage shows both how much more clearly Barth understands the *analogia entis* than in his Münster dogmatics and how far his critique of the *analogia entis* has advanced since 'Fate and Idea'. The most interesting shift between the argument of 'Fate and Idea' and the one offered here is that Barth now is arguing for a 'true *analogia entis*' in opposition to the *false* version that Augustine and Przywara offer. The dividing line between the two versions is their understanding of the implications of creation. Augustine and Przywara interpret creation as an act of revelation that results in the endowment of certain capacities upon the human being that enable her to have a relationship with God. This revelation is 'given' (a *datum*), and as such, both these capacities and this relationship are a permanent feature of human existence. The 'givenness' of God's revelation in creation is what enables Augustine to refer to his own moral attributes when he talks about his own 'ascent' to God, and it also allows Przywara to make the claims he does about the constant nature of the human's relationship to God. Specifically, Przywara is able to argue for an *analogia entis* between God and humans on the basis of observations about human existence because he believes that the shape of this relationship, the analogy, is built in, or 'given', to human existence as such as a result of God's act of

---

[111] *Ibid.*, p. 5.

creation. Barth, in contrast, argues that divine revelation is something that, in every moment, is 'to be given' (a *dandum*). It is not something that can be possessed, but rather, it occurs solely in the 'process' of God's ongoing and particular act of relating to the creature. For him, therefore, creation is not a 'fulfillment but a promise' – that is, it does not denote that a relationship has occurred but that one *will occur* at every moment as God relates to his creatures now and in the future.[112] For Barth, then, the act of creation does not give humans any special features or capacities that enable them to come to knowledge of God, and it cannot be used as the basis for a system or principle that enables us to determine the status or shape of the relationship between God and humans. Rather, creation stands simply as a sign that the human will come to knowledge of God's relationship with her in the event of God's moment-by-moment act of relating to her through the Word of God in Jesus Christ, specifically in the form of scripture and proclamation heard by the power of the Holy Spirit.

Reminiscent of Przywara, Barth describes this process of the Word proclaimed and heard as the human's 'openness or preparedness for God's grace', but unlike Przywara's description of the human as 'open upwards', Barth's description of human openness for God does not posit it as something built into human existence as such.[113] Rather, he sees it in terms of the human's 'existence *for* Christ' which occurs as 'the special work of God the Spirit'.[114] Human openness to God is precisely the human's 'being grasped in this occurrence which is the effect of the divine action'.[115] In other words, sinful human beings who exist in contradiction to God are 'made fit by God for God', and this act by God results in a true *analogia entis*: a relationship of correspondence between God's act of grace (in the Word) and the justified human's obedient response to it (in the Spirit). This relationship is thus the result of God's moment-by-moment act on *both* sides of the divide.[116] It is not built upon an always-existing, 'tranquil and assured' continuity between God and the creature, as in Augustine and Przywara, but upon the 'becoming' in which sinful humans are 'ever *acquiring* the character of divine indications, duties and promises' through their hearing of God's Word by

---

[112] For this reason, Barth says, 'none of the external or internal "urges" of our existence, as creature that we know of, can be taken by us in themselves and as they are as already the Creator's Word'. See *Ibid.*, p. 9.

[113] *Ibid.*, p. 6. It seems clear that Barth is trying to draw a sharp contrast between the two types of openness here.

[114] *Ibid.* He explains the difference sharply later: 'And really this is the state of the case, namely, that I permit the Word to be said to me because the created spirit is in no wise "open upward" in itself; it is not within the compass of any cleverness or ability of mine, but it is purely and simply the office of the Holy Spirit to be continually opening our ears to enable us to receive the Creator's word.' See *Ibid.*, p. 8.

[115] *Ibid.*

[116] *Ibid.*, p. 7.

the power of the Holy Spirit.[117] This relationship is thus a moral one, in that it consists of the divine act and human correspondence to that act, as well as an eschatological one. That is, the Holy Spirit has 'continuity with the human spirit' only as the Spirit, who is 'present in his total difference', relates to the human being in revelation by its act of pointing the human being to the promise that she will be made righteous as a child of God.[118] This future justification, Barth says, is 'present with us [now] through the Word' – meaning that God's revelation in his Word stands as a real-yet-future promise that defines the human's being as well as her relationship with God.[119] This statement can be read in light of the concern expressed by Barth's students about Przywara's decision to focus on the human consciousness: any talk about an analogous relationship between the human and God must begin with human being as it actually exists, that is, in sin. For Barth, true human being – and thus the true *analogy* of being – begins from the basis of the Holy Spirit's promise to the sinner in need of redemption.

Barth's argument provides the clearest expression thus far of the difference between the ontology undergirding his theology and the one working within Catholic theology as represented by Przywara. Barth is not thinking about 'being' in terms of a state but as 'act'. Any account of God's relationship to the human, therefore, must be understood in terms of an active relation, one 'which stresses the sovereignty of grace, the incapacity of the creature, and the miraculous history whereby grace grants what the creature lacks for the sake of love and freedom'.[120] This is where Barth is drawing the line

---

[117] *Ibid.*, p. 9.

[118] *Ibid.*, p. 59. Barth had described the eschatological nature of the relationship with God and the human – and the implications of this relationship for our understanding of human sin – in detail just a few months earlier in his lectures on ethics in Münster. There Barth compares Roman Catholic theology, which is shaped by a 'dreadfully pervasive deeschatalogizing of the whole of Christianity', to the theology of the Reformation, which invoked a 'reawakening of an awareness of the eschatological liberty of the children of God'. See Karl Barth, *Ethics*, ed. Dietrich Braun, trans. Geoffrey W. Bromiley (New York: The Seabury Press, 1981), p. 484; also see pp. 461–97, especially pp. 464–70.

[119] Barth, *The Holy Spirit and the Christian Life*, p. 62.

[120] George Hunsinger, *How to Read Karl Barth: The Shape of His Theology* (New York, NY: Oxford University Press, 1991), p. 31. Hunsinger's description of Barth's actualism represents the contours of Barth's thinking here: 'The church, the inspiration of scripture, and all other creaturely realities in their relationship to God are always understood as events. They are not self-initiating and self-sustaining. They are not grounded in a neutral, ahistorical, or ontological relationship to God independent of the event of grace. Nor are they actualizations of certain ontologically given creaturely capacities. Rather, they have not only their being but also their possibility only as they are continually established anew according to the divine good pleasure. They have their being only in act – in the act of God which elicits from the creature the otherwise impossible act of free response. God is thus the Lord – not only of the

between his view and Przywara's view. In keeping with the Roman Catholic tradition, Przywara sees God's self-revelation in terms of 'God in Christ in the Church', and he thus holds that the Church, as the 'creaturely-visible form of God', is the definitive form of God's continuing manifestation in the world.[121] Such a view stands in contradiction to the basic thrust of Barth's theology ever since his break with liberalism: he has always held that God does not hand over his self-revelation to creaturely realities but remains the subject of his revelation at all times. Revelation is not always accessible; it occurs only in the particular event of God's self-revealing act. Barth moved in the direction of this view because he saw that it cut to the root of the error that led his teachers to embrace an unrighteous war. He worked hard to figure out how to formulate a theology that prevented this kind of error through *Romans* I and *Romans* II. His view finally reached mature form with his presentation of the doctrine of the incarnation in his lectures at Göttingen. There he noted that creaturely realities 'may well be in analogy but cannot be in continuity' with God's revelation.[122] Barth now realized that Przywara's *analogia entis* posited just such a continuity in the formulation of an Augustinian tension between divine and human action. God's divine actions were seen to exist on the same plane as human actions, even to the point where God's revelation was identified with human institutions like the Roman Catholic Church. Such a view, Barth believed, would lead to a doctrine of revelation that is little more than an act of self-assertion that leads to a gospel of judgement instead of grace. Barth's motivation for his rejection of the *analogia entis* lies here, and it is not predicated upon a mistake: it goes to the heart of the difference between Protestant and Catholic theology. It is a boldly Protestant affirmation of God's grace.

Barth's Rejection of the analogia entis

Why, then, does Barth reject Przywara's *analogia entis*? He does so because he understands that it is built upon doctrinal commitments that he, as a Protestant, cannot accept. Specifically, Przywara's *analogia entis* is built upon the notion that there is something 'given' in God's act in creation – namely, the shape and structure of human existence itself – and that human reflection upon this 'given' can lead to knowledge of God. On the ground of this claim, he holds that the knowledge of God available as a result of God's act in creation stands in continuity with God's revelation in Jesus Christ, and consequently, he believes that the knowledge of God available through

---

mysterious event which constitutes the divine being, but also of the mysterious event which constitutes our being in relation to God.'
[121] Przywara, 'Das katholische Kirchenprinzip', p. 283.
[122] Barth, *Göttingen Dogmatics*, p. 94.

philosophical reflection stands in continuity with the knowledge of God given in and through revelation found in the Catholic Church. Lying behind these affirmations is Przywara's conviction that what humans know by reason on the basis of their nature can be perfected and fulfilled by what they know by faith on the basis of God's grace in Jesus Christ. This belief, in turn, is grounded in the notion that humans are, by nature, fit for God's justifying grace in Jesus Christ because they stand in an intrinsic relationship to God by virtue of their creation by God, and this relationship remains intact even after the Fall and apart from the reconciling work of Christ. Barth rejects the *analogia entis* because he rejects this line of thought and the theology behind it. The dividing line is Barth's account of the doctrine of justification. Barth believes that the Fall has left humans incapable of acquiring knowledge about God, or having a right relationship with God, apart from a *second* act in addition to creation: the miracle of our justification by grace through faith in Jesus Christ. Because Przywara's *analogia entis* is built upon the notion that God's act in creation establishes both knowledge of and a relationship with God that exists apart from this justifying work, Barth believes that Przywara is drawing an analogy between God and an *ideal* human rather than the actual human, the human as sinner. He is thus convinced that Przywara's *analogia entis* is not a 'true' *analogia entis*, but a false one, since the reality of sin means that the only 'given' that humans have access to by nature is the 'given' of their own fallen being. In short, for Barth, sin has left humans incapable of knowing anything true about God on the basis of an intrinsic capacity that they have by virtue of their creation. This rules out the notion that what humans know by reason stands in continuity with what they know by faith, and it also means that what they know by nature cannot stand in continuity with what they know by grace. Indeed, Barth thinks that if this were the case, then human action would stand in continuity with divine action in a way that contradicts the Protestant *sola gratia*, because what the human accomplishes by nature would contribute to what God accomplishes by grace. In Barth's view, humans have a capacity for God only as they are 'made fit by God for God' in and through a second miracle of grace.[123] This miracle takes visible form as God relates to humans in his specific, moment-by-moment, revelation in his Word, received by the power of the Holy Spirit. These humans, as justified sinners in the sense of Luther's *simul iustus et peccator*, stand in continuity with God, but they do so only in and through Jesus Christ.

In sum: Barth's rejection of Przywara's *analogia entis* stems from his rejection of Przywara's accounts of divine revelation, God's grace, and the person and work of Jesus Christ. The rejection of these doctrines is neither the result of a 'demented' point of view nor an irrational opposition to

---

[123] Barth, *The Holy Spirit and the Christian Life*, p. 7.

Roman Catholicism, Przywara, or the *analogia entis* itself. His serious and open engagement with Roman Catholic theology in Münster, his warm personal interaction with Przywara and enthusiastic response to their meeting, and his embrace of the *analogia entis*, as defined by him, as a principle used in his own theology both in the Münster Dogmatics and in 'The Holy Spirit and the Christian Life' all provide evidence for this fact. Rather, the reasons for his rejection of the *analogia entis* stand directly in line with the reasons Luther and the Reformers gave for turning away from Roman Catholicism centuries earlier. They feared that the Roman Catholic doctrine of justification allowed for a continuity between God's saving act and human moral action, and that such continuity undermined a proper account of God's grace. Barth correctly discerns that the same kind of continuity exists in Przywara's *analogia entis*, because Przywara's doctrine is predicated upon the notion that God's revelation can be read directly off of creaturely realities. Barth had rejected this same error 15 years earlier when he turned away from the theology of his former teachers. Doing so now was nothing out of the ordinary for him, nor was it the result of a misunderstanding or a mistake: it was the fulfilment of the convictions that had governed his theology since 1914 and would continue to govern his theology for the rest of his life.

5

PRZYWARA'S *ANALOGIA ENTIS* AND THE 'INVENTION OF THE ANTI-CHRIST'

The goodness of God, which in this case distinguishes itself from the goodness that he possesses as creator, still thoroughly belongs to the order of creation. This is observable and characteristic for the structure of Catholic thought. The outline of a description of the relation between God and the human can fundamentally be given according to it, without sin and grace, as the grace shown to sinners playing a decisive role. The great cycle of creation, revelation, and completion is closed without the problem of reconciliation having any meaningful incision in it (see Przywara's Religionsphilosophie*!).*

– Protocol from Barth's 'The Problem of Natural Theology' seminar in Bonn, 1931[1]

Introduction

Chapter 4 provided an account of the nature of Barth's rejection of the *analogia entis*. It was shown that Barth rejected the principle precisely *because* he understood it. That is, he recognized that it was built upon the foundation of Roman Catholic theological formulations that he could not accept in light of his Protestant theological commitments. Barth's rejection of the *analogia entis* thus stands in the tradition of the early Reformers' own justifications for not remaining Roman Catholic. It was not based upon a

---

[1] 'The Problem of Natural Theology Student Protocol' (unpublished manuscript in the Karl Barth Archive, Basel), p. 4; cited in Amy Marga, 'Partners in the Gospel: Karl Barth and Roman Catholicism, 1922–1932' (Unpublished Doctoral Dissertation, Princeton Theology Seminary, 2006), p. 295.

mistaken interpretation, but rather, it was based upon the foundation of a clear understanding of the theological differences between Roman Catholic and Protestant understandings of creation, revelation, justification, sanctification, and the doctrine of God.

This chapter will explore the climax of the debate between Barth and Przywara by considering Przywara's mature formulation of the *analogia entis* and Barth's clearest condemnation of it, both of which occurred in 1932. First, we will examine the prelude to this debate by means of a brief account of Przywara's visit to the Barth's seminar on 'The Problem of Natural Theology' in December 1931. We will turn then to the inner workings of the *analogia entis* as developed in Przywara's *Analogia Entis*. The central claim will be that while *Analogia Entis* represents an advance in clarity and insight over Przywara's portrayal of the *analogia entis* in *Religionsphilosophie katholischer Theologie*, it does not mark a substantive departure from that earlier account. In other words, Przywara's description of the *analogia entis* in 1932 clarifies but does not mark a break from his earlier formulations of the principle. As a result, the reasons that Barth gave for rejecting the *analogia entis* in 1929 do not need to be modified after the publication of *Analogia Entis* in 1932: the problems he saw in Przywara's earlier version of the principle remain in this newer version. This claim will lead us to Barth's famous description of the *analogia entis* as 'the invention of the anti-Christ' in the preface of *Church Dogmatics* I/1 (*CD* I/1). These remarks will be placed in their historical and theological context, and I will show that while the preface marks a polemical turn in Barth's discussion of the issue, his remarks stand in line with his earlier treatments of *analogia entis* and the unique historical context in which Barth was writing. Barth, in other words, is repeating what he had said two years earlier in a new way to address the challenges of a new situation.

The Prelude to Analogia Entis *and the Preface to* CD *I/1*

With 'The Holy Spirit and the Christian Life', Barth had rejected Erich Przywara's version of the *analogia entis* publicly and definitively. For his part, however, Przywara did not believe that he had finished the task of fully describing the principle. In the years since the publication of his *Religionsphilosophie*, he had spent time reading the prolegomena to Barth's *Die christliche Dogmatik in Entwurf*, writing major works on Kierkegaard and Kant, engaging the philosophy of Martin Heidegger, and studying Augustine even more closely.[2] Przywara's visit to Barth's seminar in 1929

---

[2] See Erich Przywara, *Analogia Entis*, in *Schriften*, vol. 3 (Einsiedeln: Johannes-Verlag, 1962), pp. 7–10. Also see Przywara, 'Die Reichweite der Analogie als katholischer Grundform', in *Schriften*, vol. 3 (Einsiedeln: Johannes-Verlag, 1962), pp. 247–8.

came near the end of this cycle of study, and we know from the letters between them that the visit provided Przywara with new insights. Barth, in fact, had sent Przywara copies of the student protocols from the seminar so that he could 'get a small picture of what we have against you', and we know that Przywara read them.[3] In 1931, Przywara finally began to write down his new ideas about the *analogia entis* in preparation for another volume.

Near the end of that year, Przywara was invited to address another one of Barth's seminars, this time at Bonn on the 'The Problem of Natural Theology'. The protocols of Barth's seminar recently have been analysed by Amy Marga.[4] Her examination reveals that Barth and Przywara did not change their positions on the *analogia entis* or each other's theology as a result of this second meeting; rather, this encounter simply confirmed each thinker's prior interpretation of the other. Barth, for example, is recorded in the seminar protocols expressing the same opinion of Przywara and Roman Catholic theology as he did in 'The Holy Spirit and the Christian Life'.[5] For his part, Przywara, who had already composed most of *Analogia Entis* by the time of his visit, offers an interpretation of Catholic thought that is consistent with what he says in that book.

Even though no major advances occur in the debate over the *analogia entis* in this seminar, two aspects of Marga's analysis of the student protocols are worth noting. First, during the students' discussions about the theology of Augustine and Vatican I, they express the same concern Barth had expressed earlier about the *analogia entis*: that in the Catholic construal, God's revelation in creation fits 'seamlessly' with God's revelation in Jesus Christ. For the students, this means that God's act of reconciliation stands as only one element within the 'wider scheme of the "great Catholic peace"' rather than at the centre.[6] Second, during his guest lecture, Przywara confirms that the students' analysis of the Roman Catholic view on this matter is correct, and he offers a spirited defence of it that corresponds to

---

[3] See the letter from Barth to Przywara on 27 February 1929 (unpublished manuscript in the Karl Barth Archive, Basel); cited in Amy E. Marga, 'Partners in the Gospel', pp. 240–1.

[4] See Marga, 'Partners in the Gospel', pp. 292–304.

[5] Barth also had already lectured over most of the material that would later be published as *Church Dogmatics* I/1 – including several sections in which he criticizes the *analogia entis*. For a brief account of Barth's lectures, Przywara's visit, and the general circumstances at Bonn during this time, see Eberhard Busch, *Karl Barth: His Life from Letters and Autobiographical Texts* (Grand Rapids, MI: Eerdmans, 1994), pp. 214–216. Hereafter *Church Dogmatics* I/1 will be cited as *CD* I/1.

[6] Marga, 'Partners in the Gospel', p. 295. While we cannot ascribe the summary of the students' discussions in the protocols directly to Barth, it is likely that they stand in line with Barth's own interpretation.

the argument he will make in *Analogia Entis*. Specifically, Przywara argues that 'natural theology' in the Roman Catholic sense of the term means that reason and faith stand in a relationship of unity with one another, and on this basis, he insists that humans have a natural 'potential' to come to knowledge of God. Therefore, just as God's grace in revelation stands in harmony with nature, faith stands in harmony with reason: what we can know of God by nature corresponds with what we know of God through supernatural revelation because that latter revelation perfects and supports the former.[7]

After Przywara's visit, Barth's seminar turned to the opening sections of Calvin's *Institutes on the Christian Religion*, and there they found a clear Protestant alternative to the Roman Catholic view as Przywara had presented it.[8] As they read him, Calvin presents the human as a sinner who can come to the knowledge both of who he is and who God is only through the Word of God found in scripture and preaching. This knowledge occurs as the result of a unique and particular event rather than by the act of creation; it is not something available to humans by natural means but something supernatural that must be received at every moment in the event of God's self-disclosure.[9] The students, in fact, located the fundamental difference between the Protestants and Roman Catholics precisely on the fault line of this distinction.

> Decisive for a response to [Przywara] is the *understanding of forgiveness*. The human comes before God as one in the fullness of his sinfulness, and is seen by God as *such*; one receives forgiveness from God as such. That is, one's sins are not reckoned to him – which is not a substantial change, and therefore also does not mean a new bestowal of power to the *ratio*. In that grace, or to use Przywara's words – the *veritas* – meets humans, one first then recognizes one's lost state, the weight of one's sins, the darkening of one's *ratio*. A call for knowledge of self or experienced reality or the depth of sin could still be nothing more than a manifestation of impenitence. Thus, indeed, with

---

[7] *Ibid.*, pp. 301–02.

[8] *Ibid.*, pp. 302–3. Barth would turn to these passages from Calvin again on the discussion of the same topic during his response to Emil Brunner's Nature and Grace. See Karl Barth, 'Nein!', in *Natural Theology: Comprising 'Nature and Grace' by Professor Dr. Emil Brunner and the Reply 'No!' by Dr. Karl Barth* (London: Centenary Press, 1946), pp. 94–109. Barth's reading of Calvin there likely was shaped by his experience in this seminar and the context in which it occurred – namely, right after Przywara's visit and defense of Roman Catholic natural theology.

[9] Marga, 'Partners in the Gospel', p. 303. Barth's influence upon his seminar's interpretation of Calvin can be seen clearly, since it parallels the arguments he made in 'The Holy Spirit and the Christian Life'.

these different understandings of grace, the central point [of disagreement] has been reached. And from here out, no further discussion is possible.[10]

Here we see that the students in Barth's 1931 Natural Theology seminar came to the same conclusion that Barth's Thomas Aquinas seminar in 1929 had reached, and their analysis parallels the critique that Barth himself had offered of Przywara's theology in 1929. The central issue for the students was the different understandings of the reality of human existence, sin, grace, forgiveness, and revelation. Forgiveness does not involve a 'substantial change', they argue, but rather, it indicates that the human as sinner is not reckoned a sinner any longer even though he remains one through and through (in Luther's sense of *simul iustus et peccator*). Because the human remains a sinner, therefore, any knowledge of the human self or the reality of the world remains a 'manifestation of impenitence' because, even after the event of grace, it remains an act based on fallen human nature. Hence, the students reject any knowledge of God or the world that comes from any source other than divine revelation in Jesus Christ. This view marks a clear rejection of Roman Catholic theology as Przywara portrays it, and it stands in line with one way of reading the traditional Protestant account of these issues. Assuming that the seminar in some sense reflects Barth's own views at the time, then we may say that as 1931 drew to a close, Barth viewed his own Protestant perspective as the clear opposite of Roman Catholic theology as represented by Przywara.

For Przywara, his visit to the seminar served as the capstone of what had been a long process of rethinking and retooling the *analogia entis*. Once again, he had defended the truth of the principle before the most prominent Protestant theologian of the day, and he believed that he was now ready to publish his definitive word on the topic, one that would be the summary and fulfilment of everything he had written earlier.[11] He was as convinced as ever

---

[10] 'The Problem of Natural Theology Student Protocol' (unpublished manuscript in the Karl Barth Archive, Basel), p. 22; cited in Marga, 'Partners in the Gospel', p. 304. The remark – 'or to use Przywara's words – the *veritas*' – demonstrates that Przywara used the same language during his visit to Barth's seminar that he would use in print later on in *Analogia Entis*, because in that book he often follows references to God or "the divine Is" with the addendum, '(*Wahrheit*, usw)'. This shows us that the distinctions and qualifications Przywara employs in the book were already in use at the time of his visit to Barth's seminar.

[11] See Przywara, *Analogia Entis*, 8–10. That Barth was the most prominent Protestant theologian of the day can be seen in his effect upon student enrollment at Bonn. Before he arrived, there were 170 students; after his arrival, enrollment reached nearly 400. See Bruce L. McCormack, *Karl Barth's Critically Realistic Dialectical Theology: Its Genesis and Development, 1909–1936* (Oxford: Oxford University Press, 1995), 415.

that the *analogia entis* was the 'primal structure' and 'total rhythm' not only of all Catholic theology, but of metaphysics in general.[12] Now he believed he was in a position to make his case clearer than he had before. In the preface to the book, he notes that he will employ the same 'method of immanent historical understanding' that he had used previously, but now he has a wider cast of characters in mind as he does so – a cast that includes not only Barth, but Husserl, Heidegger, and the many variations of Kantianism found in Germany at the time.[13] His *Analogia Entis* would stand as a challenge to them all.

Przywara's Analogia Entis

Analogia Entis is divided into two parts. The first part, consisting of §1–4, discusses 'general metaphysics', while the second part, comprised of §5–8, contains an exposition of the *analogia entis* and an examination of its manifestation in history, particularly in the thought of Augustine and Thomas Aquinas. This structure mirrors the one found in the *Religionsphilosophie*. Przywara's goal is also similar: he wants to show that the *analogia entis* is the key to answering the perennial problems in philosophy, and that it is so because it enables us to unlock false dichotomies and resolve them in the tension of analogy. This goal points to Przywara's underlying conviction that analogy can function as an ontological as well as an epistemological concept. Here Przywara is working from the same ground he was standing on when he used the distinctions of Thomist metaphysics to discuss the problems of the philosophy of religion in his *Religionsphilosophie*. He contends that the *analogia entis* is *the* central concept in metaphysics, and that the whole of Catholic theology is built upon the foundation of a 'creaturely metaphysics' that is analogical in character and thus markedly superior to all other types of metaphysics.[14]

---

[12] These phrases are taken from the subtitles to Parts 1 and 2 of the 1962 version of the work. See Przywara, *Analogia Entis*, pp. 19, 211. *Analogia Entis* was originally published as *Analogia Entis: Metaphysik* in 1932 as the first of a two-part work. Przywara never completed the second part. Instead, when his works were gathered in an edited edition in 1962, he collected several related essays composed between 1939 and 1959 to serve as Part II. Part I included the original 1932 text with a few minor changes, including a changed subtitle ('Metaphysik' to 'Ur-Struktur') and an additional final paragraph.

[13] Przywara, *Analogia Entis*, p. 10. Przywara notes that it was as a result of his dialogue with Barth that 'the theological element of the *analogia entis* was constructed to its own particular form'.

[14] *Ibid.*, p. 28.

The Failure of Philosophy

Przywara develops this account in the opening section of the book, and this section is important because it reveals why analogy is central for him and sets the stage for his larger argument. He begins with the claim that analogy holds the key to philosophy's most difficult problem: the relationship between subject and object. Przywara rejects any antithesis between subject and object because he believes that this dichotomy fails to capture the true nature of creaturely reality. To capture this reality, he believes, the relation must be interpreted in terms of the tension that exists between the *being* of the subject and the *being* of the object. This tension is produced because the knowing subject is a finite being who is seeking to know an object external to her and thus *beyond* her being – which means that her act of knowledge produces tension because it is an act that can be fulfilled only if she transcends her own being.[15] This tension, Przywara argues, points to the necessary relationship between epistemology and ontology.[16] 'Not only does [the subject's] comprehension (as self- as well as external comprehension) happen through objects . . . but the inner form of the understanding itself is objective.'[17] Neither epistemology nor ontology can be resolved into the other, meaning that one cannot treat the duality of the subject and object simply as if the ontological question is a part of or can be resolved by the epistemological question. Rather, the epistemological question of subject and object can be addressed only by maintaining a connection to the ontological context in which this question arises. To put it another way: human knowledge occurs in the midst of human experience, and the human knower cannot cut himself off from this experience to ask about his knowledge of things. In short, in Przywara's view, epistemology must always remain in tension with ontology, and as a result, any philosophy attempting to address the question of subject and object must maintain this tension. No philosophers, however, have been able to accomplish this task.[18]

---

[15] *Ibid.*, pp. 23–24. It is helpful to keep Przywara's pattern of 'essence in-over existence' in mind here, because is simply applying it to the question of knowledge between subject and object.

[16] *Ibid.*, p. 26. Przywara argues that this relationship exists in every philosophy whether it is acknowledged or not, because the act of knowledge necessarily leads to a tension of being. To illustrate, he points to the fact that the 'pure judgment categories of Kant' are understood in terms of 'being categories: Quality, quantity, modality, etc', while Hegel's expression of being takes the form of an 'expression of being: identity and opposition'.

[17] *Ibid.*, pp. 25–6.

[18] *Ibid.*, pp. 24–5. It may be helpful to recall the discussion above of the influence of John Henry Newman's *An Essay on the Development of Christian Doctrine* on Przywara's methodology. Newman argued that the full meaning of Christian doctrine only can be established when it is understood in connection to the historical context in which it

Przywara insists that he alone is able to maintain this tension because he properly accounts for both the 'How' (epistemology) and the 'What' (ontology) of knowledge in his approach to metaphysics.[19] To this end, he argues that there is a necessary dialectic between the 'How' and the 'What', and we must move from one to the other and back again without resolving them. He describes this tension by using two terms that capture the nature of the relationship: 'meta-noetic' and 'meta-ontic'. A 'meta-noetic' approach to metaphysics makes the *act* of knowledge (the 'How') primary over the context in which this act occurs, because it judges the ontological status of knowledge from the starting point of the consciousness of the subject. Augustine represents this kind of approach, but it is also the approach of most modern philosophers, as they are chiefly concerned with epistemology. A 'meta-ontic' approach to metaphysics, in contrast, is determined primarily by a 'speculative ontology' in which the priority is given to the *actual status of the object* being known – the 'What'.[20] Thomas Aquinas represents this type of thinking along with the Greek philosophers who focus primarily upon the question of 'being'. Przywara argues that a tension must exist between the two approaches, because neither one can stand on its own.[21] Nevertheless, he assigns priority to the 'meta-ontic' over the 'meta-noetic', because, he argues, ontological assumptions are required before we can know anything at all.[22] Of course, as finite creatures, our ontological assumptions are limited and incomplete, but this fact raises a critical point. Our limited perspective stands as an implicit acknowledgement that a reality exists above and beyond our subjective consciousness. Przywara puts it this way:

The becomingness of the back and forth relation is, however, the old 'become what you are': the essence [*So*] which the becoming approaches,

---

arose, because the doctrine's meaning is intrinsically tied to that history. Clearly, for Przywara, the same principle applies to philosophy.

[19] For a helpful account of Przywara's 'meta-noetic' and 'meta-ontic' distinction, see Niles C. Nielsen, 'The Analogia Entis of Erich Przywara' (Unpublished Doctoral Dissertation, Yale University, 1951), pp. 89–96.

[20] For the phrase 'speculative ontology', see Nielsen, 'The Analogia Entis of Erich Przywara', p. 93.

[21] Betz summarizes what Przywara had in mind with respect to the tension between the two: '[I]f this tension is inevitable, as Przywara claims, then there is no pure meta-ontics any more than there is a pure meta-noetics; for just as no meta-ontics can fail to consider the role of consciousness and intentionality in our perception of being, no meta-noetics can fail to consider the gratuity of being to consciousness'. See John R. Betz, 'Beyond the Sublime: The Aesthetics of the Analogy of Being (Part Two)', *Modern Theology* 22, no. 1 (2006), p. 23.

[22] Barth's judgement in 'Fate and Idea' that the *analogia entis* is a realist enterprise corresponds to Przywara's account here. This claim also marks one of the key points of divergence between them.

already yet as the existence [*Da*] of the becoming: therefore: 'essence over existence' [*So über Da*] and still 'essence in existence' [*So in Da*]: therefore 'essence in-over existence' [*So in-über Da*]. If we take into account, that the meta-ontic in any case is the objective first and comprehensive (in all methodological priority of the meta-noetic), then the formal constituting basic formula of the creaturely metaphysics, following from the basic problems of metaphysics in general is: essence in-over existence [*Sosein in-über Dasein*].[23]

What Przywara means is that the human knower reveals that her essence is 'in-over' her existence in her act of knowledge because she acts on the basis of the assumption that a reality exists that is above and beyond herself.[24] Przywara insists that 'the most formal basis of a "creaturely metaphysics"' can be found precisely here. He argues: 'it is creaturely with respect to its formal object – the tension between being and consciousness (and not the absoluteness of a self-identity of consciousness or being) – and more decisively with respect to its formal method, which runs its course in a back and forth relationship between the two in a manner of becomingness (and not in separation and self-sufficient unity)'.[25] In short, the problem of the subject and object leads us into the formula 'essence in-over existence' – and this, Przywara thinks, leads us directly into an encounter with the One who is above our existence. This is the correlated relation with otherness – what Przywara calls the ἄλλο προς ἄλλο – that he believes defines human existence.[26] The approach that can capture this coordinated relation is an analogical one, he argues, because only analogy maintains the tension internal to our situation *without* trying to resolve it. All other approaches fail to capture the relation because they inevitably attempt to overcome the tension and collapse one side into the other.

---

[23] Przywara, *Analogia Entis*, p. 28. I translated *So* as 'essence' and *Da* as 'existence' because this translation most closely captures Przywara's intended meaning. This passage serves as an example of how Przywara uses obscure and often unclear terminology. As he explains later on, he does so in part out of the worry that the words typically used in philosophy obscure the central questions at hand. To combat this problem, he employed often unclear language to shake the reader into thinking more deeply about the problem itself. This explains Przywara's arguments are summarized more often than they are quoted. See Przywara, *Analogia Entis*, pp. 88–90.

[24] *Ibid.*, pp. 27–8. Betz notes a further implication: 'there is no creaturely cognition, desire, or feeling that does not imply a regulative objectivity, respectively, of the true, the good, and the beautiful'. See Betz, 'Beyond the Sublime (Part Two)', p. 24.

[25] Przywara, *Analogia Entis*, p. 28.

[26] See Betz, 'Beyond the Sublime (Part Two)', p. 24.

Two Modes of Knowledge

Working in the background here is the same distinction that was operative in Przywara's *Religionsphilosophie*: the distinction between essence and existence. For Przywara, this distinction points us to key difference between divine and human modes of knowledge. Whereas God has complete knowledge because his essence and existence are identical, the human knows only in part because she herself exists 'in part' – that is, she *is* 'in part' because her being is completed only in and through her relation to that which is above her, namely God. To put it another way: humans are finite creatures who exist only within the limitations of history and thus have a limited perspective in their knowing of objects. A human cannot know the essence of a thing by means of a pure rational act, because she can have knowledge of an essence only as it has been made *actual* in existence.[27] Since neither essence nor existence is complete in anything other than God, it is simply impossible to know anything in this world completely. *Everything* can be known only in part because everything *is* only in part. This means that any metaphysics must account for 'being' as the formal object of metaphysics (the essence of a thing) *and* the concrete manifestation of 'being' within the context of the limited, contingent reality of history (the existence of a thing) *and* the nature of the relationship between the two.

Przywara describes this requirement for metaphysics as the mutual interdependence and relationship of *a priori* and *a posteriori* factors in knowledge, with *a posteriori* factors being derived from sense perception and *a priori* being derived from intuition and rational reflection.[28] He argues that despite attempts to undermine the mutual nature of this relationship in the history of philosophy, every metaphysics inevitably exists in the tension between 'being' as the formal object of metaphysics, on the one hand, and the concrete manifestation of being in history, on the other.[29] There is a likeness and an unlikeness – an analogy – between the two types of knowledge of being, because they exist in an 'in-over' relationship in which 'being' as a formal object is present in the concrete manifestation of being while also transcending it. He argues that if we focus on one type of knowledge of being and neglect the other (such as in Kant, whom he believes focuses on *a priori* at the expense of *a posteriori*), then we can never come to an accurate

---

[27] Przywara, *Analogia Entis*, pp. 28, 36–8.

[28] Przywara works through the distinction between *a priori* and *a posteriori* metaphysics in detail in §3. See *Ibid.*, pp. 36–60. For a helpful account of this distinction, see Nielsen, 'The Analogia Entis of Erich Przywara', pp. 108–110, and James V. Zeitz, *Spirituality and the Analogia Entis According to Erich Przywara, S.J.* (Washington, DC: University Press of America, 1982), pp. 142–4.

[29] Przywara, *Analogia Entis*, pp. 36–8.

description of the true character of our knowledge as a creature because a creature *is* a limited being; and, if we neglect the nature of their relationship, we will fail to understand in what way the one stands in the background of the other. In short, Przywara believes that humans cannot pretend to know things the way that God knows things. Rather, humans must understand their knowing in light of who they really are, and they are creatures who have their essence 'in-over' their existence – that is, they are finite creatures who are not God. *Only* analogy captures this reality, Przywara thinks, because analogy bases the act of knowing on the being of the finite, limited, and contingent creature who exists before the God who is in and above it.[30]

In Przywara's view, there are two implications for this understanding of the nature of human knowledge and the nature of a metaphysics that comprehends human knowledge.[31] First, it tells us something about the reality of the world. That is, the relation of *a priori* and *a posteriori* forms of knowledge indicates that true reality is something both in and beyond the experience of the creature. We can conclude on the basis of this relation that human experience must be 'open upwards' to something beyond it. Note the advance here: Przywara has provided firm *philosophical* grounding for his theological claim about the central shape and movement of Catholic life. Second, Przywara believes that this understanding tells us something about the nature of a true philosophy. Human being and existence cannot be considered only in rational terms, as if human existence could be placed inside the bounds of a conceptual framework. Rather, because the *true* reality is an 'in-over' reality, a true philosophy will be one that captures *both* the concrete experience of human finitude in history *and* the fact that this experience is grounded in something beyond finite history.[32] Or, as Przywara puts it:

> For truth is the realm of the pure essence [*So*], history that of the existence [*Da*]. In the formula 'truth in-over-history' is expressed, consequently, the more primary 'essence in-over existence'. It is the final primary quality of the creature, that in it the ideal and the real

---

[30] One consequence of this construal, as Bernhard Gertz notes, is that the formation of metaphysics is necessarily a humble enterprise, inasmuch as any theory is always seen in relationship to the absolute God above. Przywara's construal, he says, 'is first of all a battle against all absolutizing. With the cry of Michael, "Who is like God?", each thought draws back into the limits of its relativity'. See Gertz, *Glaubenswelt als Analogie: Die Theologische Analogielehre Erich Przywaras und ihr Ort in der Auseinandersetzung um die Analogie Fidei* (Düsseldorf: Patmos-Verlag, 1969), p. 170.

[31] I am indebted to Nielsen for helping me see these two implications. See Nielsen, 'The Analogia Entis of Erich Przywara', 82.

[32] Przywara, *Analogia Entis*, pp. 55–8.

are not identical and therefore truth and history are in tension with each other.[33]

In other words: philosophy must capture both the ideal and the real, and in doing so it captures the fundamental orientation of human life: that our essence is 'in-over' our existence. A true philosophy, therefore, will be a philosophy of *history* which directs us to the God who is *in* yet *above* history.

Przywara contrasts this view with those offered by idealism and empiricism, where one side of the relationship between the ideal and the real is emphasized over the other. Hegel is his primary target for the idealist approach. For Hegel, Przywara says, '[c]reation and God stand (ontically and noetically) in a relationship of an identity which contradicts itself and confronts itself'. The result of this view, he says, is that 'the ground of God is usurped' because the human knower is granted 'a comprehension of the inner rhythm of the divine life'.[34] Against this view, Przywara contends the finite being is marked by a tension between essence and existence, and one pole of this tension cannot be *aufgehoben* into the other, because then we are simply not talking about the finite human or the utterly transcendent God any longer.[35] The reality of human finite historical particularity and the distinction of the human from God simply cannot be overlooked or ignored in the construction of an ideal or logical construal as Hegel wants to do.[36] Against the empiricist approach, Przywara argues that metaphysics cannot be concerned with historical phenomena alone; it must also inquire about that which is beyond phenomena – the underlying ground and meaning of the empirical reality that humans see. This is possible, Przywara believes, because human beings really *do* have the ability to understand the essence that stands behind our existence, even if only in an incomplete, contingent, and fragmentary way. Such knowledge, as Niels Nielsen says, is 'knowledge in a greater not-knowing', and it testifies to the existence of the One above human existence.[37] In other words, for Przywara, human

---

[33] *Ibid.*, p. 58.

[34] Przywara, *Analogia Entis*, p. 108. Earlier, Przywara noted that for Hegel, 'the thinking in the thinker is logically a region which is exempted from the other creaturely qualities of the thinker, exempted from his individual limitation'. The same would be true of Kant and all idealists. See *Ibid.*, p. 48.

[35] See *Ibid.*, pp. 99–104.

[36] See *Ibid.*, pp. 35–, 38–48. He calls Hegel's philosophy the 'divineness of pure thinking' and sees it as a sign of the 'immanent deity in empirical man'. He concludes: 'in his attempt to resolve all existence in to essence, Hegel ultimately denies the full reality of the tensions in the being of creation'. These tensions are precisely what Przywara hopes to maintain. See *Ibid.*, p. 48.

[37] Nielsen, 'The Analogia Entis of Erich Przywara', p. 89. Also see Przywara, *Analogia Entis*, pp. 161–3 and 171–3.

knowledge – because it occurs contingently and within the limits of finitude – can be understood only in relation to the God who is above it.

> In this way it becomes clear how the 'God over-in creature' necessarily appears as final in the formal problem of metaphysics, i.e., as its forming ground. We have with this a *theologia naturalis* inherent in the concept of metaphysics in general which precedes that *theologia naturalis* through which a metaphysics is formulated. We thus have here in this forming ground the formal shape of the 'creaturely meta-physics': its 'essence in-over existence' is cut through vertically by the 'God over-in creature'. If, however, the 'God in-over creature' yielded itself in the considered 'essence in-over existence', then it appears evident also in its traits.[38]

Przywara thus believes that a limited knowledge of God and the nature of God's relationship to humanity can be derived from metaphysics alone. That is, we can come to real knowledge of God through reflection upon the fundamental nature of human existence by means of an examination of the question of human knowing, because the question of how we know things can be answered only if we first postulate that our being is one that is becoming before the God who stands over us in his perfect being. In other words, because the fundamental questions of metaphysics are 'cut through vertically' by the reality of God, metaphysics itself leads us to God, even if only in an imperfect and limited way.

What we see here is that Przywara has made his study of the failures of philosophy more specific than he did in the *Religionsphilosophie*. In that volume, the failure was of religious philosophy to come to an understanding of God and God's relationship to the world. In this volume, the failure has to do with the questions of subject and object that have been driving mod-ern philosophy since Descartes. Thus, in a bold move, Przywara has moved his argument to the philosopher's home territory and argued that the best thinkers in philosophical history – from Kant to Hegel to Heidegger – have failed to accomplish their own objectives on their own terms. He casts aside their solutions because in one way or another, these modern philoso-phers have ignored the concrete reality of the One beyond human existence. Only a philosophy that captures both the historical situatedness of the human knower and the reality towards which the knower is striving can balance the concrete situation of the human with the true meaning of human existence: its relationship to the God *above* this existence.

Przywara believes that the only philosophy that can accomplish this task is one that is based upon the *analogia entis*. 'Only analogy', he says

---

[38] Przywara, *Analogia Entis*, pp. 65–6.

'is capable of respecting both extremes. Logic deals with the immediacy of physical laws. Dialectics is an either-or of continual shifting between opposites. But analogy alone maintains a "measured" equilibrium . . . the medium between Heraclites and Parmenides'.[39] Indeed, the *analogia entis* finally gives us the key to discern the pattern that has actually been operative – but flattened or ignored – in every philosophy in human history. Only now, with the revelation from the Catholic tradition pointing the way, can the *analogia entis* be used to provide the answers to the questions philosophers have been unable to solve by demonstrating the balance and tension between the extremes that has been missing in every attempt they have offered. In other words, with the revelation of the *analogia entis*, the imperfect knowledge available through philosophy can be brought to its fulfilment. The Roman Catholic notions that 'grace does not destroy but supports and perfects nature' and 'revelation does not destroy but supports and perfects reason' remain as true as ever. Przywara has simply given them a new depth and a new relevance; they are principles that now strike at the very heart of the Western philosophical tradition.

The *analogia entis* as the Solution to Philosophy's Problems

Now that Przywara once again has established that the *analogia entis* is the key to philosophy, he has to explain again exactly what it is and how it functions. This task occupies the second half of the book. Like the argument in the first half, Przywara's account of the principle is deeper and richer than the one found in his *Religionsphilosophie*. But again, like the argument in the first half, his presentation stands in basic continuity with his earlier formulations.

In this new presentation, Przywara describes the *analogia entis* in terms of a tension that exists between the poles of similarity and dissimilarity within the analogy itself.[40] The pole of *similarity* is represented by the *analogia attributionis*. This analogy works from 'below to above': it is the analogy employed when the two things being compared stand on a common plane with one another. Przywara holds that we can use this analogy when we are thinking about the *analogia entis* between God and humans because essence is *in* existence – meaning that there is a relation of similarity between essence as such and the concrete manifestation of essence in history. The pole of *dissimilarity* is represented by the *analogia proportionis*, which is

---

[39] Przywara, *Analogia Entis*, p. 112. Eberhard Mechels thus is right to say that the '*analogia entis* implies consciously and intentionally a meta-theory of the history of Western thought'. See Mechels, *Analogie bei Erich Przywara und Karl Barth: Das Verhältnis von Offenbarungstheologie und Metaphysic* (Neukirchen-Vluyn: Neukirchener Verlag, 1974), p. 235.

[40] See Przywara, *Analogia Entis*, pp. 135–41.

used when the two things in comparison are fundamentally distinct from one another and thus can only be brought together proportionally. Przywara thinks that we must use this analogy in reference to the human relationship with God because humans have their 'essence in-*over* existence'. That is, the human manifests an incompleteness in his own being, and he is thus defined by a growth or development (becoming) as he realizes his true essence in the midst of his existence. This being-in-becoming is completely dissimilar to God's being, which is perfectly actualized because God's essence *is* his existence. The *analogia proportionis*, therefore, captures the otherness of God within the *analogia entis*, because it functions from 'above to below'. This means that all true knowledge of God's being in this analogy must be *revealed* knowledge.

Przywara believes that the *analogia attributionis* is indispensable for the *analogia entis*, because it constitutes the basic type of analogy used in the context of our daily existence and the starting point for all analogies. Given the fact that the analogy is a consideration of God, however, it cannot work without supplementation: it must be completed in an *analogia proportionis* that exists in and above it. He argues, therefore, that an '"attributive analogy" (*analogia attributionis*) reduces itself into an incomprehensible "tension" analogy (*analogia proportionis*)'.[41] What he means is that 'a positive statement about God' is offered in the *analogia attributionis*, but this statement 'is only the foundation of the *negative* statement concerning [God's] absolute otherness'.[42] This otherness is captured by the *analogia proportionis*. Hence, Przywara says:

> An 'attributive' analogy (*analogia attributionis*) stands at the beginning only in so far as the creaturely 'is (to be for)' points to the divine Is (Truth, etc.) as its original basis . . . But that is itself even already inconceivable 'tensioning analogy' (*analogia proportionis*), because in this relation the creaturely points beyond itself, therefore beyond its manner (*proportio*) of ontic as noetic into the completely different way of God. . .[43]

Note that this analogy *within* the *analogia entis* – the analogy between *analogia attributionis* and *analogia proportionis* – treats both types of analogy in a way that recognizes their similarity and dissimilarity to one another and the tension between them. The full *analogia entis*, made up of both the *analogia attributionis* and the *analogia proportionis*, manifests

---

[41] Przywara, *Analogia Entis*, p.135.
[42] *Ibid.*, emphasis added.
[43] *Ibid.*, 137.

this tension *within itself*. In this way, therefore, it also adequately manifests the tension of a finite human life lived in contingency of historical existence before God.

But how does it *work*? How, in other words, can the tension between the two types of analogies within the *analogia entis* be used to describe the relationship between God and humanity? To address this question, we must recall what Przywara's notion 'essence in-over existence' implies about both the human and God. To say that the human's essence is 'in-*over*' his existence is to say that the human stands in tension with his true self, because he possesses his essence only in part as he 'becomes' what he truly is in a relation to the God who is above him. At the same time, to say that the human's essence is '*in*-over' existence is to say that the human already, in fact, has a share of what he will become. That is, the human stands even now in a real relation to God simply by virtue of the fact that he exists, because this existence indicates that God has created the human and that the human, as a result, exists by participation in God's being.[44] This participation, which occurs simply by virtue of creation, means that 'God as the Is (Truth, etc.) is the innermost depth and deepest inner of all "is (to be for)"'.[45] In other words, the very nature of creatures points to the fact that God is their 'innermost depth', and it is for this reason, Przywara thinks, that we can talk about God as both above and *in* creation.

As a result, Przywara argues that when we draw an analogy between our being and God's being, we must account for both the 'above' and the 'in' of the relationship, with the 'in' serving as the presupposition of the 'above'. He puts it this way: 'The analogy as participating *over*-beyond-related-being has therefore as its deeper presupposition an analogy as participating relating-one's-self-*into*-from-above of the divine identity of the Is (Truth, etc.).'[46] He argues, however, that the only way to account for both aspects of

---

[44] See Thomas Aquinas, *Summa Theologicae* I.44.1.

[45] Przywara, *Analogia Entis*, p. 119. As was the case above, I translated the word 'gilt' from the phrase 'ist (gilt)' as 'to be for' rather than 'to be valid', which is more literal, because it captures Przywara's meaning more clearly. Przywara's argument on this point is offered in dialogue with Thomas Aquinas' account in the *Summa Theologicae* I.8.a.1.ad.3: 'No action of an agent, however powerful it may be, acts at a distance except through a medium. But it belongs to the great power of God that He acts immediately in all things. Hence nothing is distant from him, as if it could be without God in itself. But things are said to be distant from God but the unlikeness to him in nature or grace; as also He is above all by the excellence of His own nature.' Przywara sees this aspect of the *analogia entis* as simply a gloss upon Aquinas' original insight.

[46] Przywara, *Analogia Entis*, p. 119, emphasis mine. In the original: ‚Die Analogie als teilnehmendes Über-hinaus-bezogen-sein hat also zu ihrer tieferen Voraussetzung eine Analogie als teilgebendes Sich-von-oben-hinein-beziehen der göttlichen Identität des Ist (*Wahrheit*, usw.).'

the analogy is to draw an analogy between the human and God starting from 'below to above' that is bracketed by the fact that this analogy occurs only as a result was God's *prior* act of creation – which is an act from 'above to below'. Here the doctrines of *creatio continua* and *creatio ex nihilo* play a similar role as they did in Pryzwara's *Religionsphilosophie*. Przywara holds that creation exists because of its contingent and derivative participation in the divine being which is its first cause. He notes, however, that creation also has its *own* existence, meaning that creaturely being is its 'own cause' in the sense of a secondary cause. Thus, even though it is distinct from God, creaturely being bears a similarity to the divine being, and this similarity corresponds to the kind of similarity that exists between a first and secondary cause, because the creature has its being only by participation.[47] On this basis, Przywara thinks that we can describe the relationship between the divine being and creaturely being by an *analogia attributionis*, because in this specific sense there is a commonality between the being of God and the being of humanity. This is the 'in' which is the presupposition of the 'above'. We can start with this 'in', however, *only* if we bracket this entire analogy by the doctrine of *creatio ex nihilo* – meaning that even with the similarity that results from the creature's participation in God there is an even greater dissimilarity because there is no ontological identity between God and the humanity at all.[48] This is the 'above' that brackets the 'in'. In other words, we can draw an *analogia attributionis* between God's being and human being only when it is bracketed by an even greater *analogia proportionis*.[49] The human's similarity to God occurs in the midst of an even greater dissimilarity, leaving the analogy to culminate in the *reductio in mysterium* that defines the human encounter with the always greater God. In short, when viewed together, the *analogia attributionis* and the *analogia proportionis* appropriately describe and define the nature of the human's 'open upwards' relationship to God, and through this relationship, the knower can recognize God's transcendence by means of a reflection

---

[47] *Ibid.*, p. 134. This similarity, Przywara says, is 'the coronation which Thomas Aquinas gives to our potentiality: the doctrine of second cause (*causae secundae*)'. For Przywra, one implication of this insight is the fact that creatures really are *other* than God: 'it is the most proper mystery of the divine Is (Truth, etc.) itself, that something without remnant is always derived from him and still is so little identical with him, that it can even say No to him.' See *Ibid.*, p. 136.

[48] The reason, of course, lies in the fact that *creatio ex nihilo* guards against any notion that creation is an emanation from God's being. On Thomist grounds, then, this doctrine means that creation is distinct from God and exists only by a contingent participation in God's being.

[49] Przywara, *Analogia Entis*, pp. 134–5. Betz captures it rightly: Przywara's view is 'ultimately a proportional rhythm between two different analogies: between a *tanta similitudo* expressed in the *analogia attributionis* and a *maior dissimilitudo* expressed in the *analogia proportionis*'. See Betz, 'Beyond the Sublime (Part Two)', p. 17.

first upon God's immanence.[50] This construal of the two analogies thus provides a way for the human knower, reflecting upon human existence itself, to arrive at an accurate understanding of the relationship between God and the human.

One may think that, with such a strong emphasis on the dissimilarity between God and humanity in the above account, Przywara has at least put himself in position to begin to address some of Barth's concerns. The problem, however – at least from Barth's perspective – is that Przywara's account of the *analogia entis* is not yet complete. He takes it further by arguing that the relationship between the two analogies inevitably leads us to posit a *third* kind of analogy: a 'new' *analogia attributionis* that works from 'above to below' instead of 'below to above'. This new *analogia attributionis* is the product of the process of the original *analogia attributionis* always being seen under the prefix of the *analogia proportionis*:

> The unlimitable 'tensioning' analogy (*analogia proportionis secundum convenientiam proportonalitatis*) is the basis for a *new* 'attributive' analogy (*analogia attributionis*), but not, as the first, from below to above, but from above to below: from *Deus simper maior* [God ever greater] to the creature is 'given' his 'realm of service'. The 'ever greater dissimilarity' (*maior dissimilitudo*) here has a positive meaning: the fixing of the limits of a positive realm, into which the creature is 'sent' to 'accomplishing service'.[51]

Przywara believes that – once it has been bracketed by the reality of the *analogia proportionis* – the *analogia attributionis* can be recovered. This recovery is the unique contribution of the Roman Catholic Church to

---

[50] Przywara, *Analogia Entis*, p. 136. For this reason, he says, 'the decisive analogy for Thomas Aquinas is essentially *proportio*', because this type of analogy captures the 'restless separating line of the distinction' between God and humanity: it is an analogy that lies 'between univocality (*univocatio*) and full otherness (*aequivocatio*) of meaning, which would also "extinguish" the relation'. Barth, of course, would serve for Przywara as an example of one who 'extinguishes' the relation between God and humanity, because he posits an 'otherness' between God and creation without balancing it with God's immanence to creation.

[51] *Ibid.*, p. 139. The phrase '*analogia proportionis secundum convenientiam proportonalitatis*' is a clarifying term Przywara uses at certain points to explain what he means by *analogia proportionis*. Zeitz explains that for Przywara, any notion of proportion must be safeguarded with a notion of 'proportionality', because 'if analogy were merely a proportion between two, then the proportionate things in their community with one another would imply control from both sides. In proportionality there is proportion, but it is different from one and for the other. The only community of relation here leads continually to greater dissimilarity'. See Zeitz, *Spirituality and the Analogia Entis*, p. 157.

philosophy: whereas any philosophy could draw an *analogia attributionis* between the human and God that captures the similarity in the relationship (see Hegel), only the Catholic tradition could qualify such an analogy with the reality that God is utterly dissimilar to the human. This Christian contribution, taking the form of the assertion of the *analogia proportionis* over against the more basic *analogia attributionis*, leads to a *new analogia attributionis* that works from 'above to below'. Przywara calls this analogy the 'descending *analogia attributionis*'.[52] This analogy is not a higher synthesis of the *analogia attributionis* and the *analogia proportionis*; this new analogy *is the tension between* the *analogia attributionis* and the *analogia proportionis*. As such, it captures the similarity between God and the human only by starting from the basis of God's prior act; and by maintaining both the similarity *and* the dissimilarity of the relationship between God and the human, it captures the back and forth, oscillating rhythm that defines human being in becoming before God.

Przywara thinks human existence, when viewed in these terms, can be seen as having a 'positive meaning' because this existence leads the human who lives restlessly before an ever greater God to freely enter into 'active service' of the majesty of God. Przywara has in mind here the example provided by the lives of Augustine and the Catholic mystics.[53] The 'descending *analogia attributionis*' is thus an analogy that works in concert with the Catholic Church's tradition, but because it functions in the same way that other analogies function within human experience (because it is an *analogia attributionis*), it *also* is comprehensible to those outside the faith and can be used to express the truth about the reality of their own existence to them. This is how the *analogia entis* between God and humanity functions within Przywara's *Analogia Entis*, how it solves the central problems of philosophy, and most importantly, how it serves as a connecting point between philosophy and the theology of the Catholic Church. The culture, desperate to find meaning and purpose for its life, can discover both of these things in the truth of the *analogia entis* where the 'positive meaning' of human existence finally is explained. In the face of this reality, Przywara hopes, the Catholic Church should be both motivated to and capable of sharing this truth with the world.

---

[52] Przywara, *Analogia Entis*, p. 140.

[53] What Przywara means is that the notion that God is dissimilar leads us to strive even more into his mystery. The dissimilarity thus facilities a true relation: 'The positive "relation", discloses itself in its peak as the negative, "otherness". But exactly so is the negative "otherness" the token of the fulfillment of the positive "relation": Inconceivability, the token, that it is God. Conception, the token, that it is not God: *si . . . comprehendis, non est Deus* (Augustine in Psalm 85:12)'. See Przywara, *Analogia Entis*, p. 136. For a discussion of how this line of thinking relates to Przywara's emphasis on spirituality, see Zeitz, *Spirituality and the Analogia Entis*, pp. 156–7.

Having developed the *analogia entis* in close detail, Przywara turns in the final section of the book – as he did in his *Religionsphilosophie* – to the task of demonstrating how the tension described by the *analogia entis* was operative throughout history in the thought of figures such as Plato, Aristotle, Augustine, and Thomas Aquinas.[54] In his view, history itself serves as the definitive evidence for the truth of his claims, because in each of these thinkers and the traditions that follow from them, the pattern of the *analogia entis* can be seen clearly.[55] Consequently, he argues, the *analogia entis* should not be seen as the 'absolute starting point of an absolute metaphysics, from which we would be able to derive everything', but rather, it should be understood as 'the expression for how the restless potentiality of the creaturely is unfolded as the starting point of thought *as* thought'.[56] Przywara's point is that the *analogia entis* is simply a descriptive principle that describes the way things *are*.[57] For him, then, the Catholic tradition, through the *analogia entis*, merely perfects and fulfils the partial and incomplete accounts of human existence put forth by philosophers throughout history. It is in this sense that the Catholic dictum, 'faith does not destroy but supports and perfects reason' remains true: philosophers and theologians are attempting to describe the same truth, but only the Catholic Church describes this truth in its fullness. Przywara clearly felt that this critical point was not grasped by the readers of the 1932 edition of his book, because in the edited volume of 1962, he adds an additional paragraph to the end of the book that reiterates this claim:

[The *analogia entis*] is in no way a 'principle' meaning something static, 'from which' everything else could be deduced, or 'to which'

---

[54] See Przywara, *Analogia Entis*, pp. 142–202.

[55] *Ibid.*, p. 205. Zeitz labels Przywara's emphasis on the objective fact of the *analogia entis* in history his 'sensitivity to the living manifestations of God in the world', and he notes that it allows Przywara to do justice to God's activity as it is 'visible in the actual "disposition" of this world's cultural and spiritual events'. Here we again see the fruit of Przywara's attempt to provide a foundation for a Church that *engages* the world. If the disposition of the world itself is towards God, as it is in Przywara's construal, then a church that withdraws from the world is one that essentially turns its back on God and its own being as the 'body of Christ' in the world. See James V. Zeitz, 'Erich Przywara: A Visionary Theologian', *Thought* 58 (1983), p. 156.

[56] Przywara, *Analogia Entis*, p. 206. He continues: 'It is not a principle in the sense that the creaturely is grasped (and is thus graspable) but in the sense that it uninhibitedly hovers over the created world in its restless potentiality.'

[57] John Betz captures Przywara's intent well: 'in no way is [the *analogia entis*] a neutral "principle" by which reason is able to capture God in concepts . . . but simply the appropriate metaphysical articulation of the Christian doctrine of creation'. See Betz, 'Beyond the Sublime: The Aesthetics of the Analogy of Being (Part One)', *Modern Theology* 21, no. 3 (2005), p. 404.

everything else could be reduced. Rather, it is essentially the basic dynamism within which oscillates the 'within creation,' the 'between God and creaturely', and the Inner-God relations of Father, Son, and Spirit which are its hyper-transcendental expression. This 'Being', which all philosophers name as the basic question and basic datum of everything else that exists, does not have an analogy as one of its own properties or as an unfolding of its own being, but rather analogy is being, and here (noetically) thought is analogy.[58]

By clarifying this point, Przywara makes his intent clear: the *analogia entis* is a description *of* reality rather than merely scheme designed to explain it, because analogy *is* reality. In this sense, the *analogia entis* stands as the culmination and fulfilment of *all* human thought about God throughout human history. The different views of God throughout history have been brought together into 'one stream'.

Philosophy, Theology, and Divine Revelation

It is clear that Przywara's account of the *analogia entis* in *Analogia Entis* has a more explicit theological grounding than the one offered in his *Religionsphilosophie*. Specifically, Przywara has demonstrated that, because the *analogia entis* is understood specifically in terms of a 'descending *analogia attributionis*' – meaning that it is the product of the tension that results between an *analogia attributionis* (emphasizing similarity) that has been refined by an *analogia proportionis* (emphasizing difference) – it is not like other kinds of *analogia attributionis* that are employed when the two things being compared exist on a common plane. Thus, even though God and humanity are being compared with one another in the *analogia entis*, this comparison occurs only as a result of a movement within the analogy in which divine revelation plays the decisive role.[59] That is to say, the

---

[58] Przywara, *Analogia Entis*, p. 210. This paragraph helps explain the change in the subtitle from 'Prinzip' in the 1932 version to 'Ur-Struktur' in the 1962 version.

[59] Mechels argues that this focus on revelation makes Przywara's version of natural theology unique because 'theology for Przywara is not a question of subjective religion as teaching about the natural relationship between man to God, nor objective religion as teaching about God as the ground and meaning of the world, but rather the self-revelation of God'. See Mechels, *Analogie bei Erich Przywara und Karl Barth*, pp. 149–50. It is intriguing that the students in Barth's seminar on 'The Problem of Natural Theology' in 1931 made the same argument about Vatican I: the natural theology there is not subjective but *objective*, because it is based upon the concrete revelation that occurs in the creaturely sphere. This indicates that Barth was aware of the differences between the natural theology he discerned in Przywara and that which he discerned elsewhere. This points to the fact that the nature of divine revelation is the central issue in the debate over the *analogia entis*, because it is not Przywara's

comparison between God and humanity that is being drawn in the *analogia entis* occurs only because the *analogia attributionis* has been bracketed by the *analogia proportionis* so that it produces a 'descending *analogia attributionis*' that works from 'above to below'. This means that the comparison between God and the human that occurs via the *analogia entis* takes place on the basis of God's revelation rather than human speculation. This point has caused some interpreters argue that, despite their public disagreements, Przywara and Barth share the same pathos because both of them are trying to formulate a theology that adheres strictly to the fact of divine revelation without shaping it *a priori* by outside factors.[60] Is this, in fact, the case? Have Przywara's refinements made this version of the *analogia entis* more amenable to Barth's theology than the prior one? To put it sharply: should Barth withdraw his rejection of the *analogia entis* in light of the clarifications Przywara makes in *Analogia Entis*?

To address this question, it is important to note the nature of the divine revelation that grounds Przywara's analogy: it is the revelation that occurs in God's act of *creation*. Przywara, of course, affirms and defends the *duplex ordo cognitionis* of the First Vatican Council, which declares that God can be known with certainty, if only in part, through the light of natural reason. In line with this affirmation, Przywara's presentation of the *analogia entis* in *Analogia Entis* is built upon the concept that human essence is 'in-over' existence, and this concept is dependent upon the notion that creaturely participation in God's being is the result simply of the fact that the human is created by God. No act of revelation beyond that which occurs in creation is needed to arrive at this knowledge; the reality of human sin does not affect this knowledge; the revelation of Jesus Christ is not the basis for the acquisition of this knowledge other than in the fact that Christ provides the clearest manifestation of human 'essence in-over existence' in history; and Christ's justifying work on the cross is not necessary for this account as a whole to function. Thus, while Przywara's *analogia entis* is certainly built upon an account of divine revelation, this revelation is understood primarily with respect to God's act in creation. To be sure, in line with the thinking of Vatican I, this act of creation stands in continuity with God's act of revelation in Jesus Christ, and it finds its fulfilment in it. *Both* acts of revelation,

---

method but his understanding of the *content* of revelation that divides him from Barth. For an account of this discussion in Barth's seminar, see Marga, 'Partners in the Gospel', p. 293.

[60] See Leo Zimny, ed., *Erich Przywara: Sein Schrifttum (1912–1962)* (Einsiedeln: Johannes Verlag, 1963), p. 5. Mechels provides a helpful insight when he says that, for both Barth and Przywara, the key question 'is how the act of interpreting behaves with regard to the matter being interpreted, whether the interpreter serves it by dominating it *a priori*, or whether he correlates it and places it in the dialectical order'. See Mechels, *Analogie bei Erich Przywara und Karl Barth*, pp. 249.

however, function to provide knowledge of God. Hence, if one rejects the notion that God's revelation in creation remains operative for human beings after the Fall – as Barth does – then one also has to reject Przywara's account of the continuity between creation and reconciliation and the implications of it.[61] John Betz isolates the key distinction here: 'The issue here, of course, which lies at the heart of Barth's debate with Przywara, is to what extent one values the being of creation *as* revelation, not whether the *analogia entis* is conceived independently from revelation as such. Indeed, Przywara is explicit that the *analogia entis* is a second-order reflection that follows from the prior fact of God's revelation in creation.'[62] This judgement is correct. In *Analogia Entis*, Przywara's *analogia entis* still operates primarily upon the basis of God's act of revelation in creation. Barth, on the basis of his Protestant theological commitments, cannot accept such an account, because he rejects the notion that God's revelation in creation, due to the effects of the Fall, provides any true knowledge of God at all.

But why is this position so important for Barth? Why does Barth believe that he has to reject an account of God's relationship with creatures that is built primarily upon God's act of revelation in creation? What are the dangers of such an account, in Barth's view? Why, in other words, cannot these two views be brought together, especially since both Przywara and Barth both are building their accounts of God's relationship with human on the basis of divine revelation? One way to answer these questions is to draw out the implications of Przywara's account of the *analogia entis* for the relationship between philosophy and theology, because these implications take us to the heart of the reasons why Barth feels that he has to reject Przywara's account.

On the ground of the *analogia entis*, Przywara holds that philosophy and theology are distinct but intrinsically related disciplines. Specifically, he argues that because philosophy inevitably directs us to the reality *above* human existence, it shares the same subject matter as theology: God and God's relationship with creation. By use of reason alone, he explains, philosophers can 'confidently recognize God as the beginning and end of nature', but because they sees things only 'provisionally', they cannot acquire the full truth about God without obtaining insights acquired from theology.[63] How, then, do the two disciplines relate to one another? Przywara explains that the nature of the relationship manifests itself most clearly in the two 'formal principles' of Catholic thought: 'faith does not destroy but supports and perfects reason' and 'grace does not destroy but supports and perfects

---

[61] As Mechels notes, this distinction, more than any other, explains why Barth's and Przywara's views 'cannot be harmonized'. See Mechels, *Analogie bei Erich Przywara und Karl Barth*, pp. 248–9.

[62] Betz, 'Beyond the Sublime (Part One)', p. 404.

[63] Przywara, *Analogia Entis*, p. 75.

nature', with the former principle applying to the noetic aspects of the relationship and the latter applying to the ontological. These principles, of course, are the same ones Przywara appealed to in Barth's Thomas Aquinas seminar, but now – perhaps in response to the critique levelled Barth and his students – Przywara's account of their meaning is developed more thoroughly. He argues that, despite the inability of philosophy to obtain true knowledge of its subject matter without theology, 'reason and nature do not become something else by being lifted up by theology (*fides* and *gratia*), but rather, they are preserved in their being (*non destruit, sed supponit*)'.[64] This means that philosophy, grounded upon human reason, still maintains its own integrity as a discipline. Even so, Przywara says, it exists only as a 'negative of a positive'.[65] What he means is that, even though philosophy has a role to play in human thought about God, this role is defined at every moment by the fact that the true end of philosophy is a *theological* one: the knowledge of God and God's relationship with humanity. This knowledge is not the result of the sum of the insights of philosophy added to those of theology, however, as if one led to the other, because theology alone leads us to the actual path to the truth about God. For this reason, philosophy's contributions are determined by their relationship to theology. These contributions are still important, of course, because even though philosophy obtains only a partial picture of God, it still does, in fact, say something true about God.[66] Faith does not destroy reason, then, because the subject matter of reason is, in reality, one and the same as that of faith. For Przywara, this insight means that the primary difference between philosophy and theology is methodological.[67] Philosophy, working from 'below to above', is limited in what it can accomplish because of the limited capabilities of the finite human knower; theology, working from 'above to below', starts from the perspective of God's revelation in the Catholic Church and transcends these limitations. The subject matter and *telos* of both disciplines, however, is the same.

For Przywara, this correspondence between philosophy and theology leads to an important insight: because God is both immanent and transcendent to creation, both philosophy *and* theology are necessary in a proper construal of God and God's relationship with humanity. He argues that if we proceed solely from 'above to below' – from the ground of theology alone – we will tend towards theopanism, because the nature of God's already-existing revelation *in* creation will be ignored; if we proceed solely from 'below to above' – from the ground of what we can know only through philosophy – pantheism will be the result, because that which transcends our natural

---

[64] *Ibid.*
[65] *Ibid.*
[66] *Ibid.*
[67] *Ibid.*, pp. 66–72.

knowledge from creation will be ignored.[68] The former error is seen in Luther and Barth, while the latter is seen in Hegel; these errors are two sides of the same problem because they demonstrate what occurs when the proper relation-in-distinction between philosophy and theology is not maintained. The only way to maintain the balance between the two disciplines is through the *analogia entis*, because it captures *both* the historical reality of the human situation (God *in* creation – philosophy's primary focus) and the revelation that has occurred in Catholic tradition (God *above* creation – theology's primary focus). Hence, as Przywara says, 'the question concerning the relationship between philosophical and theological metaphysics in its inner logic has become *concrete* in the question between creaturely metaphysics and Catholic theology' – that is, in his formulation of the *analogia entis*.[69]

This relationship follows the pattern we saw in the inner-workings of the *analogia entis* described above. Human reflection upon God necessarily begins with philosophy as we reflect upon our existence, and eventually, upon the reality above our existence. This knowledge is true but incomplete because of our finite limitations; it must be supplemented by new insights from theology which perfect and overcome these limitations. This does not mean that theology supplants philosophy; rather, the two disciplines exist in a tension that takes the form of a 'transfigured philosophy' that accounts for both the immanence and transcendence of God in God's relationship to creation.[70] The pattern here is the one we saw earlier when the *analogia attributionis* ('below to above') was perfected by the *analogia proportionis* ('above to below') so that it produced a 'new' *analogia attributionis* ('above to below'). Przywara thinks that philosophy and theology relate in the same way: the *analogia entis* facilitates the formation of a 'new' philosophy, grounded in divine revelation, that works from 'above to below'.[71] As was the case before, this 'new' philosophy is not a '"third [thing]" in which the

---

[68] Przywara explains that while '[t]heopanism is the fundamental ground of an *a priori* metaphysic, pantheism is the fundamental ground for an *a posteriori* metaphysic'. Just as *a priori* metaphysics needs to be held in tension with *a posteriori* metaphysics through the *analogia entis*, any approach to God needs the *analogia entis* to avoid sliding into one of these two extremes. In Barth's case, Przywara thinks that he is guilty of a 'blending of theology and philosophy', because 'theology stands at the beginning and at the end, a philosophy that is theology and a theology that is philosophy'. See Przywara, *Analogia Entis*, p. 70.

[69] *Ibid.*, p. 72.

[70] For the phrase 'transfigured philosophy', see Nielsen, 'The Analogia Entis of Erich Przywara', p. 181.

[71] He sees this idea as consistent with the thought of the two pillars of Catholic tradition, Augustine and Thomas Aquinas, because they both upheld the possibility of a universally applicable 'Catholic philosophy'.

separation between philosophy and theology is bridged'.[72] Each discipline remains intact with its own integrity. Rather, he says, this 'new' philosophy is 'a formal *philosophical* undertaking that bears in itself a form-primacy of the *theological*, because and in so far as this theology as such encompasses the entire realm of creation. The form primacy of theology yields itself therefore as immanent to the distinguishing essence [*Wesen*] of metaphysics.'[73] In other words, the 'new' philosophy is a *theological* enterprise because theology is the '"inner *telos*" of the metaphysical'.[74] Philosophy and theology thus exist in a dynamic tension between one another, where theology is 'above' philosophy and yet 'in' it as its underlying form. This does not mean that philosophy collapses into theology, but rather, after passing through the refining fires of theology – which has the effect of 'forming it through and through' – philosophy becomes 'perfected' so that it finally is capable of fulfilling its original task.[75] In short, whereas philosophy originally was limited by the finite nature of human knowledge, now – because it has been perfected by theology – it can achieve its true end of describing the full spectrum of human experience before God. Philosophy is, as Przywara concludes, 'positively "liberated" and "beyond itself" in the theological'.[76] The insights of theology enable philosophy to achieve its true end because through it, philosophers finally are able to provide an account of that to which philosophy was implicitly ordered by its subject matter: God and the human who is 'open upwards' to God.

The key to understanding this portrayal – and how it illustrates the ongoing divergence between Przywara's and Barth's views – lies in a clear understanding of how the doctrines of creation, sin, and justification function within it. For Przywara, faith perfects reason, not in the sense that faith is added to reason or overcomes it, but in the sense that reason itself is a 'preliminary' form of faith. The basis for this claim is the fact that nature as such exists within the realm of grace, and this idea is derived directly from Przywara's doctrine of creation. He believes that creation is a revelation

---

[72] Przywara, *Analogia Entis*, p. 79.

[73] *Ibid.*, p. 79, emphasis added.

[74] *Ibid.*, p. 80. Nielsen notes one consequence of this construal: Przywara has demonstrated that 'valid philosophical interpretation does not preclude the possibility of historical revelation'. In other words, he has shown that philosophy must (or at least should) listen to and engage with theology as it goes about its own task, and that it cannot accomplish its true end without the help of theology. In a certain sense, then, Przywara's can be seen as grounds for justifying the place of theology in the Western intellectual tradition, and thus the relevance of the Catholic Church in the modern world. The continuing influence of Przywara's early goals of forming a Catholic Church that engages the world can be seen here. See Nielsen, 'The Analogia Entis of Erich Przywara', p. 370.

[75] Przywara, *Analogia Entis*, p. 83.

[76] *Ibid.*, p. 84.

of God's relationship with humanity, because the creature has its being by participation in God's being. Since the creature cannot be considered at all outside of the context of this relationship, any consideration of the creature at all must involve a consideration of God as the source of its being. In short, inasmuch as they can come to know some true aspects of the being of the creature, philosophers can arrive at some knowledge of God as well, and this knowledge is a function of God's act of creation. This knowledge of God is imperfect, because God is beyond the reaches of human observation, and the result is a partial, distorted, and unbalanced view of God. The knowledge of philosophy, therefore, needs to be supplemented by insights from theology, and specifically, by the insights gleaned through the revelation of Jesus Christ within the Catholic Church, which exists in the present as the body of Christ in the world. With this newfound knowledge, philosophy is 'transfigured' and is now able to achieve its original ends.

Note that, in this account, the philosopher's inability to arrive at a clear understanding of God and God's relationship with humanity is due not to the corruption of sin but to the imperfect character of human knowledge as it was created. That is, human reason cannot acquire true knowledge of God because its field of vision is, by nature, finite and limited. The insights provided by God's revelation in the Catholic Church provide a supplemental field of vision, and with this new 'transfigured' perspective, the philosopher can finally see the full truth about God. This new knowledge is not inconsistent with the knowledge that the philosopher obtained prior to gaining the insights from theology, but rather, it is the fulfilment of that knowledge, because God's act of revelation in creation stands in continuity with God's act of revelation in Jesus Christ. The limited knowledge of God that the philosopher obtains on his own through philosophy, therefore, stands in continuity with the knowledge of God he obtains as a result of God's revelation in and through the Catholic Church. This is the case because the subject matter is one and the same in both philosophy and theology, with the only difference being the change in perspective produced by the insights of God's revelation in the Catholic Church provided by theology.

With this account in hand, it is clear why Barth has to reject it: it commits the same error he condemned in 'The Holy Spirit and the Christian Life'. There, Barth rejected the notion that knowledge gleaned from God's act in creation stands in continuity with knowledge acquired from God's justifying act in Jesus Christ, because he believed that this kind of continuity conflates divine action and human action in the Christian life. He rejected the notion that divine action can stand in continuity with human action because he noted that such a view 'places man's own work . . . under the prefix of predestination and of grace and of the loftiest humility'.[77] As a result of

---

[77] Karl Barth, *The Holy Spirit and the Christian Life: The Theological Basis of Ethics*, trans. R. Birch Hoyle (Louisville: Westminster/John Knox Press, 1993), p. 23.

such a view, Barth believes, not only do human action and merit count for something in one's relationship with God, but human insights about God – taken from sources other than God's revelation in Jesus Christ – are inevitably imported into one's view of God. These errors are the very same errors that Barth had been fighting against since he broke away from his former teachers' theology in 1914.

In other words, Barth sees the same 'prefix' that he condemned in 'The Holy Spirit and the Christian Life' operative within Przywara's *Analogia Entis*. Przywara posits that insights gained apart from God's revelation of Jesus Christ stand in continuity with those acquired in and through this revelation because the 'nature' that philosophers are examining is, in fact, within the realm of grace *simply as a result of God's act of creation*. Here lies the problem. Barth believes that this account overlooks the effects of human sin. In his view, God's act in creation cannot lead to true knowledge of God because creation is fallen. If nature stands in continuity with grace, therefore, it can do so solely because of the justifying work of Jesus Christ. This means that any relationship with God, or any true knowledge of God, stems solely from the knowledge of our justification. *This* is where we must start. Knowledge obtained from sources other than this starting point in Jesus Christ – such as the knowledge gained by the philosophers – does not stand in continuity with the knowledge of God given in and through Christ. The revelation of Jesus Christ, rather, comes from the outside as something new and distinct, and it stands in judgement over all other sources for the knowledge of God.

In sum, Przywara's account in *Analogia Entis* clearly marks an advance over his previous accounts because he is able to explain in precise detail how the *analogia entis* is an 'above to below' movement dependent upon divine revelation at every moment. Even so, the same divisions remain between his view and Barth's view. Przywara views divine revelation in terms of God's act in creation, which stands in continuity with God's act in Jesus Christ; in contrast, Barth – because of his strong accounts of the ontological and noetic effects of sin – views divine revelation solely in terms of God's act in Jesus Christ. Przywara believes that human action outside of the context of God's justifying work in Jesus Christ has a role to play in the Christian life because these actions are a consequence, at every moment, of God's act in creation; Barth, in contrast, believes these actions have no role to play because they are a consequence, at every moment, of human sin. The fault line between these two views lies along the doctrine of justification. Przywara sees the Christian life in terms of an ascending movement of the human along the continuum between her and God, where the Christian becomes righteous as God's grace in creation is fulfilled and perfected by God's grace in Christ in the Catholic Church; Barth, in contrast, sees the Christian life in terms of the totally sinful believer's participation in the alien righteousness of Jesus Christ through Christ's justifying work on the cross. The differences between the views of Barth and Przywara remain stark, and they are the same differences that divided them from one another in 1929.

'The Invention of the Anti-Christ'

On 26 April 1932, Przywara wrote Barth to ask if he would review *Analogia Entis* in an upcoming issue of *Zwischen den Zeiten*. Barth politely declined in a letter on 6 May, saying that he did not have time to give the book proper attention under his present circumstances.[78] Although it was summer, Barth was, in fact, extremely busy. He was finishing the lectures that would be published later that year as *CD* I/1, and he also was teaching a seminar on Albrecht Ritschl's *Instruction in the Christian Religion*. That summer's work was the continuation of the hectic activity of the previous couple of years. After his arrival in Bonn in early 1930, Barth carried a busy teaching load that often included two lectures courses and a seminar in a single semester.[79] One of his seminars – on 'Anselm's *Cur Deus Homo?*' – evolved into a book project, and Barth spent months working on the manuscript.[80] His role in

---

[78] Barth also tells him, 'I can actually always only slowly and eventually take a stand on things, and often only after years do I gain clarity for myself about how I stand regarding a book.' The same may be said about his views of the *analogia entis*. See the letter from Przywara to Barth on 26 April 1932 (unpublished manuscript in the Karl Barth Archive, Basel) and the letter from Barth to Przywara on 6 May 1932 (unpublished manuscript in the Karl Barth Archive, Basel); cited in Marga, 'Partners in the Gospel', pp. 306–7.

[79] For a list of Barth's courses at Bonn, see McCormack, *Karl Barth's Critically Realistic Dialectical Theology*, pp. 415–6.

[80] See Karl Barth, *Anselm: Fides Quaerens Intellectum: Anselm's Proof of the Existence of God in the Context of his Theological Scheme*, trans. Ian W. Robertson (Richmond, VA: John Knox Press, 1960). For an account of the genesis and content of the book, see McCormack, *Karl Barth's Critically Realistic Dialectical Theology*, pp. 423–34. This book plays an important role in von Balthasar's reading of Barth, as he locates Barth's decisive turn 'from dialectic to analogy' precisely here. However, under the reading of Barth's development offered here – one that stands in line with Bruce McCormack's thesis that Barth's use of analogy was the result of dogmatic decisions that occurred much earlier in his development – this book on Anselm does not play a pivotal role as we consider Barth's interpretation of and response to the *analogia entis*. Two observations will suffice to demonstrate why this is the case.

First, Barth's interpretation of Anselm's methodology stands in line with the methodology that Barth himself employed as early as 1924. For example, in a section on 'The Conditions of Theology', Barth notes that when it comes to the knowledge of God, Anselm understands that the human cannot understand this knowledge 'as such', but rather 'has to understand it in its very incomprehensibility'. This knowledge would not occur, in Anselm's view, 'if God did not "show" himself, [and] if the encounter with him were not in fact primarily a movement from his side'. That the intellect can reach this knowledge, therefore, stems from '"grace", both with regard to the perception of

Protestant theology was more prominent than ever, and he felt the pressure of this responsibility as some of the 'dialectical theologians' with whom he had once identified began to move in directions he could not accept.[81] All of this occurred while Barth was following through with his decision to 'begin again at the beginning' with his dogmatics, and he was realizing that this decision was more momentous than he had initially thought.[82]

It is this decision, in fact, that gives us clearest insight into his mindset as he approached the topic of the *analogia entis* during this time. The roots of

---

the goal and the human effort to reach it' (pp. 38–40). These descriptions of Anselm's thought could be lifted and placed into Barth's lectures on dogmatics in Göttingen as representative of Barth's own. In other words, if Barth's description of Anselm's method in some way reflects Barth's own views (a tricky, if often ignored, question underlying any reading of this book), then it reflects the theology he had articulated six years earlier.

Second, Barth's discussions of the way analogy is used in Anselm correspond to the way he already had used analogy in Göttingen and 'The Holy Spirit and the Christian Life'. To illustrate: in a discussion of Anselm's interpretation of 'the revelation of God in his world', Barth notes that this occurs *'per analogiam'* only 'as far as God *wills* to reveal himself and has in fact revealed himself'. Note the language here, and how it focuses on the event of God's self-revelation *per analogiam* rather than the always-existing fact of it. It must take place in *event*, Barth notes, 'because of the Fall'. That is, humans cannot acquire the knowledge of God apart from God's activity because they are, in and of themselves, incapable of it in their sinful state (p. 117). This use of analogy falls directly in line with the account of analogy in Göttingen as well as in Barth's account of the 'true *analogia entis*' in 1929. Inasmuch as this book represents a development in Barth's own theology, therefore, it represents simply a confirmation of insights Barth had already developed and defended earlier. It does not mark a break or a shift in his theology – or in his interpretation of the *analogia entis*.

Przywara's opinion of Barth's book on Anselm was negative. He says that this book is 'no accidental work', and that it represents an attempt by the Protestant Barth to 'extract a program of theology in general connection with Anselm'. In the end, however, he concludes that Barth is unable to avoid '[t]he terrible tear of Calvinism' – namely, 'election by the abolishment of the distance to God – damnation by the insurmountable blindness against God generally'. See Erich Przywara, 'Sein im Scheitern – Sein im Aufgang', *Stimmen der Zeit* 123 (1932), pp. 138–9.

[81] Interestingly, Przywara notes the same problem in Barth's *Die christliche Dogmatik im Entwurf*, and his review of it in 1929 may have helped Barth come to the realization that there were problems with the text. He argues that for Barth in this book, 'eternal life' is reduced to 'conversation'. He argues: 'unconsciously for Barth, the old ghost of the "Correlation" [rises] again. Certainly it is not, like in liberal Protestantism, a Correlation "from below to above"' where in the '"God for Us"' a secret pantheism appears'. It is rather a 'revelation conversation' that takes the form of an 'above to below' correlation. See Erich Przywara, 'Problematik der Gegenwart', *Stimmen der Zeit* 116 (1929), p. 105. Barth responded to Przywara's review in *Church Dogmatics* I/1, p. 172; *Die Kirchliche Dogmatik* I/1, p. 178. Hereafter *Die Kirchliche Dogmatik* I/1 will be cited as *KD* I/1

[82] *CD* I/1, p. xi; *KD* I/1, p. vi.

it can be found in the summer of 1929 in the period between 'Fate and Idea in Theology' and 'The Holy Spirit and the Christian Life'. Barth was already disturbed by the way that *Die christliche Dogmatik in Entwurf* had been received by his fellow Protestant theologians, some of whom had used that book's insights to defend a theology based on 'existential thinking'.[83] Now, with the clearer picture Augustine and Luther gave him of the consequences of Przywara's *analogia entis*, Barth perceived a surge of interest in natural theology across the theological spectrum. Such interest, he worried, was occurring at precisely the wrong time in history. The political situation in Germany was tumultuous and uncertain, and the threat that would eventually blossom into the Nazi takeover of the German government was on the horizon. Barth began to worry that certain Christian groups would rely on a sophisticated natural theology as the basis for justifying their own political ideology in God's name.[84]

In 'The Holy Spirit and the Christian Life', this worry is expressed with Barth's caution about the use of the word 'Christian'.

What, then, is meant by such phrases as a 'Christian' view of the universe, 'Christian' morality, 'Christian' art? Where are 'Christian' personalities, 'Christian' families, 'Christian' groups, 'Christian' newspapers, 'Christian' societies, endeavors, and institutions? Who gives us permission to use this adjective so profusely? Especially when we must know that to confer this adjective, in its peculiarly serious import, is withdrawn altogether from any authority we have. This, if you like, unimportant misuse of language: does it not become evil to anybody who reflects at all? Is it not just a presumption that can allude to a most general thing as though existing . . . Ought not a serious consideration of the office of the Holy Spirit to the pardoned sinner to have

---

[83] This refers to an analysis by Theodore Siegfried that Barth discusses in *CD* I/1. Barth notes that this misinterpretation of his intention is partially his fault, since he had used these concepts in the book: 'I ought to have had the better judgment to see that to drag in those concepts at that point in relation to what I wanted to say there was a superfluous and dangerous game'. See *CD* I/1, pp. 125–6; *KD* I/1, p. 129.

[84] McCormack notes that Barth expressed these worries clearly in a July 1930 lecture, 'Die Theology und der heutige Mensch': 'Barth was very concerned at the time of this address with a situation which he say to be developing in the evangelical churches in Germany. Everywhere, he noted, there were people in the Church who, having grown weary of atheism and liberalism, were "rediscovering their Catholic hearts". By this, Barth meant that from every corner and in every possible way, the cry for natural theology was being heard with increasing intensity. This development represented, to his mind, the "most dangerous possibility in a most dangerous moment"'. See Karl Barth, 'Die Theologie und der heutige Mensch', *Zwischen den Zeiten* 8 (1930), p. 395; and McCormack, *Karl Barth's Critically Realistic Dialectical Theology*, pp. 416–9.

this small result, at least, namely: to make it more difficult in the future for such an adjective as this to drip from our lips and our pen?[85]

Barth is protesting here against *generality*: the use of 'Christian' is withdrawn from its specific basis in God's self-revelation, and it is used to affirm and support almost anything 'existing' at all. By invoking the distinction between the Holy Spirit and the 'pardoned sinner' as the basis for his caution, Barth is reflecting on the argument he had just made against the *analogia entis*: it opens the door to a continuity between God's action and human action, so that our moral acts can be seen as an visible manifestation of and, in fact, an extension of God's own activity in the world. This theology, in other words, allows *our* activity to become *God's* activity. The use of the word 'Christian' in relation to so many of those activities serves as witness of what happens when this kind of thinking holds sway. When God's particular revelation is made general so that it can be identified with the 'natural' world – and especially with our own consciousness – then the door is open to using God to endorse almost any human activity.

Of course, such an approach was not new for Barth. The link between humanity and God he recognized in 1929 followed the pattern he had seen in 1914 when his former teachers enlisted God in support of their own cause by giving their blessing to the war. Barth's theology, from that moment on, had been driven by his goal of overcoming this mistake. In Przywara's *analogia entis*, he discovered a sophisticated version of the same error, and in the Germany of 1932, the political winds were stirring in much the same way they had in 1914. Hence, when he received Przywara's letter announcing the publication of *Analogia Entis*, Barth likely became apprehensive. Would Przywara's book be the catalyst that would take this trend to new heights? Would natural theology become *the* theology in Germany – at precisely the *wrong* time, in Barth's view? The time had passed for a polite disagreement: a dramatic statement had to be made.

Barth seized the opportunity when the time came to write the preface to *CD* I/1 in August 1932. That the above worries were on his mind as he wrote is clear. He notes how seeing the prolegomena to the Münster dogmatics in print 'showed me plainly . . . how much I myself still have to learn both historically and materially'.[86] He then offers 'some general observations' about the change between the first and second editions, starting with the change in title. 'In substituting the word "Church" for "Christian" in the title,' he says, 'I have tried to set a good example of restraint in the lighthearted use of the great word "Christian" against which I have protested'.[87]

---

[85] Barth, *The Holy Spirit and the Christian Life*, pp. 37–8, emphasis added.
[86] *CD* I/1, p. xi; *KD* I/1, p. vi.
[87] *CD* I/1, pp. xii–xiii; *KD* I/1, p. viii.

His remarks from 'The Holy Spirit and the Christian Life' clearly are on his mind, and the content of his argument in that text is on his mind as well. He notes that this change 'means above all that I now think I have a better understanding of many things, including my own intentions, to the degree that in this second draft I have excluded to the very best of my ability anything that might appear to find for theology a foundation, support, or justification in philosophical existentialism'.[88] Seen in context of his broader argument in 'The Holy Spirit and the Christian Life', this statement seems to be a thrust at the heart of any natural theology that might take Christian experience and make it the basis of theology – and thus open the door to allowing any human action to be placed in continuity with *God's* action. Barth, in short, thinks that he has finally shut the door to this type of theology by removing any trace of it in his own thought. It is at this point that Barth makes his famous statement about the *analogia entis*:

'The Word or existence?' The first edition had the brilliance – or, perhaps, the stupidity, to offer ground for this question. I hope that now, at least as it concerns my own intentions, the answer is clear. Because in the previous undertaking I can see only a resumption of the line which leads from Schleiermacher to Ritschl to Herrmann; because I can see in any conceivable continuation along this line only the clear destruction of Protestant theology and the Protestant Church; because I can see no third possibility between the tolerance of the *analogia entis* which is legitimate only on the grounds of Roman Catholicism – that is, between the greatness and misery of a so-called natural knowledge of God in the sense of the *Vaticanum* – and a Protestant theology which draws from its own source, stands on its own feet, and is finally liberated from this secular misery; for all of these reasons, I can only say 'No' here. I regard the *analogia entis* as the invention of the anti-Christ, and I think that because of it, one cannot become Roman Catholic. Whereas, at the same time, I do not approve of any of the other reasons that one can have for not becoming Catholic, as they are short-sighted and trivial.[89]

This passage is not Barth's most lucid piece of writing, but even so, the logic of it is not difficult to follow. The statement has two parts, and each of them is centred on the question above: 'Word or existence?' Now that his first edition has raised the question, Barth must answer it. First, he has to explain why he cannot avoid answering it; and second, he has to explain why he chooses one answer over the other.

---

[88] *CD* I/1, p. xiii; *KD* I/1, p. viii.
[89] *CD* I/1, p. xiii; *KD* I/1, pp. viii–ix, translation mine.

To understand the first part – the clauses linked by the repetition of 'because' – one must recall the context discussed above. Barth is explaining why he started again with a new dogmatics that replaces the one he articulated at Münster. He believes that his former attempt left the door open to 'philosophical existentialism' – that is, to a theology that makes human experience its starting point. His confused embrace of the *analogia entis* in his lectures there serves as an example of this error. Now, after seeing how that edition had been received and learning more about the *analogia entis* from Przywara, Barth recognizes that what he said there stands on the same ground he had been trying to avoid since he broke with the theology of Herrman and his other teachers. He realizes, in other words, that this theology made it possible to see human activity in continuity with God's activity. Any theology that has room for that possibility, in Barth's view, is not a *true* Protestant theology. Why not? On the basis of the distinctions he drew earlier between his Protestant theology and Przywara's Roman Catholic theology, the answer can be found in Barth comment about a Protestant theology that 'draws from its own source'. A *true* Protestant theology is one that is drawn from the Word of God in Jesus Christ that comes to sinners. This is the *only* ground for theology. It is the ground that his teachers abandoned when they looked *also* to human experience in their theology. As their actions demonstrated, such a theology is false. It is also clear that a true Protestant theology, one based on the Word of God, stands as the opposite of Roman Catholic theology. Why? Barth's reference to Vatican I, 'natural knowledge', and the *analogia entis* make it clear that Barth is thinking of the Roman Catholic continuum between God's activity and human activity that he criticized in the two lectures from 1929. He is thinking, in other words, of a theology that leaves room for the natural capabilities and experience of the human to play a part in God's act of reconciliation. Between this view and the true Protestant view, Barth thinks there can be no 'third possibility'. Why not? They are fundamentally different approaches: one is talking about a Word of God that comes to sinners who have no capabilities; the other is talking about the Word that comes with the human who has some capability for God by virtue of her creation. Moving to a 'middle ground' as a 'third possibility', therefore, simply won't work: the two traditions stand as fundamentally different approaches to the relation of God's grace and human sin. For this reason, Barth must say 'No' to the 'third possibility'.

It is here that Barth turns to the second part of this statement: he must explain why he chooses 'Word' over 'experience'. In other words, now that he has said 'No' to a third way, he has to explain why he has chosen the Protestant option over the Roman Catholic option. He locates the reason in the *analogia entis*. Why? Because he has been convinced by Przywara that this principle is the summation and synthesis of all Catholic thought, since it is the one insight that captures the basic and fundamental rhythm of

Roman Catholic life. At this point, the reason he would reject this doctrine should be clear: he believes it leaves room for precisely the kind of continuity that he does not think possible if one adheres to the Word of God in Jesus Christ in a truly Protestant way. That is, as he already noted, the *analogia entis* is 'legitimate only on the grounds of Roman Catholicism', and it works only if one assumes a Catholic framework of justification and sanctification that stands in contradiction to the Protestant understanding. But why call the *analogia entis* 'the invention of the anti-Christ'? Is that not an overtly polemical statement? Two comments may be offered. First, it *is* a polemical statement – but it is one that stands squarely in line with many other statements about the *analogia entis* that Barth had already made publicly. For example, in 'Fate and Idea', Barth had said, that a 'theology ignorant that even its best concept of God, informed by the pinnacle of human thought, is in itself no witness to God can only be, strictly speaking, a witness to the devil'.[90] His critique is clear: any theology that works from any ground other than God's revelation in Jesus Christ is essentially a witness to Satan. It is clear from 'Fate and Idea' onward that Barth believes that the *analogia entis* fits this precise description. Calling it 'the invention of the anti-Christ', therefore, simply is another way of saying what Barth had already said. It does not mark, in other words, a departure – even in tone – from Barth's previous condemnations of the principle.

Second, and more importantly, Barth's remark is a direct function of his context. In the summer of 1932, Adolf Hitler's Nazi Party was only months away from seizing total control of the German government. The political turmoil around him had to be on Barth's mind, and in his view, the church appeared to be complicit in the events that were unfolding. Indeed, immediately after his statement about the *analogia entis* in the preface, Barth mourns the state of 'modern Protestantism' and notes that 'many of its preachers and adherents have finally learned to discover deep religious significance in the intoxication of Nordic blood and their political *Führer*'.[91] The language here echoes Barth's language about his teachers' failures when they embraced World War I. In his view, the same kind of theology that fuelled that error is flourishing once again. Przywara's *Analogia Entis* stands as the most recent and perhaps the most magnificent manifestation of this theological trend. Such a theology, in his mind, is nothing more than a tool of the devil, because it keeps the church from adhering to its true Word – the Word that would prevent the church from embracing political movements like fascism. What we see is that Barth's condemnation, while polemical, is not 'demented'. It is not based on a misunderstanding. His rejection is

---

[90] Karl Barth, 'Fate and Idea in Theology', in *The Way of Theology in Karl Barth: Essays and Comments*, ed. H. Martin Rumscheidt (Allison Park, PA: Pickwick Publications, 1986), p. 59.
[91] *CD* I/1, p. xvi; *KD* I/1, p. x.

rooted in real-life worries and based in substantive theological concerns. Barth's condemnation was intended to sound his dramatic and polemical opposition to the complicity between the church and the government and God and the human. To protest against such complicity – even polemically – was nothing new for him. He had been shouting the same loud 'Nein!' since 1914.

6

BARTH'S *ANALOGIA FIDEI*
AND ITS IMPLICATIONS

*In the Bible, however, it is not a being common to God and man which
finally and properly establishes and upholds the fellowship between
them, but God's grace.*

– *Karl Barth*[1]

Even according to Catholic doctrine, there is no theologia naturalis *that
can be unmoored from salvation history.*

– *Gottlieb Söhngen*[2]

Introduction

This chapter marks the turning point between the two parts of this study. In
the first part, we addressed the question of whether or not Barth's rejection
of the *analogia entis* was the result of a mistaken understanding of it. Our
investigation focused on the *analogia entis* as presented by Erich Przywara,
both because Barth learnt about the *analogia entis* from Przywara and
because Przywara's version was the one that Barth rejected. We showed that
Barth understood Przywara's *analogia entis* – as well as its theological motivations and implications – correctly. He did not reject it because he saw in it
something that was not there; he rejected it because he accurately concluded
that it allows divine and human action to stand in continuity with one
another in the Christian life. This error was a form of the same error the
Reformers had rejected when they broke from the Roman Catholic Church.

---

[1] Karl Barth, *Church Dogmatics* II/1 (Edinburgh: T&T Clark, 1957), p. 243; *Die
Kirchliche Dogmatik* II/1 (Zürich: Evangelischer Verlag, 1940), p. 275. Hereafter,
these volumes will be cited as *CD* II/1 and *KD* II/1 respectively.

[2] Gottlieb Söhngen, 'Natürliche Theologie und Heilsgeschichte: Antwort an Emil Brunner',
in *Catholica* 4 (1935), p. 111.

Barth's rejection of the *analogia entis* was not based upon a misunderstanding, therefore, but rather, it was based upon his firm adherence to the basic theological convictions that had governed Protestant theology from its inception.

In the second part of the book, we will turn to a second question: did Barth, either in response to the realization that he had made a mistake or due to changes in his own theology, implicitly withdraw his critique of the *analogia entis* and accept a version of it as his own? The background to this question was discussed in Chapter 1, and it stands in close relation to the question addressed in the first part of the book. Indeed, on the basis of the insights obtained in the first part, we already are in a position to address at least one aspect of this question. We can conclude that Barth did not change his mind, withdraw his critique, and accept a version of the *analogia entis* into his own theology because he realized that his initial rejection of it was based upon a misunderstanding. This answer, however, leaves the other aspect of this question remaining: did Barth's theology *change* in such a way that he no longer felt a need to criticize the *analogia entis*? And did Barth eventually incorporate a version of the *analogia entis* into his own theology? As we saw in Chapter 1, many interpreters of Barth, both Roman Catholic and Protestant, believe that this is the case. They argue that Barth's *analogia fidei* necessarily implies an *analogia entis*, and that once Barth realized this fact, he quietly stopped criticizing the principle. In fact, they claim that Barth *had* to cease this criticism, because when he developed his full account of the relationship of God to humanity in his doctrine of creation in *Church Dogmatics* III/1–4 (*CD* III/1–4), it became clear that he himself was working with an *analogia entis* that stands in continuity with the *analogia entis* he had rejected in *CD* I/1. These arguments are associated most prominently with Hans Urs von Balthasar, but his claims are built upon the work of Gottlieb Söhngen, who advanced an early form of them in 1934. What are we to make of these claims? Does Barth, either wittingly or unwittingly, employ an *analogia entis* in the *CD*? And if so, does this mean that he simply is confused about the *analogia entis* and what it entails? Or does it mean that changes in his own theology forced him to withdraw his earlier critique and adopt a version of the *analogia entis* as his own?

These questions will be addressed in this and the following chapter, and the following claims will be advanced: Barth *never* withdrew his rejection of Przywara's early version of the *analogia entis*. What he rejected first in 1929 and again in 1932 he still rejected in 1968, the year of his death, and for the same reasons. Barth did not change his mind. He did, however, change his response to the *analogia entis* in three ways. First, he dropped his polemic against the *analogia entis* as 'the invention of the anti-Christ' because he believed that the Roman Catholic interpretation of it shifted in positive ways as a result of his criticism. Second, Barth publicly admitted that his alternative to the *analogia entis*, the *analogia fidei*, implies a *participatio entis*, and that he must account for this participation – and thus 'being' – in his theology if he is to maintain an *analogia fidei* at all. Third, Barth accounts for this participation in 'being' by positing a relationship of continuity between God and the human. However, the fact that Barth now accepts a type of continuity between God and the human does not mean that he has retreated from his earlier critique of Przywara's position, because a crucial difference remains between the two views. In Przywara's construal – as well as in those of Söhngen, von Balthasar, and many other Roman Catholics – the human as created stands in continuity with the human in grace as a function of God's act of creation. Barth posits a continuity of a different sort, and the difference arises from the doctrine of election formulated in *CD* II/2. After developing this doctrine, Barth realized that what humans *are* intrinsically is not a function of their creation by God; it is a function of God's election of them in Jesus Christ. What we can know of God and ourselves through reflection upon our created nature, therefore, is not fulfilled and perfected by what we know through revelation and faith, as in the Catholic view, because what humans are *internally* is, at every moment in time, a function of their *external* relation to God in Jesus Christ – and this relation is something that can be known only in and through the revelation of Christ's reconciling work. In short, Barth posits continuity between God and the human, but his type of continuity precludes the possibility that knowledge of God obtained apart from the revelation of God's reconciling act in Jesus Christ can be perfected and fulfilled by knowledge of this revelation. In sum, Barth does not adopt a version of the analogy that Przywara originally offered, but rather, he offers the strongest possible rejection of it, because nothing at all like Przywara's analogy can exist on the ground of Barth's account of creation. Barth's mature views of continuity thus stand as the *fulfilment* of his early rejection of the *analogia entis* rather than a retreat from it.

This argument will be developed as the chapters progress, and it lead to the conclusion that Barth's later theology does, in fact, contain an *analogia entis*, but that his formulation is in no way compatible with the *analogia entis* as presented by Przywara, Söhngen, or von Balthasar. Barth's discussion of 'being' stands against theirs, and his view is the outworking of the same theological commitments that led him both to reject Przywara's *analogia entis* and to distinguish his own formulation from Söhngen's and, by extension, von Balthasar's formulation. For this reason, this change in response *to* the Roman Catholic *analogia entis* does not indicate a change in his interpretation *of* it; rather, it marks a clearer and deeper articulation of the same, basically Protestant, commitments that have been driving his theology since his break with Protestant Liberalism.

These three changes in Barth's response – and their relation to my larger claim – should become clear in the course of this chapter and the next.

The first two changes in Barth's response to the *analogia entis* will b
cussed in this chapter; the third will be discussed in Chapter 7. The argument
in this chapter will proceed in three sections: first, I will offer an account
of Barth's *analogia fidei*; second, I will explain the nature of Gottlieb
Söhngen's critique of Barth's position; and third, I will examine Barth's
response to Söhngen and the implications of it for his understanding and
critique of the *analogia entis*.

Barth's analogia fidei

As we consider Barth's doctrine of analogy in the CD, there are two important
points that must be kept in mind. First, Barth's analogical formulations –
including the *analogia fidei* and the *analogia relationis* – should be seen not
as principles or doctrines that stand or function independently. Instead, they
should be seen simply as tools or instruments that Barth uses to serve his
larger dogmatic objective: to adhere to his proper theological subject matter,
the Word of God in Jesus Christ. Barth never intends, in other words,
to offer a self-contained concept of analogy that can stand on its own outside of the context of his own dogmatics. Second, Barth's use of analogy is
governed at every moment by two central doctrines of Protestant theology:
Luther's *sola gratia* and *simul iustus et peccator*. On the basis of *sola gratia*,
Barth rules out the idea that human action can contribute in any way to
one's relationship with God, and this includes the human ability to come to
the knowledge of God. In the same way, Luther's *simul iustus et peccator*
governs how Barth understands the nature of Jesus Christ's saving work.
The human does not become righteous in and of himself as a result of this
work, but rather, he is reckoned as righteous because of his participation in
the alien righteousness of Christ even though he remains a sinner through
and through. From the beginning to the end of Barth's CD, these two doctrines shape the uses of analogy that Barth rejects, those he defends, and the
development of his own use of analogy. Simply put: Barth's discussion of
analogy cannot be understood if the influence of these two doctrines is not
kept in mind at all times, because they are governing his use of analogy at
every moment.

In the early volumes of the CD, Barth's account of analogy is built with
one purpose in mind: to close the door to the type of continuity between
divine and human action that he condemned when he rejected Przywara's
account of the *analogia entis*. To this end, he lays out his account of the
proper starting point and subject matter for dogmatics, and he is unequivo-
cal about what the proper starting point *cannot* be: metaphysics. He argues
that since the Enlightenment and the advent of 'Modernist' dogmatics, Protestant theology had been formulated so that 'the church and faith are to be

understood as lines in a greater nexus of being'.[3] Dogmatics was understood to be part of a larger and more basic question – 'that of an ontology' – and as a result, the theologian's first task was to articulate a 'comprehensively explicated self-understanding of human existence'.[4] Then, with this answer in hand, the theologian had to explain how theology could be possible by outlining the limits and rules that the ontology necessarily places upon the practice of dogmatics.[5] Only then could the theologian actually begin the task of dogmatic reflection.

As Barth sees it, however, this approach 'stands or falls with the answer to the question whether there really *is* a nexus of being superior to the being of the church and consequently a nexus of scientific problems superior to dogmatics'.[6] His theology constitutes a break with this tradition because he insists that there is no such 'being'. Instead, for Barth, *God* is the one who is superior to both the church and dogmatics, because God is the one who determines both of them in their innermost depths. A proper theology in service to the church, therefore, must begin with God and God's revelation rather than any other source. In other words, questions of ontology that attempt to lay a foundation from 'the general historicity of human existence' cannot be part of the dogmatic task, but rather, dogmatics must focus solely on that which is 'outside all human possibilities' – 'the actuality of revelation'.[7] This revelation – the Word of God in Jesus Christ – is the sole and proper subject matter of dogmatics.

Divine Revelation and the *analogia entis*

What does Barth's account about the proper starting point for dogmatics have to do with the *analogia entis* and his rejection of it? Barth believes that Roman Catholic theologians are committing a variation of the same error that 'Modernist' Protestant theologians have been committing, and he believes that the *analogia entis* is the clearest manifestation of this error. Przywara's theology illustrates Barth's concern. Przywara holds that 'God in Christ in the Church' demonstrates the pattern of the *analogia entis*, and that this pattern can be applied to the rest of human existence because creation as such exists in relationship to God in the same way. The clear and perfect revelation in the Catholic Church, therefore, serves as an 'objective principle of knowledge' that is used to supplement and perfect the unclear

---

[3] Karl Barth, *Church Dogmatics* I/1, rev. ed. (Edinburgh: T&T Clark, 1975), p. 36; *Die Kirchliche Dogmatik* I/1 (Zürich: Evangelischer Verlag, 1932), p. 35. Hereafter these volumes will be cited as *CD* I/1 and *KD* I/1 respectively.

[4] *CD* I/1, p. 36; *KD* I/1, p. 36.

[5] *CD* I/1, p. 37; *KD* I/1, pp. 36–7.

[6] *CD* I/1, p. 38; *KD* I/1, p. 37.

[7] *CD* I/1, pp. 38–9; *KD* I/1, p. 38.

and imperfect account of this revelation discerned by philosophers in their account of human being and existence.[8] Barth notes that 'at least in intention', this view attempts to take seriously 'the concept of the acting God'.[9] That is, Roman Catholics like Przywara believe that the Catholic Church exists as the concrete and visible form of God's self-revelation in the world, and they hold that this revelation serves as a pattern for how God relates to creation as a whole. Dogmatic reflection may begin with human existence, therefore, only because we know that God has acted in the Catholic Church in the same way that he acts in his relationship to creation as a whole. This is one reason why Przywara can label his approach an 'above to below' movement, and it is also why he would reject the argument that his approach is grounded in anything other than divine revelation.[10]

Barth's problem with such a view, however, is that in Przywara's or any other Roman Catholic construal, divine revelation no longer freely stands over the church as something other than it, but rather, it has become *a part of* the church's existence.

> Their presupposition is that the being of the church, Jesus Christ, is no longer the free Lord of its existence, but that He is incorporated into the existence of the church, and is thus ultimately restricted and conditioned by certain concrete forms of the human understanding of his revelation and of the faith which grasps it . . . grace here becomes nature, the action of God immediately disappears and is taken up into the action of the recipient of grace, that which is beyond all human possibilities changes at once into that which is enclosed within the reality of the church, and the personal act of divine address becomes a constantly available relationship.[11]

Barth's worry, in other words, is that if divine revelation is incorporated into the being of the church, then the church 'can recognize itself and God's

---

[8] *CD* I/1, p. 40; *KD* I/1, p. 39. See Erich Przywara, 'Das katholische Kirchenprinzip', *Zwischen den Zeiten* 7 (1929), pp. 283–4.

[9] *CD* I/1, p. 40; *KD* I/1, p. 40.

[10] The ultimate 'objective principle of knowledge' is, of course, the incarnation, and the Catholic Church, as the body of Christ in history, is a form of the incarnation continued in history. In his discussion of the incarnation in *Church Dogmatics* I/2, Barth rejects this understanding of the incarnation, because 'we do not find that the Word of God has become man in general, but flesh'. On this basis, he argues that Przywara's move of using the Catholic Church as the pattern for how God relates to creation generally does 'not prove what has to be proved', because it mistakenly takes a unique event and then applies it universally. See Karl Barth, *Church Dogmatics* I/2 (Edinburgh: T&T Clark, 1956), p. 43; *Die Kirchliche Dogmatik* I/2 (Zürich: Evangelischer-Verlag, 1938), p. 48. Hereafter these volumes will be cited as *CD* I/2 and *KD* I/2 respectively.

[11] *CD* I/1, pp. 40–1; *KD* I/1, p. 40.

revelation in this constantly available relationship between God and man, in this revealedness'.[12] This view leads to the Catholic variant on the Modernist error: once we can talk about God's revelation in terms of its ongoing existence and availability *in* the church, we then can talk about the 'being' of revelation in the same way that we talk about any other 'being' in the world. That is, we can use the 'general structure of laws' that are applicable to every other aspect of human existence to talk about divine revelation as well, and as a result, divine revelation quickly becomes contained within the boundaries of human existence. In Barth's view, then, even though Przywara seeks to maintain a focus on the 'acting God' who works from 'above to below' by starting with the pattern of God's relation to the Catholic Church and then applying that pattern to human existence as a whole, he falls into the same fatal error as the liberal Protestants because, in his construal, God's revelation in Jesus Christ becomes a part of the larger 'nexus of being' in which humans exist. Indeed, for Przywara, human existence as such – because it also exists as the 'window' of the self-revelation of God – stands in continuity with human existence in the church, and thus with God himself. As we have seen, this means that a theologian can legitimately begin dogmatic reflection with human existence (metaphysics) and then move to the more specific insights of special revelation (theology) without loss, because the subject matter of both disciplines is the same.[13]

Barth concludes that this approach must be rejected because it applies 'the secular "There is" to God and the things of God as the presupposition, again ontological, of that change or transformation, of that depriving of revelation and faith of their character as decision by evasion and neutralization'.[14] In other words, because God's self-revelation takes a concrete and always-available form within human existence, it becomes a part of the world in such a way that a human can apply the presuppositions of modern philosophy to God's action and say, 'There is revelation' in the same way he

---

[12] *CD* I/1, p. 41; *KD* I/1, p. 40.

[13] Przywara would argue that because, in his view, philosophy stands in an analogous, 'in-over' relationship with theology – meaning that, it remains an 'above to below' event – it is not guilty of the fault that Barth lays at its feet. Barth's response to Przywara would be that, because true knowledge of God in philosophy occurs only 'retrospect from revealed truth' in Przywara's construal, it occurs by 'recapitulation and not anticipation', thus disqualifying it as 'an instrument of the knowledge of God' altogether. In other words, the fact that, in retrospect, philosophical knowledge can be brought into correlation with theological knowledge does not mean that philosophy rightly can be seen as part of dogmatics, nor does it alter the need for a purely theological starting point. Barth concludes that 'it is hard to see what theological foundation could be found' for including philosophy in the process at all. See *CD* I/1, pp. 39–40; *KD* I/1, pp. 38–9.

[14] *CD* I/1, p. 41; *KD* I/1, p. 40. This comment is specifically directed towards the *analogia entis*.

might say 'There is' in reference to any other thing in the world. The out-ward form of human existence becomes the ontological presupposition for God's self-revelation: God is no longer free, because his act of self-revelation occurs within the constraints of human existence. Barth rejects this approach because he insists that revelation and faith are 'not ours' to possess or know in this way, and their content cannot be understood – even in a limited and imperfect way – by means of an ontology or reflection upon human experi-ence.[15] The ability to come to such knowledge, he insists, 'has been taken from us by the Fall', and this ability 'is restored to us only in the Gospel, in *revelatio specialis*'.[16] We simply cannot understand God's revelation in the same way that we understand the other 'general truths' of human existence, because God's act of revelation is *sui generis*, it is 'comprehensible only from and through itself'.[17]

For Barth, this characteristic does not mean that God does not reveal himself to humans, because this revelation does, in fact, occur. If it does so, however – and it does so in such a way that it does not exist in the same way that other things exist in this world – then in what manner does it occur? And what form does it take when it occurs? Barth addresses these questions by explaining his distinct way of understanding the existence of the church. This account allows him to draw a distinction between his understanding of revelation and those found in both Protestant Liberalism and Roman Catholicism. For him, the church is 'pure act'. That it is 'act', he says, means that the being of the church is 'an event of personal address' rather than 'a continuously available relationship' or 'a transmitted material condition'.[18] That it is 'pure' means that it is distinct from all other events in history – indicating that the church as a *human* institution is distinct from the *true* church which exists and is maintained solely by the act of God. At every moment, therefore, the church 'depends on God's ongoing act' for its true being and existence, and in this act, God in no way divests himself 'into the historical contingency of the church' so that, in the being of the church, God or God's revelation can be recognized as part of this world.[19] The actualistic nature of the church's existence points us, Barth says, to a basic truth: 'God and His Word are not given to us in the same way as natu-ral or historical entities'.[20] To say otherwise – that is, to hold that revelation

---

[15] *Ibid*. He notes later: 'If a man, the church, church proclamation and dogmatics think they can handle the Word and faith like capital at their disposal, they simply prove thereby that they have neither the Word nor faith.' See *CD* I/1, p. 225; *KD* I/1, p. 236.

[16] *CD* I/1, p. 130; *KD* I/1, p. 134.

[17] *CD* I/1, p. 41; *KD* I/1, p. 41.

[18] *Ibid*. The church, he says, is visible 'not in itself and as such' but only 'in virtue of the divine confirmation and preservation'. See *CD* I/1, p. 49; *KD* I/1, p. 49.

[19] *CD* I/1, p. 41; *KD* I/1, p. 41.

[20] *CD* I/1, p. 132; *KD* I/1, p. 136.

'exists' as other creaturely realities exist – would be a 'deverbalizing' of God's Word. It would mean, in other words, God's 'allowing us to gain control over His Word, to fit it in with our own designs, and thus to shut up ourselves against Him to our own ruin'.[21] A revelation that becomes a visible and concrete part of the 'nexus of being' of the world, therefore, would not be a true revelation at all, and this is precisely what Barth believes happens in both 'Modernist' Protestant and Roman Catholic dogmatics.

It is helpful to put the distinctions Barth draws here within the context of his larger argument about the nature of divine revelation. Barth's view of revelation as *event* in the early volumes of the *CD* means that dogmatics can occur only on the basis of 'the present moment of the speaking and hearing of Jesus Christ Himself, the divine creation of light in our hearts'.[22] This claim stands in line with his argument in 'The Holy Spirit and the Christian Life' that human knowledge of God takes place only by the 'miracle of the Holy Spirit' who works in the event of God's revelation by bringing the human to faith in Christ.[23] God's revelation and our understanding of it, therefore, are an act of God on *both* sides. This distinguishes Barth's construal from Roman Catholic formulations because in the Catholic view, at least some knowledge of God can result from the concrete and always-available revelation available in creation. This means, as we have seen, that knowledge of God is the result of divine *and* human action seen in continuity with one another.[24] For Barth, in contrast, the 'co-existence' that occurs between God and the human in the event of revelation does not occur 'on the same plane' and 'it cannot be viewed in the same way as that of two other entities' that relate to one another in the world.[25] There is no continuity between God and the human as such in the event of revelation, as would be the case if the imperfect knowledge of God available by means of reflection upon human existence were fulfilled by the knowledge of

---

[21] *CD* I/1, p. 139; *KD* I/1, p. 143. The verbal character of divine revelation helps Barth draw an important distinction between his and the Roman Catholic understanding of revelation in the church. For Barth, revelation takes place by the preaching: the proclamation of the Word of God that is received in faith. In Catholic liturgy, he notes, revelation may be 'complete without [preaching]' because the most important aspect of worship is the sacrament – an event of revelation focused more on the *being* of the elements than their verbal character. The difference is that in the Protestant worship, revelation occurs 'between person and person', while in Catholic worship, revelation occurs 'materially between God as author on the one hand and the ground of being in the human person on the other' with the Catholic Church serving as the 'medium and channel of this influence'. See *CD* I/1, pp. 67–9; *KD* I/1, pp. 68–71.

[22] *CD* I/1, p. 41; *KD* I/1, p. 41.

[23] *CD* I/1, p. 182; *KD* I/1, p. 190, translation mine.

[24] *CD* I/1, p. 42; *KD* I/1, p. 42. This prior knowledge, Barth says, 'can be known and said in advance, before actually embarking on dogmatics'.

[25] *CD* I/1, p. 201; *KD* I/1, p. 209.

God available in special revelation. Rather, in Barth's account, God's self-revelation to the human occurs as a wholly unique encounter that takes place through the power of the Holy Spirit. It is an encounter, therefore, that could 'never be dissolved in union' such that it could be viewed in the same terms any other encounter in this world.[26]

Barth's account makes sense in light of his earlier commitments because it clearly follows the same line as the dialectic of veiling and unveiling he employed in his Göttingen lectures. While the Word of God is revealed within 'secular reality', he argues, this does not mean that it 'meets us in the garment of creaturely reality' as if that reality in and of itself revealed God.[27] Rather, because creaturely reality is *fallen* reality, it 'has as little ability [in and of itself] to reveal God to us as we have to see God in it'.[28] If God's Word comes to us through creaturely reality, therefore, it is revealed 'in such a way that this "through it" means "in *spite* of it"'.[29] Divine revelation in creaturely realities, therefore, must be seen as an act of God in the 'reality which *contradicts* God, which conceals him, and in which his revelation is not just his act but his miraculous act, the tearing of an untearably thick veil'.[30] Barth describes this veil as a 'twofold indirectness', meaning that, in the event of revelation through creaturely realities, 'God veils himself and that in so doing . . . he unveils himself'.[31] Human knowledge of God, therefore, must be seen as an act of God at every moment. If this were not the case – if, that is, God revealed himself directly in creaturely realities without a veil so that humans could access this revelation apart from his specific action upon them – then Barth believes that this revelation could be known in the same way that other creaturely realities are known. Such a revelation, he notes, could 'be pierced by the *analogia entis*'.[32] This would mean, Barth argues, that God's revelation would be something that the humans would have to move *towards* by reflecting upon its always-available reality instead of something that 'has really come to us' as a new and distinct reality.[33]

---

[26] *CD* I/1, p. 141; *KD* I/1, p. 146.

[27] *CD* I/1, p. 166; *KD* I/1, p. 172.

[28] *CD* I/1, p. 166; *KD* I/1, pp. 172–3.

[29] *CD* I/1, p. 166; *KD* I/1, p. 173, emphasis added.

[30] *CD* I/1, p. 168; *KD* I/1, p. 174, emphasis added.

[31] *CD* I/1, p. 169; *KD* I/1, p. 175.

[32] *Ibid.*

[33] *Ibid.* Thus Barth: 'God's Word is no longer grace, and grace itself is no longer grace, if we ascribe to man a predisposition towards this Word, a possibility of knowledge regarding it that is intrinsically and independently native to him'. This idea stands in line with Barth's discussion of the 'fatal self-assertion' of a theology that stands in continuity with philosophy in 'Fate and Idea'. See *CD* I/1, p. 194; *KD* I/1, p. 202, and Karl Barth, 'Fate and Idea in Theology', in *The Way of Theology in Karl Barth: Essays and Comments*, ed. H. Martin Rumscheidt (Allison Park, PA: Pickwick Publications 1986), p. 56.

That is how Barth sees Przywara's formulations, and his critique is a form of the same one he issued in 'The Holy Spirit and the Christian Life'. If we place divine revelation in the same 'nexus of being' that humans exist in – even if this occurs in the 'above to below' manner described by Przywara – then the inevitable result is that human action stands in continuity with God's action as we obtain knowledge of God. This is simply another form of the error of blending justification with sanctification, and it is an error, Barth thinks, that leads to judgement instead of grace.

'Capacity of the Incapable'

When the above arguments are kept in view, the meaning and content of Barth's *analogia fidei* is not difficult to grasp: in the same way that Luther held that humans do not contribute in any way to faith or salvation and that human action does not stand in continuity with divine action in the event of salvation, Barth believes that the knowledge of God has its beginning in God's Word alone and that, at every moment, it occurs 'independently of the inborn or acquired characteristics and possibilities' of the human.[34] He argues that faith is not the result of self-contemplation or 'an openness, a positive or at least a negative point of contact [*Anknüpfungspunkt*] for God's Word' that is intrinsic to the human as such.[35] For Barth, there simply is no *natural* capacity for faith, nor is there any inherent capability to hear and understand God's revelation. This does not mean, however, that this capacity is not a part of human life at all, because, in fact, this capacity does exist. It exists, however, as something that is *given* to the human anew and afresh in each moment in the event of God's self-revelation. The reception of this capacity takes analogous form: 'Hearing the Word of God could not take place if there were not something common to the speaking God and the hearing person, an *analogy*, a similarity in and with this event for all the dissimilarity implied by the difference between God and humanity – if we may now adopt this term – a "point of contact" between God and humanity'.[36] This is what Barth means by the *analogia fidei*: it is the 'point of contact' [*Anknüpfungspunkt*] between God and the human that takes place solely because of and within the ongoing event of God's self-revelation to the human.

Note that Barth intends his account of the *analogia fidei* to remain focused on the 'first article' concern of how humans come to knowledge of God. His concern is epistemological, and his argument is that there is no *inherent*

---

[34] *CD* I/1, p. 236; *KD* I/1, p. 249.

[35] *Ibid*. Both Przywara and Brunner appear to be on his mind here.

[36] *CD* I/1, p. 238; *KD* I/1, p. 251, translation mine. Unfortunately, Geoffrey Bromiley's translation leaves out the critical word 'analogy', with the result that Barth's meaning in this passage and its connection to what follows is obscured for the English reader.

point of contact, capacity, or openness to the knowledge of God in the human as such. 'In *faith*', Barth says, 'there takes place a conformity of man to God', and 'in *faith*, as he really receives God's Word, man becomes apt to receive it'.[37] Barth turns to the *analogia fidei*, then, to explain in a concrete way how humans become capable of hearing God's Word. The reason that faith is required for this knowledge is that humans 'lost their capacity for God' in the Fall.[38] The *analogia fidei* enables Barth to show how, in the event of faith, this destroyed capacity, or *Anknüpfungspunkt*, is restored by God's grace in Jesus Christ – and by this grace alone (*sola gratia*).

> [T]his point of contact is not real outside faith; it is real only in faith. In faith man is created by the Word of God for the Word of God, existing in the Word of God and not in himself, not in virtue of his humanity and personality, not even on the basis of creation, for that which by creation was possible for man in relation to God has been lost by the fall. Hence one can only speak of this point of contact theologically and not both theologically and also philosophically, as of all else that is real in faith, i.e., through the grace of reconciliation.[39]

This grace does not change the human recipient so that she now *possesses* a new capacity that she did not have before.[40] If she did possess this capacity as her own, then it would exist like anything else in the world – and thus it could be examined by philosophy as well as theology. But the human recipient of grace is still a fallen sinner in the sense of Luther's *simul iustus et peccator*. She is and remains a sinner through and through, and as such, she has no intrinsic or inherent capability or capacity to know God. She knows

---

[37] *CD* I/1, p. 238; *KD* I/1, p. 251, emphasis added. Hunsinger captures how faith is functioning here for Barth: 'Since no inherent human openness or capability exists to be exercised, grace is the sole condition for the possibility of faith. Faith is conceived as grounded in grace alone, and the mediating term with respect to the analogy is conceived not as "being" but as "miracle".' See George Hunsinger, *How to Read Karl Barth: The Shape of His Theology* (New York, NY: Oxford University Press, 1991), p. 283, fn. 2.

[38] *Ibid.* He explicitly rejects Brunner's notion of it: 'as a possibility which is proper to man *qua* creature, the image of God is not just, as it is said, destroyed apart from a few relics; it is *totally annihilated*'. This is why there can be no common basis between human disciplines like philosophy and theology when it comes to the knowledge of God: philosophy has its own 'dignity and justification' in its own sphere, but it is the philosophy 'of sinful and lost man'. See *CD* I/1, p. 256; *KD* I/1, p. 270.

[39] *CD* I/1, p. 239; *KD* I/1, pp. 251–2.

[40] McCormack makes this point: 'The "analogy of faith", once realized, does not pass over into human control. It must continue to be effected moment by moment by the sovereign action of the divine freedom if it is to be effected at all'. See Bruce L. McCormack, *Karl Barth's Critically Realistic Dialectical Theology: Its Genesis and Development, 1909–1936* (Oxford: Oxford University Press, 1995), p. 17.

God only through God's act upon her, and this knowledge is a gift of grace. It is for this reason, Barth thinks, that this knowledge can be discerned only on the grounds of theology, and specifically on the ground of a theology of God's revelation in Jesus Christ, which is addressed to sinners.

Does the fact that God's self-revelation does not exist like other things in the world mean that it cannot take visible form like these other things? For Barth, the answer is no. Indeed, God's revelation becomes visible precisely in the fact that, in the event of grace, a *correspondence* occurs between God's act of revelation and the human response to it. The fallen human hears God's Word as God gives him in each moment the capacity to hear it, and through the power of the Holy Spirit, he responds by conforming his life to this Word in obedience. The correspondence takes place in the event in which the human recipient of God's revelation is, through the power of the Holy Spirit, 'raised up from real death' and 'restored or created anew'.[41] This event is the visible manifestation of the Christian's participation in Christ. He now truly is 'capable of so corresponding in his own decision to the decision God has made about him in the Word', but he is so only by grace.[42] This correspondence by grace through faith is the visible form of the analogy between God and the human, since this action marks the point of commonality between God and the human. For Barth, therefore, only humans who have been reconciled – that is, only humans who are *in Christ* – stand in analogy and conformity to God. The *analogia fidei* is the reestablishment of an *Anknüpfungspunkt* between God and the human in Christ, and it marks a real human capacity to know God. It is, however, a 'capacity of the incapable', a 'miracle that cannot be interpreted anthropologically' but nevertheless exists as 'a real capacity which is already actualized in faith'.[43] This distinction helps Barth show how his own construal stands over against Przywara's formulations, and he believes it also shows how his account avoids the errors that plague liberal Protestant and Roman Catholic dogmatics.

Gottlieb Söhngen: 'analogia entis *within the* analogia fidei'

After reading Barth's account of the *analogia fidei,* some Catholic theologians argued that Barth's rejection of the *analogia entis* was unnecessary,

---

[41] *CD* I/1, p. 239; *KD* I/1, p. 252. This argument is made again in *CD* I/2, where Barth argues that the connection between God and humanity is a 'free and undeserved distinction, based only upon grace and not at all upon nature, a distinction which *happens* to "nature"'. The active nature of this 'happening' is the essential characteristic of Barth's view. See *CD* I/2, p. 37; *KD* I/2, p. 41.

[42] *CD* I/1, p. 240; *KD* I/1, p. 253.

[43] *CD* I/1, p. 241; *KD* I/1, p. 254.

that Catholic theology *also* had an *analogia fidei*, and that the controversy between Barth and Przywara misrepresented the true state of affairs between Protestants and Roman Catholics. In fact, in their view, Barth's rejection of the *analogia entis* simply was an unfortunate byproduct of Przywara's overly metaphysical presentation of the principle. If Przywara's account could be corrected by a more balanced presentation of the *analogia entis*, they believed, then Barth's rejection of it – and his reasons for not becoming Roman Catholic – could be mitigated.

The most prominent exponent of this view was Gottlieb Söhngen, who published a pair of essays on the topic in 1934.[44] Söhngen's essays arose from his participation in a seminar with Arnold Rademacher at Bonn, where Barth was also teaching at the time.[45] The seminar participants read *Analogia Entis* and concluded that Przywara's presentation, because it focused on metaphysics at the expense of theology, was too one-sided in its presentation. It was this one-sidedness, they believed, that provoked Barth into labelling the *analogia entis* 'the invention of the anti-Christ' and positing the *analogia fidei* as its corrective. This result is tragic, because Przywara and Barth *both* have it wrong: the *analogia entis* and *analogia fidei* are *complementary* rather than mutually exclusive ideas, and the Catholic tradition has always maintained both concepts in balance with one another. The seminar concluded, therefore, that an account that could look back to this tradition and, through it, place *theological* rather than philosophical concerns at the forefront would be able to capture this fact. It was this interpretation of Przywara and Barth that inspired Söhngen's essays: he wants 'to make the connection between the *analogia entis* and the *analogia fidei* visible' again, and by doing so, to build a bridge between Barth and Roman Catholicism.[46]

That Söhngen had thoughtfully considered Barth's position is clear in his first essay, because he begins with the right person: Martin Luther. Söhngen correctly recognizes that Luther's key doctrinal distinctions are driving both Barth's critique and his alternative. He explains that Barth's rejection of the *analogia entis* stems from the fact that he takes Luther's theology

---

[44] Gottlieb Söhngen, 'Analogia Fidei: Gottähnlichkeit allein aus Glauben?', *Catholica* 3, no. 3 (1934), pp. 113–36, and Söhngen, 'Analogia Fidei: Die Einheit in der Glaubenswissenschft', *Catholica* 3, no. 4 (1934), pp. 176–208. Söhngen is not every well known outside of German theological circles, but his influence lives on in one of his students, Joseph Ratzinger, who later became Pope Benedict XVI. Söhngen chose the topic for Ratzinger's dissertation as well as his *Habilitationsschrift*. See Fergus Kerr, *Twentieth Century Catholic Theologians: From Neoscholasticism to Nuptial Mysticism* (Malden, MA: Blackwell Publishing Ltd., 2007), p. 185.

[45] Söhngen notes this influence in his essay. See Söhngen, 'Analogia Fidei: Gottähnlichkeit', p. 114.

[46] *Ibid.*

'completely seriously', as opposed to Emil Brunner, whom he thinks affirms natural theology and an *analogia entis* 'at the expense of the Reformation' because the logic of his thought demands the 'relinquishment of *sola fide* in the strict sense of *simul iustus et peccator*'.[47] This does not mean, however, that Söhngen believes that Barth is correct in his judgement about the *analogia entis*. He argues that placing the *analogia entis* in opposition to the *analogia fidei* is, in fact, to place 'faith against being, or the reality of faith against the being of the world and human reality'.[48] Such an opposition is unfortunate, he argues, because it means that the faith of the Reformation does not talk about the actual 'being' of the human at all; rather, it talks only about a being *extrinsic* to human. For this reason, Barth's *analogia fidei* can only be 'an *analogia attributionis mere extrinsecae*, a correspondence relationship of purely external allocation'.[49] This point is significant, because it helps us understand why Söhngen believes that Barth's doctrine of analogy cannot stand on its own, as well as how Söhngen hopes to correct Barth's *analogia fidei* by connecting it to the more robust Roman Catholic version.

To this end, Söhngen contends that there are two points of connection between Protestant and Roman Catholic uses of analogy, and that they reveal the solution to Barth and Luther's problem. First, he argues that in both traditions, analogy implies participation.[50] The Roman Catholic *analogia entis*, for example, implies that the creature participates, at least in a derivative and contingent way, in the 'being' of God. It would be impossible to draw such an analogy if this were not the case. The Protestant *analogia fidei also* implies participation in the divine life, although in its case, this participation occurs through Christ by grace through faith alone. Regardless of how the participation occurs, however, Söhngen believes that on this point, both traditions stand on the same ground. This leads him to the

---

[47] *Ibid.*, p. 119. Barth refers to Söhngen's conclusion in his response to Brunner's *Nature and Grace*: 'Brunner has been unable to adhere to *sola fide – sola gratia* . . . In addition to the applause of the "German Christians" and their ilk he should make a point of reading what my Roman Catholic colleague at Bonn, Gottlieb Söhngen, wrote concerning his understanding. This should convince him that I am not wantonly branding him as a heretic, but that this really is how the matter stands'. See Barth, 'Nein!', in *Natural Theology: Comprising 'Nature and Grace' by Professor Dr. Emil Brunner and the Reply 'No!' by Dr. Karl Barth* (London: Centenary Press, 1946), p. 90.

[48] Söhngen, 'Analogia Fidei: Gottähnlichkeit', p. 120.

[49] *Ibid.*, p. 124. One of the implications of Barth's extrinsic analogy is that it precludes the possibility for a certain kind of ecclesial visibility – a point, of course, that Barth himself established in *CD* I/1. As a Catholic theologian, Söhngen's motivation for objecting to this view is obvious. It is significant, however, that he attempts to incorporates Barth's insights into his own Catholic theology instead of simply rejecting them.

[50] *Ibid.*, p. 125. He appeals to Thomas Aquinas, *Summa Theologica*, trans. Father of the English Dominican Province (New York: Benziger Brothers, Inc., 1948), I.85.ad5 in support of this claim.

second point of connection between the two traditions: Christian mysticism. He employs Luther's commentary on the Psalms as an illustration of how Protestants join Catholics in affirming the possibility of mysticism. Both traditions, he insists, think that mystics in some sense participate in God's life, and Catholics and Protestants alike believe that this participation occurs by *faith*.[51] He insists, however, that this participation cannot occur only *as* faith, because this would 'strictly exclude' any *true* mysticism.[52] The mystic, as a fully human being, must participate by faith *in the divine life* – meaning that the mystic must, by definition, participate in 'being'. A 'right understanding of *participatio fidei*', therefore, is one that includes within itself the notion of a *participatio entis*. The incarnation provides the ground for this idea, because just as Jesus Christ participated in human nature, so too does the human *in* Christ participate in the divine life.[53] For Söhngen, this insight leads us to his central claim about analogy: 'the *analogia fidei* is not absolutely against the *analogia entis*', but rather, the *analogia fidei* implies the *analogia entis*.[54] The two concepts are complimentary because, on the one hand, the *analogia fidei* cannot account for participation in the divine life without reference to 'being', and on the other hand, the *analogia entis* cannot function on its own because the participation in 'being' is the result of faith alone.

This is the argument of the first essay, and Söhngen believes it shows that the *analogia entis* need not – and indeed cannot – be construed as the opposite of the *analogia fidei*. In the second essay, he extends his argument further by showing that the *analogia fidei* is not just a Protestant doctrine. Catholic theology offers a version of the *analogia fidei* as well, and it is one, Söhngen argues, that can 'stand and speak for itself' in such a way that the contradiction between the *analogia fidei* and the *analogia entis* is avoided.[55] After working through several primary texts demonstrating the existence of the *analogia fidei* in the Catholic tradition, Söhngen summarizes four implications it has for Catholic theology. It indicates, first, that there is a unity within the Bible and within the broader meaning of the Bible; second, that a unity exists between the Bible and the teaching of the church; third,

---

[51] *Ibid.*, pp. 131–3.

[52] *Ibid.*, p. 133.

[53] Joseph Palakeel, who offers a helpful summary of Söhngen's argument, makes this aspect of the argument clear: 'In this sense analogy of faith alone cannot refer to Christian participation, nor is analogy of being utterly contrary to the Christian understanding of faith, because as Christ truly participated in human nature, man in Christ really participates in God through Christ.' See Joseph Palakeel, *The Use of Analogy in Theological Discourse: An Investigation in Ecumenical Perspective* (Rome: Pontificia Università Gregoriana, 1995), p. 133.

[54] Söhngen, 'Analogia Fidei: Gottähnlichkeit', p. 133.

[55] Söhngen, 'Analogia Fidei: Die Einheit in der Glaubenswissenschft', p. 176.

that there is a unity in the understanding of the mysteries of the faith and their 'secret connection' to one another; and fourth, that there is a unity between obedience to natural knowledge of God and knowledge of God stemming from grace and faith.[56] Söhngen's emphasis on 'unity' is important: it demonstrates the fact that, in the Catholic *analogia fidei*, the various orders of knowledge, including those orders that have to do with divine revelation as well as creaturely being, stand in continuity with one another. That is, whereas in Barth's understanding the *analogia fidei* has to do with epistemological concerns – how we come to knowledge of God – the Catholic *analogia fidei* is based upon the notion that faith implies *being*. Hence, whereas Barth's view separates revelation from being, the Catholic view brings revelation and being together *in faith*. Söhngen describes this idea in terms of the Christian's life before God:

> [God's revelation] announces to us the inner-divine life of the mystery of the Trinity and our participation *in* the inner-divine life as the mystery of the children of God. Precisely in this participation in the divine nature there appears to us clearly an unmistakable *analogia fidei*, namely the supernatural divine-likeness rooted in Godly faith or the image of God in human beings.[57]

For Söhngen, in short, the Catholic *analogia fidei* has ontological as well as epistemological implications. Revelation is not only a divine Word that transmits knowledge; it is also a divine act that has implications for human 'being', because it signifies human participation in the life of God.[58]

This argument leads him to draw a distinction between the relation of being and act in philosophy and theology. In the order of being, he says, '*Operari sequitur esse* – act follows being'.[59] This order, of course, is the basis for all metaphysics, inasmuch as metaphysics marks an attempt to know the true being of creaturely realities. However, the fact that metaphysics must begin with these creaturely realities and only then, by reflection, move to a consideration of their being, indicates that the order of knowledge

---

[56] *Ibid.*, p. 177.

[57] *Ibid.*, p. 190.

[58] Söhngen has to consider the ontological as well as epistemological implications of analogy because, as a Catholic theologian, he has to account for the concrete visibility of the Catholic Church. As he notes later on, '[t]he visible assertion of God's Word in the living word of the Church obviously stands and falls on this point: that grace and faith do not stand simply against nature and reason, but rather that the *analogia fidei* is *sanans et elevans analogiam entis*'. Söhngen, in other words, simply cannot accept Barth's construal of the *analogia fidei* – or his wholesale rejection of the *analogia entis* – because Barth's account leaves no room for a tangible church. See *Ibid.*, p. 208.

[59] *Ibid.*, p. 198.

works in reverse: '*Esse sequitur operari* – the knowledge of being follows from the knowledge of act.'[60] Söhngen insists that 'if this counts in the *natural* order of knowledge, then it counts all the more in the order of knowledge in faith'.[61] Why? The reason lies in the nature of God's revelation in creation. Natural revelation, he explains, should be seen as an act of communication from God in the sense that God 'imparts a subsistent realm of being' to creation. This means that creaturely being 'is in its deepest roots dependent upon God, because God created and maintains it'.[62] This does not mean, however, that human reflection upon creaturely being – such as that which occurs in metaphysics – will lead to God. Here Söhngen reveals a different interpretation of the doctrine of creation – as well as a different view of the relationship of philosophy to theology – than the one Przywara holds. Recall that Przywara holds that creation serves as a 'window' to God because creaturely being has its essence 'in-over' its existence, meaning that creaturely 'being' – because it is being by participation – is a revelation of God's being. This is why he holds that philosophy stands in continuity with theology: they have the same subject matter. Söhngen, in contrast, argues that creation provides a 'window' into creaturely being – *and nothing more.* 'The metaphysical *analogia entis*', he says, 'is therefore actually an analogy of *being*' – that is, it is an analogy of *creaturely being.*[63] Philosophy, therefore, will lead the knower to *himself*, not to God.

He illustrates this claim by drawing an analogy between God's creation of the world and an artist's creation of his artwork.[64] If we look at the analogy from one angle, we can see that God's relationship to creation is closer than an artist's relationship to his art, because while an artist can create a work of art, he cannot sustain and maintain it from *within* as God sustains and maintains creation. From another angle, however, we can see that when the artist creates a work of art, both the artist and the artwork remain 'within the realm of human nature and activity'. For this reason, an artist's artwork 'somehow gives form to his inner life'. That is, because the artist and his artwork exist in the same realm of being, the artist can 'impart himself in his work of art' in such a way that someone viewing it can know the inner being of the artist. But, Söhngen argues, this is precisely *not* the way God relates to creation because 'God's revelation in nature is *not* a communication of himself'.[65] God does not exist in the same realm of being as creation because God's being is not 'created and sustained' like creaturely

---

[60] *Ibid.*

[61] *Ibid.*

[62] *Ibid.*

[63] *Ibid.*, p. 199. I translated the term '*analogia entis*' into English here so Söhngen's emphasis could be captured.

[64] *Ibid.*

[65] *Ibid.*

being is. God thus does not impart his 'inner life' in the act of creation; rather, he 'shows only his exterior [life] to us here'.[66] For Söhngen, this illustrates the crucial difference between the type of knowledge available in philosophy and that which is available in theology.

> God is, according to the metaphysical concept of Thomas Aquinas, not the *subiectum* of metaphysics (as in holy theology), but only the *obiectium* or *praedicatum*, wherein we must understand the difference between subject and object in the sense of the ancients. The *subiectum* of metaphysical evidence is the '*ens commune*'; and because metaphysics as a science seeks after the causes, it so happens that God falls in its horizon as the cause of everything that is. Therefore, Thomas knows of no (natural) theology alongside ontology as an independent philosophical or metaphysical discipline.[67]

The difference between Przywara's and Söhngen's views centres upon their different interpretations of Thomas Aquinas. On the basis of his reading of Aquinas, Przywara believes that metaphysics gives us a limited but real knowledge of God, because it is reflection upon human being – which, by definition, is a being by participation in God's being. Söhngen, conversely, uses Aquinas to argue that we cannot reach any true knowledge of God on the basis of metaphysics, because reflection upon the existence of created realities is nothing more than reflection on creaturely being as such. In metaphysics, therefore, the human 'is directed to *himself*, to his human nature and to the whole realm of nature and being in which he stands'.[68] Philosophy not only fails to give us *full* knowledge of God; it fails to give us *any* knowledge of God.

Söhngen's argument clearly stands over against Przywara's position on this point, but it also leads him to an incisive critique of Barth's theology. Specifically, on the one hand, Söhngen believes that any understanding of the relationship between human being and God's being cannot be derived from philosophy; it can occur only within the context of faith and by revelation alone. On the other hand, however, he also believes that knowledge of true human 'being' really *is* given in revelation – as he demonstrated in his argument about revelation showing us the nature of human participation in the divine life. For this reason, he argues, a proper approach to analogy has to include both an *analogia entis* as well as an *analogia fidei* – as long as both terms are understood in a particular sense. Specifically, because '[h]uman nature as such does not participate at all in divine nature', we

---

[66] *Ibid.*, p. 200.
[67] *Ibid.*
[68] *Ibid.*, p. 198, emphasis added.

cannot understand the *analogia entis* in terms of its connection to philosophy.[69] It must instead be understood strictly *theologically*, because our participation in the divine being only occurs solely by faith and through Christ. We must conclude, therefore, that the *analogia entis* occurs only because of and within the *analogia fidei*. It does not describe human being as such, as Przywara contended; rather, it describes the being of the Christian who participates by faith through Christ in the triune life. Hence, the proper formula for the relation of the two analogies is '*analogia entis* within *analogia fidei*'. This construal, Söhngen argues, follows the pattern we see in the incarnation: just as Jesus Christ assumed a concrete human nature, so the *analogia fidei* assumes the concrete *analogia entis*.[70] It also, unlike Barth's view, leaves room for the Catholic Church to exist as a visible manifestation of Christ's being in the world.

Söhngen's argument shifts the debate about the *analogia entis* in two important ways. First, Söhngen's version of the *analogia entis* falls outside the scope of Barth's prior criticism of the principle. Przywara's *analogia entis* draws an analogy that involves human being as such – that is, human being as created – while Söhngen's *analogia entis* is strictly a theological concept that draws an analogy about human being *in faith*. As a result, Barth's concern that Przywara does not account for the human *in actu* – the human as sinner – does not pertain to Söhngen. Likewise, Barth's worry that Przywara's *analogia entis* establishes a relationship between God and humanity apart from God's saving action in Jesus Christ does not apply to Söhngen, since Söhngen's *analogia entis* occurs only *within* and *because of* Christ's saving action. Of course, this does not mean that Barth can simply accept Söhngen's account or his *analogia entis*; this much will become clear in due course. It does mean, however, that the two doctrines driving Barth's critique of Przywara – *sola gratia* and *simul iustus et peccator* – do not impel Barth to criticize Söhngen in exactly the same way, because Söhngen accounts for the theological implications of these doctrines in his argument.

Second, Söhngen's argument issues a strong challenge to Barth, because he rejects the notion that the *analogia fidei* can stand on its own without a corresponding account of being. Söhngen believes that, as was the case with Luther, Barth *must* talk about being when he talks about faith, because any understanding of *participatio fidei* necessarily includes within itself an account of *participatio entis*. If Christians really are justified sinners, then they are those who have their true being in Christ; this means that the *analogia fidei* cannot stand alone but must include an *analogia entis*.

---

[69] *Ibid.*, pp. 201, 204–5.

[70] See *Ibid.*, p. 208: 'That is to say: Jesus Christ, *Deus et homo, Verbum Divinum assumens humanam naturam est nostra analogia fidei assumens analogiam entis.* [Jesus Christ, God and man, divine word assuming human nature is our *analogia fidei* assuming the *analogia entis*]'.

By denying this fact, Barth is simply falling into a form of the same error he committed in his early theology: the denial of *any* tangible or visible manifestation of faith in human existence. And does this not, in effect, constitute a denial of the possibility of the incarnation as well? Does it not undermine the church as a visible institution? Does it not leave faith completely unconnected to human life? These are the questions that Söhngen's account issues to Barth, and they are questions that will be picked up by Roman Catholic readers of Barth from this point on. Does not Barth's theology – or any theology – require an *analogia entis* to speak about faith and God's relationship to the human in faith at all? Söhngen believes that it does, and for this reason, he believes not only that Barth implicitly has an *analogia entis* running throughout his theology, but that Barth's reasons for rejecting it cannot stand. In short, Söhngen believes that by Barth's own standards, Barth no longer has any reason not to become Roman Catholic.

Barth's Response to Söhngen

What are we to make of Söhngen's critique and his charge that Barth implicitly has an *analogia entis* operative within his *analogia fidei*? Barth himself issues two responses: yes and no. On the one hand, he was impressed with Söhngen's argument – enough so, in fact, to give it an extended treatment in a small-print passage in *CD* II/1. There, after working through Söhngen's argument closely, Barth draws the following conclusion:

> If this is the Roman Catholic doctrine of the *analogia entis*, then naturally I must withdraw my earlier statement that I regard the *analogia entis* as 'the invention of the anti-Christ'. And if this is what that doctrine has to say to our thesis, then we can only observe that there is every justification for the warning that participation in being is grounded in the grace of God and therefore in faith, and that substance and actuality must be brought into right relationship. If we are going to present our thesis correctly we certainly must not neglect to take heed to this warning and comply with it.[71]

Barth is making two important concessions here. First, by saying that he must withdraw his earlier statement, Barth is acknowledging that Söhngen's version of the *analogia entis* does not fall into the same category as Przywara's version. Whereas Przywara's *analogia entis* connected the insights of philosophy and theology, Söhngen's version of it functions strictly within the realm of theology. It thus does not become 'anti-*Christ*' in the technical

---

[71] *CD* II/1, p. 82; *KD* II/1, p. 90.

sense that Barth believes that Przywara's principle does; that is, whereas Przywara's version provides a way to know God apart from the revelation of God in Jesus Christ, Barth recognizes that Söhngen's *analogia entis* functions *only* because of Christ's saving work and *only* within the context of faith. This was an important development over the version of the *analogia entis* that Przywara had defended, and Barth's willingness to 'withdraw' his earlier condemnation stands as an acknowledgement of that fact.

Indeed, the primary reason that Barth stopped criticizing the *analogia entis* after *CD* II/1 is that he believed Söhngen's argument that the *analogia entis* is subordinate to the *analogia fidei* marked the beginning of a critical development in Roman Catholic theology. It was so new, in fact, that Barth initially found it 'incomprehensible how, if we look at it from the historical and practical standpoint, this conception can be accepted as authentically Roman Catholic'.[72] His attitude became more hopeful later on, however, as other young theologians, including von Balthasar, began to make arguments in the same vein as Söhngen. By the end of his career, Barth was calling Söhngen's recovery of the *analogia fidei* the harbinger 'of a new Catholic theological learning'[73] and labelling von Balthasar's theology 'a promising but, of course, unofficial movement which is apparently aiming in the direction of what we might call a Christological renaissance'.[74] This hopeful attitude does not mean, as we will see, that Barth accepts that their views stand in line with his own, because he does not do so even late in his career. It does mean, however, that a simple critique and corrective, as opposed to a polemic, is required to deal with the questions at hand.

Barth's discussion of von Balthasar's 'Christological renaissance' in *CD* IV/1 stands as a case in point. There Barth notes that von Balthasar and 'quite a chorus' of younger Catholic theologians 'wish to look again at the center, to the "author and finisher of our faith", who alone can make possible either theology itself or any attempt at ecumenical agreement'. He worries, however, about von Balthasar's insistence upon seeing the Catholic Church's saints as 'repetitions or re-enactments of [Jesus Christ's] being and activity'.[75] He is concerned, in other words, that even with his Christological focus, von Balthasar is committing a form of the same error Barth pointed out in *CD* I/1 with his warnings about Christ absorbed into the being of the church. If this is the case, Barth says, 'it unfortunately means that this

---

[72] *Ibid.*

[73] This comment is from a letter to Markus Barth in 1957, cited in Eberhard Busch, *Karl Barth: His Life from Letters and Autobiographical Texts* (Grand Rapids, MI: Eerdmans, 1994), p. 428.

[74] Karl Barth, *Church Dogmatics* IV/1 (Edinburgh: T&T Clark, 1956), p. 768; *Die Kirchliche Dogmatik* IV/1 (Zürich: Evangelischer Verlag, 1953), p. 858. Hereafter these volumes will be cited as *CD* IV/1 and *KD* IV/1 respectively.

[75] *CD* IV/1, p. 768; *KD* IV/1, pp. 858–9.

promising new beginning in Roman Catholic theology is in danger of returning to, or it may be has never left, the well-worn track on which the doctrine of justification is absorbed into sanctification – understood as the pious work of self-sanctification which man can undertake and accomplish in his own strength'. This language should sound familiar: it is *identical* to the language Barth used against Augustine, Przywara, and the *analogia entis* in 'The Holy Spirit and the Christian Life' in 1929. Barth's critique of Roman Catholic theology *has not changed*; it remains as focused as ever on problems with the Catholic construal of justification. His response to these problems, however, has become more hopeful in tone and intent. In this case, Barth ends his comment upon von Balthasar's movement with a remark about what he would do if *he* were a Roman Catholic theologian.[76] This signifies a change, not in Barth's theology, but in his approach: his objectives and his convictions remain the same, but his methods have turned from polemics to encouragement in the hope that he might help this fledgling movement catch hold in Roman Catholicism. In short, both this remark in *CD* II/1 and Barth's later work reveal that, while Barth changes his tone about the *analogia entis* after Söhngen's critique, he does so *not* because he realized he had made a mistake and changed *his* view, but because he believed that the *Roman Catholic* position had changed.

The second important concession that Barth makes to Söhngen is to accept, at least in part, Söhngen's argument about the implications of the *analogia fidei*. Barth admits that God's act of grace does, in fact, imply a *participatio entis*, and for this reason, he must heed Söhngen's warnings and account for this 'being' in his own theology. What does this mean? Barth simply is acknowledging that, by talking about the human in faith who has her true, reconciled being by participation in Christ, he is, in fact, *talking about being*. Indeed, to talk about a capacity or *Anknüpfungspunkt* at all, even if it occurs ever anew by God's act of grace, is to talk in a very particular sense about the being of the human. And to draw an analogy that involves a fallen human being who is capable of hearing and corresponding to the Word of God because she has her *true*, justified being in Christ by participation – a being that she never possess as her own but one that is truly hers inasmuch as she truly *is* justified in Christ – is to draw an analogy of *being*. In short, and to make the matter concrete: Barth realized that his talk of the correspondence of the human to the divine – the one that occurs first and perfectly in the perfect obedience of Jesus Christ and only then in the sinner as she corresponds to God on the basis of her participation in Christ's being – means that any discussion of faith necessarily includes a discussion of the human's *being in Christ*. In this sense, Söhngen was right: the *analogia fidei* implies and contains within itself an *analogia entis* – even

---

[76] *CD* IV/1, p. 768; *KD* IV/1, p. 859.

if the 'being' in the analogy is not intrinsic to the human as such, occurs only in faith, only by participation, and takes the form of correspondence in action.

That this was the case was not a surprise to Barth. After all, after rejecting Przywara's *analogia entis* in 'The Holy Spirit and the Christian Life', Barth had offered his own version of a 'true *analogia entis*', and it was nearly identical in form to the *analogia fidei*: a correspondence between God and the human that is an act of God on both sides.[77] Even in *CD* I/1, Barth notes that his presentation of the *analogia fidei* leaves him 'only a hair's breadth from the Roman Catholic doctrine of the *analogia entis*'.[78] Why does he not talk about a 'true *analogia entis*' in that volume as well? His condemnation of the *analogia entis* in the preface – and its basis in his worries about the growing attraction to natural theology in Germany – explain why he would want to avoid the term. Barth's recent experience with the misinterpretations of *Die Christliche Dogmatik* also made him careful about unclear or imprecise terminology. Barth wanted to leave no room for misunderstanding or confusion, and using the term *analogia entis* might make it possible for interpreters to conflate his very specific version of the *analogia entis* with the version offered in Roman Catholicism.

In fact, this insight about the particular nature of Barth's *analogia entis* points us to the 'no' that he says to Söhngen: while Söhngen may be correct that Barth does have to talk about a *participatio entis* – and, by implication, an *analogia entis* – if he talks about an *analogia fidei*, he is incorrect to think that Barth's definition of either term stands in line with his own. The key difference is that the *analogia entis* implied within Barth's *analogia fidei* is one that *cannot* be understood as part of the larger 'nexus of being' in which all other things exist, while Söhngen's version can. The reason this is the case is found in Söhngen's explicit rejection of the *analogia attributionis extrenseca*. Söhngen rejects this type of analogy because he believes that it sets 'faith against being, or the reality of faith against the being of the world and human reality'.[79] The analogy must be an *intrinsic* one, he argues, because otherwise the human's being in Christ stands in opposition to human being as such. Söhngen, in short, wants to retain an account in which the grace available through Jesus Christ does not stand in contradiction to, but in line with, the grace found in nature by virtue of God's act of creation. As we have seen, however, Barth simply cannot accept such an account.

---

[77] Karl Barth, *The Holy Spirit and the Christian Life: The Theological Basis of Ethics*, trans. R. Birch Hoyle (Louisville: Westminster/John Knox Press, 1993), p. 5.

[78] *CD* I/1, p. 239; *KD* I/1, p. 252.

[79] Söhngen, 'Analogia Fidei: Gottähnlichkeit', p. 120.

Barth's Extrinsic Analogy of Attribution

The reason Barth cannot accept Söhngen's account becomes clear when it is seen in the light of Barth's critique of Johann Andreas Quenstedt's analogy doctrine in a passage subsequent to his response to Söhngen in *CD* II/1.[80] Indeed, it is Barth's engagement with this seventeenth-century Lutheran theologian, whom Barth refers to as 'a summarizer of the older Protestant theology', that provides the clearest account of why Barth thinks that important differences remain between Söhngen's Roman Catholic view and his own.[81]

Quenstedt turned to analogy to address the question of whether words like essence, substance, spirit, goodness, wisdom, and justice can be predicated of God and creatures at the same time. Univocal predication is not acceptable, he argued, because a creature has characteristics in common with God only because those characteristics exist first in God, and then only secondly – and through God – in the creature. At the same time, equivocation is not acceptable because that would mean that these terms could not justly be used in reference to God at all; all predicates that humans apply to God would be null and void. The only remaining option is analogy, which for Quenstedt means that 'the same term, applied to two different objects, designates the same thing in both but in different ways'.[82] Analogical predication enables us to use single word or concept in reference to both God and the creature in such a way that the difference between God and the human is included in and with that usage. But how can this be the case? How can a term apply to God and the creature at the same time, even if it applies to each one differently?

To answer these questions, Quenstedt turns to several traditional Scholastic definitions of analogy, including many of the same definitions that Przywara used in his exposition of the *analogia entis*. Quenstedt argues that the analogy between God and creature cannot be an *analogia inaequalitatis*, because this analogy is used when there is a similarity between two species of the same genus. Clearly, this is not the case with God and the creature. The analogy also cannot be an *analogia proportionalitatis*, because this analogy is used when some predications agree but others disagree – and this would mean that we could not apply the words in question to both God *and* the creature. The analogy, therefore, must be an *analogia attributionis*, which he takes to mean 'a similarity of two objects which consist in the fact

---

[80] See Johann Andreas Quenstedt, *Theologica Didactio Polemica sive Systema Theologicum* (Lipsiae: Thomam Fritsch, 1715). All of Barth's citations from Part I, *caput 9*, *sectio 2*, *quaestio 1*. I am grateful for to the Special Collections Library at Princeton Theological Seminary for granting me access to this rare manuscript.

[81] *CD* II/1, p. 238; *KD* II/1, p. 269.

[82] *CD* II/1, p. 237; *KD* II/1, p. 268.

that what is common to them exists first and properly in the one, and then, because a second is dependent upon it, in the second'.[83] For Quenstedt, the fact that it exists 'properly' in each analogue means that the characteristic in common exists in each one *intrinsically*. In other words, for there to be a comparison between two objects, each one really must *possess* the characteristic in common – even if that possession occurs in a definite order, with one dependent upon the other. For this reason, Quenstedt holds that the most precise formulation of the analogy between God and the creature is *analogia attributionis intrinsecae*. Only this kind of analogy, he believes, makes it possible to apply a single word to both God and the creature, because it is the only one that captures the fact that God and the creature really do share a characteristic in common, although the characteristic exists in God first and the creature second.

This account of analogy stands in line with Söhngen's argument where he criticized Barth for having an '*analogia attributionis mere extrinsecae*' because it set 'faith against being'.[84] Like Quenstedt, Söhngen believes that any analogy drawn between God and the human must be an *intrinsic* analogy of attribution, because the comparison must involve a characteristic that is proper first to God and then to the human.[85] He also believes that Barth, whether he is willing to admit it or not, also employs this kind of intrinsic analogy in his version of the *analogia fidei*. Barth clearly understands this criticism and its relevance, as his remarks about Söhngen's argument demonstrates, and he uses his analysis of Quenstedt to respond to it. Specifically, when he asks in reference to Quenstedt, 'Have we said the same thing as he?' he also, in effect, is asking: 'Is Söhngen's argument against my position correct?'[86]

Barth's answer begins with a point of commonality: he agrees with Quenstedt about the necessity of analogy when it comes to talk about God. The use of analogy is appropriate, he says, because neither univocal nor equivocal predication is adequate.[87] He also concurs with Quenstedt that

---

[83] *CD* II/1, p. 238; *KD* II/1, p. 268.

[84] Söhngen, 'Analogia Fidei: Gottähnlichkeit', p. 120.

[85] As we saw in the exposition of *Analogia Entis*, Przywara also employed an *analogia attributionis intrinsecae*, although he does not use that term. In his construal, the creature possess its being as a result of God's act of creation, although this possession is not complete in the midst of existence, because the creature's essence is 'in-over' its existence. Even so, in its limited, contingent, and dependent existence, the creature's being truly is *intrinsic* to it, because if it did not possess its being at all, the creature would not exist as a being distinct from God. To be a creature at all, therefore, is to posses one's being, even if only in part. Clearly, then, the final form of Przywara's *analogia entis* falls within this type of analogy.

[86] *CD* II/1, p. 238; *KD* II/1, p. 269.

[87] The reason stems from his own dialectic of veiling and unveiling in revelation: 'We are forced to decide against the *univoce* because it conflicts with the confession of God's

the analogy between God and the creature must be an *analogia attributionis*, since an *analogia inaequalitatis* and an *analogia proportionalitatis* fail for precisely the reasons Quenstedt noted. He rejects, however, Quenstedt's argument that this analogy has to be an *analogia attributionis intrinsecae*, and it is here that Barth's argument against Quensted applies to Söhngen. Quenstedt believes that for the analogy to apply at all, it has to apply to characteristics that both God and the creature possess intrinsically, even if the creature possesses those characteristics 'dependently and by participation'.[88] Söhngen holds the same view, and in fact, this idea is working in the background of his argument that the *analogia fidei* cannot be set against 'the being of the world and human reality'.[89] His worry is that, by divorcing faith from human being as such, faith no longer has any connection to real human being at all. Note, however, that Söhngen assumes that the 'being' of the human remains constant both inside and outside of faith. That is, the being of the human as created stands in continuity with the being of the human in faith, so that any analogy drawn from within the context of faith must connect to the 'being of the world' – the being shared by all creatures by virtue of their creation by God. This assumption marks the dividing line between Söhngen's and Barth's views, because Barth rejects it. He does so because he believes that, if this assumption were true, the truth about God and God's relationship to humanity revealed in Jesus Christ would inevitably become 'only a modification of the general truth of being'.[90] Barth's concerns about the larger 'nexus of being' determining the shape of God's self-revelation – as well as his longstanding worries about the misuse of theology to enlist God as a partner in one's own sinful endeavours – come to the fore here. If an *analogia attributionis intrinsecae* could be drawn between God and the human with the result that God and God's revelation stands in continuity with human existence as such, then the believer's knowledge of God in faith would be of the same genre as her knowledge of other things in this world. For Barth, this means that almost anything in human existence has the potential to stand in continuity with divine revelation. As a result, he argues that the 'being' of the human in faith – because it stands in continuity with human being as such – could be interpreted so that it fits into preconceived notions of a moralistic, humanistic, transcendental, or even 'German' being.[91] For this reason, Barth says, the most worrisome

---

veiling in His revelation, and against the *aequivoce* because it contradicts the confession of His unveiling; against the one as against the other because it cannot be united with the confession of God's grace in His revelation'. See *CD* II/1, p. 240; *KD* II/1, p. 271.

[88] *CD* II/1, p. 238; *KD* II/1, p. 269

[89] Söhngen, 'Analogia Fidei: Gottähnlichkeit', p. 120.

[90] *CD* II/1, p. 241; *KD* II/1, p. 272.

[91] *Ibid.*

aspect of Quenstedt's analogy is the fact that 'it is an arbitrary presupposition'.[92] The same critique applies to Söhngen's analogy as well, and given the historical context, this criticism carries a special significance.

To correct the problem that he sees in Quenstedt's and Söhngen's account of analogy, Barth turns to Luther's *sola gratia* and *simul iustus et peccator*, and these doctrines serve his argument in two ways. First, they provide a basis for his affirmation of an extrinsic analogy between God and the human, because he believes that this kind of analogy avoids the problem of placing human being as such in continuity with human being in faith; and second, they provide him a way to explain why his view does not divorce faith from human being in the way Söhngen had claimed. To this end, Barth insists that if Quenstedt had 'remembered the Lutheran doctrine of the forgiveness of sins by grace alone', then he would have avoided an intrinsic analogy between God and the human, because this analogy stands in stark contradiction to 'grace of revelation' – that is, to the Word of God in Jesus Christ. Specifically, he argues that those characteristics which 'convert the creature into an analogue of God do not lie in [the creature] itself and its nature'.[93] Instead, that which 'converts the creature into an analogue of God' is something that lies completely outside the creature as such. Any analogy between God and the human, therefore, must have its basis 'in the doctrine of the justification of the sinner by faith', and this means that it must be an *analogia attributionis extrenseca*.[94]

What does Barth mean by this term? It is clear what he does *not* mean. He does not mean that Söhngen's description of his view as an '*analogia attributionis mere extrinsecae*' is accurate. If this were the case – that is, if he were saying that he believes that this view is correct, despite Söhngen's critique – it would constitute an immediate retraction of the remarks Barth *had just made* about the need to 'take heed' and 'comply' with Söhngen's arguments about the need to account for 'being' of the human in his account of the *analogia fidei*.[95] Barth clearly does not mean, then, that his account of analogy has no real connection to the being of the human at all. Barth also does not mean that there is no connection at all between characteristics or concepts that apply to the human and those that apply to God, as if there were no continuity between the meaning of those characteristics or concepts as they are applied to the two parties in the analogy. While many

---

[92] *CD* II/1, p. 243; *KD* II/1, p. 275. Barth explains that the arbitrariness is derived from the fact that this view establishes 'a relationship between creator and the creature which as such can be known even apart from the knowledge of God in Jesus Christ'. See *CD* II/1, pp. 239–40; *KD* II/1, p. 271.

[93] *CD* II/1, p. 239; *KD* II/1, p. 270.

[94] *CD* II/1, p. 242; *KD* II/1, p. 274.

[95] See Söhngen, 'Analogia Fidei: Gottähnlichkeit', p. 124, and Barth, *CD* II/1, p. 82; *KD* II/1, p. 90.

interpreters believe that this is precisely what Barth is saying in this passage, this view is based on a misunderstanding of Barth's argument.[96] The key to grasping Barth's true meaning here is to keep the pattern of Luther's *simul iustus et peccator* in mind, because this doctrine is governing his argument. For Luther, the believer's righteousness is not something he possesses in and of himself, but rather, it is his only by virtue of his *participation* in the being of Jesus Christ (*participatio Christi*). In line with this pattern, Barth argues that the believer becomes 'objectively another man' in the event of revelation, because this revelation reveals the 'unveiled reality' of the believer's true existence in Christ.[97] This 'reality' is not the believer's possession, however, but something that he has only in and through his relationship to Christ.

> There can be no doubt that the biblical witnesses remain true to themselves on this point. By pointing to the man in the cosmos, they point to a certain extent through him to the man of the revelation of God, i.e., to the man who, in the covenant of God with His people, in the unity of the members of the body of Christ with their Head, is a participant in the divine good-pleasure and therefore in the knowledge of God. They do not consider taking man in the cosmos seriously and addressing him in his 'nature' – which really means in his self-understanding. Rather, they say to him that he no longer really exists as such; that in his self-understanding he now exists only in one monstrous misunderstanding. For his original and proper truth has been opened up to him by God's revelation. They point through him to the One with whom God is well pleased, to the man Jesus of Nazareth, to the judgment fulfilled in Him, to the grace which man has found before God in Him . . . They do not point to a truth which man in the cosmos already possessed somewhere and somehow . . . His truth to which they point is not his truth as he had fetched it out from somewhere within himself, but his lost truth as it has now become new to him and come upon him.[98]

For Barth, the *true* reality of the believer, therefore, is not what the human is by virtue of his creation, but rather, it is what the human is *in Christ*. This

---

[96] Richard H. Roberts, for example, argues that such a view provides the 'illusory security of a theology which unfolds itself apart from the natural order and which, in attempting to recreate everything, appears to find itself in possession of nothing'. See Richard H. Roberts, *A Theology on its Way? Essays on Karl Barth* (Edinburgh: T&T Clark, 1991), p. 64. For a related critique, see Jay Wesley Richards, 'Barth on the Divine "Conscription" of Language', *Heythrop Journal* 38, no. 3 (1997), pp. 247–66.

[97] *CD* II/1, p. 110; *KD* II/1, p. 122.

[98] *CD* II/1, pp. 112–13; *KD* II/1, p. 124.

insight helps us see how Barth conceives of the *analogia attributionis extrenseca*. By affirming an extrinsic analogy, Barth is not saying that concepts or characteristics that apply to God do not apply in any way to human creatures, such that there is no continuity between them. This would mark a retreat back into the equivocation he had just rejected, and as Barth says, 'we do not attribute to our views, concepts, and words a purely fictional capacity, so that the use we make of them is always hedged in by the reservation of an "as if"'.[99] Barth does, in fact, hold that, in an analogy between God and the human, the concepts and characteristics used in that analogy apply to both parties so that there is continuity between their application to God and their application to the human. His key distinction, however, is that this continuity is the result of God's grace in Jesus Christ *alone*. In other words, Barth denies that an analogy can be drawn between God and the human as a function of those characteristics that are understood to belong to the human by virtue of his or her creation by God, because the human in analogy with God is the human *in Christ*, and the being of this human is *objectively distinct* from the being of the human as such. This distinction between the being of the human as created and the being of the human in Christ is what Barth is affirming in his use of an extrinsic analogy of attribution. That is, since knowledge of God occurs by way of the revelation of Jesus Christ alone, any analogy between God and the human has its basis on the relationship that the believer has with Christ and that relationship alone. This relationship does not stand in continuity with human being as such, because the human 'in Christ' is an objectively different human than the human as such.[100]

---

[99] *CD* II/1, p. 228; *KD* II/1, p. 257.

[100] Quenstedt, of course, is not alone among Protestant theologians in holding a view contrary to this one. Barth calls him merely an example of the 'happy inconsistency of Protestant orthodoxy in its general handling of natural theology'. This inconsistency explains the reasons behind Barth's disagreement with Brunner, who argues in 'Nature and Grace' that the being of the human in faith cannot stand in contradiction to the being of the human as such, and that this position stands in line with the one held by the Reformers. Barth's counter-argument is that Brunner's position rests 'fundamentally upon an insufficient appreciation of the place of the Reformers in the history of dogma'. That is, the Reformers 'could not clearly perceive the range of the decisive connection which exists in the Roman Catholic system between the problem of justification and the problem of the knowledge of God, between reconciliation and revelation'. But now, with the perspective gained through an encounter with the 'secularized Thomism' of their own time, a modern theologian who seeks to uphold the Reformers' basic insights has to hold a position *different* than that of the Reformers themselves. 'If we really wish to maintain the Reformers' position . . . we are not in a position today to repeat the statements of Luther and Calvin without at the same time making them more pointed than they themselves did.' Quenstedt provides a clear illustration of why this is the case, and Barth's 'Nein!' to Brunner – as well as his critique of the *analogia entis* – is the product of his desire to make the

This distinction marks the fault line dividing Barth's view of analogy from the one offered by Söhngen. Specifically, while Barth says 'yes' to Söhngen's notion that the *analogia fidei* implies a participation in 'being', he says 'no' to the idea that the 'being' of the Christian stands in continuity with the 'being of the world' in such a way that it could be seen as one element within the 'greater nexus of being'. It is helpful to recall that the motivation behind Barth's criticism of Augustine in 'The Holy Spirit and the Christian Life' was the fact that Augustine saw the Holy Spirit merely as *distinct from* rather than *opposed to* the human spirit; this allowed Augustine to posit the existence of a continuity between human action and divine action that blended justification with sanctification in the Christian life. Inasmuch as he believes that Söhngen holds that the faith – and the believer's being in Christ – stands not in complete opposition but rather in continuity with human being as such, then he is committing a form of the same error. The form of Söhngen's error, of course, is different from the one Przywara committed. For Przywara, the error occurred because the *analogia entis* between God and the creature applied to creation as a whole, meaning that philosophy and theology ultimately had the same subject matter. Söhngen, as we have seen, rejects such a view. For him, the *analogia entis* occurs only within the context of faith and God's justifying act. Even so, like Augustine and Przywara, Söhngen believes that God's justifying act does not stand in opposition to the 'being of the world and human reality'; rather, God's act stands in continuity with human reality because it manifests itself in and through that reality in the believer's moral life. Such continuity *has* to exist, of course, because otherwise the Roman Catholic notion that God's grace manifests itself through the visible righteousness of the Christian – not to mention the doctrine that the Catholic Church exists as the visible manifestation of the 'body of Christ' in the world – could not be maintained. From Barth's point of view, however, this means that the 'being' under discussion in Söhngen's analogy of being is in the same genre as the 'being' of humans and institutions like the church. Both the analogy and these human entities are defined strictly in terms of faith; but even so, they both can be seen as 'lines in a greater nexus of being' shared by other entities in this world.[101] This is why Barth cannot accept the notion that Söhngen's version of '*analogia entis* within *analogia fidei*' stands in continuity with the version of that formula operative in his own theology. Indeed, Söhngen's argument, while helpful in pointing out formal similarities between their views, fails to recognize the material differences between them.

Reformers insights 'more pointed' to address the challenges of his own time. See *CD* II/1, p. 242; *KD* II/1, p. 273, and Barth, 'Nein!', pp. 100–1.

[101] *CD* I/1, p. 36; *KD* I/1, p. 35.

The Nature of Barth's Change with Regard to the analogia entis

Barth's response to Söhngen demonstrates clearly that his rejection of the *analogia entis* – that is, his rejection of Przywara's version of it – has not been lifted. He still rejects the principle, and he does so for the same reasons as before. He has changed, however, the nature of his response to the problem of the *analogia entis*. Specifically, Barth has realized that there are other ways of construing the *analogia entis* than the one Przywara offered, and he believes that, in the case of Söhngen and eventually von Balthasar, these new versions have been influenced by his own position inasmuch as they are making real attempts to incorporate his basic insights into their construal.

Barth's preface to Hans Küng's volume on Barth's doctrine of justification provides a helpful insight here. In the book, Küng makes an argument that is similar to Söhngen's argument in that he is attempting to show that the Roman Catholic doctrine of justification stands closer to Barth's own view than Barth realizes. In response to this argument – and in line with his response to Söhngen – Barth wryly remarks that if Küng's presentation is correct, then he will have to make a 'contrite confession' that he has misrepresented Roman Catholic theology. However, before he does so, he wants to ask Küng a question: 'How do you explain the fact that all this could remain hidden so long, and from so many, both outside and inside the [Catholic] Church? And now, for my own salvation, may I just whisper a question . . . Did you yourself discover all this before you so carefully read my *Church Dogmatics* or was it while you were reading it afterward?'[102] Barth's point is clear: even if Küng's presentation of the Roman Catholic doctrine of justification is correct, Barth believes that he may not have arrived at it without first encountering Barth's critique. Barth suspects, in other words, that Küng's reading of the *CD*, and his desire to respond to it, gave him eyes to see aspects of his own Roman Catholic tradition that both he and other Catholics were unable to see before.[103] Barth could ask Söhngen a similar question. Would he have been able to discover that the *analogia fidei* is so prominently embedded in the Catholic tradition had he not been prompted to do so by Barth? Would he, and later von Balthasar,

---

[102] Karl Barth, 'A Letter to the Author', in Hans Küng, *Justification: The Doctrine of Karl Barth and a Catholic Reflection*, 40th Anniversary Edition (Louisville, KY: John Knox Press, 2004), pp. lxviii–lxix.

[103] Henri de Lubac's observation that dogmatic disputes with Protestants often put Roman Catholics on guard 'against one-sided formulates which, though harmless in the past, can be fraught with danger today' is helpful here, because something similar occurred in both Söhngen's and Küng's case. See Henri de Lubac, *The Mystery of the Supernatural*, trans. Rosemary Sheed (New York: Herder & Herder, 1998), p. 26.

have seen the need to subordinate the *analogia entis* to the *analogia fidei* if Barth had not issued such a strong rejection of the *analogia entis*? In this light, as Barth sees things, those who criticize him for failing to recognize the fact that the *analogia entis* is embedded in an *analogia fidei* within the Roman Catholic tradition are, among other things, blaming him for not recognizing something that *they themselves* were unable to see before he helped them see it.

Regardless of how Söhngen came to his formulation, however, it is clear that the change in Barth's response to the *analogia entis* stems from the fact that he sees a new potential for true dialogue with his Roman Catholic interlocutors. To this end, he realizes that repeating his prior criticism of the *analogia entis* will not be helpful to promoting such dialogue. He also thinks, however, that the question of whether his *analogia fidei* implies an *analogia entis* fails to strike at the heart of the difference between his view and the Catholic position. For Barth, the key issue involves a clear understanding of the implications of justification by grace through faith alone. This doctrine, he believes, marks the dividing line between his view of analogy and *every* Roman Catholic construal. The same issue that divided Luther from Rome divides Barth from Przywara, Söhngen, and von Balthasar – although in different ways in each case. For Barth, the key question is not whether an *analogia entis* exists; the question is whether an *analogia entis* is understood in light of the particularity of God's grace in Jesus Christ.

7

ANALOGY IN COVENANT

Through him all things were made; without him nothing was made that has been made.

– Jn 1.3

Analogy, even as the analogy of relation, does not entail likeness but the correspondence of the unlike.

– Karl Barth[1]

Introduction

The question occupying the second part of the book is whether Barth, due to the realization that he had made a mistake or due to shifts in his theology, changed his mind about the *analogia entis* and adopted a version of it as his own. The previous chapter provided an answer to this question with respect to Barth's theology in the years between his rejection of Przywara's *analogia entis* in *Church Dogmatics* I/1 (*CD* I/1) and his response to the arguments of Gottlieb Söhngen in *CD* II/1. There we saw that Barth conceded that he must heed Söhngen's 'warning' that the *analogia fidei* implies a *participatio entis*, and he agreed that, in light of the formula '*analogia entis* within *analogia fidei*', his condemnation of the *analogia entis* as 'the invention of the anti-Christ' should be withdrawn.[2] This concession, however, does not signal a change of mind about his rejection of Przywara's *analogia entis* in 1929 and again in 1932. Barth retained this criticism, even as he softened his critique of Roman Catholic formulations, because he rightly believed that Söhngen's version of the *analogia entis* was a departure from Przywara's interpretation of the doctrine. The softening of Barth's critique of the

---

[1] Karl Barth, *Church Dogmatics* III/1 (Edinburgh: T&T Clark, 1958), p. 196; *Die Kirchliche Dogmatik* III/1 (Zürich: Evangelischer-Verlag, 1945), p. 220. Hereafter these volumes will be cited as *CD* III/1 and *KD* III/1 respectively.

[2] *CD* II/1, p. 82; *KD* II/1, p. 90.

analogia entis, therefore, reveals only that Barth believed that the *Roman Catholic* position had changed to the extent that he no longer needed to criticize it in the same way as he had before. We also saw that, with respect to Barth's engagement with Söhngen's version of the *analogia entis*, the key question is not whether Barth has an *analogia entis* at all in his theology, because Barth does, in fact, have one; rather, the question is whether his version of the *analogia entis* stands in continuity with Söhngen's version of it. To this end, we demonstrated that Barth's version of the '*analogia entis* within an *analogia fidei*' is substantively different from Söhngen's because Barth's version is understood strictly in light of the particularity of God's grace in Jesus Christ, which means that, for Barth, human 'being' in faith does not stand in continuity with human 'being' as such because of the effects of the Fall and Christ's work of justification.

In this chapter, I will argue that the same conclusions can be drawn about Barth's mature theology: in the later volumes of the *CD*, Barth remains committed to his rejection of Przywara's *analogia entis*, and the version of the *analogia entis* operative within Barth's theology does not stand in continuity with Roman Catholic versions of it. In other words, Barth never changes his mind about what he had previously rejected, and while Barth's theology shifts in the later volumes of the *CD*, this shift does not alter the fundamental distinction between his construal of the relationship between God and humanity and the construal offered by his Roman Catholic critics. These claims, however, stand in stark opposition to arguments made by Hans Urs von Balthasar on the same topic. Von Balthasar believes that Barth at least implicitly changed his mind about the *analogia entis* in the later volumes of the CD, and he also insists that Barth's account of the relationship between God and humanity corresponds to Roman Catholic accounts to such an extent that Barth's formulation is 'Catholic in the fullest sense of the word'.[3] He argues, in fact, that in light of the changes in Barth's theology, Roman Catholics now can 'harmonize the inalienable demands of the Church as promulgated above all by Vatican I with the essential insights of Karl Barth without artificial or forced syncretism'.[4] In other words, von Balthasar believes that, in the later volumes of the *CD*, Barth's theology has changed to such an extent that he now accepts Roman Catholic formulations of the core doctrinal issues at stake in the debate over the *analogia entis*.

Clearly, von Balthasar's account of Barth's theology stands in contradiction to my own. To establish my claims, I will show that von Balthasar's reading of Barth on these matters is incorrect, and that Barth's use of

---

[3] Hans Urs von Balthasar, *The Theology of Karl Barth: Exposition and Interpretation*, trans. S. J. Edward T. Oakes (San Francisco: Ignatius Press, 1992), p. 118.

[4] *Ibid.*, p. 382.

analogy does not correspond to Roman Catholic formulations. This argument will be developed by means of three sections: in the first section, I will provide a summary of von Balthasar's interpretation of Barth on the matters relevant to the debate about the *analogia entis*; in the second, I will show how and why von Balthasar's interpretation of Barth misses the mark; and in the third, I will demonstrate that my claims correspond to the theology of the volumes of the *CD* written subsequent to von Balthasar's critique of Barth while von Balthasar's claims do not. This argument will show that although Barth posits continuity between God and the human, this continuity has its basis solely in God's election of humanity in Jesus Christ. This construal, as we will see, stands as the fulfilment of Barth's rejection of Przywara's *analogia entis* rather than a retreat from it, and it also demonstrates the stark differences between Barth's theology and Roman Catholic theology.

Von Balthasar's Interpretation of Barth

Von Balthasar's arguments about Barth's use of analogy began with a series of essays in the 1940s and culminated with his book *The Theology of Karl Barth*, which incorporated the earlier material in a revised form. When analysing von Balthasar's claims in this book, it is important to keep two factors in mind. First, von Balthasar's arguments are shaped at every turn by his ecumenical intentions. One of von Balthasar's primary reasons for writing the book is to convince Roman Catholics that Barth's theology is worth reading, and to this end – even though he is not afraid of offering critical judgements about Barth's theology – his underlying intent is to build bridges between Barth and Roman Catholics. One consequence of this goal is that von Balthasar is often led to argue that Barth's criticisms of Roman Catholic theology are based upon a misunderstanding of it. These arguments are meant to convince his Roman Catholic readers, and perhaps Barth himself, that the differences between them are more apparent than real. These claims, however, often misrepresent Barth's criticisms, because they fail to account for the historical context in which those criticisms were initially issued.

To illustrate this problem, consider von Balthasar's argument that Barth's rejection of Przywara's *analogia entis* is based upon a misunderstanding of it. This argument is central to von Balthasar's interpretation of Barth, and to entitle himself to it, he regularly cites texts from Przywara that demonstrate that the latter is not guilty of Barth's charges. Many of the texts that von Balthasar cites, however, were written years *after* Barth's critique was issued. For example, in his summary of 'what Erich Przywara actually meant by his formula, analogy of being', von Balthasar uses texts written in 1940 and 1949 to clarify some of Przywara's key claims from *Analogia Entis*, and he then uses *this* account to make the case that 'nothing whatever can be found of that ogre that Barth has made of the analogy of being'.[5] These later texts, however, reflect the fact that Przywara continued to clarify his account of the meaning and content of the *analogia entis* in the years following both Barth's and Söhngen's criticism of it. This clarification resulted in a significantly different description of the doctrine. Indeed, von Balthasar himself divides Przywara's development into two phases: there is a 'first phase', culminating with the publication of *Analogia Entis*, during which Przywara's *analogia entis* can 'seem like a philosophical constructed system'; and there is a 'second period', taking place in the years *after* the publication of *Analogia Entis*, where Przywara's *analogia entis* is 'set out more clearly in all its theological contexts'.[6] Barth's rejection of Przywara's *analogia entis*, of course, is based upon texts from the 'first phase' of Przywara's development. Thus, when von Balthasar cites texts from Przywara's 'second period' to make the case that 'nothing' can be found in Przywara's account that resembles Barth's description of it, he is citing texts that present an account of the *analogia entis* that *did not exist* when Barth issued his critique. This leads to the incorrect judgement that Barth misunderstood Przywara. In reality, as we have seen, Barth understood Przywara's early formulations of the *analogia entis* correctly. Przywara's account of the *analogia entis* in his 'second period' has a theological clarity to it that simply is not present in the early formulations, and this clarity is a function, in part, of Przywara's desire to respond to the criticism he had received from Barth and other theologians.[7] To accuse Barth of misunderstanding Przywara on the basis of these later texts, then, is to accuse him of failing to understand a version of the *analogia entis* that arose only in the future and only as a product of his critique. We may assume that Von Balthasar is not trying to misrepresent Barth's view here, but rather, he simply is trying to build bridges between Barth's theology and Roman Catholic theology by making the case that Barth's critique does not apply to how Przywara *currently* understands the *analogia*

---

[5] See *Ibid.*, pp. 255–7. The texts cited are Erich Przywara, 'Philosophy', in *Philosophisches Jahrbuch* (1949), pp. 1–9; and Przywara, 'Die Reichweite der Analogie als katholischer Grundform', in *Scholastik*, vol. 3 (1940), p. 527.

[6] Balthasar, *The Theology of Karl Barth*, p. 255.

[7] In his 'second period', Przywara developed his own version of the *analogia fidei*, one that is subordinate to the *analogia entis*. Bernhard Gertz notes that this move to 'biblical theology' and the *analogia fidei* 'became important for Przywara as a way of responding to Barth and Söhngen'. See Gertz, *Glaubenswelt als Analogie: Die Theologische Analogielehre Erich Przywaras und ihr Ort in der Auseinandersetzung um die Analogie Fidei* (Düsseldorf: Patmos-Verlag, 1969), p. 105. Also see Eberhard Mechels, *Analogie bei Erich Przywara und Karl Barth: Das Verhältnis von Offenbarungstheologie und Metaphysic* (Neukirchen-Vluyn: Neukirchener Verlag, 1974), pp. 40–63 and 188–99. For an example of Przywara's 'biblical theology', see *Alter und Neuer Bund: Theologie der Stunde* (Wien: Verlag Herold, 1956).

entis. Even so, because it does not do justice to the historical context in which Barth's interpretation occurred, von Balthasar's account leads to a misrepresentation of the true state of affairs. This example illustrates why it is important to keep the ecumenical impulses driving von Balthasar's argument in mind as we encounter his arguments about Barth's theology. Regardless of von Balthasar's intentions, these impulses often cause him to bend his interpretation of both Barth and Roman Catholic sources in ways that can be misleading.

Second, it is important to remember that, because von Balthasar's book was published in 1951, his conclusions about Barth's theology were drawn on the basis of an incomplete picture of it. That is to say, none of the volumes published after *CD* III/3 had been released by the time von Balthasar composed his book, and this means that von Balthasar's claims about Barth's theology were made without the benefit of seeing the volumes that make up *CD* IV. This is unfortunate, because many of the dogmatic decisions made from *CD* II/2 onward become clearer when seen in the light of their culmination in Barth's Christology. Hence, even though von Balthasar's book is the result of nearly two decades of thinking about Barth's theology in conversation with a 'sensitive awareness of the most important Catholic replies, above all those of Erich Przywara and Gottlieb Söhngen', his judgements about Barth were made while Barth was 'midstream' in his theological development, and they provide only a partial picture of Barth's thought.[8]

This second point perhaps explains why von Balthasar came to some of the conclusions he did about Barth's theology, and specifically about this interpretation of the *analogia entis*. As he approached his study, the debate about the *analogia entis* remained largely unchanged since Barth's response to Söhngen in *CD* II/1. Barth had conceded that his use of analogy implied a participation in 'being' – and thus that he had an analogy of being in his theology – but he still insisted that his account of human 'being' did not correspond to Roman Catholic accounts, because he defined human 'being' in terms of God's act in Jesus Christ rather than in terms of God's act in creation. Von Balthasar seeks to challenge Barth's self-interpretation and show that Barth's *analogia fidei* and *analogia relationis* both contain an implicit *analogia entis* that is a function of God's act in creation. If proven accurate, this argument will enable him to claim that, despite what Barth himself may believe, Barth's theology operates upon the same ground as Roman Catholic theology to such an extent that it is 'not really possible to construct any genuine contradiction' between them.[9] To this end, von Balthasar sees his task as two-fold. First, he must undermine Barth's account of an *extrinsic* analogy of attribution between God and the creature, because this

---

[8] *Ibid.*, p. xviii.
[9] *Ibid.*, p. 308.

analogy enables Barth to claim that, even though the *analogia fidei* implies a 'participation in being', it does not correspond to the Roman Catholic *analogia entis*. Second, he must show that Barth's *analogia relationis* implies an *analogia entis* in the same way that the *analogia fidei* does, because it is predicated upon the assumption, shared by Roman Catholics, that God's act in creation and God's act in Jesus Christ take place within 'one interlocking order'.[10] These two tasks work together to form one overarching claim: that Barth's theology, like Roman Catholic theology, views God's act in creation as the presupposition of God's act of reconciliation in Jesus Christ. If von Balthasar can establish this claim, then it undermines the distinction that Barth pointed to when he distinguished his doctrine of analogy from Söhngen's doctrine.

To accomplish the first of these tasks, von Balthasar makes the case that Barth's 'extrinsic' analogy of attribution presupposes an already-existing *intrinsic* analogy that corresponds to the one found in the Roman Catholic *analogia entis*.[11] Recall that Barth understood his analogy to be 'extrinsic' in the sense that he rejected the idea that the characteristics drawn together in the analogy between God and the human are inherent to the human as such; he claimed, rather, that they are given to the human by grace and must be understood in terms of the believer's participation in the being of Jesus Christ. Von Balthasar challenges the notion that the being of the creature can be defined in terms of Christ's being, because he believes that the revelation of Christ to the creature already presupposes that the creature is intrinsically related to God. 'For if it is in fact true', he argues, 'that the "authentic" truth of the creature resides in God, then it is indeed *God's* truth, created and established by Him. This being so, this truth must be, not extrinsic, but intrinsic. In other words, it is the very expression of the creature's essence that it be God's creature'.[12] The issue von Balthasar is pressing here is Barth's insistence that he can define the being of the human by reference to Jesus Christ. Von Balthasar rejects that notion, because if the human were defined in terms of its reference to Jesus Christ – and if this truth about the human is the fulfilment of God's will *for* the human – then this truth is, in fact, the essential and intrinsic truth of the human as such. Indeed, as von Balthasar interprets it, Barth's account of divine revelation illustrates this point. He argues that even though Barth claims that creation is 'dependent ontically and noetically on God's revelation in Christ, it is just as true that we can glimpse in this revelation a presupposition lying at its foundations that makes revelation possible'.[13] What is this presupposition?

---

[10] *Ibid.*, p. 165. For von Balthasar, as we will see, this interlocking order takes shape in Barth's theology in the relationship between creation and covenant.

[11] *Ibid.*, p. 110.

[12] *Ibid.*

[13] *Ibid.*, p. 112.

Von Balthasar points to the fact that the event of revelation itself presupposes that God acted to create an 'other' to whom he would reveal himself. This act of creation thus reveals a divine will *for* the human, and it establishes that there is a pre-existing 'compatibility between God and the creature' *before* the event of revelation of Jesus Christ takes place.[14] Since this compatibility defines human being as such, it demonstrates that Barth's understanding of the 'extrinsic' being of the creature 'in Christ' presupposes an 'intrinsic' relationship between God and the creature that exists as a result of creation alone. In other words, in von Balthasar's view, Barth's 'extrinsic' analogy is incoherent, because God's act in Jesus Christ presupposes God's prior act in creation. 'For if revelation is centered in Jesus Christ', he argues, 'there must by definition be a periphery to this centre. Thus, as we say, the order of the incarnation presupposes the order of creation, which is not identical with it'.[15] This presupposition means that creation itself stands in continuity with God, because God's will for creation – that which defines it by nature – is that creation be brought to fulfilment in Jesus Christ. In short, even though Barth believes that his 'extrinsic' analogy of attribution divided his *analogia fidei* from the Roman Catholic *analogia entis*, his view actually presupposes the same intrinsic relationship between God and creation that Roman Catholics use to derive the *analogia entis*.

Von Balthasar approaches the second task – to explain why Barth's *analogia relationis* presupposes an *analogia entis* – in the same way, because he believes that Barth's mistake is the same: he has failed to realize the Catholic assumptions underlying his affirmations about God's relationship to humans in Jesus Christ. In *CD* III/1–2, Barth develops the *analogia relationis* as way of maintaining his commitment to the notion that any analogy between God and the human must be a function of God's action upon the human rather than any innate characteristics of the human.[16] The logic of Barth's analogy works as follows: the relation between God and the human Jesus corresponds to the relations between the eternal Father and the eternal Son; the relation between the human Jesus and humanity in general corresponds to the relation between the human Jesus and God; the relation between humans to other humans correspond to the relationship between the human Jesus and humanity; and thus, the relation between humans to other humans correspond to the relations within the Trinity. This correspondence in relationship, with Jesus Christ at the centre, is how a human

---

[14] *Ibid.*, p. 114.

[15] *Ibid.*, p. 163.

[16] Barth adapted his account of this analogy from Dietrich Bonhoeffer, who posited an *analogia relationis* in opposition to the *analogia entis* in his theological exegesis of Gen. 1–3. See Bonhoeffer, *Creation and Fall: A Theological Interpretation of Genesis 1–3*, trans. John C. Fletcher (New York: Macmillan, 1959), p. 37.

exists in analogy to God.[17] The human is not in an analogy of 'being' with God, Barth thinks – as if it were the characteristics in correspondence in the analogy were intrinsic to human being itself – but rather, the human is in analogy to God inasmuch in her self-giving relationships to others she corresponds, through Christ by the power of the Holy Spirit, to the relationships of self-giving within the Trinity. For von Balthasar, however, this formulation again is based upon an underlying ontological presupposition.

> For example, interhuman relationships – between man and woman or between friends – are a true presupposition for the fact that Jesus can become our brother. It is *because* man is a social being who lives by intersubjective relationships that he is capable in the first place of entering into a covenant with God, as God has intended. And *this* natural order is for its part only possible on the basis of God's own interpersonal nature, his true nature, of which the human being is a true image. Certainly one can call this an *analogia relationis*, as Barth admits. But this way of talking is all too Scholastic and expresses nothing but a relation of being.[18]

Von Balthasar's claim is that Barth believes that a human is capable of entering into the covenant with God because he is a social being; and he is a social being only because he is a 'true image' of the being of God. Hence, the possibility of the covenant – as well as the possibility of reconciliation in Christ – exist for Barth only because God's acts of creation and reconciliation stand in continuity with one another to such an extent that the human's *created* being is a 'true image' of God's being. Barth's *analogia relationis*, therefore, functions as it does *only* because it is based upon a presupposed *analogia entis* between God and the human that is a function of the fact that God's act in Jesus Christ presupposes God's act in creation. In this sense, once again, Barth's view stands in line with the Roman Catholic view.

To illustrate the accuracy of his claims, von Balthasar points to two important shifts in Barth's thought in the later volumes of the *CD*. First, he notes that Barth 'increasingly came to sing the praises of the goodness of creatureliness as such'.[19] He makes the case that, beginning with his doctrine of creation in *CD* III/1–3, Barth abandons the notion that sin annihilates the human's natural capacity for God. Barth now believes that 'humanity

---

[17] A more detailed account of Barth's *analogia relationis* will follow below. Here I am following the summary of Eberhard Jüngel, who describes the relationships within Barth's *analogia relationis* in a series of theses. See Eberhard Jüngel, 'Die Möglichkeit theologischer Anthropologie auf dem Grunde der Analogie', in *Barth-Studien* (Gütersloh: Benzinger Verlag, 1982), p. 216.

[18] Balthasar, *The Theology of Karl Barth*, p. 163.

[19] *Ibid.*, p. 112.

is good in itself', and that although humanity has been 'thoroughly abused by sin, it has not been destroyed' by it.[20] As von Balthasar interprets him, this shift is the result of Barth's desire to affirm that the human exists in relationship to God simply by virtue of his creation by God and that sin does not completely destroy this relationship. This means that Barth now understands that the incarnation is the 'authentic truth of human nature' because it 'grounds and justifies *all* human nature'.[21] This shift, he says, shows that Barth 'has taken an immense step forward' towards 'a rapprochement with Catholicism and humanism, [and] with their respective natural theologies'.[22] Specifically, the strict distinction between God and humanity that had driven him to reject the *analogia entis* now has been 'bracketed in the truth of the Redeemer' so that it no longer functions in the same way.[23] This 'bracket' is similar to the 'prefix' that Barth had criticized in the theology of Augustine and Przywara.[24] Barth rejected their views, in part, because he thought that they placed human action in continuity with God's redemptive action. Now, von Balthasar argues, Barth himself has embraced the same kind of continuity because, with his covenant of grace, Barth has placed the same kind of 'prefix' before God's act in creation by placing it in continuity with God's act in Jesus Christ so that human action stands in continuity with God's action.

The second shift is an implication of Barth's concession to Söhngen that his *analogia fidei* implies a *participatio entis*. Does not this concession mean that, despite Barth's protests to the contrary, theology stands in continuity with philosophy? That is, if metaphysics marks an attempt to determine the true nature of 'being', and if Barth's theological reflections imply a participation in 'being', then does not theology have an implied relationship with metaphysics? Could not a philosophy that remains subordinate to and within faith, therefore, stand in continuity with theology? Despite the fact that Barth had strongly opposed this kind of continuity throughout his career, von Balthasar argues that his doctrine of creation opens the door to it. For example, in *CD* III/1, Barth acknowledges that philosophical reflection upon human existence causes the human to be open to the concept of God, because the human recognizes that he requires something above and beyond himself to guarantee that he does, in fact, exist.[25] In other words,

---

[20] *Ibid.*, p. 118.

[21] *Ibid.*, p. 116, emphasis added.

[22] *Ibid.*, p. 116.

[23] *Ibid.*, p. 157.

[24] See Karl Barth, *The Holy Spirit and the Christian Life: The Theological Basis of Ethics*, trans. R. Birch Hoyle (Louisville: Westminster/John Knox Press, 1993), p. 23.

[25] Barth is thinking specifically of Descartes' arguments in his *Mediations* here, and he later offers an extended engagement with them to illustrate his point. See *CD* III/1, pp. 350–63; *KD* III/1, pp. 401–15.

to say that humans exist 'with any sense of security' requires a demonstration that human being is grounded in 'an originally and intrinsically and therefore indubitably existent being'.[26] The various attempts to demonstrate the existence of God throughout history demonstrate this fact, because they show that philosophers recognize the truth of the notion that '[i]f we are the creation of a real Creator, we ourselves are real'.[27] Barth, of course, does not believe that such proofs are adequate to arrive at a true knowledge of God, and he thinks this is especially the case if the proof is derived from 'the content of an immediate consciousness of God which is bound up with our consciousness of ourselves and the world'.[28] Even so, he now seems to accept the assumption that metaphysics stands in an intrinsic relationship with theology inasmuch as he accepts the notion that the human who reflects upon his existence knows by nature that an 'indubitably' real God can guarantee his own reality. Von Balthasar interprets this to mean that Barth now recognizes that metaphysics can serve in a preparatory role for grace, because reflection upon human existence leads the human to seek knowledge of God. Indeed, from von Balthasar's point of view, this line of thought simply is the consequence of Barth's admission that any discussion of grace or faith implies a participation in being: if grace implies being, then some sort of continuity between metaphysics and theology is required. In this sense, he argues, creation marks the 'onset of God's intimate revelation of his Word', because God's act of creation establishes a 'capacity inherent in the human being' that becomes 'the preparation, foundation and onset of a *higher* capacity given to him in grace also to grasp God through faith in his personal Word'.[29] God's revelation in creation, therefore, stands in continuity with – and serves as the foundation for – God's revelation in Jesus Christ. From von Balthasar's perspective, Barth's discussion of the implications of a metaphysics that begins with reflection on human existence functions in the same way: it shows that Barth recognizes that reflection upon human existence provides a foundation for the knowledge of God because it enables the human to recognize that God's revelation 'in created nature itself' prepares the human to recognize that 'the meaning and movement of God's revelation in creation is his will finally to reveal himself in the incarnation of Christ'.[30] In this sense, just as in the Roman Catholic view, creation serves as the presupposition of reconciliation for Barth, because within the context of Barth's covenant of grace, the 'whole order of reason is theologically embedded in the order of faith, just as the

---

[26] *CD* III/1, p. 346; *KD* III/1, p. 397.
[27] *Ibid.*
[28] *CD* III/1, p. 347; *KD* III/1, p. 397.
[29] Balthasar, *The Theology of Karl Barth*, p. 310, emphasis added.
[30] Balthasar, *The Theology of Karl Barth*, pp. 309–10.

order of creation lies embedded in the order of grace'.[31] Von Balthasar also believes that Barth's construal stands in line with the classic Roman Catholic principles 'grace does not destroy but supports and perfect nature' and 'faith does not destroy but supports and perfects reason'. These were the principles Przywara had used to defend the *analogia entis* in Barth's Thomas Aquinas seminar and again in *Analogia Entis*; now, because it has been shown that Barth's theology clearly contains the pattern of '*analogia entis* within *analogia fidei*', it is clear to von Balthasar that these principles function in Barth's theology as well.[32]

Von Balthasar's interpretation of Barth – when placed in conjunction with his claims about Barth's misinterpretation of Przywara and von Balthasar's own innovative account of the Catholic theological tradition – makes for a convincing argument. Von Balthasar takes himself to have shown that Barth's claim that his doctrine of analogy is distinct from the Roman Catholic doctrine is incorrect, and he is convinced that Barth's theology as a whole corresponds with Roman Catholic theology in spirit if not in letter. This correspondence, he believes, carries significant ecumenical implications. As we noted in Chapter 1, these implications help explain the influence of von Balthasar's account of Barth's development since its publication. The acceptance of this account, in turn, has served as the foundation for many of the contemporary assumptions about Barth's doctrine of analogy. But is von Balthasar's interpretation correct? We already demonstrated in the first part of the book that his arguments about Barth's misinterpretation of Przywara's *analogia entis* are off the mark. What about his claims about Barth's mature theology? Does Barth really accept that God's act in Jesus Christ presupposes God's prior act in creation? Does his theology really contain an *analogia entis* that corresponds to the *analogia entis* found in Roman Catholic theology, whether it be Przywara's version or the one offered by Söhngen and von Balthasar? To address these questions, we must turn to the later volumes of Barth's *CD*.

Barth's Mature Use of Analogy

The distinction between von Balthasar's interpretation of Barth and Barth's interpretation of his own views about the nature of God's relationship with humanity centres upon the question of whether Barth is able to define the being of the human in faith strictly in terms of the being of Jesus Christ *without* presupposing a prior determination of human being in God's act of

---

[31] *Ibid.*, p. 325.

[32] See, for example, his argument that Barth's construal of creation and covenant in *CD* III/1 functions as a 'relationship whereby grace supports and perfect nature'. See *Ibid.*, p. 323.

creation. Von Balthasar's key mistake is that he failed to recognize that Barth's entire account of creation is predicated precisely upon avoiding this presupposition. That is to say, von Balthasar failed to see the full implication of what Eberhard Jüngel calls Barth's 'decisive innovation' in his doctrine of creation: Barth's decision to make the human Jesus of Nazareth the condition for the possibility of knowledge of human being as such.[33] What von Balthasar failed to realize is that this innovation enables Barth to posit that God's eternal decision to reconcile humanity in the person of Jesus Christ is the presupposition *of creation*. In other words, Barth reverses the order of the Roman Catholic account, and this means that, on his account of 'being', there can be no true knowledge of God or the human through reflection upon human existence or the created order in and of itself. Instead, because what humans are *intrinsically* is a function at every moment of the *extrinsic* relation of God to them in Jesus Christ, this knowledge comes through the revelation of Christ alone. 'What *we* consider to be the truth about the created world is one thing', Barth insists. 'Quite another is the covenant of grace, the work of Jesus Christ, for the sake and in fulfilment of which creation exists as it is'.[34] It is on the basis of this distinction that Barth is able to posit the continuity between God and the human that von Balthasar rightly recognized. But, contrary to what von Balthasar assumed, this continuity is not a function of God's act of creation *per se* – as it is in the Roman Catholic accounts – but rather, it is a function of God's act in Jesus Christ, which is seen in terms of God's eternal decision to be in relationship with human beings in and through the person of Christ. There clearly is a 'bracket' in front of Barth's doctrine of creation, as von Balthasar believes, but the meaning and content of this 'bracket' is substantively different from the one found in Roman Catholic accounts, and this difference shows that Barth is not working from the same theological ground as these accounts.

Creation and Covenant

To explain these differences and the reasons for von Balthasar's misinterpretation in more detail, it is necessary to turn to Barth's account of creation and the relationship of creation to the covenant of grace.[35] Barth's claims in this regard are grounded upon insights that he developed in his doctrine of

---

[33] See Jüngel, 'Die Möglichkeit theologischer Anthropologie auf dem Grunde der Analogie', p. 212: 'The being of the human Jesus is the ontological and epistemological ground of all analogy.'

[34] *CD* III/1, p. 370; *KD* III/1, p. 423.

[35] Jüngel also argues for a distinction between Barth's and von Balthasar's views here. See Jüngel, 'Die Möglichkeit theologischer Anthropologie auf dem Grunde der Analogie', p. 217.

election in *CD* II/2.[36] There Barth argues that when we talk about God's 'grace', we are talking about something specific: the 'institution of the covenant' between God and humanity that has its basis in the 'primal decision "in Jesus Christ", which is the basis and goal of all his works'.[37] This 'primal decision' is God's free election of 'another to fellowship with himself', and it signifies that God 'draws it upwards to himself, so as never again to be without it, but to be who he is in covenant with it'.[38] This decision means not only that all knowledge of God must begin with knowledge of God's electing decision, but it also means that the 'being and nature' of creation itself is 'predetermined' by it.[39]

> From the standpoint of this beginning and this subject these ways and works [of God] are *per se*, in all circumstances and in all forms and stages, the ways and works of grace. Since it is the divine self-determination, the primal decision from which they derive cannot be over-ridden, abrogated, weakened, or altered by any other decision. Always and from every point of view they derive from the fact that from and to all eternity God has moved toward man freely and therefore definitively. Always and from every point of view they derive from Jesus Christ, the One who in the will of God was to be, was, is, and will be both very man and very God. Always and from every point of view they are what from all eternity they were necessarily foreordained to be. And that applies to all God's works without exception. There is no such thing as a created nature which has its purpose, being or continuance apart from grace, or which may be known in this purpose being or countenance except through grace.[40]

---

[36] For an excellent treatment of the relationship between Barth's doctrine of election and his mature use of analogy, see Hans Theodor Goebel, *Vom freien Wählen Gottes und des Menschen: Interpretationsübungen zur 'Analogie' nach Karl Barths Lehre von der Erwählung und Bedenken ihrer Folgen für die Kirchliche Dogmatik* (Frankfurt: Peter Lang Publishing Co., 1988). Also see Goebel's essay, 'Trinitätslehre und Erwählungslehre bei Karl Barth: eine Problemanzeige', in *Wahrheit und Versöhnung: Theologische und philosophische Beiträge zur Gotteslehre*, ed. Dietrich Korsch and Hartmut Ruddies (Gütersloh: Gütersloher Verlagshaus Gerd Mohn, 1989), p. 164, where he argues that every analogy that Barth draws between God and the human after *CD* II/2 'finds its basic form in the eternal history of the election of Jesus Christ'.

[37] Karl Barth, *Church Dogmatics* II/2 (Edinburgh: T&T Clark, 1957), p. 9; *Die Kirchliche Dogmatik* II/2 (Zürich: Evangelischer-Verlag, 1942), p. 8. Hereafter these volumes will be cited as *CD* II/2 and *KD* II/2 respectively.

[38] *CD* II/2, p. 10; *KD* II/2, p. 8.

[39] *CD* II/2, p. 50; *KD* II/2, p. 53.

[40] *CD* II/2, p. 92; *KD* II/2, p. 99.

Barth thus defines creation as such strictly in terms of God's eternal decision to enter into covenant with humanity in Jesus Christ. Any consideration of the nature and being of creation in distinction from this covenant is an abstract one, in Barth's view, because it has no connection at all to the true being of God, humanity, or the relationship between them. For him, there is no 'being' of creation apart from God's eternal decision that determines it, and there is no knowledge of this decision apart from the revelation of Jesus Christ.

But what does it *mean* to say that creation itself is defined by the covenant? How does this idea work? Barth addresses these questions in his account of the relationship between creation and covenant in CD III/1. He argues that, while creation should be seen as the external basis and possibility of the covenant, the covenant should be seen as the internal basis and possibility of creation. He explains that, on the one hand, to say that creation is the external basis of the covenant is to say that creation exists as 'the work of [God's] own will and achievement'.[41] Creation is not self-existent; it does not have its own *telos*. It exists, rather, for a purpose: 'the fact that God as the Creator has turned toward it with *his* purpose',[42] which is 'the execution of the eternal covenant which God has decreed in himself as the covenant of the Father with his Son as the Lord and Bearer of human nature, and to that extent the Representative of all creation'.[43] To say that creation is the external basis of the covenant, therefore, is to say that it exists because God determined that it serve as 'the space' within which the execution of the divine will that Jesus Christ be the representative of human beings in history takes place.[44] On the other hand, to say that the covenant is the internal basis of creation is to say that the existence and being of creation, as well as its meaning, derives solely from the fact that God makes creation 'the exponent of his intention plan and order. It could not exist if it were not, in virtue of its being, this exponent'.[45] Creation exists, in other words, because it actually fulfils God's purpose for it in the election of Jesus Christ for humanity. Creation 'was not created other than to be the recipient of this gift', Barth says, and 'it does not exist otherwise than as the recipient of this gift'.[46]

> It is and exists solely by reason and in accomplishment of the revelation of the glory of God's free love: the love which God has shown toward it without being under any obligation to do so; the love of the

---

[41] *CD* III/1, p. 96; *KD* III/1, p. 105.

[42] *CD* III/1, p. 94; *KD* III/1, p. 103, emphasis added.

[43] *CD* III/1, p. 97; *KD* III/1, p. 106.

[44] See *CD* III/1, p. 44; *KD* III/1, p. 46.

[45] *CD* III/1, p. 230; *KD* III/1, p. 260.

[46] *Ibid.*

Father and the Son in the Holy Spirit; the love which already in the eternal decree of the giving of his Son for the sake of man did not will to be without a concrete extra-divine object. It was when this love began to be deed and event and therefore to be revealed that creation took place and the creature received its being and existence. The creature owes both the fact *that* it is, and *what* it is, to the revelation which has this content.[47]

To say that the covenant is the internal basis of creation, therefore, is to indicate that the content of the covenant – God's election of humanity in Jesus Christ – is the 'material presupposition' of creation as such.[48] The covenant is not something that supplements or perfects that which creation already *is*, but rather, it exists as creation's most basic ground.

This description of the relationship between creation and covenant puts us in a position to recognize the difference between Barth and von Balthasar's construal of the relationship between the orders of creation and reconciliation, and it also helps us see why von Balthasar's conclusions about the implications of Barth's account of the covenant miss the mark. While it is correct to say that both Barth and von Balthasar believe that humanity stands in relationship to God simply by virtue of its createdness, something more must be said: we must also account for the *nature* of this relationship. This is the step that von Balthasar failed to take. For von Balthasar, the relationship between humanity and God is an intrinsic feature of humanity as such by virtue of God's act of creation viewed in distinction from God's act in Jesus Christ. That is, God's act in creation reveals that the human exists in relationship with God, and this relationship is not defined strictly in terms of God's reconciling act in Jesus Christ, because while God's act in creation is *fulfilled* by God's work in Christ, it remains distinct from it. Here lies the difference between von Balthasar and Barth. Although Barth also believes that creation signifies that the human exists in relationship with God, it does so solely because creation as such cannot be defined in distinction from the covenant of grace. Simply put, for Barth, there is no presupposed relationship between God and humanity on the basis of God's act of creation viewed in distinction from God's reconciling act in

---

[47] *Ibid.*, emphasis added. Adam Neder summarizes Barth's line of thinking here well: 'Jesus Christ's fulfillment of the covenant of grace establishes the context within which human beings exists, and that context is determined fundamentally by the relationship of lordship and obedience that Jesus Christ embodies . . . The essence of human life is to be drawn into the covenant, to exist within the sphere of this relationship'. See Neder, *Participation in Christ: An Entry into Karl Barth's Church Dogmatics* (Louisville: Westminster/John Knox, 2009), p. 31.

[48] *CD* III/1, p. 232; *KD* III/1, p. 262.

Jesus Christ.[49] Indeed, such an account would be impossible, because for him, the covenant is not a programme but a *person*: Jesus Christ. The covenant of grace is God's eternal decree that Jesus Christ condescend to humanity in order to exalt humanity in him, and as very God and very man, Christ stands in relation both to God and to every human being.[50] Since creation as such is defined by *this* particular action, the relationship between God and humanity cannot be considered on the basis of what the human naturally possesses by virtue of her creation considered in abstraction from the person of Jesus Christ and his act in the covenant. This relationship, rather, must be seen strictly and solely in the light of human's relation to *this* man Jesus. For Barth, then, this relationship consists of 'not a oneness of being but a genuine togetherness of being with God' that happens through the action of Jesus Christ.[51]

This 'togetherness of being', in Barth's view, takes visible form in human life in the action of the human as he or she corresponds to Jesus Christ's action. In the covenant, he says, 'the being of man in all its independence and particularity, in all its difference from the being of God, is the being which is acted upon in this action of God, ruled in this rule of God and drawn into this history inaugurated and controlled by God'.[52] In other words, the content of God's act in Jesus Christ itself points to the fact that the human's relationship with God is not the result of an intrinsic character-istic which she has by virtue of her creation, as it is for von Balthasar, but the result of God's action towards and upon her in and through the person of Jesus Christ. This act, as it occurs in history, compels the human, in turn, to be drawn into this history and to act in correspondence to God's act upon her. This divine action and the human correspondence to it *is* the relationship between God and the human, and it takes visible form in the event in which the human hears the Word of God and responds to it by the power of the Holy Spirit. Barth's covenant of grace, therefore, does not presuppose a 'mutual co-ordination of two spheres or factors', such as is the case in von Balthasar's account of the relationship between creation

---

[49] As Jüngel notes, this insight helps explain why Barth never allowed his lectures on ethics from Münster to be made public during his lifetime: he 'never published them because of their reliance on the doctrine of the orders of creation, which he was soon to reject'. See Jüngel, *Karl Barth: A Theological Legacy*, trans. Garrett E. Paul (Philadelphia: The Westminster Press, 1986), p. 39. These lectures were published posthumously as *Ethics*, ed. Dietrich Braun, trans. Geoffrey W. Bromiley (New York: The Seabury Press, 1981).

[50] See Jüngel, 'Die Möglichkeit theologischer Anthropologie auf dem Grunde der Analogie', p. 216.

[51] Karl Barth, *Church Dogmatics* III/2 (Edinburgh: T&T Clark, 1960), p. 141; *Die Kirchliche Dogmatik* III/2 (Zürich: Evangelischer Verlag, 1948), p. 169. Hereafter these volumes will be cited as *CD* III/2 and *KD* III/2 respectively.

[52] *Ibid.*

and reconciliation; rather, it signifies 'a *history* which is enacted between God and man under the transcendent leadership of God, in which decisions are made first by God and then also by man'.[53] For Barth, then, the reality of human existence – and the human's existence in relationship to God – has its basis in the concrete dealings between God and humanity initiated by God in his eternal election of humanity in Jesus Christ, and neither God nor the human can be considered apart from this particular history and its particular form of Word and Spirit.

Barth's 'Bracket' and the Doctrine of Justification

Von Balthasar's question, however, hangs in the air: does not Barth's account of the covenant of grace mean there is now a 'bracket' standing before creation itself that functions in the same way as the Roman Catholic 'prefix' that Barth once condemned in Augustine and Przywara?[54] The answer is both yes and no. In one sense, von Balthasar is correct to think that, for Barth, in fact, all creation and human existence as such stands under God's electing decision, and that this decision thus serves as a kind of 'bracket' over creation. His account of the implications of this 'bracket' is incorrect, however, because he failed to recognize that the critical question is not the existence of it but whether Barth means the same thing by it as he does. Barth himself poses this question: 'What is the creaturely nature of man to the extent that, looking to the revealed grace of God and concretely to the man Jesus, we can see in it a continuum unbroken by sin, an essence which even sin does not and cannot change?'[55] To put this question another way: what must we say about human nature if we are to say that the human continues to be in relationship with God even after sin? This is the key question, because Barth and von Balthasar's answer explains how they understand the nature of the 'bracket' existing over creation.

For von Balthasar, the answer is that God's act in creation is an act of grace, and that the human stands in relationship to God as a result of it. Sin affects this relationship, but it does not destroy it. God deals with the sin in and through Jesus Christ, and this act of reconciliation thus stands as the perfection and fulfilment of God's initial act of grace in creation. Indeed, God's act in creation is the presupposition of this act of reconciliation,

---

[53] *CD* III/2, p. 124; *KD* III/2, p. 149. Thus Barth: 'Those who regard God's creation as an eternal but timeless relation of the creature and its existence can certainly boast of a very deep and pious conviction, but they cannot believe it in the Christian and biblical sense. For this timeless relation has nothing whatever to do with God's decree of grace in which God from all eternity has condescended to His creature in His Son in order to exalt it in His Son; nor with the acts in which God has accomplished this decree according to the revelation of Himself.' See *CD* III/1, p. 60; *KD* III/1, pp. 64–5.

[54] Balthasar, *The Theology of Karl Barth*, p. 157.

[55] *CD* III/2, p. 43; *KD* III/2, p. 50.

because the relationship established between God and the human in God's act of creation sets the stage for God's reconciling work in Jesus Christ. In short, human nature stands in relationship with God even after sin because God's act of creation establishes a relationship that sin does not destroy, and God's act in Jesus Christ presupposes this prior relationship. Von Balthasar believes that Barth holds to the same view, because Barth's affirmation that creation as such is determined by the covenant means that he also believes that sin does not fundamentally alter the relationship of humanity with God. He sees Barth's affirmation that 'humanity is good in itself' as evidence for this interpretation.[56] That is, Barth's account of sin shows that he believes that the human by nature stands in relationship with God by virtue of creation alone, and the fact that sin does not cancel this relationship out reveals that the covenant of grace – which consists of the justification of sinners – is not necessary for this relationship to exist. In short, the 'bracket' created by Barth's covenant of grace functions in the same way as the Roman Catholic 'bracket', such that there is a continuity between the human as created and the human in grace that stems from the fact that creation exists as the presupposition of reconciliation.

As evidence for his interpretation, von Balthasar points to Barth's remarks in the later volumes of the *CD* that sin does not fundamentally alter the relationship between God and creatures. For example, Barth says that while the human's 'corruption is radical and total' as a result of sin, the human 'is still real' and a 'creature of God' after sin.[57] This is the case, he explains, because 'in the radical depravity of man there is necessarily hidden his *true nature*' that sin does not destroy.[58] This 'true nature' is the fact that the human is at every moment defined by God's grace.

> We cannot forget how man is revealed to us in the light of God's Word – that he is a sinner, but that as such and in spite of himself he is also the object of divine grace, the partner in the covenant which God has made with him. Sinful man in himself, without regard to the fact that he is also this covenant-partner and as such still the creature of God, is an abstract concept which must be excluded . . . Even the fact that he is a sinner is true only when seen in connection with the truth that he is the object of the grace of God . . . The grace of God, the covenant of God with man, is primary. The sin of man is secondary. It is not ultimate, and therefore it is not primary. This excludes the abstraction of man as merely sinful, and implies the pardon of man, who even as a sinner does not cease to be the creature of God.[59]

---

[56] Balthasar, *The Theology of Karl Barth*, p. 118.
[57] CD III/2, p. 28; KD III/2, pp. 30–1.
[58] CD III/2, p. 29; KD III/2, p. 32, emphasis added.
[59] CD III/2, p. 32; KD III/2, p. 36.

Barth's argument on this point is shaped by the implications of his doctrine of election. If the human is elected from eternity in Jesus Christ, then the primary truth about the human is the fact that, in and through Christ, he is a covenant partner with God. While God's Word in Jesus Christ reveals the human's sin, therefore, it also reveals that his sin is not the primary word spoken about him: the primary word about him is God's 'Yes' in Jesus. This means that the human's knowledge of his sin is dependent upon his knowledge of his election in Christ, so that his status as a sinner stands at all times under the *prior* reality that he is a creature whom God has determined to stand in relationship with in Jesus. One implication of this account, Barth notes, is that it shows that God's Word in Jesus Christ stands 'in continuity with His purpose in creation to the extent that it takes place on the presupposition and in the framework of certain relationships of the being of man which are influenced by sin but not structurally modified by it'.[60] In other words, because the fundamental nature of the human being is determined in God's electing act, God's attitude towards the human being does not change because of sin. Her created 'nature and essence' is certainly 'distorted by sin', but it cannot be 'destroyed or transmuted into something different' by it.[61]

Von Balthasar took these claims to mean that Barth held that the human exists in a relationship with God that occurs as a result of God's act of creation alone. That is, because sin does not fundamentally alter this relationship – and because the covenant of grace is God's act to reconcile sinners – this relationship must be something that exits in distinction from the covenant of grace. This interpretation, however, fails to grasp Barth's meaning. The key to Barth's claims about sin is to return to his 'decisive innovation' of defining human being as such in terms of the 'supreme particularity' of the 'one man Jesus'.[62] For Barth, any talk about human being must begin with a clear affirmation: 'there can be no question of a direct equation of human nature as we know it in ourselves with the human nature of Jesus'.[63] The reason, Barth explains, is that 'human nature as it is and in ourselves is always a debatable quantity' because 'the human experience as we know and experience it is dialectical'.[64] In other words, if what it means to be human is defined in terms of the human relation to God, then it is simply a fact that 'human nature in [Jesus] is determined by a relation between God and himself such as has never existed between God and us, and never will exist'.[65] We do not exist as a 'real' human in and of ourselves,

---

[60] *CD* III/2, p. 40; *KD* III/2, p. 46.
[61] *CD* III/2, p. 42; *KD* III/2, p. 48.
[62] *CD* III/2, p. 44; *KD* III/2, p. 51.
[63] *CD* III/2, p. 47; *KD* III/2, p. 54.
[64] *Ibid.*
[65] *CD* III/2, p. 49; *KD* III/2, p. 57.

because we do not exist in relationship to God in the same way that the *true* human being, Jesus Christ, exists in relationship to God. If we have a true human nature, therefore, it has to take place by means of a participation in *his* human nature.

This insight is important for Barth's account of sin because it leads him directly to the same doctrine that has been the key for his account of the human relationship with God – as well as analogy – from the very beginning: the doctrine of justification.

> The first thing which has to be said about human nature in Jesus is that in Him an effective protest is lodged against our self-contradiction and all the self-deception in which we try to conceal it. It is a protest because the antitheses in which we live are no antithesis in Him, and therefore do not require any attempted solution, so that in Him all illusions about the success of these attempts are quite irrelevant. And it is effective because His human nature shows us the dialectic of our situation and the hopelessness of our illusions by showing them to be the sin which in Him is no longer imputed to us but forgiven, being taken from us and removed and eliminated, like a vicious circle which is ended by Him, so that by right we can no longer move in it. The human nature of Jesus spares us and forbids us our own. Thus it is our justification.[66]

This passage points to the key difference between Barth's and von Balthasar's understanding of the 'bracket' that exists over creation, because it demonstrates why Barth's statements about sin do not show that he believes that the creature stands in relationship with God by virtue of God's act in creation viewed in distinction from his act of reconciliation. Von Balthasar assumes that human nature as such is something that humans possess as an intrinsic characteristic by virtue of their creation. For this reason, if one holds that human nature remains 'good' in some sense after the Fall because human existence stands under the 'bracket' of God's redemptive will, then one must say that this same fallen human nature – the one they possess as their own – stands in continuity with the nature that is perfected by God's grace in Jesus Christ. In other words, this 'bracket' means that human nature and action stands in continuity with divine nature and action because God's act in creation is the presupposition of God's act in Jesus Christ. This is precisely what von Balthasar believes that Barth's covenant of grace entails, even though it is the same kind of view that Barth rejected in Przywara's account in 1929 and again in 1932. What he fails to see, however, is that, even in the light of Barth's remarks about sin, Barth *still*

---

[66] *CD* III/2, p. 47; *KD* III/2, p. 55.

rejects this position. For Barth, human nature is not something that the human possesses; it something given to the human only in and through her relation to Jesus Christ. It is not an intrinsic characteristic that the human has as her own, therefore, but a gift given to her from without that comes to her anew at every movement by her participation in Christ. In short, humans are truly human only in virtue of their *justification.* This justification is not something that is their own, because within the context of this life they are and remain sinners through and through in the sense of Luther's *simul iustus et peccator.* Rather, their justification is something they have at each moment only inasmuch as they participate in Jesus Christ's being as a result of God's action in Christ in the covenant of grace. Their human nature is their own, then, only as event and history, and this fact 'reminds us', as Barth says, 'of the reserve which is incumbent upon us if we are really to venture, on the basis of that judicial pardon, to think about man as created by God'.[67] In sum, Barth remains strongly opposed to the existence of a continuity between God and humanity that has its basis in characteristics that are intrinsic to the human as a result of God's act of creation viewed in distinction from God's act in Jesus Christ.

In short, for Barth, the fact that human sin does not 'modify' God's covenantal determination for the creature does not mean that the human stands in relation to God by virtue of his creation alone, but rather, it means that human sin is always viewed in light of Jesus Christ's act to address that sin. This act leads him directly to the doctrine of justification. Jesus Christ acted to take on human sin – the sin that marked the human breaking of the covenant – and remove it in his person. In *him,* therefore, humans are free to be human, and the truth of *their* existence is found in *his* existence in perfect and true relation to God. 'This judicial pardon', Barth says, 'gives us the courage and shows us the way to think about man as God created him'.[68] That is, it shows us that Jesus Christ's relationship with God as a human being does not remain his alone but becomes the human's own by imputation as she relates to Jesus by grace through faith. Luther's basic insights remain as true as ever for Barth: as God relates to Jesus – and as we relate to Jesus – God relates to us. Jesus Christ is our sole mediator, and he is so in and through the intercessory relationship accomplished in his

---

[67] *CD* III/2, p. 49; *KD* III/2, p. 57. Neder explains Barth's line of thinking here: 'Humanity exists only in relationship with Jesus Christ. To think of humanity apart from this relationship is merely to entertain an abstraction. Jesus Christ "clothes" humanity with himself and therefore with righteousness, holiness, and truth. Humanity does not possess these things any more than it possesses Jesus Christ. Yet while it does not possess them, it does receive them, and therefore it is not without them. That is the specific function of the *simul iustus et peccator* doctrine as Barth employs it'. See Adam Neder, *Participation in Christ*, p. 48.

[68] *CD* III/2, p. 49; *KD* III/2, p. 56.

person. Barth thus accepts that there is continuity between God and humanity, but this continuity is a function at every moment of the fact that God's act in Jesus Christ is the presupposition of creation itself.

The centrality of the doctrine of justification for Barth's view helps us see why von Balthasar's interpretation of his account of the relationship between philosophy and theology is also off the mark. Specifically, even though Barth acknowledges that, without the benefit of divine revelation, humans can realize that they need to prove the existence of God in order to exist 'with any sense of security', this does not mean that he believes that their attempts to know God through philosophical reflection stand in continuity with the knowledge of human being given to us in and by faith, as von Balthasar supposes.[69]

> It may well be that it belongs to the essence of the creaturely mind to conceive this idea and indeed the idea of the existing God which itself implies this existence. It may well be the case that in such an argument we have to do with the most characteristic and immediate act of the creaturely mind. There is no question that we always desire to be certain of existence, reality and being. Our very self-consciousness and consciousness of the world with its grand conceptions is witness to this. And so it may be that our consciousness of God – or, if we like to put it this way, our consciousness of a perfect being which as such also exists – is the crowning testimony to this supreme desire which in itself is so obviously deep rooted and inescapable. Why should it not be so? But to desire and to attain our desire are two different things even when the desire is thought to be so deeply rooted in our inmost being, and to be the most proper and immediate act of the creaturely mind. That fact that existence is integral to our idea of God as the most perfect being does not at all distinguish [this idea] from our ideas of the self and the world.[70]

Barth clearly acknowledges that the human may have an innate desire to come to the knowledge of a 'perfect being' because this being can guarantee the reality of human existence. This acknowledgment, however, does not mean that these attempts to acquire knowledge of God in this way actually accomplish their goal, that this supposed knowledge stands in continuity with the knowledge available through revelation, or that these attempts prepare the way or provide the foundation for the revelation of God in Jesus Christ. Barth still rejects the notions that faith and grace 'perfect and fulfil' reason and nature in the way that Roman Catholics understand those

---

[69] *CD* III/1, p. 346; *KD* III/1, p. 397.
[70] *CD* III/1, pp. 347–8.

ideas, because he rejects the notion there is reason and nature at all apart from God's covenant of grace in Jesus Christ. Simply put, there is *no* knowledge of the true God or true human being apart from the revelation of this covenant. Theology is 'noetically distinguished' from philosophy, he argues, 'by the fact that here, if we are to know who and what man is, it is essential that God should have spoken and that we should have listened to his Word'.[71] True knowledge of both God and creation, therefore, occurs as a revelation of something new that confronts the human from outside his own perception of his existence. If the human's relation with God was 'a relation given in and with being as such', Barth says, then it 'would be a kind of attribute of man'.[72] This is certainly how von Balthasar sees the relation, and this is how he wants to read Barth as well. In reality, however, Barth believes that this relation occurs only in the unique history of God's specific and particular encounter with the human being in Christ. This revelation does not include within itself an 'account of the cosmos' or an 'ontology of the created totality' but simply 'an ontology of man'.[73] And this ontology – because it occurs in the context of the covenant of grace – centres upon the 'very man that God Himself has become in the perfect and definitive revelation of this Word of his.[74] In short, for Barth, any account of 'being' available through reflection on human existence as such is of a completely different order than the account of 'being' that is given to the human by God's revelation in Jesus Christ. This means that the being of Jesus Christ is 'ontologically decisive' for all humans, not because they find the fulfilment of their already-possessed being in him, but because Jesus shows that human being as such is defined by the relationship to God that occurs through him.[75]

Analogy in Relation

The distinction between Barth's view of the relationship between God and humanity and von Balthasar's interpretation of it help us see how and why von Balthasar misunderstood Barth's doctrine of analogy. The underlying insight is Barth's commitment to the notion that, in the incarnation,

---

[71] *CD* III/2, p. 123; *KD* III/2, p. 146.

[72] *Ibid.*

[73] *CD* III/2, p. 6; *KD* III/2, p. 5. When we try to branch out beyond this particularity to say something more, Barth says, we lose our 'axis' – namely, God. Theology must stay focused on its own unique task: 'faith cannot have any other relation with philosophies but an external, provisional, non-committal and paradoxical one'. See *CD* III/2, p. 11; *KD* III/2, p. 10.

[74] *CD* III/2, p. 13; *KD* III/2, p. 13.

[75] *CD* III/2, p. 135; *KD* III/2, p. 161. This is why Barth says that '[t]o be a man is to be with Jesus'. See *CD* III/2, p. 145; *KD* III/2, p. 173.

Jesus Christ 'does not destroy the difference between divinity and humanity'.[76] The basic insights that the Council of Chalcedon attempted to uphold still apply for Barth: Jesus' entrance into human history does not mean that 'Godhead has taken the place of His manhood, that his manhood is as it were swallowed up or extinguished by Godhead'.[77] Barth's dialectic of God's veiling and unveiling in revelation functions here just as it did in Göttingen: the humanity of Jesus is in the image of God, but it is also 'only indirectly and not directly identical with God'.[78] That is, while Jesus Christ is fully God, he does not reveal God within history so that God becomes a part *of* history like any other object in it. Rather, God remains the subject of his self-revelation at every moment, even as he is revealed in the human Jesus. Barth insists, therefore, that while the humanity of Jesus 'belongs intrinsically to the creaturely world', it 'does not belong to the inner sphere of the essence' of God.[79] This means that the humanity of Jesus 'does not present God in himself and in his relation to himself, but in his relation to the reality distinct from himself'.[80] Barth is simply following the logic of his doctrine of election here: God's election of humanity in Jesus Christ was not a decision by God to relate to God, but a decision by God to relate to humanity *in* Jesus. The humanity of Jesus, therefore, stands in real difference from the divinity of God, and the humanity of Jesus takes the form of 'correspondence and similarity' rather than identity with God.[81] 'Between God and God', Barth says, 'the Father and the Son and the Son and the Father, there is unity of essence . . . but there can be no question of this between God and man, and it cannot therefore find expression in the humanity of Jesus, in his fellow-humanity as the image of God'.[82]

At the same time, however, Barth says that 'it is in the humanity, the saving work of the man Jesus Christ that the connection between God and man is brought before us'.[83] That is to say, there really is a point of similarity between God and humanity, and this similarity occurs in and through the humanity of Jesus. How so? Barth explains that for all the dissimilarity between God and the human Jesus, there is 'a correspondence and similarity

---

[76] *CD* III/2, p. 207; *KD* III/2, p. 247.

[77] *CD* III/2, pp. 207–8; *KD* III/2, pp. 247–8.

[78] *CD* III/2, p. 219; *KD* III/2, p. 261.

[79] *Ibid.*

[80] *Ibid.*

[81] *Ibid.* This does not mean, as Barth cautions later, that there exists a 'distance, alienation or neutrality, let alone opposition, between the human definition and the divine' in the person of Jesus. It means, rather, that 'his humanity is in the closest correspondence with his divinity. It mirrors and reflects it. Conversely, His divinity has its correspondence and image in the humanity in which it is mirrored.' See *CD* III/2, p. 216; *KD* III/2, p. 258.

[82] *CD* III/2, p. 219; *KD* III/2, pp. 261–2.

[83] *CD* III/2, pp. 219–20; *KD* III/2, p. 262.

between the two relationships'.[84] That is, the relationship between the eternal Father and the eternal Son within the Trinity is similar to the relationship between God and the human Jesus. They stand in analogy with one another – but only in a particular way.

> This is not a correspondence and similarity of being, an *analogia entis*. The being of God cannot be compared with that of man. But it is not a question of this twofold being. It is a question of the relationship within the being of God on the one side and between the being of God and that of man on the other. Between these two relationships as such – and it is in this sense that the second is the image of the first – there is correspondence and similarity. There is an *analogia relationis*.[85]

Barth's logic here is not difficult to follow: he is drawing an analogy between two relationships. In one relationship, the two parties in the relation – the Father and the Son – have the same being, because they relate to one another as God to God; in the other relationship, the two parties in relation – God and the human Jesus – do *not* have the same being, because the humanity of Jesus Christ does not belong to the inner sphere of the essence of God.[86] The point of similarity and dissimilarity between the two parties is not their *being* but their *relationship*: the *relation* between God and the human Jesus is analogous to the *relation* between the eternal Father and the eternal Son because it is both similar and dissimilar to it. The difference between this analogy and the one that Przywara offered is clear. Przywara drew the analogy between God, whose *being* is marked by the fact that his essence and existence are identical, and the human, whose *being* is marked by the fact that his essence and existence are in tension. The two parties in this analogy are *God* and the *human*. Barth is drawing an analogy between the *relation* between the eternal Father and the eternal Son and the *relation* between God and the humanity of Jesus. The two parties in this analogy are the *relationships*. This is why Barth argues that this analogy is an *analogia relationis* instead of an *analogia entis*.

The fact that Barth's analogy is strictly an analogy of relationship that centres upon the human Jesus, however, does not preclude drawing an analogy between God and humans in general. 'A common factor is presupposed here', Barth says, 'a similarity in spite of and in all dissimilarity: not merely between Jesus and other men, but – because of that which occurs between Jesus and other men – also between God and man generally'.[87] What is the point at which both God and the human are similar and

---

[84] *CD* III/2, p. 220; *KD* III/2, p. 262.

[85] *Ibid*.

[86] This distinction, of course, is in the terms of Chalcedon's 'without confusion'.

[87] *KD* III/2, p. 269, translation mine; see *CD* III/2, p. 225.

dissimilar, and thus in analogy? Barth explains that inasmuch as the human Jesus is the true human being – and inasmuch as his existence fulfils God's eternal will to exist in relation to creatures – then the 'minimal definition of our humanity, of humanity generally, must be that it is the being of man in encounter, and in this sense the determination of man as a being with the other man'.[88] What does he mean? It is helpful here to recall the original pattern of the 'true *analogia entis*' in 'The Holy Spirit and the Christian Life'. There Barth argued that a human exists in analogy to God when, by the power of the Holy Spirit, she corresponds to the Word of God in Jesus Christ. Now, in light of Barth's doctrine of election, this Word of God not only has a name but a *history*: Jesus Christ is the one who entered into the world as a human being to exist *for* humans so that he could bring them in relation with God through himself. If a human is to correspond to this Word of God, therefore, she must do so by existing in the *same way* that Christ did: by being *for* other human beings. This correspondence in action is the point of contact for the analogy between God and the human. Just as the relationship between the eternal Father and the eternal Son is analogous to the relationship between God and the human Jesus, so the relationship between the human Jesus and humanity in general is analogous to the relationship between the human and other human beings. Jesus Christ, fully God and fully human, is the connecting point between the various analogies, and through him, the human who exists *for* others in the same way that Jesus did stands in analogy to the triune God who eternally determined to be God-*for*-us by relating to humanity in Jesus. The human is not in analogy to God because of her being, therefore, but rather, she is in analogy to God inasmuch as she corresponds, through Christ by the power of the Holy Spirit, to God's action *for* her by her own act of existing *for* others. A human in analogy to God is one whose life is marked by 'the character of obedience, this active form of hearing God's Word'.[89] What visible form does this obedient action take? It takes the form of the proclamation of the Word of God to a sinful world. In short, for Barth, the human being exists in analogy to God only when she corresponds to the Word she has heard by proclaiming it, in the power of the Spirit, to her fellow humans. The analogy is one of act and relation. This action does not stand in continuity with God's action, either as the fulfilment of God's action or the presupposition of it; it merely corresponds to it as the human relates to her fellow humans in the same way that Jesus Christ, the elect of God, relates to her: by proclaiming God's 'Yes' to the world.

This puts us in a position to assess von Balthasar's argument that Barth's *analogia relationis* depends upon a presupposed *analogia entis*. Specifically,

---

[88] *CD* III/2, p. 247; *KD* III/2, p. 296.
[89] *CD* III/2, p. 182; *KD* III/2, p. 217.

von Balthasar argued the 'interhuman relationships' between human beings are a 'true presupposition for the fact that Jesus can become our brother', that it is only '*because* man is a social being who lives by intersubjective relationships that he is capable in the first place of entering into a covenant with God'; and thus that '*this* natural order is for its part only possible on the basis of God's own interpersonal nature, his true nature, of which the human being is a true image'.[90] The basic claim here is that it is only because the human exists in the image of God as a relational being – and thus stands in an analogy to God's being – that he can enter into a relationship with the human Jesus, and then, through Jesus, into a relationship with God. By now the problems with this argument should be clear. Any notion of human 'being' that exists apart from Jesus Christ is foreign to Barth's covenant of grace or the analogies that function within it, because for Barth, there *is* no such being: humans 'are' what they are only in their relationship to Christ. Humans, Barth argues, 'are not simply and directly the covenant-partners of God' but only destined 'to become' covenant-partners solely because they

> are destined to participate in the benefits of the fellow-humanity of that One – destined, that is, to be rescued by him. They in their creatureliness have need, and they in their creatureliness are promised, that he, the One who is the image of God, is for them. What they themselves are in their relationship to God depends on this determination, which has its reality not in themselves, but *in him*, that One.[91]

The fact that God creates humans does not give humans an inherent ability or capacity that serves as the presupposition for the establishment of God's relationship with them in the covenant of grace. This ability, rather, is a function of the fact that they are the ones who have been determined from all eternity to be justified by Christ by participation in his salvific benefits. A 'participation in the benefits' of Christ, of course, is nothing other than a participation in Jesus Christ himself. Humans are not 'capable' of entering into relationship with God because they are in the image of God, therefore, but rather, they enter into this relationship *only* because 'the One who is the image of God' exists *for* them by entering into time as a human being and then exalting them in and through his own exaltation. Luther's *sola gratia* still governs Barth's doctrine of analogy even here. For Barth, human

---

[90] Balthasar, *The Theology of Karl Barth*, p. 163.

[91] *KD* III/2, pp. 268–9, translation and emphasis mine; see *CD* III/2, p. 225. Barth draws an analogy to help capture the nature of the participation occurring here: 'From the very first, even in their creatureliness, [humans] stand in the light which is shed by Him. But if they are in His light, they cannot be dark in themselves but bright with His light. We thus ask concerning their brightness in *his* light.' See *KD* III/2, p. 269, translation mine; see *CD* III/2, p. 225.

existence itself, because it takes place 'in Christ', presupposes human reconciliation, and this means that his account actually reverses the order of the relationship between creation and reconciliation found in the Roman Catholic accounts.

This reversal marks a fundamental distinction between Barth's account of the relationship and von Balthasar's account, and it shows that von Balthasar's claims about the correspondence between Barth's analogy and Roman Catholic analogies are misplaced. Von Balthasar failed to realize that, even though Barth admits that any account of grace and faith necessarily includes an account of a participation in 'being', Barth means something completely different by the word 'being' than von Balthasar does. For Barth, it is impossible to talk about 'being' at all outside the context of the covenant of grace, and to talk about it within this covenant is to talk about the being of one man – Jesus Christ – and every human's relationship to him. As such, Barth believes that, because 'being' itself is determined by God's free and eternal decision to enter into human history in Jesus Christ in order to reconcile humanity to himself, true human 'being' has its basis in the human's free decision to correspond to this act in faith and obedience. For Barth, then, 'being' is always 'being-in-act', and a true analogy of 'being' consists primarily of divine action and the corresponding human action. Any talk of 'being' at all, and any talk about of an 'analogy of being' between God and the human, must be based solely upon Christ's act of reconciliation and the human's act in correspondence to it. 'If the analogy is not merely to be an edifying game', Barth says, 'it cannot be ventured except from the knowledge of Jesus Christ. But on this ground it should be ventured, and there should be no hesitation'.[92] Even though the use of analogy does have ontological implications for Barth, therefore, these implications are not what von Balthasar assumed. Barth is not adopting the kind of *analogia entis* that von Balthasar supposes, because what humans are internally is, at every moment in time, a function of the *external* relation of God to humanity in Jesus Christ.

The Culmination of Barth's Analogical Thinking

In an afterword to the second edition of *The Theology of Karl Barth* written in 1961, von Balthasar briefly analyses the volumes of the *CD* that had been published after the release of the first edition. He notes that the key insights he treated from Barth's earlier volumes 'converge' in the Christology of the later ones, and he makes the case that this convergence confirms that his earlier interpretation was correct.[93] To this end, he argues that Barth's mature use of analogy still presupposes a prior analogy based upon God's

---

[92] *CD* III/1, p. 30; *KD* III/1, p. 32.
[93] Balthasar, *The Theology of Karl Barth*, p. 392.

act in creation, because it still contains the 'inner presupposition' of an 'analogy in the order of creation' that provides its 'external ground'.[94] This presupposed analogy shows that, even in his doctrine of reconciliation, Barth is still operating with assumptions that are shared by Roman Catholics. 'What more', von Balthasar asks, 'could a Scholastic theologian ask for?'[95]

What are we to make of von Balthasar's claims? A close reading of CD IV/1–3 shows that, once again, his interpretation of Barth is off the mark, because these volumes demonstrate that Barth's theology diverges from von Balthasar's interpretation of it in precisely the same manner as it did in Barth's doctrine of creation. In fact, Barth's doctrine of reconciliation stands as the *culmination* of the rejection of Roman Catholic accounts of the relationship between God and humanity that Barth issued in the earlier volumes, because in this doctrine, Barth finally makes his account of the relationship between Jesus Christ and humanity concrete by showing precisely *how* Jesus becomes the condition for the possibility of knowledge of human being as such. The implications of this affirmation remain the same as they were before. Barth still believes that God's covenant with humanity in Jesus Christ is the presupposition of creation and the condition for the possibility of the knowledge of human being as such, because he still holds that the 'ordaining of salvation for man and man for salvation is the original and basic will of God, the ground and purpose of his will as creator'.[96] He also still contends that there is no presupposed relationship between God and humanity on the basis of God's act in creation viewed in distinction from God's reconciling act in Jesus Christ. 'It is not that he first wills and works the being of the world and man, and then ordains it to salvation', Barth says. 'But God creates, preserves and over-rules man for this *prior* end and with this *prior* purpose, that there may be a being distinct from himself ordained for salvation, for perfect being, for participation in his own being'.[97] These implications are more concrete than before, however, because Barth now anchors them in a particular account of the being and work of Jesus Christ organized in terms of the *munus triplex*, the 'threefold office' of Christ as priest, king, and prophet.[98] Barth uses his account of Jesus Christ's reconciling work in the priestly and kingly offices to set up his description of the correspondence of divine and human action that takes place in the

---

[94] *Ibid.*, p. 396.

[95] *Ibid.*, p. 394.

[96] Karl Barth, *Church Dogmatics* IV/1 (Edinburgh: T&T Clark, 1956), p. 9; *Die Kirchliche Dogmatik* IV/1 (Zürich: Evangelischer Verlag, 1953), p. 8. Hereafter these volumes will be cited as *CD* IV/1 and *KD* IV/1 respectively.

[97] *Ibid.*, emphasis added.

[98] The first three volumes of the doctrine of reconciliation correspond to this organization: *CD* IV/1 describes the priestly work of Christ, *CD* IV/2 the kingly, and *CD* IV/3 the prophetic.

prophetic office, and this correspondence in action is precisely how Barth understands the analogy between God and the human in light of God's covenant of grace in Jesus Christ. This account of the analogous relationship between God and humanity demonstrates that Barth continues to diverge from von Balthasar's interpretation of him, because Barth's account of the relationship between God and humanity, as well as his articulation of the analogy between them, remains consistent with his earlier formulations, his rejection of Przywara's *analogia entis*, and the distinction he drew between Söhngen's doctrine of analogy and his own.

The key to understanding Barth's doctrine of reconciliation is to realize that, once again, Barth's description of it has its basis in dogmatic decisions prompted by his doctrine of election. In line with his earlier arguments, Barth argues that the covenant of grace reveals the decision that was 'freely determined in eternity by God himself before there was any created being', and as such, the covenant is the 'revelation and confirmation of the most primitive relationship between God and man'.[99] Any discussion of the human, God, or their relationship with one another, therefore, must begin with the knowledge of this covenant and thus with the knowledge of the person and work of Jesus Christ. Of course, as Barth established in his doctrine of creation, this starting point means that the true nature of human being is known only 'in the light of the particular being of man in Jesus Christ'.[100] This is not all that the covenant of grace tells us, however, and here Barth extends his argument further than before. Not only does the covenant give insights into the being of humans, Barth says, but it also provides knowledge of the 'mystery of the inner being of God'.[101] God's act in Jesus Christ in time gives insight into the relationship between the Father and the Son in eternity, and it shows us that 'for God, it is just as natural to be lowly as it is to be high, to be near as it is to be far, to be little as it is to be great, to be abroad as to be at home'.[102] In other words, the fact that God became incarnate in Jesus Christ signifies that humility in the form of obedience is proper to the eternal being of God. 'If, then, God is in Christ', Barth explains, 'if what the man Jesus does is God's own work, this aspect of the self-emptying and self-humbling of Jesus Christ as an act of obedience is not alien to God'.[103] This claim about the nature of God's being is important, because Barth uses it to enclose both the 'above to below' movement of God to the human *and* the 'below to above' movement of the human to God in the person of Jesus Christ. The distinction between these two movements, of course, had once been used by Barth to divide his own 'above to

---

[99] *CD* IV/1, p. 10; *KD* IV/1, p. 8.
[100] *CD* IV/1, 92; *KD* IV/1, p. 98.
[101] *CD* IV/1, p. 177; *KD* IV/1, p. 193.
[102] *CD* IV/1, p. 192; *KD* IV/1, p. 210.
[103] *CD* IV/1, p. 193; *KD* IV/1, p. 211.

below' construal of the relationship from the 'below to above' construal he discerned in Przywara's *analogia entis*. Now, in the light of the knowledge of the being of God provided by the revelation of the covenant of grace, Barth accepts *both* movements as essential to an understanding of the relationship between God and humanity – but they are so only in the sense that they both occur within the history of Jesus Christ.

Barth understands the 'above to below' movement as the priestly work of Jesus Christ in which God reconciles sinful humans to himself. The most basic truth of human existence, Barth explains, is that God 'does not will to be God without us' but rather intends to 'share with us and therefore with our being and life and act his own incomparable being and life and act'.[104] The problem is that the human has demonstrated that he is unworthy of this life through his sin. This sin means that the relationship between God and the human must occur as the result of the atonement of this sin and the justification of the sinner rather than as the result of an ongoing 'interconnection of creator and creature' that results from God's act of creation alone.[105] Atonement and justification happen in and through Jesus Christ, who obediently lowers himself to take the place of the sinner. This act, Barth says, marks Christ's 'participation in our being, life and activity and therefore obviously our participation in his'.[106] Jesus Christ takes the consequences of the human's sin upon himself, and in him, 'man the covenant-breaker is buried and destroyed'.[107] Through the power of the Holy Spirit, the once-dead human is 'summoned' and 'awakened' in faith to the reality that his 'truest being' is in Jesus Christ.[108] The fact that this relationship occurs through the work of Christ and the Holy Spirit means that it is 'an event between God and man, not the static relationship of their being, but the being of God and man in a definite movement'.[109] That this movement is from 'above to below' is signified by that fact that God's act, rather than any human capacity, establishes this relationship.

Barth describes the 'below to above' movement in terms of Jesus Christ's kingly work in which the believer is sanctified and thus restored to her proper status as a covenant partner with God. Barth's description of the covenant of grace as a 'history' plays a key part here. As Barth sees it, Christ's act of obediently lowing himself to take the sins of the world upon himself puts him in position to transform human nature, because as Christ is exalted as the victorious king in his resurrection and ascension, humanity is exalted by their participation in him. This 'below to above' movement is

---

[104] *CD* IV/1, p. 7; *KD* IV/1, p. 5.

[105] *CD* IV/1, p. 11; *KD* IV/1, p. 10.

[106] *CD* IV/1, p. 13; *KD* IV/1, p 13.

[107] *CD* IV/1, pp. 93–4; *KD* IV/1, p. 99.

[108] *CD* IV/1, p. 14; *KD* IV/1, p. 14.

[109] *CD* IV/1, p. 545; *KD* IV/1, p. 608.

thus a function of the fact that 'there took place first the opposite movement from God to man, from heaven to earth, and therefore from above to below'.[110] In other words, because Jesus is the one who came to save sinners through his death, he is also, in his resurrection and ascension, the 'type and dynamic basis for what will take place and is to be known as the exaltation of man in his reconciliation with God'.[111] The history of Christ's life and being is thus the 'history of the placing of the humanity common to him and us on a higher level'.[112] Humans experience a 'real alteration of their being' through Christ's work, because their participation in him means that they also have a 'participation in his exaltation'.[113] This alteration occurs through the power of the Holy Spirit, who gives humans a 'subjective assurance which corresponds to this objective being'.[114] The Spirit, in short, enables the Christian to live the 'authentically human life' that is a covenant relationship with God.[115] This relationship is a movement from 'below to above' because it consists of the restoration of sinful humanity to God's intended plan for it, but it can be known only through the revelation of Jesus Christ because this movement is the work of Christ alone.

Since both the 'above to below' and the 'below to above' movements occur in and through Jesus Christ, Barth argues that they must be seen as 'a *single* action in which each of the two elements is related to the other and can be known and understood only in this relationship: the going out of God only as it aims as the coming in of man; the coming in of man only as the reach and outworking of the going out of God; and the whole in its original and proper form only as the being and history of the one Jesus Christ'.[116] Note what Barth has accomplished here: he has used the knowledge of both human being and the 'inner being' of God provided by the covenant of grace to formulate an account of the relationship between God and humanity that incorporates *both* sides of the relationship while remaining rooted in the particularity of Jesus Christ in the history of the covenant of grace. Martin Luther's key insights still apply in the same way as before. This

---

[110] Karl Barth, *Church Dogmatics* IV/2 (Edinburgh: T&T Clark, 1958), p. 29; *Die Kirchliche Dogmatik* IV/2 (Zürich: Evangelischer Verlag, 1955), p. 30. Hereafter these volumes will be cited as *CD* IV/2 and *KD* IV/2 respectively. Paul Dafydd Jones captures the significance of Barth's move here: 'Humiliation and exaltation no longer relate to the course of Christ's life; they now anchor dogmatic descriptions of the modes of existence that respectively characterize his divine and human essences.' See Jones, *The Humanity of Christ: Christology in Karl Barth's Church Dogmatics* (London: T&T Clark, 2008), p. 125.

[111] *CD* IV/2, p. 19; *KD* IV/2, p. 19.

[112] *CD* IV/2, p. 28; *KD* IV/2, p. 29.

[113] *CD* IV/2, pp. 529, 280; *KD* IV/2, pp. 598, 311.

[114] *CD* IV/2, p. 282; *KD* IV/2, p. 313.

[115] *CD* IV/2, p. 452; *KD* IV/2, p. 509.

[116] *CD* IV/2, p. 21; *KD* IV/2, p 21, emphasis mine.

relationship is by grace alone, because it is the work of God alone. The human also stands justified before God, but she does so only because, while she remains a sinner, her true being is 'in Christ'. Barth, in short, offers an account of both the 'above' and 'below' aspects of the relationship between God and the human, and he does so while remaining firmly planted on the same Protestant ground he has been standing on his entire career.

Barth does not stop there, however. He argues that there is a *third* movement of Jesus Christ's work that 'rests on the distinctness and difference of the first two' but 'is not identical with either'.[117] Barth understands this movement as the prophetic work of Jesus Christ. This aspect of Christ's work does not add anything to the other two, Barth explains, because the work of justification and sanctification have 'no need of supplement'; rather, it simply reveals the fact that Christ's reconciling act necessarily 'expresses, discloses, mediates and reveals itself'.[118] By this Barth means that, because it reveals the 'inner being' of God and the nature of God's relationship with humanity, the covenant of grace has 'the character of revelation'.[119] Jesus Christ 'speaks for himself' in and through his work, and as the living Lord, he is 'his own authentic witness'.[120] Even so, Barth explains, Christ 'does not will to be alone' in this witness.[121] Through the power of the Holy Spirit, Christ summons believers to serve as heralds who, alongside him, proclaim the reality this work of reconciliation to the world. 'To live as man', Barth argues, 'is to belong to this sphere, to the sphere of the life and activity of this other, so that, whether we realize it or not, the decision is made that God will accomplish his personal life-act only together with us,

---

[117] Karl Barth, *Church Dogmatics* IV/3.1 (Edinburgh: T&T Clark, 1961), p. 7; *Die Kirchliche Dogmatik* IV/3.1 (Zürich: Evangelischer Verlag, 1959), p. 6. Hereafter these volumes will be cited as CD IV/3.1 and KD IV/3.1 respectively.

[118] CD IV/3.1, p. 8; KD IV/3.1, p. 6. John Webster explains that Barth sees Christ's work as 'complete' not only in the sense of its 'being finished' but in its 'effective power in renewing human life by bringing about human response to itself'. As a result, for Barth, 'the relation of "objective" and "subjective" shifts. The objective is not a complete realm, separate from the subjective and, therefore, standing in need of "translation" into the subjective. Rather, the objective includes the subjective within itself, and is efficacious without reliance on a quasi-independent realm of mediating created agencies.' This insight explains why Barth turned away from notions of sacramental mediation: it contradicts the finished and self-attesting nature of Christ's work. See John Webster, *Barth's Ethics of Reconciliation* (New York: Cambridge University Press, 1995), pp. 127–8.

[119] CD IV/3.1, p. 38; KD IV/3.1, p. 40.

[120] CD IV/3.1, p. 46; KD IV/3.1, p. 49.

[121] Karl Barth, *Church Dogmatics* IV/3.2 (Edinburgh: T&T Clark, 1961), p. 606; *Die Kirchliche Dogmatik* IV/3.2 (Zürich: Evangelisher Verlag, 1959), p. 695. Hereafter these volumes will be cited as CD IV/3.2 and KD IV/3.2 respectively.

and we can accomplish ours only together with God'.[122] In other words, for Barth, the fulfilment of the covenant of grace occurs as humans – taken up into the life of God through their participation in Jesus Christ – cooperate with God's work in Christ through the power of the Holy Spirit by sharing in the task of proclaiming the reality of Christ's work to the world. The human participates in this divine work as 'active subject, in the action of Christ and therefore in the history of salvation, doing things with Christ even if not himself effecting them'.[123] It is in this precise sense that the human corresponds to Christ: just as Christ exists for others by proclaiming his work of reconciliation to the world, so too does the human in Christ exist for others by proclaiming the reality of Christ's work to the people around her.[124] The human does not add anything to Christ's work or make it effective, but she still has an active role in it because she participates as a partner in its proclamation to the world.

Analogy as Vocation

This participation in the prophetic work of Christ is how Barth conceives of the analogous relationship between the human and God. The basic framework of the analogy is the same as in his *analogia relationis*, but Barth's description of the analogy is more concrete, because he uses his account of Jesus Christ's reconciling work to draw a direct connection between the being and action of Jesus in the history of the covenant of grace and the being and action of Christians who, by virtue of their participation in Jesus, also participate in this same covenantal history.

> [T]he distinctive feature of the being of Christians as the children of God thus consists decisively and dominatingly in the fact that, as those whom Jesus Christ has called and calls to himself in the work of his Spirit, they exist in particular proximity to him and therefore in analogy to what he is. He is originally – not merely in the counsel of

---

[122] *CD* IV/3.1, p. 41; *KD* IV/3.1, p. 43. For this reason, as Hans Theodor Goebel says, the Christian 'lives as a witness to God' inasmuch 'attests the self-determination of God in history in his own life's story as a witness in time'. See Goebel, *Von freien Wählen Gottes*, p. 37.

[123] *CD* IV/3.2, p. 600; *KD* IV/3.2, p. 688.

[124] Neder rightly connects this correspondence between divine and human action back to its basis in the doctrines of election and participation: 'Election and obedience are related to one another as ground and consequence. Jesus Christ's fulfillment of the covenant of grace is a work of faithful obedience. As such it establishes true humanity as a life of faithful obedience. The *telos* of election is Jesus Christ's life history, and the *telos* of objective participation in Christ is subjective participation in Christ. In both cases, the *telos* is realized in obedience.' See Adam Neder, *Participation in Christ*, p. 18.

God but in the eternal being of God, and then in time, in the flesh and within the world in virtue of the counsel of God – that which men become as they are called to be Christians. That is to say, he is originally the Son of God. And in analogy and correspondence, which means with real similarity for all the dissimilarity, they may become sons of God. Their new and distinctive being as Christians is their being in this real similarity, for all the dissimilarity, to his being as the Son of God. They may become and thus be what he is originally and does not have to become.[125]

It is important here to keep in mind how Barth conceives of the being of Jesus Christ. Jesus Christ's being is his act: he *is* the one who exists *for* humans as he executes God's eternal plan in the covenant of grace. *This* is what it means to be the Son of God. The human exists in analogy to Christ inasmuch as she, through her participation in Christ, is taken up into the divine life and cooperates with Christ as an active partner in the outworking of the covenant of grace in history. *This* is what it means to be human. Her partnership with Christ takes the form of the proclamation of the Word of God, and it is precisely in this proclamation that she is in analogy to God, because in and through this act she exists *for* others in a way that is analogous to Christ's own existence. That is, her being as a human is in her free and obedient act of correspondence to Christ's work upon her in and through the power of the Holy Spirit. The analogy is thus an analogy of being-in-action: the 'divine-human action in divine-human sovereignty when we speak of the being and life of Christ, and human action in human freedom when we speak of the being and life of the Christian'.[126] This means that the analogy is *event*, and it takes visible form as 'repetition, confirmation, and revelation' as the human hears the Word of God in Jesus Christ and corresponds to it through the power of the Holy Spirit.[127] The analogy is not based upon an intrinsic capacity given to the human by God in the act of creation, therefore, but upon the always-extrinsic relationship between the human and Jesus Christ that takes place in and through Christ's fulfilment of God's eternal decision to exist in relationship to the human in the covenant of grace.

This account of analogy makes it clear that Barth's development of the implications of the covenant of grace for the relationship between God and humanity in the later volumes of his *CD* do not signal a retreat from his

---

[125] *CD* IV/3.2, pp. 532–3; *KD* IV/3.2, p. 612.

[126] *CD* IV/3.2, p. 597; *KD* IV/3.2, p. 685. This human act is free, not in the sense of absolute self-determination, but as a free self-determination within the context of God's self-determination. See Eberhard Jüngel, '. . . keine Menschenlosigkeit Gottes . . . ', in *Barth-Studien*, pp. 339–40 and 344–6.

[127] *CD* IV/3.2, p. 533; *KD* IV/3.2, p. 613.

rejection of the Roman Catholic *analogia entis*.[128] Barth is just as certain as ever that valid knowledge of God must be distinguished from all other human knowledge because it must proceed from the revelation of God's Word in Jesus Christ alone; he still holds that sinful humanity is incapable of any knowledge of God at all apart from revelation, and on this basis, he still rejects the notion of a philosophical prolegomena to theology or any permanent or lasting continuity between philosophy and theology; he still believes that the Word of God confronts the human as something new in each moment so that it never becomes something that the human possesses, but only something she receives. For him, the human's relationship with God is still the result of God's act in Jesus Christ alone; the human response to it does not stand in continuity with this action, as if it contributes to it, but it simply corresponds to it in the power of the Holy Spirit and on the basis of the human's justification. Barth also still believes that grace is self-validating, occurs moment-by-moment in event, that there is no condition or precondition for its reception, and that its reception is guaranteed only by itself. Barth still has no interest in analogy in general; he has interest only in the analogy as determined and given by Jesus Christ. And while he acknowledges that to talk about faith in analogy is also to talk about a participation in 'being', he is very specific about what, or more specifically whose, 'being' he is talking about: the being of Jesus Christ. Barth embraces an analogy of being, but his is an analogy of human being *in Christ*, and it takes the form of correspondence in action as the Christian finds her true being in her act of cooperating with the prophetic work of Jesus Christ in the outworking of God's covenant of grace in history.

---

[128] Peter Oh argues that Barth, in fact, did retreat from this rejection in the 1956 lecture 'The Humanity of God' when Barth notes his shift from an 'abstracted and absolutized' view of God to one rooted in the notion of God's '*togetherness* with man'. For Oh, these remarks demonstrate that von Balthasar's argument has 'convinced' Barth that 'the *analogia fidei* is not antithetical but complementary to the *analogia entis*', and Oh then uses this claim to say that 'Barth's own works written on the ground of the *analogia fidei*' should now be read 'as implying the complementary aspects of the *analogia entis*'. The above account has demonstrated how and why this argument is incorrect with respect to the content of Barth's mature theology. This reading of Barth's remarks in the 'The Humanity of God' also is historically implausible, however, because in transcripts of discussions at Princeton in 1962 and with students from Tübingen in 1964, Barth explicitly denies that he has changed his view of the *analogia entis*. If his 1956 lecture signalled a change of heart, therefore, then Barth himself did not know about it. It is better to read Barth's remarks about the 'togetherness' of God and humanity as describing the insights about 'inner being' of God derived from God's revelation in the covenant of grace rather than a change of heart about the *analogia entis*. See Karl Barth, *The Humanity of God* (Richmond, VA: John Knox Press, 1960), p. 45, and Peter S. Oh, *Karl Barth's Trinitarian Theology: A Study in Karl Barth's Analogical Use of the Trinitarian Relation* (London: T&T Clark, 2006), p. 16.

These conclusions allow us to return to the question about the *analogia entis* that Barth received in Princeton in 1962, which was discussed in Chapter 1. Recall that Barth responded to the questioner by saying that, while he has softened his critique of the *analogia entis*, he has not changed his mind about it. After making this claim, he then continues with a description of the kind of analogy that he thinks is necessary.

> If analogy is understood as analogy between two marks or two points in the doings of God and the doings of man, then it is acceptable and I think it is necessary to speak of it. For example, if we speak of God's grace, of God's behavior as a graceful God, and if we think of man as the partner in the covenant over against God and speak of man who is destined to be thankful to God; and if we then translate these two terms 'grace of God' and 'thankfulness of man' into Greek, then we see χάρις on the one side and εὐχαριστία on man's side. Here you have an example of *analogia relationis*, you see, between these two behaviors of God and man. Well, if somebody will say: 'But in being graceful and in being thankful God and man *are*, and so the notion of "being" reenters the scene', I will not resist. But the point is that the relation between God and man is a question of common history between God and man – something that happens from God's side and then should also happen from man's side.[129]

Our examination in this chapter stands in line with Barth's description of his own position, and it shows that he is correct to say that it does not signal a change of mind about the *analogia entis*. Indeed, the same theological commitments and distinctions that have been governing his thought since he rejected Przywara's original version of the *analogia entis* are present here. Barth rejected Przywara's *analogia entis* and distinguished his own view from Söhngen and von Balthasar's *analogia entis* because he thought that they placed God's action on the same plane as human action so that human action, rooted in intrinsic human capabilities given in creation, stood in continuity with God's grace in Jesus Christ. He was worried that this kind of continuity made God's action merely distinct from, rather than opposed to, human action, and it thus opened the door to the theological errors that he had been fighting against since he rejected the theology of his teachers. Barth's answer in response to the question at Princeton shows that this critique is still operative at the very end of his career. He had not changed his mind about what he had rejected earlier, and he has not incorporated a

---

[129] Karl Barth, *Gespräche: 1959–1962*, Gesamtausgabe (Zürich: Theologischer Verlag Zürich, 1995), pp. 499–500. Barth's comments here stand in line with his remarks in *CD* IV/1, p. 41; *KD* IV/1, p. 43.

form of this view into his own theology. He has, however, changed the nature of his own formulations in significant ways. Now, instead of thinking of the human only as standing 'over against' God, Barth also thinks of him as a partner in God's covenant of grace. The human is a partner with God not because he contributes something to God's grace, as if his own action is necessary to the execution of this covenant; he is a partner because God wills that the human be an active subject as the Word of God prompts him, in the power of the Holy Spirit, to act in correspondence to it by witnessing to God's reconciling act in Jesus Christ.[130] These actions constitute a history of encounter between two distinct subjects, and these subjects stand in analogy with one another inasmuch as their *actions* are similar to one another in the midst of an even greater dissimilarity. It is certainly correct to say that 'being reenters the scene' here, but we must immediately clarify that this being is not the 'being' given to the human by God in God's act of creation, as it is in the Roman Catholic accounts. It is the being of Jesus Christ, who as true God and true human is the being at the centre of the 'common history' between God and humanity and the mediator of their relationship.

Analogy and the Church for the World

This account of Barth's mature doctrine of analogy brings us full circle, because it provides a point of connection between Barth's theology in the CD and Erich Przywara's early version of the *analogia entis*. Recall that Przywara turned to the *analogia entis* because, in the face of the cultural and philosophical horrors exposed by the war, he wanted to provide the Catholic Church with the theological resources it needed to engage world with the truth of the Christian gospel. He rejected Barth's position, in part, because he believed that Barth's theology so divorced God from creation that the church was led to 'shrink back' from the culture rather than engage it.[131] This criticism, as we saw in Chapter 2, prompted Barth to rethink his portrayal of God, and this rethinking began a long course of development in his theology. Now, with Barth's mature doctrine of analogy in hand, we

---

[130] This description of the human's active role in the outworking of the covenant of grace explains the basis for Barth's rejection of Przywara's charge of 'theopanism'. He says: 'It is apparent at once that the formula "God everything and man nothing" as a description of grace is not merely a "shocking simplification" but complete nonsense . . . in reconciling the world to himself in Christ, God is indeed everything but only in order that man may *not* be nothing, but rather, that he may be *God's* man, and as such that he may – in his own place, on his own level and within his own limits – be *everything*.' See *KD* IV/1, pp. 94–5, translation mine, emphasis original to the German text; *CD* IV/1, p. 89.

[131] Erich Przywara, 'Gott in uns oder über uns? (Immanenz und Transzendenz in heutigen Geistesleben)', in *Stimmen der Zeit* 105 (1923), p. 350.

see his final answer to Przywara's criticism. Barth still rejects Przywara's *analogia entis* for all of the reasons he gave earlier in his career, but he does not reject Przywara's vision of a church that engages the world. In fact, Barth's final vision of the analogy between God and humanity *fulfils* Przywara's original vision for the church, but it does so in such a way that it also stands as the fulfilment of Barth's rejection of Przywara's *analogia entis*.

For Barth, to be a Christian at all is to be one who exists *for* others by reaching out to them with the truth of the Christian gospel. There is no such thing as a Christian who lives for himself or for his own spiritual fulfilment, because to the extent that the Christian is 'engrossed in himself, rotating about himself and seeking to assert and develop himself, he alienates himself from what makes him a Christian'.[132] What makes one a Christian is the event of the Word of God in Jesus Christ and the human correspondence to that Word that occurs through the power of the Holy Spirit. This correspondence takes visible form in the proclamation of Jesus Christ to those who do not know about him. This means that, at the most basic level, the Christian is 'referred, not to himself, but to God who points him to his neighbor'.[133] The church exists in the same way. The church is the community of believers gathered together by the Holy Spirit who, in response to the proclamation of God's Word in Jesus Christ to them, exist *for* the world by proclaiming that same Word to others. 'The church *is* when it *takes place*', Barth says, 'and it takes place in the form of a sequence and nexus of definite *human activities*'.[134] These activities are not the ones directed towards the church's own members for their own spiritual growth or edification; rather, these activities are the ones directed towards those *outside* the church who have yet to hear the gospel. The being of the church, therefore, is characterized by its act of 'leaping out to those to whom it is sent. In every respect, even in what seems to be purely inner activity like prayer and the liturgy and the cure of souls and biblical exegesis and theology, its activity is always *ad extra*'.[135] The church, in short, is the community that has been called out from the world by the Holy Spirit, and it exists precisely in and through its activity of reaching out to the world that exists outside the community.

Barth's mature vision of the church leaves no room for any 'shrinking back' from the culture, therefore, because for him, the church *is* only in and through its act of engaging the world around it. This vision for the church is a function of his doctrine of analogy. Barth can describe the church's being as its act precisely because he views the relationship between God and humanity as an analogy of relation: the relationship between the eternal

---

[132] *CD* IV/1, p. 652; *KD* IV/1, p. 747.
[133] *Ibid.*
[134] *CD* IV/1, p. 652; *KD* IV/1, p. 728, emphasis original to the German text.
[135] *CD* IV/3.2, p. 780; *KD* IV/3.2, p. 892.

Father and the eternal Son is analogous to the relationship between God and the human Jesus, and the relationship between human Jesus and the believer is analogous to the relationship between the believer and other humans. To be a human in analogy to God, therefore, means to be in relationship with others, and if this relationship follows the form of the relationships within the Trinity, then it is a relationship that has the form of an existence *for* others. This act for the other is essential to the being of the Christian rather than secondary to it, because this act constitutes the being of the Christian as such. If Barth were to embrace an analogy of being along the lines of Przywara, Söhngen, or von Balthasar, he could not hold such a view. In these views, the Christian's act of reaching out to the other is *secondary* rather than essential to Christian being, because the Christian's relationship with God is something that already exists in distinction from this action for the other. This act, in other words, is a *second* step that is not constitutive of the Christian's being in relationship to God. Thus, while Barth's conception of analogy is predicated upon an understanding of the human relationship with God that *requires* the act of reaching out to the other, Roman Catholic views of analogy are predicated upon an understanding of the human relationship with God that exists prior to and in distinction from this act. That is to say, while Barth's doctrine of analogy *requires* a church that engages the world, the Roman Catholic doctrine of analogy makes this engagement secondary, and thus optional, for Christian life. Barth's mature doctrine of analogy thus stands as the fulfilment of his original rejection of the Roman Catholic *analogia entis*, because his entire vision of the Christian life and the church stands in opposition to it.

8

CONCLUSION

For there is one God and one mediator between God and humans, the
man Christ Jesus, who gave himself as a ransom for all humans.
– 1 Tim. 2.5–6

The first part of this study, occupying Chapters 2 through 4, focused on the
question of whether Karl Barth's rejection of Erich Przywara's *analogia entis*
was the result of a mistaken understanding of it. Through an examination
of the theological development of both Barth and Przywara, their personal
encounters with one another, and a close analysis of Barth's early responses
to Przywara's *analogia entis*, we demonstrated that Barth did not reject
Przywara's *analogia entis* because he misunderstood it. Rather, Barth understood it correctly, and his rejection of it stands upon the foundation of the
Reformers' prior criticism of Roman Catholic theology and of their constructive alternative to it. The second part of this study, occupying Chapters 6
and 7, addressed the question of whether Barth changed his mind about his
rejection of the *analogia entis* and incorporated a form of it into his own
theology. Through an examination of Barth's doctrine of analogy in the
Church Dogmatics (CD) in conversation with Catholic critiques of it, we
demonstrated that, while Barth's theology changed throughout the course of
his career, he did not change his mind about his rejection of the Roman
Catholic *analogia entis*. Barth's mature theology does, in fact, contain an
analogia entis, but his version of it is substantively distinct from Roman
Catholic formulations, and it thus stands as a deepening of, rather than a
departure from, the same theological commitments that initially prompted
him to reject Przywara's *analogia entis*.

In addition to providing a correction to many of the ongoing mispercep-
tions about Barth's interpretation of the *analogia entis* and his later response
to it, this argument sets the stage for future discussion of this topic in three
ways. First, this study highlights the need for concreteness and specificity
in future examinations of Barth's interpretation of the *analogia entis*. For
example, this study shows how critical it is for any examination of Barth's
interpretation of the *analogia entis* to begin with a clear account of *which*

231

version of the *analogia entis* is being discussed. As we have seen, this matter is complicated, because the description of the *analogia entis* found in Przywara's *Analogia Entis* is distinct from the *analogia entis* defended by Gottlieb Söhngen and Hans Urs von Balthasar in the early parts of their careers, and both of these versions are different from the *analogia entis* that Przywara defended late in his career as well as the one found in von Balthasar's *Theo-Drama*.[1] There are, of course, other theologians and other versions of the *analogia entis* that could be mentioned on the Roman Catholic side alone. Since Barth's remarks about the *analogia entis* are directed to one but not all of these versions at any given time, an analysis of his interpretation of the doctrine needs to take account of *which* version he is interacting with in a particular passage. A lack of clarity on this point, as we have seen, leads to confusion and false conclusions about his interpretation. The same principle applies to an assessment of Barth's use of analogy within the *CD*. It is simply incorrect to conclude that, because Barth's mature theology contains an *analogia entis*, his critique of Przywara was misplaced and that there is no real difference between his assumptions and those adopted by Roman Catholics. Such conclusions are misplaced, as we have seen, because Barth's mature theology remains distinct from the Roman Catholic alternatives precisely because his version of the *analogia entis* is different from Roman Catholic versions of it. To put it sharply: not every *analogia entis* is the same, and care must be taken when describing the various versions offered by theologians involved in the debate about the doctrine.

This same concreteness and specificity is necessary for an analysis of the broader theological positions of the figures involved in this debate. For example, any description of Przywara's theology needs to take into account the fact that his description of the *analogia entis* developed and changed in significant ways over the course of his career. This means that those who embrace Przywara's early version of the *analogia entis*, in fact, are endorsing formulations that Przywara himself did not endorse in the same way late in his career; and likewise, those who reject Przywara's early account of the *analogia entis* on the basis of Barth's criticism are rejecting formulations that he later revised precisely to respond to that criticism. The same principle applies to Barth. The Barth of *Romans* II is different from the Barth of *CD* I/1, who is different again from the Barth of *CD* IV/1–3. While the later Barth did not abandon the basic insights that motivated his early theology,

---

[1] The shape of Przywara's later versions of the *analogia entis* is clearest in his essay, 'Die Reichweite der Analogie als katholischer Grundform', in *Schriften* III (Einsiedeln: Johannes-Verlag, 1962), pp. 247–301, and the volumes *Alter und Neuer Bund: Theologie der Stunde* (Vienna: Herold Verlag, 1956) and *Logos, Abendland, Reich, Commercium* (Düsseldorf: Patmos-Verlag, 1964). For von Balthasar's mature account of the *analogia entis*, see his *Theo-Drama: Theological Dramatic Theory*, Vol. III: *Dramatis Personae: Persons in Christ* (San Francisco: Ignatius Press, 1992), especially pp. 220–9.

he did supplement and modify these insights in significant ways in order to respond to the criticisms he received from Przywara and others. Any rejection or endorsement of Barth's early conclusions, therefore, needs to be aware of these later developments in his thought and account for them.

The need for concreteness and specificity on the issue of the *analogia entis* and the figures involved speaks to a second way this argument sets the stage for future discussions of this topic: it demonstrates the uselessness of the injudicious and sometimes harsh rhetoric that has characterized both sides of this debate. Jüngel's remark about the 'horrifying carelessness' that has characterized 'Barthian' descriptions of the *analogia entis* clearly could apply to many of Barth's critics as well.[2] Barth, of course, bears much of the blame for the tone that this debate has taken over the decades, and he admitted as much late in his career. The nature of the topic, along with the fact that the theologians involved were complex thinkers who developed their theology over the course of many decades, speaks to the care with which an analysis of this debate must be approached.[3] Adding to the complexity is the fact that it is simply impossible to consider the theology of any of the major figures in this debate in isolation from the influence of the others. For example, as we noted above, Barth lists Przywara as one of the 'Catholic reviewers' who prompted him to reconsider his portrayal of God in *Romans II*, and Przywara acknowledges that the arguments of *Analogia Entis* are the result, in part, of his interaction with Barth.[4] It also is clear that Söhngen's description of the Catholic tradition of the *analogia fidei* owes much to his desire to respond to Barth's criticisms, and it is simply impossible to understand von Balthasar's theology, early or late, apart from his engagement with Barth. In short, these theologians are who they are precisely *because* they interacted with one another, and none of them would have come to the conclusions that they did apart from this interaction. Polemical statements about someone's 'vacuous' and 'barbarous' views – not to mention the notion that a position of another theologian is 'the invention of the anti-Christ' – tend to obscure just how intertwined the figures of this debate are with one another.

---

[2] Eberhard Jüngel, *God as the Mystery of the World: On the Foundation of the Theology of the Crucified One in the Dispute between Theism and Atheism*, trans. Darrell L. Guder (New York: T&T Clark, 1983), p. 281.

[3] On this point, see von Balthasar's remark that '[t]he more deeply one enters into the dialogue, the less one will be tempted to think one can get anywhere with slogans'. See von Balthasar, *The Theology of Karl Barth: Exposition and Interpretation*, trans. S. J. Edward T. Oakes (San Francisco: Ignatius Press, 1992), p. xix.

[4] See Karl Barth, *The Epistle to the Romans*, 6th edn, trans. Edwyn C. Hoskins (London: Oxford University Press, 1933), pp. 20–1; and Erich Przywara, *Analogia Entis*, in Schriften, vol. 3 (Eisiedeln: Johannes-Verlag, 1962), p. 8.

The third contribution that this study makes is that it demonstrates that the debate between Barth and Przywara, Söhngen, and von Balthasar is really not about *analogy* at all, but about the content of the key theological doctrines that have distinguished Protestants from Roman Catholics for centuries. Barth himself recognized that this was the case. In a question and answer session with students from Tübingen in 1964, Barth received a question about his interpretation and use of the *analogia entis* similar to the one he had received in Princeton two years earlier. Barth's answer was largely the same as it was in Princeton: he said that he had not changed his mind, but if his critics want to call an *analogia fidei* or an *analogia relationis* an *analogia entis*, then he will not object to it. He then adds another insight.

> If now someone says with good grace, '*summum esse*' and suchlike, I no longer turn up my nose as I did thirty years ago and say, 'Huh, metaphysics! Terrible!' Instead, I say, 'Let us talk further about what "*esse*" and what "*nosse*" mean, and what "act" can mean. We want to understand one another; we do not want to fight about words'. Therefore I have now discontinued the battle against the idol of the *analogia entis*. I no longer fire along this front. In the end, this entire discourse about analogy became boring to me.[5]

This answer, of course, stands in line with the shift in Barth's approach to the debate about the *analogia entis* after Söhngen's critique that was noted above. This comment gives us new insights, however, about the way in which Barth thought the debate should continue in the future. Barth realized that if future debates between Protestants and Roman Catholics focus on the question of *analogy*, then the critical issues that actually distinguish Protestant theology from Roman Catholic theology are obscured. Rather, the most important questions concern different interpretations of key doctrines. What do we actually mean by 'being'? What do Roman Catholics mean when they speak of God's 'act', and how does their understanding of this act relate to what Barth means by 'act'? What is the nature of divine revelation? What is true theological knowledge? How do the insights gained through philosophical reflection relate to the insights given in and through revelation? What is 'grace'? How should we understand God's act in creation? How does God's act in creation relate to God's act of reconciliation in Jesus Christ? What role does human sin play in our account of the human relationship with God? What role does human action have in the outworking of God's plan of salvation? How should the church relate to the culture around it? The different answers Barth, Przywara, Söhngen,

---

[5] Karl Barth, *Gespräche 1964–1968*, Gesamtausgabe (Zürich: Theologischer Verlag Zürich, 1995), pp. 88–9.

and von Balthasar gave to *these* questions are what distinguished them from one another, and they are what distinguish their theological heirs from one another in the present. The debate about the *analogia entis* was and is a manifestation of these more central and basic differences, and these differences provide the subject matter for the *real* dialogue that needs to take place between Protestant and Roman Catholic theologians. If future discussions of Barth's interpretation of the *analogia entis* simply focus on the issue of analogy or the rhetoric involved in the debate, therefore, then they will miss the most relevant aspects of the debate altogether. The same will be true if the core differences between Barth's theology and the theology of his Roman Catholic interlocutors are blurred or downplayed in the name of ecumenical agreement. There are, in fact, real and critical differences between Barth's theology and Roman Catholic theology, and the only way to have *true* ecumenical dialogue is to put those differences on the table and discuss them.

Theologians approaching this topic in the future should not be afraid of such a debate about these doctrines, nor of having different views on them. Years after his visit to Barth's seminar in 1929, Przywara remembered that Barth seemed to think that his visit was a symbolic event. He recalled that Barth had intentionally arranged the room so that they both sat behind a single desk, and he remembered Barth telling his students that 'the Evangelical and Catholic theologians were sitting "at one table" after centuries for a strictly dogmatic "conversation" that would not be about cheap compromises but final clarity about the opposing standpoints'.[6] In the decades since their encounter, the debate between Przywara, Barth, and their followers on both sides has been marked more by cheap shots than cheap compromises. Perhaps, by focusing once again on the key doctrinal differences motivating Barth's and Przywara's initial disagreement, clarity can be achieved in a debate in which clarity has been hard to find. As Barth recognized, such clarity occurs only when we, in the midst of our differences, sit as brothers and sisters in Christ at the same table.

---

[6] Erich Przywara and Hermann Sauer, *Gespräch Zwischen Den Kirchen* (Nürnberg: Glock und Lutz Verlag, 1956), p. 7.

BIBLIOGRAPHY

Anzinger, Herbert, *Glaube und kommunikative Praxis: eine Studie zur vordialektischen Theologie Karl Barths* (München: Chr. Kaiser Verlag, 1991).

Augustine of Hippo, *The Augustine Catechism: Enchiridion of Faith, Hope and Love*, The Augustine Series, vol. 1, ed. John E. Rotelle (Hyde Park, NY: New City Press, 1999).

—*The Confessions*, trans. O. S. B. Maria Boulding, Vintage Spiritual Classics (New York: Vintage Books, 1997).

—'The Spirit and the Letter', in *The Works of Saint Augustine*, vol. 23, ed. John E. Rotelle, trans. Roland J. Teske (Hyde Park, NY: New City Press), pp. 150–202.

—*The Trinity*, trans. Edmund Hill (Brooklyn, NY: New City Press, 1991).

Barth, Karl, *Action in Waiting* (Rifton, NY: Plough Publishing House, 1969).

—*Anselm: Fides Quaerens Intellectum: Anselm's Proof of the Existence of God in the Context of His Theological Scheme*, trans. Ian W. Robertson (Richmond, VA: John Knox Press, 1960).

—*Die christliche Dogmatik im Entwurf* (München: Chr. Kaiser Verlag, 1927).

—*Church Dogmatics* I/1, revised edn (Edinburgh: T&T Clark, 1975).

—*Church Dogmatics* I/2 (Edinburgh: T&T Clark, 1956).

—*Church Dogmatics* II/1 (Edinburgh: T&T Clair, 1957).

—*Church Dogmatics* II/2 (Edinburgh: T&T Clark, 1957).

—*Church Dogmatics* III/1 (Edinburgh: T&T Clark, 1958).

—*Church Dogmatics* III/2 (Edinburgh: T&T Clark, 1960).

—*Church Dogmatics* IV/1 (Edinburgh: T&T Clark, 1956).

—*Church Dogmatics* IV/2 (Edinburgh: T&T Clark, 1958).

—*Church Dogmatics* IV/3.1 (Edinburgh: T&T Clark, 1961).

—*Church Dogmatics* IV/3.2 (Edinburgh: T&T Clark, 1961).

—'Concluding Unscientific Postscript on Schleiermacher', in *The Theology of Schleiermacher: Lectures at Göttingen, Winter Semester of 1923/24*, ed. Dietrich Ritschl (Grand Rapids, MI: William B. Eerdmans Publishing Co., 1968), pp. 261–79.

—*The Epistle to the Romans*, 6th edn, trans. E. C. Hoskyns (London: Oxford University Press, 1933).

—*Ethics*, ed. Dietrich Braun, trans. Geoffrey W. Bromiley (New York: The Seabury Press, 1981).

—*Evangelical Theology: An Introduction*, trans. Grover Foley (London: Fontana Library, 1965).

—'Evangelical Theology in the 19th Century', in *The Humanity of God* (Richmond, VA: Westminster John Knox, 1960)

—*Gespräche: 1959–1962*, Gesamtausgabe (Zurich: Theologischer Verlag Zürich, 1995), pp. 11–33.

—'Fate and Idea in Theology', in *The Way of Theology in Karl Barth: Essays and Comments*, ed. H. Martin Rumscheidt (Allison Park, PA: Pickwick Publications, 1986).

—'Foreword', in Heinrich Heppe, *Reformed Dogmatics* (Grand Rapids, MI: Eerdmans, 1978).

—*Gespräche: 1959–1962*, Gesamtausgabe (Zürich: Theologischer Verlag Zürich, 1995).

—*Gespräche 1964–1968*, Gesamtausgabe (Zürich: Theologischer Verlag Zürich, 1995).

—*The Göttingen Dogmatics: Instruction in the Christian Religion*, ed. Hannelotte Reiffen, trans. Geoffrey W. Bromiley, vol. 1 (Grand Rapids, MI: Eerdmans, 1991).

—*The Holy Spirit and the Christian Life: The Theological Basis of Ethics*, trans. R. Birch Hoyle (Louisville, KY: Westminster/John Knox Press, 1993).

—'The Humanity of God', in *The Humanity of God* (Louisville, KY: John Knox Press, 1960), pp. 37–65.

—*Die Kirchliche Dogmatik* I/1 (Zürich: Evangelischer Verlag, 1932).

—*Die Kirchliche Dogmatik* I/2 (Zürich: Evangelischer Verlag, 1938).

—*Die Kirchliche Dogmatik* II/1 (Zürich: Evangelischer Verlag, 1940).

—*Die Kirchliche Dogmatik* II/2 (Zürich: Evangelischer Verlag, 1942).

—*Die Kirchliche Dogmatik* III/1 (Zürich: Evangelischer Verlag, 1945).

—*Die Kirchliche Dogmatik* III/2 (Zürich: Evangelischer Verlag, 1948).

—*Die Kirchliche Dogmatik* IV/1 (Zürich: Evangelischer Verlag, 1953).

—*Die Kirchliche Dogmatik* IV/2 (Zürich: Evangelischer Verlag, 1955).

—*Die Kirchliche Dogmatik* IV/3.1 (Zürich: Evangelischer Verlag, 1959).

—*Die Kirchliche Dogmatik* IV/3.2 (Zürich: Evangelischer Verlag, 1959).

—'A Letter to the Author', in Hans Küng, *Justification: The Doctrine of Karl Barth and a Catholic Reflection*, 40th Anniversary Edition (Louisville, KY: John Knox Press, 2004), pp. lxvii–lxx.

—'No!', in *Natural Theology: Comprising 'Nature and Grace' by Professor Dr. Emil Brunner and the Reply 'No!' by Dr. Karl Barth*, trans. Peter Fraenkel (London: Centenary Press, 1946), pp. 65–128.

—*Predigten 1914*, Gesamtausgabe (Zürich: Theologischer Verlag Zürich, 1974).

—*The Theology of the Reformed Confessions*, trans. Darrell Guder and Judith Guder, Columbia Series in Reformed Theology (Louisville, KY: Westminster John Knox Press, 2002).

—*Die Theologie Zwinglis 1922/1923: Vorlesungen Göttingen Wintersemester 1922/1923*, Gesamtausgabe (Zurich: Theologischer Verlag Zürich, 2004).

—'The Righteousness of God', in *The Word of God and the Word of Man*, ed. Douglas Horton (Gloucester, MA: Peter Smith Publishing, 1978), pp. 9–27.

—'The Problem of Natural Theology Student Protocol' (unpublished manuscript in the Karl Barth Archive, Basel).

—*Römerbrief. Erste Fassung, 1919*, ed. Hinrich Stoevesandt, Gesamtausgabe (Zurich: Theologischer Verlag, 1985).

—'Die Theologie und der heutige Mensch', *Zwischen den Zeiten* 8 (1930), pp. 374–96.

—'Thomas Aquinas Seminar Protocol' (unpublished manuscript in the Karl Barth Archive, Basel).

BIBLIOGRAPHY

—*Unterricht in der christlichen Religion: Erster Band: Prolegomena, 1924*, in Gesamtausgabe (Zurich: Theologischer Verlag, 1985).

Barth, Karl and Rudolf Bultmann, *Karl Barth-Rudolf Bultmann Letters 1922–1966*, ed. Bernd Jaspert, trans. Geoffrey W. Bromiley (Grand Rapids, MI: William B. Eerdmans Publishing Co., 1981).

Barth, Karl and Eduard Thurneysen, *Karl Barth – Eduard Thurneysen Briefweshsel: 1921–30*, Gesamtausgabe (Zürich: Theologischer Verlag Zürich, 1974).

Berkouwer, G. C., *The Triumph of Grace in the Theology of Karl Barth* (Grand Rapids, MI: William B. Eerdmans Publishing Co., 1956).

Betz, John R., 'Beyond the Sublime: The Aesthetics of the Analogy of Being (Part One)', *Modern Theology* 21, no. 3 (2005), pp. 367–411.

—'Beyond the Sublime: The Aesthetics of the Analogy of Being (Part Two)', *Modern Theology* 22, no. 1 (2006), pp. 1–50.

Bonhoeffer, Dietrich, *Creation and Fall: A Theological Interpretation of Genesis 1–3*, trans. John C. Fletcher (New York: Macmillan, 1959).

Bradley, Denis, *Aquinas on the Twofold Human Good* (Washington, DC: The Catholic University of America, 1997).

Brunner, Emil, *The Christian Doctrine of Creation and Redemption: Dogmatics Volume II* (Philadelphia, PA: Westminster Press, 1952).

Busch, Eberhard, 'God Is God: The Meaning of a Controversial Formula and the Fundamental Problem of Speaking about God', *Princeton Seminary Bulletin*, no. 7 (1986), pp. 101–13.

—*Karl Barth: His Life from Letters and Autobiographical Texts* (Grand Rapids, MI: Eerdmans, 1994).

—*The Great Passion: An Introduction to Karl Barth's Theology*, trans. Geoffrey W. Bromiley (Grand Rapids, MI: William B. Eerdmans Publishing Co., 2004).

Calvin, John, *Institutes of the Christian Religion*, ed. John T. McNeil (Philadelphia, PA: Westminster Press, 1960).

Collins, James, 'Przywara's "*Analogia Entis*"', *Thought*, no. 65 (1990), pp. 265–77.

de Lubac, Henri, *The Mystery of the Supernatural*, trans. Rosemary Sheed (New York: Herder & Herder, 1998).

Dutari, Julia César, *Christentum und Metaphysik Das Verhaltnis beider nach der Analogielehre Erich Przywaras (1889–1973)* (Münich: Berchmanskolleg Verlag, 1973).

Freudenberg, Matthias, *Karl Barth und die reformierte Theologie: Die Ausseinandersetzung mit Calvin, Zwingli und den reformierten Bekenntnisschriften während seiner Göttinger Lehrtätigkeit* (Neukirchen-Vluyn: Neukirchener Verlag, 1997).

Gertz, Bernhard, *Glaubenswelt als Analogie: Die Theologische Analogielehre Erich Przywaras und ihr Ort in der Auseinandersetzung um die Analogie Fidei* (Düsseldorf: Patmos-Verlag, 1969).

—'Erich Przywara (1889–1972)', in *Christliche Philosophie im katholischen Denken des 19. und 20 Jahrhunderts*, vol. 2, ed. Emerich Coretch (Graz: Styria, 1988), pp. 575–89.

Gilson, Etionne, *Being and Some Philosophers*, 2nd edn (Toronto: Pontifical Institute of Medieval Studies, 1952).

Goebel, Hans Theodor, 'Trinitätslehre und Erwählungslehre bei Karl Barth: eine Problemanzeige', in *Wahrheit und Versöhnung: Theologische und philosophische*

BIBLIOGRAPHY

Beiträge zur Gotteslehre, ed. Dietrich Korsch and Hartmut Ruddies (Gütersloh: Gütersloher Verlagshaus Gerd Mohn, 1989).

—*Vom freien Wählen Gottes und des Menschen: Interpretationsübungen zur 'Analogie' nach Karl Barths Lehre von der Erwählung und Bedenken ihrer Folgen für die Kirchliche Dogmatik* (Frankfurt: Peter Lang Publishing Co., 1988).

Hart, David Bentley, *The Beauty of the Infinite: The Aesthetics of Christian Truth* (Grand Rapids, MI: William B. Eerdmans Publishing Co., 2003).

—'The Offering of Names: Metaphysics, Nihilism, and Analogy', in *Reason and the Reasons of Faith*, ed. Paul J. Griffiths and Reinhard Hütter (New York: T&T Clark, 2005).

Hauerwas, Stanely, *With the Grain of the Universe: The Church's Witness and Natural Theology* (Grand Rapids, MI: Brazos Press, 2001).

Heppe, Heinrich, *Reformed Dogmatics* (Grand Rapids, MI: Eerdmans, 1978).

Hunsinger, George, *How to Read Karl Barth: The Shape of His Theology* (New York, NY: Oxford University, 1991).

—'Toward a Radical Barth', in *Karl Barth and Radical Politics*, ed. George Hunsinger (Philadelphia, PA: Westminster Press, 1976), pp. 181–233.

Jenson, Robert, *God after God: The God of the Past and the God of the Future, Seen in the Work of Karl Barth* (New York: The Bobbs-Merrill Company, 1969).

Jones, Paul Dafydd, *The Humanity of Christ: Christology in Karl Barth's Church Dogmatics* (London: T&T Clark, 2008).

Jüngel, Eberhard, *God as the Mystery of the World: On the Foundation of the Theology of the Crucified One in the Dispute between Theism and Atheism*, trans. Darrell L. Guder (New York: T&T Clark, 1983)

—*Karl Barth: A Theological Legacy*, trans. Garrett E. Paul (Philadelphia, PA: Westminster Press, 1986)

—'. . . keine Menschenlosigkeit Gottes . . . ', in *Barth-Studien* (Gütersloh: Benzinger Verlag, 1982), pp. 332–47.

—'Die Möglichkeit theologischer Anthropologie auf dem Grunde der Analogie', in *Barth-Studien* (Gütersloh: Benzinger Verlag, 1982), pp. 210–232.

Kerr, Fergus, *Twentieth Century Catholic Theologians: From Neoscholasticism to Nuptial Mysticism* (Malden, MA: Blackwell Publishing Ltd., 2007).

Lee, Jung Young, 'Karl Barth's Use of Analogy in his *Church Dogmatics*', *Scottish Journal of Theology* 22 (1969), pp. 129–51.

Long, Stephen A., 'Obediential Potency, Human Knowledge, and the Natural Desire for God', *International Philosophical Quarterly* 37, no. 1 (1997), pp. 45–63.

—'On the Possibility of a Purely Nature End for Man', *The Thomist* 64, no. 3 (2000), pp. 211–37.

Lovin, Robin W., 'Foreword', in *The Holy Spirit and the Christian Life* (Louisville, KY: Westminster/John Knox Press, 1993), pp. ix–xx.

Marga, Amy E., 'Karl Barth's Second Dogmatic Cycle: Münster 1926–1928: A Progress Report', *Zeitschrift für dialektische Theologie* 21, no. 1 (2005), pp. 126–37.

—'Partners in the Gospel: Karl Barth and Roman Catholicism, 1922–1932' (Unpublished Doctoral Dissertation, Princeton Theology Seminary, 2006).

Maury, Piere, *Predestination*, trans. Edwin Hudson (Richmond, VA: John Knox Press, 1960).

BIBLIOGRAPHY

McCormack, Bruce, 'The Being of Holy Scripture is in Becoming: Karl Barth in Conversation with American Evangelical Criticism', in *Evangelicals and Scripture: Tradition, Authority and Hermeneutics*, ed. Vincent E. Bacote, Laura C. Miguélez, and Dennis L. Okholm (Downers Grove, IL: InterVarsity Press, 2004), pp. 55–75.

—*Karl Barth's Critically Realistic Dialectical Theology: Its Genesis and Development, 1909–1936* (Oxford: Oxford University Press, 1995).

Mechels, Eberhard, *Analogie bei Erich Przywara und Karl Barth: Das Verhältnis von Offenbarungstheologie und Metaphysic* (Neukirchen-Vluyn: Neukirchener Verlag, 1974).

Mondin, Battista, *The Principle of Analogy in Protestant and Catholic Theology*, 2nd edn (The Hague: Martinus Nijhoff, 1968).

Neder, Adam, *Participation in Christ: An Entry into Karl Barth's Church Dogmatics* (Louisville, KY: Westminster John Knox, 2009).

Neuser, Wilhelm, *Karl Barth in Münster 1925–1930* (Zürich: Theologischer Verlag Zürich, 1985).

Newman, John Henry, *An Essay on the Development of Christian Doctrine*, 6th edn (Notre Dame, IN: University of Notre Dame Press, 1989).

—*Meditations and Devotions of the late Cardinal Newman* (London; New York: Longmans, Green, 1893)

Nielsen, Niles C., 'The Analogia Entis of Erich Przywara' (Unpublished Doctoral Dissertation, Yale University, 1951).

O'Meara, Thomas F., *Erich Przywara, S.J.: His Theology and His World* (Notre Dame, IN: Notre Dame University Press, 2002).

Oakes, Edward T., *Pattern of Redemption: The Theology of Hans Urs von Balthasar*, 2nd edn (New York: Continuum, 1997).

Oh, Peter, *Karl Barth's Trinitarian Theology: A Study in Karl Barth's Analogical Use of the Trinitarian Relation* (London: T&T Clark, 2006).

Palakeel, Joseph, *The Use of Analogy in Theological Discourse: An Investigation in Ecumenical Perspective* (Rome: Pontificia Università Gregoriana, 1995).

Przywara, Erich, *Alter und Neuer Bund: Theologie der Stunde* (Wien: Verlag Herold, 1956).

—*Analogia Entis*, in *Schriften*, vol. 3 (Einsiedeln: Johannes-Verlag, 1962).

—*A Newman Synthesis* (New York: Longmans, 1931).

—'Die Reichweite der Analogie als katholischer Grundform', in *Schriften*, vol. 3 (Einsiedeln: Johannes-Verlag, 1962), pp. 247–301.

—'Die Reichweite der Analogie als katholischer Grundform', in *Scholastik*, vol. 3 (1940), pp. 339–62, 508–32.

—'Die religiöse Krisis in der Gegenwart und der Katholizismus', in *Katholische Krise: In Zusammenarbeit with dem Verfasser herausgegeben und mit einem Nachwort versehen*, ed. Bernhard Gertz (Düsseldorf: Patmos-Verlag, 1967), pp. 41–53.

—*Eucharistie und Arbeit*, in *Schriften*, vol. 1 (Eisiedeln: Johannes-Verlag, 1962), pp. 3–25.

—*Gott*, in *Schriften*, vol. 2 (Eisiedeln: Johannes-Verlag, 1962), pp. 243–372.

—*Gott: Fünf Vorträge über das religionsphilosophische Problem* (Köln: Oratoriums-Verlag, 1926).

—'Gott in uns oder über uns? (Immanenz und Transzendenz in heutigen Geistesleben)', *Stimmen der Zeit* 105 (1923), pp. 343–62.

—'Gott in uns und Gott über uns', in *Ringen der Gegenwart: Gesammelte Aufsätze 1922–1927*, Band II (Augsburg: Filser, 1929), pp. 543–78.

—'Gotteserfahrung und Gottesbeweis', in *Schriften*, vol. 2 (Eisiedeln: Johannes-Verlag, 1962), pp. 3–13.

—'Gottgeheimnis Der Welt: Drei Vorträge über die Geistige Krisis der Gegenwart', in *Schriften*, vol. 2 (Eisiedeln: Johannes-Verlag, 1962), pp. 121–242.

—*In und Gegen* (Nürenberg: Glock und Lutz, 1955).

—'J. H. Newmans Problemstellung', in *Ringen der Gegenwart: Gesammelte Aufsätze 1922–1927*, Band II (Augsburg: Filser, 1929), pp. 826–34.

—'Das katholische Kirchenprinzip', *Zwischen den Zeiten* 7 (1929), pp. 277–302.

—'Katholizität', in *Katholische Krise: In Zusammenarbeit with dem Verfasser herausgegeben und mit einem Nachwort versehen*, ed. Bernhard Gertz (Düsseldorf: Patmos-Verlag, 1967), pp. 20–40.

—*Logos, Abendland, Reich, Commercium* (Düsseldorf: Patmos-Verlag, 1964).

—'Metaphysik und Religion', in *Schriften*, vol. 2 (Einsiedeln: Johannes-Verlag, 1962), 14–26.

—'Philosophy', in *Philosophisches Jahrbuch* (1949), pp. 1–9

—*Polarity: A German Catholic's Interpretation of Religion*, trans. A. C. Bouquet (London: Oxford University Press, 1935).

—'Problematik der Gegenwart', *Stimmen der Zeit* 116 (1929), pp. 99–115.

—*Religionsphilosophie katholischer Theologie* (Münich: Oldenbourg, 1926).

—*Religionsphilosophie katholischer Theologie*, in *Schriften*, vol. 2 (Eisieldeln: Johannes-Verlag, 1962), pp. 373–511.

—*Ringen der Gegenwart: Gesammelte Aufsätze 1922–1927*, Band II (Augsburg: Filser, 1929).

—'Sein im Scheitern – Sein im Aufgang', *Stimmen der Zeit* 123 (1932), pp. 152–61.

—'St. Augustine and the Modern World', in *A Monument to Saint Augustine*, ed. M. C. D'Arcy (London: Sheed & Ward, 1930), pp. 251–86.

Przywara Erich and Hermann Sauer, *Gespräch Zwischen den Kirchen* (Nürnberg: Glock und Lutz Verlag, 1956).

Quenstedt, Johann Andreas, *Theologica Didactio Polemica sive Systema Theologicum* (Lipsiae: Thomam Fritsch, 1715).

Richards, Jay Wesley, 'Barth on the Divine "Conscription" of Language', *Heythrop Journal* 38, no. 3 (1997), pp. 247–66.

Roberts, Richard H., *A Theology on its Way? Essays on Karl Barth* (Edinburgh: T&T Clark, 1991).

Rocca, Gregory P., *Speaking the Incomprehensible God: Thomas Aquinas on the Interplay of Positive and Negative Theology* (Washington, DC: Catholic University of America Press, 2004).

Rolnick, Philip A., *Analogical Possibilities: How Words Refer to God* (Atlanta, GA: Scholars Press, 1993).

Schroeder, H. J., *Canons and Decrees of the Council of Trent* (Rockford, IL: Tan Books and Publishers, 2009).

Schwöbel, Christoph (ed.), *Karl Barth-Martin Rade: Ein Briefweschel* (Gütersloh: Gütersloher Verlagshaus Gerd Mohn, 1981).

BIBLIOGRAPHY

Söhngen, Gottlieb, 'Analogia Fidei: Gottähnlichkeit allein aus Glauben?', *Catholica* 3, no. 3 (1934), pp. 113–36.

—'Analogia Fidei: Die Einheit in der Glaubenswissenschft', *Catholica* 3, no. 4 (1934), 176–208.

—'Analogia entis oder analogia fidei?', *Wissenschaft und Weisheit: Zeitschrift für augustinisch-franziskanische Theologie und Philosophie in der Gegenwart* 9 (1942), pp. 91–100.

—'*Analogia Entis in Analogia Fidei*', in *Antwort: Karl Barth zum Seibzeigsten Geburtstag* (Zurich: Evangelischer Verlag AG, 1956), pp. 266–71.

—'Natürliche Theologie und Heilsgeschichte: Antwort an Emil Brunner', in *Catholica* 4 (1935), pp. 97–114.

Thomas Aquinas, *Scriptum super libros Sententiarum*, Books 1–2, ed. P. Mandonnet (Paris: Lethielleux, 1929).

Thomas Aquinas, *Summa Theologica*, trans. Father of the English Dominican Province (New York: Benziger Brothers, Inc., 1948).

Torrance, T. F., *Karl Barth: An Introduction to his Early Theology 1910–1931* (London: T&T Clark, 2000).

von Balthasar, Hans Urs, *Theo-Drama: Theological Dramatic Theory, Vol. III: Dramatis Personae: Persons in Christ* (San Francisco: Ignatius Press, 1992).

—*The Theology of Karl Barth: Exposition and Interpretation*, trans. S. J. Edward T. Oakes (San Francisco: Ignatius Press, 1992).

Webster, John, *Barth's Earlier Theology* (New York: T&T Clark International, 2005).

—*Barth's Ethics of Reconciliation* (Cambridge: Cambridge University, 1995).

Winn, Christian T. Collins, '"Jesus is Victor!": The Significance of the Blumhardts for the Theology of Karl Barth' (Unpublished Doctoral Dissertation, Drew University, 2006).

Zechmeister, Martha, *Gottes-Nacht: Erich Przywara Weg Negativer Theologie* (Münster: Lit Verlag, 1997).

—'Przywara, Erich S. J. (1908)', in *Lexikon für Theologie und Kirche*, vol. 9, ed. Klaus Ganzer and Bruno Steimer (Freiburg: Herder, 1999).

Zeitz, James V. 'Erich Przywara: A Visionary Theologian', *Thought* 58 (1983), pp. 145–57.

—'Erich Przywara on Ultimate Reality and Meaning: "Deus Semper Major"', *Ultimate Reality and Meaning* 12 (1989), pp. 192–201.

—*Spirituality and the Analogia Entis According to Erich Przywara, S.J.* (Washington, DC: University Press of America, 1982).

Zimny, Leo, *Erich Przywara: Sein Schriftum, 1912–1962* (Eisiendeln: Johannes-Verlag, 1963).

INDEX

Printed in Great Britain
by Amazon.co.uk, Ltd.,
Marston Gate.